GREECE IN THE MAKING,
1200–479 BC

Greece in the Making is an accessible and comprehensive account of Greek history from the end of the bronze age to the classical period. The first edition of this book broke new ground by acknowledging that, barring a small number of archaic poems and inscriptions, the majority of our literary evidence for archaic Greece reported only what later writers wanted to tell, and so was subject to systematic selection and distortion. This book offers a narrative which acknowledges the later traditions, as traditions, but insists that we must primarily confront the contemporary evidence, which is in large part archaeological and art-historical, and must make sense of it in its own terms.

By reading later traditions in the light of what we now know of early iron age Greece from archaeology and of what early Greek poetry, including the Homeric epics, reveals, this book creates a new history of this crucial period in which the Greek city-states developed the political and cultural forms which gave birth to the earliest democracies and to such seminal literary forms as Greek tragedy.

In this second edition, as well as updating the text to take account of recent scholarship, and reordering some material, Robin Osborne has addressed more explicitly the weaknesses and unsustainable interpretations which the first edition chose merely to pass over. He now spells out why this book features no 'rise of the *polis*' and no 'colonisation', and why the treatment of Greek settlement abroad is necessarily spread over various chapters. Students and teachers alike will particularly appreciate the enhanced discussion of economic history and the more systematic treatment of issues of gender and sexuality.

Robin Osborne is Professor of Ancient History at the University of Cambridge, and a Fellow of King's College Cambridge and of the British Academy. He has published widely on ancient Greek history, archaeology and art, including *Classical Landscape with Figures: The Ancient Greek City and its Countryside* (1987), *Archaic and Classical Greek Art* (1998), and *Greek History* (Routledge Classical Foundations, 2004).

ROUTLEDGE HISTORY OF
THE ANCIENT WORLD
Series editor: Fergus Millar

GREECE IN THE MAKING, 1200–479 BC

Second Edition

Robin Osborne

Routledge
Taylor & Francis Group

LONDON AND NEW YORK

First published 1996
Reprinted 1999, 2001, 2003 (twice), 2005, 2006 (three times)
This second edition published in 2009
by Routledge
2 Park Square, Milton Park, Abingdon, Oxon OX14 4RN

Simultaneously published in the USA and Canada
by Routledge
711 Third Ave, New York, NY 10017

Routledge is an imprint of the Taylor & Francis Group
© 1996 and 2009 Robin Osborne

Typeset in Garamond by
HWA Text and Data Management, London
Printed and bound in Great Britain by
CPI Antony Rowe, Chippenham, Wiltshire

British Library Cataloguing in Publication Data
A catalogue record for this book is available from the British Library

Library of Congress Cataloging-in-Publication Data
A catalog record for this book has been requested

ISBN 10: 0-415-46992-9 (pbk)
ISBN 10: 0-415-46991-0 (hbk)
ISBN 10: 0-203-88017-X (ebk)

ISBN 13: 978-0-415-46991-3 (pbk)
ISBN 13: 978-0-415-46992-0(hbk)
ISBN 13: 978-0-203-88017-3(ebk)

FOR JOHN,
AFTER ALL THESE YEARS

CONTENTS

FIGURES

The following were reproduced with kind permission. While every effort has been made to trace copyright holders and obtain permission, this has not been possible in all cases. Any omissions brought to our attention will be remedied in future editions.

A number of colleagues have generously assisted me in obtaining photographs. I am particularly grateful to John Boardman, Lucilla Burn, Bill Cavanagh, Nicolas Coldstream, Jim Coulton, Charles Crowther, Hans Rupprecht Goette, Henry Kim, Helmut Kyrieleis, Andrew Meadows, Nick Pollard, Mervyn Popham, David Ridgway, Brian Sparkes, Nigel Spivey, Andrew Stewart, Michael Vickers, and Bob Wilkins.

TABLES

TEXTS

PREFACE

This book has been a long time in the making. The list of those who did not write the Methuen book on Archaic Greece is a distinguished one: H. A. Ormerod and H. T. Wade-Gery were supposed to write for the old Methuen series, and J. K. Davies was initially commissioned to write for the new. That I have ended up at the end of this line I owe to Fergus Millar, who has waited patiently, has encouraged persistently but gently, and has read, and commented extensively on, the whole book.

Since Ormerod was commissioned in the 1920s, our understanding of archaic Greece has been immeasurably transformed several times over, not simply by the work of archaeologists but also by work on oral traditions. In the 1930s the leading protagonist in the use of archaeology to illuminate early Greek history was my Corpus predecessor Alan Blakeway, samizdat copies of whose lectures on the theme long influenced thinking on the subject in Oxford. Blakeway's own untimely death, and the untimely deaths of too many of his colleagues both before and during the Second World War, took the heart out of the archaeology of Iron-Age Greece in Britain. But in recent years interest in the area has been revived, in no small part as a result of the giant's stride forward in the bold use of the archaeological record to understand eighth-century BC Greece made by Anthony Snodgrass's *Archaic Greece: The Age of Experiment* of 1980. Here I attempt to consolidate that advance, and at the same time to face, more determinedly than has previously been done, the fact that what literary texts tell us about the events of the years before the Persian wars is a product of what individuals and groups in the fifth century BC found it in their interest to tell, and not of what actually happened.

This book ends with the Persian wars. That is the conventional point at which to end histories of archaic Greece, and it is the point at which Simon Hornblower's *The Greek World 479–323 BC*, the successor volume to this in the series, begins. But I will argue, in 1.4 and in the epilogue, that the Persian wars mark a change both in the nature of Greek history and in the nature of the source material from which Greek history can be written. I begin, less conventionally, with the Dark Age of the twelfth to ninth centuries BC. I have begun there, rather than with the traditional beginning of Greek history in 776 BC, because it is following the fall of the Mycenaean palaces that the greatest discontinuity in the archaeological record occurs, and because, for all that many things change in eighth-century Greece, there is no fundamental change in the sources for the study of Greek society in the eighth century.

Although there is a line of argument running through the book, I hope that it will be of service to those interested only in part of the world which it surveys.

Such readers are, however, advised that they should read the opening chapter before attempting to use the rest of the book. Discussion of various topics, such as trade, is inevitably spread over the book, and readers are encouraged to make use of the index in order to put these discussions together again. I have endeavoured to ensure that my text adequately indicates the basis for the views which it expounds; my text has not been written in opposition to 'rival' histories and I have not made any attempt systematically to signal how my views relate to those expressed by other scholars who have written on the same topics. I hope that readers will find the different choices which other scholars writing about the period make in their histories *more* interesting, rather than less, as a result of reading this book. But I hope, even more strongly, that they will go away and read the Greek sources, Homer, Hesiod, Herodotos and the rest, with a new fascination and new insight. Throughout I have employed, rather than footnotes, a running bibliography, to be found at the end of the book and to be read in parallel with the chapters. This bibliography is intended to suggest the best place for an English-speaking reader to go for further information on the topics discussed; it is not intended to be exhaustive, and has not been limited to works which argue for the view of the particular issue which my text has adopted.

I am grateful to Jim Coulton, Franco De Angelis, Henry Kim, Irene Lemos, John Lloyd, David Percik, Oliver Taplin, and Stephen Todd for assistance with various topics and criticism of various draft chapters. Many other colleagues have influenced this book in less direct ways, through the stimulus of their work and through conversation, and I am grateful to them all for the generosity with which they have shared information and views. My pupils over the past decade have contributed more than they would guess to the arguments presented here, and if some parts are better constructed than others it is as a result of their work. I owe the felicitous title to my daughter Elizabeth. I am particularly grateful to Simon Hornblower, who read and commented on the whole of the first draft and whose sensitivities to style and content have not only saved me much embarrassment but have saved the reader from a much more turgid book. My knowledge of Thasos and the Cyclades has been enhanced with the assistance of the British Academy, of Sicily with that of the Oxford University Craven Committee, and of Khios and Samos with that of Corpus Christi College; I gratefully acknowledge the help of all these bodies.

In November 1977, as an undergraduate at King's College Cambridge, I wrote an essay in answer to the question 'Account for the differences between Coelius Antipater 11 and Livy 21.21 and between Quadrigarius 10(b) and Livy 7.9.8f'. All down the margin at one point my supervisor wrote: 'We have a homeostatic oral culture here – aristocrats jealously hoarding their claims to pedigree and never in a position to sort out consciously where fact merged with pious fiction. The past is adjusted to the present, but not necessarily consciously or at any controllable level?' That remark has lived with me ever since and might stand as the epigraph to this book, which is dedicated to that incomparable supervisor, John Henderson, in the hope that he may find it a step in the right direction.

Corpus Christi College Oxford
October 1995

PREFACE TO THE SECOND EDITION

The first edition of this book has enjoyed a dozen years of use and abuse. My chief aim in revising this book has been to increase its usefulness to all sorts of readers. I have attempted to bring the bibliographical notes up to date, to clarify arguments which readers have found difficult to follow, to signal more clearly why it is that certain traditional topics of discussion do not figure here (notably 'colonisation' and 'the rise of the *polis*'), to offer more systematic discussion of the economy and of gender relations, and to facilitate the use of the book as a textbook by reversing the orders of Chapters 2 and 3. I have not attempted to defend myself against those who dismiss my account as one that is simply sceptical; I can only ask that they read more closely. I am grateful to all who offered suggestions and in particular to Paul Cartledge, Simon Hornblower, and Peter Rhodes for both detailed corrections and more general challenges to my views to which I have attempted to respond.

It is a particular pleasure to have been able to make these revisions back in the collegial company of John Henderson.

King's College Cambridge
September 2008

ABBREVIATIONS

AA	*Archäologische Anzeiger*
ABSA	*Annual of the British School at Athens*
AJA	*American Journal of Archaeology*
AM	*Athenische Mitteilungen*
ANE	Amélie Kuhrt, *The Ancient Near East* (London, 1995)
BCH	*Bulletin de Correspondance Hellénique*
BICS	*Bulletin of the Institute of Classical Studies*
BR	T. J. Cornell, *The Beginnings of Rome* (London, 1995)
Buck	C. D. Buck, *The Greek Dialects* (3rd edn, Chicago, IL, 1955)
CEG	P. A. Hansen (ed.), *Carmina Epigraphic Graeca saeculorum VIII–V a. Chr. n.* (Berlin, 1983)
FGH	F. Jacoby, *Die Fragmente der griechischen Historiker* (Berlin and Leiden, 1923–)
Fornara	C. W. Fornara (ed. and trans.), *Archaic Times to the End of the Peloponnesian War. Translated Documents of Greece and Rome*, vol. 1 (Cambridge, 1983)
GW	S. Hornblower, *The Greek World 479–323 BC* (3rd edn, London, 2002)
IG	*Inscriptiones Graecae* (Berlin, 1873–)
JDAI	*Jahrbuch des deutschen archäologischen Instituts*
JHS	*Journal of the Hellenic Society*
LSCG	F. Sokolowski (ed.), *Lois sacrées des cités grecques* (Paris, 1969)
ML	R. Meiggs and D. M. Lewis (eds), *A Selection of Greek Historical Inscriptions to the End of the Fifth Century BC* (rev. edn, Oxford, 1988)
OJA	*Oxford Journal of Archaeology*
P. Oxy.	*The Oxyrhynchus Papyri* (London, 1898–)
PCPS	*Proceedings of the Cambridge Philological Society*
SEG	*Supplementum Epigraphicum Graecum*

1

THE TRADITIONS
OF HISTORY

WHAT IS POLYKRATES TO ME?
THE NECESSITY OF ARCHAIC GREEK HISTORY

As soon as you ask why a nation's political or economic institutions, or social relations, are the way they are today, you start to delve into history. If you want to understand why the British Parliament has the powers it does, or operates in the way it does, then one of the first things you need to know is what happened in the seventeenth century with the Civil Wars and the Glorious Revolution. If you want to know why the countryside looks as it does, why country roads meander, why fields are odd shapes, you need to look back into the past history of the ownership and exploitation of the land. If you want to know why non-conformism is so strong in Wales, then you have to look at patterns of evangelism in the past, but also at patterns of political power and of economic deprivation. Studying British history is not a patriotic duty engaged in by chauvinists, it is something any inquisitive person, who wants to understand the society of which he or she is part, continually finds it impossible to do without.

But the history of a foreign country, 2,500 years ago and more? Is that not a luxury, merely a way of keeping the inhabitants of ivory towers out of mischief? Comforting though it might be to think that we can isolate our own history from what has happened to the rest of the world, we cannot. If what Parliament is in Britain today has been shaped by past events, it has also been shaped by what people have thought and written about government and its institutions. And as soon as you look into what has been thought and written on such matters in this country you find that it has been profoundly influenced by what has been thought and written elsewhere. And what has been written elsewhere has itself been shaped by what has happened elsewhere again. Because ancient Greece and ancient Rome have in the past enjoyed a special status in European thought, in a very few moves one finds oneself back with the political writings of Aristotle, and the practice of democracy at Athens. Time and again, in pursuing the history of our own society in order to understand its present forms, we find ourselves pursuing myths about ancient

1

Greece and through them the history of ancient Greece. John Stuart Mill was even prepared to claim that the Battle of Marathon, when the Athenians and Plataians defeated a Persian invasion force, was a more important event in English history than the Battle of Hastings.

You may imagine that, on this argument, there will be no end to the pursuit of the past: are we not entering an infinite regress that will end with us shuffling through the history of man from the stone age on? The answer to that is 'No', and it is 'No' for two very significant reasons, which themselves point up the importance of Greek history. The first is that it is only with the Greek world that we begin to get the sort of source materials that enable us to do the sort of history that lets us ask our own questions and hope to get answers. We have chronicles from earlier times, such as those available in the history books of the Old Testament, but it is from the Greeks of the classical period that we first get critical history, history that is conscious that people tell different stories about past events, history that tries to understand why events occurred and what their significance was, and is not satisfied with answers in terms of the commands of a political or religious leader. It is with the self-governing Greek states of the classical period that we begin to be able to see how a political system worked in detail, and to understand the structures of power on more than a personal level.

The second reason is still more striking. It is not entirely a European myth that in the classical Greek world we find the origins of very many features which are fundamental to our own western heritage. Whole modes of thought and expression have their fount and origin in Greece between 500 and 300 BC: self-conscious abstract political thought and moral philosophy; rhetoric as a study in its own right; tragedy, comedy, parody, and history; western naturalistic art and the female nude; democracy as theory and practice.

But this western tradition of the Greek origins of western civilisation, like the classical Greeks' own traditions about their past (see below, pp. 4–8), is also political, and no respecter of history. It is not only absurd to pretend that the buck stops dead in classical Greece, it is also to turn a blind eye to the socially embedded nature of human achievement. In Greek mythology the goddess Athene was born direct from the head of Zeus, but in ancient history as in modern history even the most startling discoveries and inventions have antecedents, and would not have occurred had previous conditions not been right. Therein lies the fascination with the Greece of the pre-classical period: can we recover the conditions which made the developments, the inventions, of the years 500 to 300 BC possible? What were the circumstances that brought about the revolution in the way the whole western world has thought and expressed itself ever since? We owe it to ourselves as humans to refuse the strategy of our tradition, a strategy which is far from politically innocent, which points to Athens' democracy as if that explained everything; and we owe it to ourselves to acknowledge the place which the heterogeneity of Greek experience within a pan-Mediterranean context had in the creation of that far from uniform classical Greek world.

If much of the attraction of studying archaic Greece lies in its *end*, and we must be unashamedly teleological, there is no less attraction in its beginning. In 1200 BC Greece looked much like any near-eastern society. The Mycenaeans were highly organised and, in their way, highly civilised. The language they spoke was Greek but, like several near-eastern neighbours, they wrote in a syllabary (so-called Linear B) and used writing to record the accounts of a complex and very hierarchical state organisation. Although their monuments and their figurative art certainly differ in detail from that of their near-eastern neighbours, it is difficult to feel that they differ in kind. But then something remarkable happened which we still cannot pretend that we understand: Mycenaean civilisation on the Greek mainland and islands collapsed. For the best part of two centuries, the traces of human occupation in Greece are exiguous, and, when the material remains increase again, the debt in material culture to the Mycenaean world is small. The Greeks kept their language, but they lost the tradition of writing it, and apart from some convenient ruined monuments upon which to hang their myths, the Greeks of the eighth century seem to have owed little other than that language and those myths to the Greeks of the twelfth century.

The Greeks of the ninth and eighth century were hardly in a 'state of nature', but they do give us a chance to see, from almost the very beginnings, the development of a political society and of a cultural identity. Through close examination of the material remains we can trace the formation and reformation of social groups, the contacts between groups both within and outside the Greek mainland, the links with other cultures of the near and middle east, and the effect which those contacts had at the material level. And, by a stroke of extraordinary fortune, we can get into the structures of thought of these communities through the survival of the two great epics, the *Iliad* and the *Odyssey*, both the result of a single mind working upon materials which had been transmitted and elaborated orally over a period of centuries, and also through the two much more individual works of a single historical figure, the long hexameter poems known as the *Theogony* and the *Works and Days*, by a man named Hesiod who lived in a small community in central Greece around the year 700 BC.

The challenge that faces the student of archaic Greece is this: how to understand how the small communities of men and women scattered over mainland Greece, the Greek islands, the coast of Asia Minor, and, before long, over the coasts of Sicily, south Italy, and the Black Sea too, developed from the low level of organisation and poverty of material culture that we see in the ninth century BC, to the communities that laid the foundations of the culture and political organisation of the western world of the fifth and fourth centuries. In studying the society and conditions of archaic Greece, we study also the conditions of our own emergence as a civilised society and as civilised individuals in the western world.

3

HISTORY AND THE TRADITIONS OF PREHISTORY

Knowing what questions we need answered is not difficult for archaic Greece: that is the advantage of starting from where you wish to get to, of the teleological approach. Answering those questions is a very different matter, and for much the same reason. In insisting above that understanding what happened in Greece is essential to understanding the modern western world, I have carefully focused not on archaic but on classical Greece. The confidence that we can reasonably feel about our knowledge of what happened in classical Greece, and about how classical Greek institutions worked, cannot be extended to the archaic period.

To all intents and purposes, archaic Greece is a prehistoric period, for it is a period before history was ever written. The earliest history in the western world is the work of Herodotos of Halikarnassos, written in the second half of the fifth century BC with the explicit aim of explaining how the Greeks and Persians came into conflict in what we call the Persian wars at the beginning of that century – the wars with which this book ends. Those wars are the earliest historical wars which any ancient author attempted to understand, and, whatever we think in detail of that attempt, the result is that those wars are the first wars where we can sensibly attempt to weigh up the factors which influenced either side, the first wars where we can sort out the crucial questions, even if we can never come to a definitive answer. And once Herodotos had attempted to understand the events of the generation immediately preceding his own, others, and most notably Thucydides, began to write accounts of their own times, based on observation as well as on others' stories. History had begun.

We are, of course, told plenty about Greece before the Persian wars; indeed, we are told much by Herodotos himself. But nothing that we are told comes from, or forms part of, a critical history, and we cannot treat it as if it does. What we have are traditions, and fragments of traditions, and we have them for the perfectly good reason that traditions were all that later authors had available, and that for most later authors it was the traditions that mattered. So, for Herodotos himself, the important factors which affected Greek relations with Persia at the beginning of the fifth century were what was being said about what had happened in the past and about past contacts between Greek and barbarian; whether or not what was said was true, in the sense of being an accurate account of what had taken place at some particular moment in the past, was of secondary importance at best. Herodotos does comment, from time to time, on the credibility of the stories he tells, but he tells the stories whether he believes them or not, often also carefully telling us, as itself a fact of historical importance, where he got the stories from. That perceptions are context-dependent is something some early Greek philosophers had insisted upon (below, p. 299); Herodotos' implicit recognition of this in the way he writes down his researches is one that we ignore at our peril.

4

It is not simply that no history of the archaic period has come down to us; no history of the archaic period was ever written. Writing half a century or so after the Persian wars, Herodotos, from Halikarnassos in Asia Minor, 'the father of history', hung his account of the achievements of Greeks and Persians, and why they came to fight each other, not on a continuous narrative of Greek events but on a narrative of Lydian and Persian history. The history of Greek cities is introduced by Herodotos as the Greek cities become relevant to his story about the eastern powers. Herodotos gives no absolute dates before 480 BC, does not deal with events in Greece before the Persian wars themselves in any chronological order, and is often vague about the relationship between one event and another, even when both events concern the same people or the same state.

All that Herodotos and later authors tell us about events down to 479 BC is derived from tradition, and tradition is of its essence selective. Stories are handed down because the teller thinks that they are worth telling, and they remain worth telling as long as they can make some impact on the understanding of the present. Present conditions determine what is remembered of the past, and how much is remembered. The shape of the past, as handed down, changes as the shape of the present changes, and an element of tradition that is once lost, because no longer relevant, can never be recovered. All who try to write history out of tradition have to try, with the paste of the imagination, to make up for the depredations of the scissors of time. And since in later antiquity, too, people attempted to write histories of early Greece, the modern scholar has additionally to distinguish traditions about past events from the accretions which ancients who related those traditions have themselves pasted on.

We can be fairly confident that Herodotos derived most of his information from live informants. He is thus an excellent guide to what the Greeks and others to whom he talked thought worth telling in the middle of the fifth century BC. Later writers may tell us what people were talking about in their own day, but very often they take over stories from Herodotos or other earlier authors, and interpret them in the light of their own interests and concerns. I will find occasion to explore what a fourth-century writer from Aristotle's school made of Herodotos when I discuss the Athenian sixth-century tyrant Peisistratos in Chapter 8. It is often important to distinguish where an extant writer got his information from, since that both tells us the date by which a particular version of past events had obtained currency and may warn us of a possible particular personal slant in the information given or its interpretation. I will sometimes in these pages note, for example, that information given to us by a writer of the early Roman empire, such as Diodoros or Nikolaos of Damascus, seems to derive from the lost work of the fourth-century BC historian Ephoros of Kyme, a writer whose interests and prejudices, already partly noted in antiquity, emerge even from the indirect testimony of those who relied on his work. But whether authors relied on live tradition or on what others had written is not so much dependent on the date at which they wrote as on their concerns. Plutarch and Pausanias both wrote in the second century AD, but Plutarch wrote his *Parallel Lives* of Greek and Roman statesmen on the basis of what he had read, while Pausanias, although not short of book-learning, was much more heavily dependent on what people told him as he travelled around, looking at the monuments of a past age and compiling his guide to the buildings and mythology of mainland Greece.

Although there was no history in the archaic period, there were plenty of other records, and it is these which the historian today must use to answer her questions. These records take two main forms: writing became available to the Greeks in the eighth century, and from then on literature of various types survives, all in verse; and there are diverse material remains. The surviving verse literature was composed for a variety of occasions, some of it directly engaging with current events (as in Pindar's early fifth-century odes celebrating victories in games), some of it purporting to describe a mythical world. The material remains are still more various, including some written material, from casual graffiti to formal public decisions, and a rich store of images which enhances our knowledge both of what stories were told and of the apparatus of daily life. Surviving literary and material remains are as subject to systematic bias as is the evidence of tradition: only certain types of literature have survived, and these were themselves the traditional products of very restricted social groups; and only certain sorts of materials have survived, and then only from certain contexts. But the massive advantage of these materials over the material from oral traditions is that the biases which have determined their survival are very largely biases that were the product of the society which created them, not the biases of a later society using its past to reshape its present.

The history which the literature and the material remains offer is a history that is very different from that offered by tradition. Traditions offer a dynamic view of the past, they concentrate on moments of crisis and change, and because moments of crisis and change are good to think with, their lesson is readily apparent to the audience. The history which material remains and literary remains offer is not like that, for they give direct access not to change but to the state of play at a particular moment in time. What we get is a series of still pictures, not a newsreel. To create dynamic history from these still pictures is the task of the historian, and it is an extremely difficult task. It may appear easy enough to compare one assemblage of material remains with another, but, unless one can be sure that one is comparing like with like, it is perilous to draw any substantial conclusions from their difference: that the material assemblage from a house of 650 BC is impoverished compared to a temple dedication of 700 BC does not indicate that the society as a whole was impoverished between 700 BC and 650 BC. Similarly with poetic remains, where the difference in the circumstances of composition, and the group for which the poetry was composed, always has to be taken into account in comparing the assumptions made by one text with those made by another. Using both the literary and the material remains together, to create a picture

6

of a changing archaic society, is more perilous yet. Perilous, but a challenge precisely because possible: for both the material assemblages and the poetry were products of the same society, both are fragments remaining from a once coherent world, and our aim must be to make them cohere once more.

To resort to tradition in the attempt to make the material and poetic fragments cohere is tempting but dangerous. It is all too easy to assume, and is all too often assumed, that the picture offered by tradition is a picture of the same society from which we have the material and poetic remains, and that the material and poetic remains can, indeed must, straightforwardly fill out the picture offered by tradition, and put flesh on its skeleton of events. But this assumption is fundamentally wrong. The selection and arrangement of events in the traditions were not determined by the societies to which the traditions directly relate, but by the last person who handed the tradition on before it reached a definitive form in the literature which has survived to us. In as far as tradition can be expected to cohere with any set of material remains, it is with the remains contemporary with the last person to hand it on, not with those contemporary with the events it purports to describe.

It would be absurd, on the other hand, to discard tradition altogether; particularly absurd in a history which is interested in the archaic period not least for what it became. Much of the tradition about archaic Greece received its definitive form in the classical period, and that tradition was itself part of what made classical Greece what it was. But we cannot pretend that tradition is the same as history, and we must acknowledge the fragility of the links which connect tradition to the events it claims to record. Neither the details, nor the major outlines, of traditions can be trusted unless they can be independently corroborated. When traditions can be checked against records it can be shown that on occasions they reverse the results of wars, introduce actors who were not and often cannot have been there, claim as absent figures who were active, claim as important events of no significance, and pass over events of the utmost importance. Traditions make good telling and good reading, for they would never otherwise have been handed on from one generation to another; but although traditions tell us an enormous amount about the concerns of those, both in antiquity and since, who told and retold them, they can give us few sure historical insights into the societies which they claim to be about.

But this dry theorising about tradition needs the illumination of an example, and, by way of introducing both tradition and some of the recurrent themes of this book, it will be profitable to subject to close scrutiny the traditions about one particular historical event: the foundation of a Greek settlement at Cyrene.

THE CASE OF CYRENE

Using the traditions

Greekness was largely a matter of self-identification. Use of the Greek language, recognition of a particular set of gods and of particular ways of worshipping them, and claims to a common ancestry played a part in getting that self-identification widely accepted, but place of residence did not. By 500 BC Greeks could be met enjoying a variety of natural environments in settlements all round the Mediterranean, from Egypt to Spain, from North Africa to southern France or the Adriatic, as well as at more than fifty settlements on all four shores of the Black Sea (see below, pp. 23–5, pp. 111–18 and Figure 32).

If the Greek settlement at Cyrene in Libya (Figure 1), traditionally founded in 631 BC, stood out from other settlements, it did so only because it was exceedingly prosperous. But it stands out for us because of the unique wealth and unusually early date of traditions which relate to it. The earliest allusions we have to the circumstances in which Cyrene was founded come in two poems written by the poet Pindar in 462 BC to celebrate the prestigious victory of the then ruler of Cyrene, Arkesilas, in a chariot race at the Pythian games at Delphi. Then, about forty years later, Herodotos recorded for us both what the people of Cyrene told him about how their city came to be founded, and what was said by the people of the small south Aegean island of Thera (Santorini), who claimed to have sent out the people who settled at Cyrene. From the fourth century BC a decree survives in which the people of Cyrene agreed to give land and rights to people from Thera who wished to join them. In this decree they included the text which the Therans, who came as a deputation to Cyrene to request the rights, passed off as the sworn agreement made by the Therans before the settlers were sent out. Finally, what one Menekles of Barke said in the third century BC about the foundation of Cyrene happens to be preserved in an ancient commentary on one of Pindar's odes for Arkesilas. These numerous and various texts give us a chance to see what was said about the foundation both at different times and by those with different relationships to the places involved.

In one of the two odes (*Pythian Odes* 4.1–8, 259–62), Pindar refers, as might be expected in a poem celebrating a victory at Delphi, to the role of the oracle of Apollo there in guiding the founder of the settlement at Cyrene, Battos, and declaring him king. In the other (*Pythian Odes* 5.55–69, 85–93), he celebrates Battos' scaring away the lions to found the city, Apollo's role in the foundation and the establishment of 'good government without war', the piety of Aristoteles (apparently another name for Battos) in giving cult places and processions to the gods, and his burial place in the agora (civic centre and market place) (Text 1). Piety and victory go together in Pindar's odes, and Pindar regularly celebrates victors by celebrating their real or mythical ancestry, but the choice of context here is significant. Pindar's references and

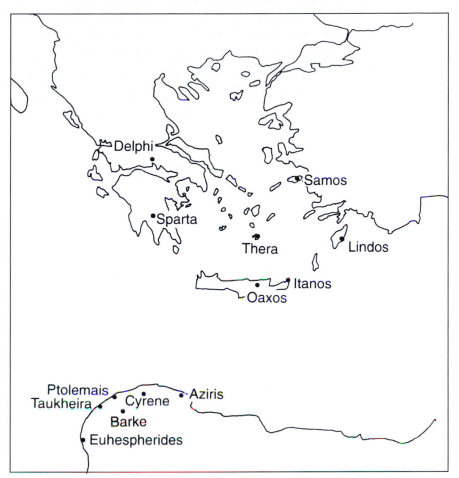

Figure 1 Parties involved in the account of settlement at Cyrene.

allusions bring out that the foundation of Cyrene was in a deserted place, inhabited by wild beasts. In addition, they bring out the personal bravery of Battos and imply that good government without war at Cyrene is rule by the Battiads, and they put much emphasis on the Spartan connection. Pindar may well use Karneios as the cult epithet of Apollo because the ode was written for performance at a festival called 'Karneia', but Apollo Karneios was a god particularly associated with Sparta, and together with the rather obscure reference to a cult of the Trojan sons of Antenor, whose visit to Cyrene seems to have occurred when they were being transported by Menelaos to Sparta after the end of the Trojan war, it marks very clearly the claim of fifth-century Cyreneans to links with Sparta. Sparta was reputedly the 'mother-city' from which Thera was founded; it was also one of very few other Greek cities ruled by kings. But there may be more involved in the invocation of

We received the feast of the Karneia, with its many sacrifices, from our Theran ancestors, and now at your banquet worship the well-founded city of Cyrene. The Trojan sons of Antenor who fight in bronze armour possess it: for they once came with Helen, after they had seen their homeland going up in smoke in war. The men whom Aristoteles brought in swift ships, opening the deep path of the sea, accepted the horse-driving people with sacrifices and approached them with gifts. Aristoteles established greater groves of the gods and laid down a straight-cut paved way to resound with the hooves of horses in processions to Apollo warding off evil from men; and his own tomb lies apart at the stern of the agora.

Text 1: Pindar, Pythian Odes *5.77–93 written to celebrate the victory of Arkesilas, Battiad ruler of Cyrene, in the chariot race at the Pythian games in 462/461 BC.*

Apollo Karneios, for both the alternative stories about how he got that epithet (Pausanias 3.13.4–5) stress the need to propitiate Apollo for harming a person or thing dear to him; in one case this is the grove from whose wood the Trojan horse, vital to the capture of the sons of Antenor, was constructed. Implicit in this story is an acknowledgement of the damage which founding a colony necessarily inflicts, and of the way in which a foundation which the god has ordered may nevertheless require propitiation of the gods. In this context, Pindar's reference to Battos as 'Aristoteles' may be intended to bring out the peculiar piety of the founder: the etymological meaning of the name ('one who brings things to the best of conclusions' or 'the one performing the best of rites') is appropriate and propitious; third-century BC Cyrene had a priest named Aristoteles performing the Karneian *telesphoria* (*SEG* 9.65).

Herodotos, whose purpose in asking about the past of Cyrene and in relating it to his readers was somewhat broader than Pindar's celebratory brief, tells us very much more (4.150–9). He first relates 'what the Therans say': that their King Grinnos went to Delphi to consult the oracle about something else, and was told to found a city in Libya; that when he said he himself was too old, the finger was pointed at Battos; that when Grinnos and Battos did nothing about all this Thera suffered a seven-year drought in which all but one of the trees died; that a consequent consultation with Delphi produced a further instruction to found a settlement in Libya; that the Therans then got expert advice from a Cretan purple-fisher named Korobios, from the city of Itanos, whom they paid to guide an advance party which settled temporarily on the island of Platea off the African coast; that Korobios was left on this island while the Therans went back for more men, and was saved from starvation only by a chance visit from a Samian called Kolaios who was sailing to Egypt; that the Therans raised settlers equally from each region of the island and from each family, and that two fifty-oared ships (*pentekonters*) sailed to Platea.

Herodotos follows the Theran story with 'what the Cyreneans say': that when widowed King Etearkhos of Oaxos in Crete remarried, his new wife made life difficult for his daughter Phronime; that her father handed

When Battos reached manhood, he went to Delphi about his stutter. In reply to his question the Pythia responded: 'Battos, you have come about your voice. But Lord Phoibos Apollo sends you to found a settlement in the sheep pastures of Libya.' … He replied in the following words: 'O Lord, I came to you to ask about my voice, but you give me other impossible commands, telling me to found a settlement in Libya. What resources do I have? What support?' But he did not persuade Apollo to give him any other command. So, when he received the same oracular response as before, Battos went away back to Thera. Afterwards things went badly for Battos himself, and for the other Therans. Not knowing the reason for the misfortunes, the Therans sent to Delphi about their present troubles. The Pythia gave an oracular response that things would go better for them if they helped Battos to found Cyrene in Libya. After this the Therans sent Battos off with two fifty-oared ships. They sailed to Libya but, at a loss what else to do, returned back to Thera. But the Therans threw stones at them as they came to land, did not allow them to put in to land, and ordered them to sail back.

Text 2: Herodotos 4. 155–6: part of the Cyrenean version of the founding of Cyrene.

Phronime over to a Theran trader named Themison to drown; that he evaded his oath to do so and brought her to Thera; that on Thera Phronime became concubine to one Polymnestos and bore him a son, Battos, who had a speech impediment; that Battos went to Delphi to consult the oracle about this impediment and was told to found a city in Libya; that Battos did not obey and subsequently Thera suffered ill fortune; that when the Therans consulted Delphi they were told it would be better if Battos founded Cyrene in Libya; that the Therans sent off Battos with two fifty-oared ships; that when these tried to return the Therans drove them off with stones; that Battos and his companions sailed back and established themselves on the island of Platea (see, in part, Text 2). Herodotos then claims that the story from that point, of moving from Platea to Aziris on the African coast on Delphic advice, and then from Aziris to the site of Cyrene, a place where they were told that 'the sky leaks' (see below, p. 25), on the advice of the Libyan natives, was one about which Therans and Cyreneans agreed.

There is very little in common between Theran and Cyrenean accounts down to the settlement of Platea. Both stories involve consultations with Delphi, both make Battos the leader, both agree about where the first settlement was. Otherwise the stories do very different things. The Theran story emphasises that the idea of sending settlers to Libya came from outside; that only after years of hardship did they agree to do so; that they sought expert advice first, and made a trial trip before selecting settlers; and that those selected to be settlers were chosen fairly from all regions and kin groups. The Cyrenean story, on the other hand, emphasises the royal ancestry of Battos and the charmed life of his mother; it makes founding a settlement a duty of Battos and not of the Theran community; and it suggests that once the Therans realised that Battos was to go they took steps to ensure he would not come back.

It is not difficult to see why, by some 150 years after the settlers had first arrived in Africa, the people of Thera and the people of Cyrene should tell such different stories. The Therans had an interest in keeping alive links with Cyrene, which had proved a prosperous place. It was vital for them to maintain that they had acted reasonably, and had done all that could conceivably be expected of a city which was sending out settlers in order to make sure that the settlement would be successful. The people of Cyrene, on the other hand, had made good. They had no need of Thera. They needed to assert their independence, not their dependence. What is more, until the middle of the fifth century the people of Cyrene were, very unusually, ruled by a royal family, the Battiads, who traced themselves back to the founder of the settlement (on fifth-century Cyrene see *GW* 59–63). It was strongly in the political interests of this dynasty to stress the personal role of the first Battos in the establishment of the settlement, for it was upon his special role that they based their claim to the monopoly of power.

Once we appreciate the factors which shape these stories, we can see that it is vain to seek historical truth from either account. Neither account was interested in a full and frank record of what happened; both parties were telling stories of the past to suit the present, stories that were not only selective in their memories but free in their elaboration. Some of that elaboration is transparent: every character in the story of Battos' mother has a name fitted to the role they play: Etearkhos means 'True ruler', Phronime 'Sensible woman', Themison 'The man who does what is right', Polymnestos 'The man who woos much'. The purple-fisher surely has his place in the story by his plausibility: where else would one go to look for advice about Africa than to Crete, already part-way there? And who else talk to but a man whose maritime specialism demands a knowledge of off-shore as well as in-shore waters?

The way that the past was something to be latched on to for present purposes is nicely revealed by one further curious detail, which is given as part of the Theran story in Herodotos: the tale of Kolaios the Samian. His part in the story is minor – he simply keeps Korobios alive while Korobios is waiting for the Therans to return to Platea. It is hard to see why the Therans should remember this, and it plays no structural part in the story. However, the visit to Platea is not all we are told about Kolaios. We are also told that when he left Platea, bound for Egypt, he was blown off course and through the Pillars of Herakles (Straits of Gibraltar), and landed up at Tartessos in Spain. There he made an enormous profit, presumably selling Greek objects such as the Tartessians had never seen before in return for the precious metal which they had in no short supply. On return to Samos he made a dedication at the sanctuary of Hera of a large bronze mixing bowl of Argive type, with griffin-head attachments and supported by three great bronze kneeling figures. Herodotos does not explicitly claim to have seen this object, but his description makes it very likely that he has done so, and that the story about Kolaios came attached to the bowl. What Herodotos does say is that Kolaios' visit to Platea was the origin of the great friendship between Samos and Thera and Cyrene. It looks as if the memory of a Samian merchant's having been somehow involved in the early stages of the foundation of Cyrene has been preserved by attaching it to a tangible record of Samian trading activity, and that the Samians were able to make this claim the basis for establishing good relations with both communities (in fact Samian sub-geometric pottery has been found on Thera, suggesting that contact goes back before Cyrene's foundation).

Sometime in the fourth century BC the Therans had occasion to try to turn their links with Cyrene to material advantage. They sent a deputation to Cyrene claiming that there had been an original sworn undertaking when the first settlers were dispatched, which allowed other Therans subsequently to claim land and citizenship, and which provided that, if the new settlement was unsuccessful, the settlers could return to Thera. The Therans even produced a text of this sworn agreement (Text 3). The people of Cyrene decided not only to accept the rights of the Therans to join them but also to have the original agreement inscribed and displayed in their sanctuary of Pythian Apollo (ML 5/Fornara 18). The authenticity of the original agreement which the Therans quoted has been much discussed but to treat this question as a question of whether it was a genuine seventh-century document or a fourth-century forgery misunderstands the process by which this text was created. The sworn agreement as inscribed certainly contains some features – the claim to originate from a meeting of the Assembly on Thera, the claim that the Delphic oracle was spontaneous, the naming of the new settlement as Cyrene – which can hardly have been in a seventh-century agreement which had been made before the settlers were dispatched. More importantly, it contains nothing which does not assist the case that the Therans are making in the fourth century: it establishes that the leader was chosen by public decision, those sent out were not expelled but chosen fairly, that the Therans did not undertake the new foundation lightly, that all Cyreneans have family links to Thera, that had the settlement failed Thera would have welcomed the settlers back and given them their property. In tone, and in some details, this claimed original agreement is very close to the account which Herodotos heard from the Therans in the fifth century, and for all that it contains more formal language and some archaizing elements, it seems best understood as an elaborated lineal descendant of the same Theran oral tradition.

Why were the people of Cyrene willing to accept this version of their past, a version directly in conflict, on some matters at least, with their own traditions? We do not know the detailed political situation in Cyrene when the Theran deputation came, or how that deputation was being used in any current political debate. We can note, however, that the story which Herodotos picked up in Cyrene in the fifth century BC will have lost much of its political relevance after the fall of the Battiads perhaps in the 430s BC: it had built into it an emphasis on Battos' charmed life and the way he was specially picked out by the god to found Cyrene, an emphasis hardly appropriate once the dynasty he founded was no longer in power. The story which the Therans

The Assembly decided: since Apollo spontaneously commanded Battos and the Therans to found Cyrene, the Therans have decided to send Battos to Libya as leader of the people and king, and the Therans shall sail as his comrades. They are to sail on equal and similar terms, by family, one son to be chosen [-*lacuna*-] those in their prime and free men from the rest of the Therans [-*lacuna*-] to sail. If the settlers establish a settlement, any of their relatives who later sails to Libya is to receive citizenship and rights and a share of undistributed land. If they do not establish a settlement, and the Therans are unable to help them, but they are driven by necessity for five years, they may freely leave the land for Thera and recover citizenship and their own property. Anyone who is unwilling to sail when the city sends him out shall be liable to the death penalty and his property shall be confiscated. Anyone who harbours or conceals, either a father a son or a brother a brother, shall be liable to the same penalty as one unwilling to sail. Sworn agreements were made to this effect both by those remaining there and by those who sailed to found the settlement, and they invoked curses upon those, either among those settling in Libya or those remaining there, who broke the agreement and did not abide by it. They made wax models and burnt them and all together, men and women, boys and girls, invoked the curse that the person who did not abide by the sworn agreement but broke it should be melted and flow away like the models, both himself and his offspring and his property, but that to those who kept the sworn agreements, both those sailing to Libya and those staying in Thera, many good things should come, both to them and their offspring.

Text 3: ML 5.23–51 The sworn agreement which the fourth-century Theran embassy to Cyrene said had been made when Battos took settlers from Thera to Libya.

tell, by contrast, stresses the equality of the original settlers – they were to sail 'on equal and fair terms'; such equality was normal in fifth-century and later settlements, but it is also well suited to Cyrene's fourth-century constitution. Changing interests demand different versions of the past, and the Therans were giving the people of Cyrene a chance to recover, and adopt, a version of their past which fitted their new interests in a way which no amount of selection from the fifth-century Cyrenean tradition could match.

Yet one more stage of the rewriting of past history in terms of the interests of a particular time and place is visible in the account of the third-century-BC North African writer Menekles of Barke (*FGH* 270 F6/Fornara 17). Menekles claimed that Battos was driven from Thera after factional strife which his own faction lost, and founded Cyrene after Delphi advised him that that was better than carrying on the struggle in Thera. Menekles came from a city which tradition (Herodotos 4.160) held to have been founded from Cyrene after factional strife…

What then can we say about the establishment of a Greek settlement at Cyrene? That there was an important, but not exclusive, connection with Thera, a starring role for someone who came to be known as Battos, and a rather lengthy process of finding the ideal site, seems safe, but little else. The other elements in the stories, from Pindar on, tell us not about the original establishment, but about politics at Cyrene and the position of Cyrene in the discourse of others in the fifth century and later. If we want to know more about what happened in the seventh century then we have to turn to archaeological data.

USING THE ARCHAEOLOGY

There is much about the history of Greek settlement in Libya which the rather limited archaeological work that has gone on there is not yet in a position to illuminate. But what the archaeology has revealed is striking. First of all, finds of Greek objects from the first half of the seventh century BC at Ptolemais and at Cyrene itself suggest that this North African coast was not nearly as unknown before the foundation of Greek settlements as the traditions suggested. Even without excavation of the site, pottery which is almost certainly to be dated to c.650 has been found at the place most likely to be Aziris. This provides material confirmation that Odysseus' lying claim to have been shipwrecked while being taken to Libya to be sold (*Odyssey* 14.295) reflects actual Greek knowledge of the southern coast of the Mediterranean. Second, although tradition had it that other sites on the Libyan coast were founded from Cyrene, the evidence for occupation from Tocra (ancient Taukheira) and from Ptolemais seems to date back as early in pottery terms as does the evidence for permanent occupation at Cyrene – that is, to c.620 BC. The selection of pottery found in the rich sanctuary deposit excavated at Tocra differs in slight but significant ways from that at Cyrene (in particular it receives a quite different range of pottery from islands in the Cyclades, with none from Thera), which suggests independent links with the Greek world. Third, the literary tradition maintains that for some fifty years the population of Cyrene remained only the initial Theran settlers and their offspring, before a general invitation to all Greeks to join was issued: not only does this make it hard to see how Cyrene could have founded Taukheira so soon after Cyrene itself was established, but the pottery reaching Cyrene and Tocra before 580 BC came from as wide a range of sites as that reaching them after 580, and the peculiarly wide variety of pottery vessels and of personal items (pins, etc.) imported from Sparta, in particular, from soon after the foundation has led archaeologists to speculate that there must have been residents from Sparta or Lakonia from the beginning. There may have been other stories, not related by Herodotos, which did more justice to the archaeology: the second-century AD writer of a guide to Greece, Pausanias, in fact preserves the claim that a Spartan athlete, Khionis, victorious in the Olympic games in 664, 660, and 656 BC, was involved with Battos in the foundation (Pausanias 3.14.3), and an inscription known as the Lindian Chronicle (*FGH* 532 F1.17), which records dedications (many of them certainly mythical) made at the sanctuary of Athene at Lindos on Rhodes, quotes a dedication made by Lindians who took part in the settlement of Cyrene by Battos.

Archaeology therefore would seem to confirm that there is a strong political slant in the later traditions. The claim to have pioneered settlement in the unknown was good for the status of both Therans and Battiads, magnifying the achievement. Keeping non-Therans out of the story certainly suited the Theran claim to be the origin of Cyrene; it may well also have suited both internal political arguments at Cyrene and the general claim not to have been a rag-bag settlement. Claiming to be the origin of other settlements along this coast similarly suited Cyrene's claim to pre-eminence in the area. Without the literary traditions to distort our view, we would still recognise a peculiar role for Thera in the settlement of this area, for Theran pottery is otherwise rarely found outside Thera, but we would also recognise a special role for Cretans (Cretan sixth-century pottery, rare enough even in Crete itself, is found at Cyrene) and for Lakonians, and all three would have to play alongside a wide range of others. Whatever stimulated Greeks to upgrade the earlier periodic contacts with the area and settle in numbers, it was not economic pressure on, or the political initiative of, one city, let alone one man.

Archaeology and literary texts almost always pull against one another. Literary texts, and the oral or written traditions on which any particular text relies, pick out whatever is of use for their argument, tend to stress the peculiar, and are retrospective; the archaeological record does not offer a random sample of the past – not all material survives equally well, and not all actions are equally directly reflected in material culture – but it does tend, despite the bias of archaeologists towards exceptional sites, to show the run-of-the-mill, and to stress overall similarities. So, using traditions to write history demands an acute awareness of the fact that men are doing things with traditions. Sometimes doing something with a tradition means preserving valuable information; it was probably the way Cyrenean tradition in the fifth century was a support for the Battiads that preserved accurately the lengths of their reigns, and so the foundation date for Cyrene. On many occasions tradition promotes disinformation. Using archaeology runs the risk of flattening out history, of failing to perceive social or political dramas which have no direct effect on material culture. To be healthy, scepticism about what traditions tell us has to be matched with a full awareness of what archaeology can never tell us. As in this example, and as throughout this book, the literary and the archaeological pictures have to be separately constructed before they can be put together; rarely do they directly illuminate each other, but together they may in different ways illuminate the same world.

OUR WORLD UNDER CONSTRUCTION

In 800 BC the Greek world was poor, small, and lacking in general organisation. Its communities were small, and hard pressed to survive in a hostile natural environment. Greeks had few contacts in the wider world and no special advantages, unless we count as advantages a good fund of traditional tales and a strong line in travelling bards. By 479 BC, after turning back the attack of the Persian empire on the Greek mainland, the Greek world was extensive and dynamic, complex in organisation, increasing in population, and immensely creative. In a sense, indeed, classical Greece created the modern western world.

The story of how it came about that the impoverished and relatively isolated groups of ninth-century Greeks grew into the flourishing and vigorous Greeks of the fifth century is the story that is told here. It is a story of small groups responding to the pressures of the natural environment, turning to communities elsewhere out of need, and returning with ideas and artefacts which they mercilessly exploited and often entirely transformed, in a spirit of competition and rivalry. It is a story of how those small groups struggled to distinguish themselves and to remain distinct, as individuals within communities, as communities among other Greek communities, and as Greeks among barbarians who were at least as wealthy, as organised, and as skilled as themselves. Because the struggle to be distinct operated at every level, this story is not simply the story of the rise of the Greek city-state, of the struggle to find a political form which both enabled and restricted individual distinction in the interests of the preservation of the distinctness of the community as a whole; it is also the story of the development of cultural distinction in expression as well as in action or in identity. To tell such a story it is necessary to try to write a 'total' history, a history which recognises that politics and social organisation, social organisation and economic pressures on the means of life, economic pressures and cultural expression, cultural expression and religious cult activity, all these are part of the same story, and none can be understood without the others or studied in isolation.

2

SETTING THE STAGE

THE NATURAL ENVIRONMENT

Geology

It is easy to look at J. W. Waterhouse's painting *Hylas and the Nymphs* (Figure 2) and to ridicule the way in which he sets his classical scene in a shaded lily pond somewhere in the south of England, but it is far more difficult to evoke the natural environment of ancient Greece successfully in a single image. There is a good reason for that: for all that Greece is a small country, it is immensely various, encompassing a whole range of environmental conditions, from desert to permanent snow, and offering highly contrasting conditions at very short distances from each other.

The thinly fleshed skeleton of Greece is formed from a series of limestone mountains, folded in ridges which run from north-west to south-east and

Figure 2 J. W. Waterhouse's painting *Hylas and the Nymphs.*

18

gradually decrease in height until they appear only as island humps breaking through the surface of the sea. These mountain ranges divide the country and create a diversity of ecological zones. Other forces too have contributed to the shape and nature of the Greek peninsula, in particular volcanic forces, and local changes in landform continue to occur today in what is the most active earthquake zone in Europe.

These geological forces have left Greece with a highly irregular coastline, and have ensured that few parts of the peninsula are far from the sea. Access to the sea is not always easy, however, and good harbours are relatively few and far between. The omnipresence of the sea does a lot to temper the climatic conditions, and most of Greece has a broadly Mediterranean climate, with wet winters (October to March) and hot dry summers. But not even this pattern is ensured for all of Greece (north-west Greece enjoys much summer rain in its more mountainous areas), and, in those places which do show this distribution pattern, the precise amounts and distribution of rain vary so much that they enable very different plant growth.

Climate

The major factors governing climatic variation are relief and aspect. The south and east of Greece are much drier than the north and west. Not only are they drier in absolute terms, but they are sufficiently much drier to be marginal for such staple crops as wheat. The north, and particularly the north-east, is significantly colder in winter, so that even at sea level frost-sensitive crops, such as olives and figs, are practically ruled out. Such crops are everywhere sensitive to relief: not only will they not grow at high altitude because of frost, but they will not grow in basins at low altitude either, because of the 'frost hollow' effect. But high altitude also means more rain, and so makes possible the growth of crops with a high water demand, particularly trees. How far the summer drought limits crop growth depends on how well the soil retains water; soils formed on volcanic rocks retain water better than those formed on limestone, and soils formed on hard limestone tend to store very little water.

Greece contains a wide variety of different ecological niches, and environmental conditions repeatedly change, sometimes dramatically, over very short distances. This is true not just of the broad patterns, but of the variations from year to year and month to month. Climatic conditions in a single place can vary significantly from year to year, and this is particularly

Table 1 Rainfall on the Methana peninsula, September 1972 to August 1974.

Rainfall in mm	S	O	N	D	J	F	M	A	M	J	J	A	Annual
1972–3	2.0	169.3	31.7	29.2	131.2	66.8	74.4	24.9	10.2	1.5	25.6	1.5	568.5
1973–4	2.0	24.6	65.2	27.9	79.2	23.9	98.7	13.7	13.5	0.8	0	2.0	352.8

true of amounts and distribution of rainfall, where the annual totals regularly vary by a factor of at least two, and monthly totals vary by a very much larger factor. Consider the rainfall on the Methana peninsula in the successive agricultural years September to August 1972–3 and 1973–4 (Table 1). Here we see not only how much drier 1973–4 was than 1972–3, but that the autumn rains came distinctly later in 1973–4 and in markedly smaller quantity; the summer drought of 1974 was much deeper and longer than that of 1973, when a July storm made a very significant contribution to local resources – albeit one that would have little agricultural effect.

So local are the variations that it is by no means guaranteed that a wet year in one place will also be a wet year twenty miles away. Some local variations are the product of physical relief: Thebes, in the middle of a basically flat central Greek landscape, receives on average only 63 per cent of the annual rainfall of Levadhia, which is twenty-five miles west of it and in the rain-excess belt of Mount Parnassos. Other local variations are less easy to account for: in 1957, when Athens had only 80 per cent of its mean annual rainfall, Eleusis, fifteen miles or so north-west, was having an average year; five years previously Eleusis had had only 83 per cent of its mean annual rainfall when Athens had 114 per cent of its average precipitation. Since such variations meant, in effect, that one place could support a wheat crop while in the other wheat, and even barley, had its yield restricted by lack of water, these bald statistics have a real importance for the local community.

Natural vegetation

Relief and climate not only affect what man can grow, but they, and other factors which are in some cases still not fully understood, also affect the wild plant communities. This is most striking, and most important for the human community, in the case of trees. Beech trees are not to be found south of Thessaly; the common pine of Europe, *Pinus silvestris*, does not penetrate further south than Macedonia. The common pine of southern Greece is the Aleppo pine, a rather stunted creation with a distinct preference for coastal environments: good for resin, it is of little use for timber. More use is the black pine, *Pinus nigra*, found on mountains to considerable heights: this was the pine favoured for merchant ships and house construction. Travellers to Athens and the surrounding countryside come to regard the Aleppo pine as part of the essential Greek countryside, yet once one is over the Parnes/Kithairon mountain range, travelling north, the Aleppo pine disappears, even though neither soils nor climate are noticeably different. By contrast, the Greek fir, *Abies cephalonica*, is not at all fussy about the soil it grows in, and is found in mountain and upland regions of Attica, Boiotia, and the whole of northern Greece at altitudes from 600 m to almost 2000 m. Fir was lighter than pine and stronger, and for those reasons was preferred for triremes, and particularly for trireme oars; but it was the silver fir, *Abies alba*, found within Greece only in Macedonia, which was the shipbuilder's favourite.

20

Whenever Orion and Sirius come to mid-heaven, and Dawn with her rosy fingers looks upon Arcturus, Perses, then cut off all the bunches of grapes and carry them home; show them to the sun for ten days and ten nights, shade them for five, and on the sixth draw off into jars the gifts of cheerful Dionysos. But when the Pleiades and Hyades and strong Orion sink in the sky, then is the time to remember the plough's season: may the seed lodge well in the earth.

Text 4: Hesiod, Works and Days *609–17. The end of Hesiod's description of the tasks of the farming year.*

We can happily assume that the basic physical geography of Greece has remained unaltered ever since humans appeared on the scene, but how confident can we be that the climate and plant communities have stayed the same? How can we be sure that Waterhouse was wrong to imagine a Greece of shady deciduous woods, lily ponds, and pale Pre-Raphaelite maidens? We have no ancient climatic statistics, but we do have a number of descriptions of plant communities and of the agricultural year from archaic and classical Greek writers, and in particular from the poet Hesiod, living in Boiotia in *c.*700 BC (Text 4), and from Aristotle's pupil Theophrastos, born on the island of Lesbos, and resident in Athens in the late fourth century BC. Such descriptions do not always give as precise information as we would like (ancient writers did not distinguish between species of pine or oak, did not differentiate juniper from cedar, and so on), but they tell enough for us to be fairly confident that the seasonal pattern in antiquity was much the same as the seasonal pattern today, and the range of wild plants to be found was also much as it is today. As we will see below, the great changes that have occurred have been less in natural vegetation and more in agricultural crops.

If we want to go further back than surviving literary sources, we have to turn to archaeological investigation of changing landforms and of pollen deposits from permanently damp areas, which have preserved organic matter in chronological sequence of deposition in an oxygen-free environment. From such sources, which may go back several thousand years, it is broadly clear that the last glaciation saw a Greece which was drier and cooler, and corresponded with a period of soil erosion and consequent alluviation (often known as the 'Older Fill'), which is found not only in Greece but also elsewhere in the Mediterranean. The Greek landscape 30,000 years ago looked decidedly different: sea level was some 120 m lower than its present level, giving large areas of coastal plain, and grassland rather than woodland seems to have been dominant in the very dry conditions. The warming of the climate, and the rise of the sea, was slow, finally completed only 8,000 years ago. The warming made trees dominant, both deciduous and coniferous. Unfortunately, while pollen cores are good at providing a broad-brush picture of such fundamental changes, they are extremely blunt tools with which to investigate those changes in detail: different plants distribute different amounts of pollen in different ways, and factors other than the amount of pollen in the local atmosphere may affect the deposition of pollen at a lake bed. Pollen diagrams do, however, suggest such curiosities as a total absence of Greek fir from the area around Lake Kopais in central Boiotia.

Major changes in the natural environment of Greece thus occurred long before human beings were in any position to influence it; and when they did arrive on the scene, it is unclear what influence either their presence or their development of sedentary agriculture had on the world around. Signs of human settlement are already well scattered across the landscape in the early Bronze Age, and these suggest that, if the natural environment of 8,000 years ago was dominated by woodland, considerable human effort must have been employed in its clearance during the neolithic.

The broad picture is of great change in the remote past, but not very much substantial change, in either climate or natural environment, during the last 3,000 years, until the last fifty years. The detailed picture is less certain. Granted that the general climatic pattern has remained the same, and that the plant communities have largely been altered by evolution and addition rather than by deletion, we remain in a very poor position when it comes to answering questions about particular areas of the countryside.

The effects of agriculture

Particular farming regimes undoubtedly have their own effects on landscape. Arable farming means the removal of timber trees, the planting of fruit trees and vines, repeated tilling of the land, which increases its water retention, and the planting of cereals and legumes, which take out and put in various nutrients. On sloping soils, continued arable cropping demands that measures be taken to retain the topsoil if erosion is not to occur, and hence brings about the construction of terrace walls – walls which not only alter the appearance of the landscape but themselves create a new environmental niche. Pastoral farming may compete with arable farming for lowland pasture, but it primarily exploits the non-arable landscape, as sheep and goats graze land that is neither suitable nor wanted for arable agriculture. Sheep, and more particularly goats, are practically omnivorous, and will consume a very wide range of scrub and tree material. The trees that are most palatable (lime, holm oak, and the like) get restricted by browsing to areas inaccessible to goats. Trees that can withstand being eaten off to the ground continue to be present, but in shrub rather than tree form. The reduction of tree species to shrubs allows light into areas which have previously been shaded, and hence allows other plants, intolerant of shade, to develop. In particular, a good case has been made for considering that the so-called *garriga* communities of plants, such as Jerusalem sage and thyme, which develop on soils too short of moisture for woodland plants, have been brought into existence solely by the pasturing of animals.

If there had never been any agricultural activity, the Greek landscape would be more highly wooded, with more deciduous trees and a pattern of woodland and grassland, where grasses occupied the areas too dry, or with too restricted soils, for trees to grow. The situation would not be static: certain trees (notably pines) cannot grow in the shade produced by their own species, and hence can grow again only once mature trees have reached the end of their life and fallen in large enough numbers to open up the ground to the light. What would be lost from the present wild landscape are the areas of aromatic plants, the *garriga*, so evocative of the Greek countryside and the whole Greek way of life today.

It is more subject to dispute whether the landscape itself has been physically altered by humans. Many have suggested that, in the last 3,000 or so years of human exploitation, human activity has not only removed trees but has removed the soil, which has been washed away once the tree roots are no longer there to retain it, and the trees' well-clothed branches no longer there to protect it from the force of summer storms. There has certainly been a good deal of soil erosion in Greece. Pleistocene erosion before people ever appeared on the scene has already been mentioned; erosion and alluvial deposition caused by marine transgression can be traced in certain places during the historical period; but the relationship between erosion and agricultural or pastoral activity is not at all a straightforward one. There is no doubt that cultivation on slopes leads to soil movement downhill, something that can been seen very clearly in the accumulation of soil in lynchets at those field boundaries which run across slopes, especially if those boundaries are hedged. There is also no doubt that when a formerly terraced landscape goes out of cultivation, and the terraces are no longer maintained, the terraces rapidly get breached, and soil is washed out from behind them before the slope can stablize itself again. But have factors such as these dramatically altered the landscape since the Greek Dark Age? On the whole, there seems to be a good chance that the answer is 'No'. Individual examples can certainly be found of areas where woods were recorded in antiquity but now there are no trees in sight, but there is good reason not to believe that all the mountains which are now bare, or which now support only *macchia* and *garriga*, were soil-covered and well-wooded in antiquity. When erosion can be studied in action today, it is often very difficult to discover what makes a particular landscape liable to erosion, or why erosion suddenly stops. Some of the most dramatic examples of soil erosion are very clearly the product of particularly severe weather conditions, which have not simply removed soil but have taken away full-grown trees and substantial buildings at the same time.

A lot has happened in the Greek landscape since the Dark Age, but if we want to conjure up a picture of any particular area of Greece at that time we could probably do a lot worse than start from the appearance of that landscape today. In many areas more environmental change was probably to be seen by moving twenty miles or so in the Dark Age than is to be seen by moving from the Dark Age to the present day in the same place.

Table 2 Rainfall on the south and east coasts of Sicily and on the coast and plateau of Cyrenaica.

Rainfall in mm	S	O	N	D	J	F	M	A	M	J	J	A	Annual
Agrigento averages, 1931–40	24	46	81	94	57	61	40	21	23	6	1	4	458
Syracuse averages, 1931–40	47	58	125	90	115	63	41	29	21	5	1	11	606
Ptolemais 1932–3	4.5	3.9	90.7	23.7	11.4	11.3	4.2	0.4	11.1	0.4	0	0.1	161.7
Ptolemais 1934–5	1.0	55.1	14.3	168.7	141.8	31.3	31.8	1.7	0	0	0.5	0	446.2
Cyrene 1946–7	0	42.2	62.0	178.2	179.5	27.4	6.0	1.0	0	0.5	0	0	496.8
Cyrene 1948–9	0.4	3.0	143.1	146.6	196.6	76.5	86.3	2.2	26.8	3.6	0	7.4	692.5

The wider Greek world

Familiarity with a wide variety of environmental conditions was perhaps one of the factors which enabled Greeks easily to move around the Mediterranean world and to settle outside the Greek mainland and islands. Greekness was seen to be a product of descent, customs, language, and religion: it was by demonstrating shared descent with the Argives that the Macedonian kings got themselves accepted as Greeks, and able to compete at the Olympic festival (Herodotos 9.45.2, and 5.22 with *GW* 89; compare what the Athenians say at Herodotos 8.144.2). For much of the period covered by this volume very large numbers of those who would call themselves Greek lived outside modern-day Greece. When Greeks settled in Sicily, South Italy, North Africa, or the Black Sea, they met climatic patterns and climatic conditions significantly at variance with those to be found in any part of the Greek peninsula. The plant communities in those places offered both constraints, particularly on the growing of the olive, and possibilities, such as the plant called silphium, locally restricted to Libya, to which they were not accustomed. Fully to survey the geographical background of this wider Greek world would be to survey the geography of a very large part of the Mediterranean basin, but comparing climatic data from Sicily and North Africa with those given above will reveal some of the conditions in which Greeks came to live compared with those they were used to at home.

In Sicily and Libya, as in Greece itself, rainfall varied from area to area (Table 2). Greeks did not in fact settle in the wettest regions of Sicily, which tend to be the higher land in the interior. Nevertheless, on the east coast of Sicily, where they first settled, at sites such as Syracuse itself, the climate is significantly damper than that of the south-east part of Greece. Even in dry years, when rainfall at Syracuse drops to just below 400 mm, cereal cultivation is not seriously in danger of being insufficiently well supplied with water, and in wet years, when precipitation may exceed 1,000 mm, rainfall is such as only mountainous areas of Greece itself enjoy. As the Greeks moved west, however, the coastal settlements which they founded enjoyed significantly less rain, without becoming seriously risky for cereal cultivation – dry years at Agrigento may receive as little as 300 mm of rain, wet years get about 600 mm.

In Libya the contrast is much more striking. The coast, where the first settlements were made and where almost all the Greek settlements, other than Cyrene itself, were placed, is a place where drought is frequent and serious. This is clearly shown by the figures for Ptolemais for 1932–3, when the drought was such that no cereals, not even barley, could have survived. The average rainfall per year for Ptolemais in the years 1921 to 1940 was 350 mm, which makes it very closely comparable to Athens itself. The Aziris area, where the first settlement was traditionally made, was even drier; modern Derna has an average rainfall of 283 mm a year – insufficient to support wheat. By contrast to this, Cyrene itself, on an inland plateau, is very much better supplied with water, explaining why it was said to enjoy a 'hole in the sky' (Herodotos 4.158). The average rainfall at Cyrene in the years 1915–39 was 595 mm, although here there was not only great variation from year to year but from quinquennium to quinquennium: in 1915–19 the average was 422 mm, in 1920–24 it was 804 mm! Yet even at Cyrene the summer drought is liable to be, if anything, even longer than on the Greek mainland, lasting in some years from April to October; the high annual rainfall is achieved by particularly heavy rainfall in the winter months. That is a significantly different pattern from Sicily, where rain can regularly be expected in September; it is different enough, indeed, to demand adjustments in standard agricultural practices. It is likely that life in Libya demanded active co-operation between Greek settlers and the nomadic pastoralists, who alone could exploit the areas of low rainfall, in a way not demanded in Greece itself or in Sicily.

LIVING OFF THE LAND

Traditional and ancient farming methods

If we are wise to be cautious about the extent to which the natural landscape of Greece has altered, we should also be aware of the extent of agricultural change. It is relatively easy to think away developments during the last century, such as the mechanisation that, even in Greece, has vastly reduced the agricultural labour force, or the chemical pesticides and fertilisers, or the easy transport of bulky goods, which has enabled production of relatively perishable goods for wide markets. But it is tempting to believe that the traditional agriculture of pre-modern Greece, still to be studied on certain islands and in some other remote communities, operates in just the same way, and with the same constraints, as agriculture in prehistoric and historic Greece. Although there is much that is unchanged, the changes are important. The most important changes are in farming methods, in the variety of crops grown, in the reliability of crop yield, and the ability to move agricultural produce over the countryside.

Traditional Greek agriculture, as observed even on the smallest farms and even in modern Greek communities where mechanisation is minimal, is extensive agriculture. The lands of any family tend to be scattered in small parcels, so that the furthest plots may be several miles distant from the residence of the farmer. Crops which require a high labour input tend to be restricted to nearer fields. Farmers are heavily reliant on beasts of burden as the motive power for the plough, and to transport themselves and their agricultural produce, but sheep and goats tend to be kept as an enterprise separate from the family lands. Such extensive agricultural regimes were familiar in Roman antiquity, and the production figures preserved in Roman agricultural writers seem generally to refer to such regimes. But even in the Roman period it is clear that this was not the only pattern of exploitation, and in archaic Greece extensive agriculture was probably the exception rather than the rule.

For much of the period covered by this book the population density was not great, the landscape not fully exploited, and land-holdings probably more concentrated. A more intensive cultivation was possible for the whole farm area, enabling such things as employing rotation of labour-hungry pulses with less labour-hungry cereals, rather than bare fallow, as a means of maintaining the fertility of the soil. Moreover, when continuous tracts of lands are in the hands of a single farmer, it is possible to keep animals on, rather than off, the farm, and so secure their manure for crop production. There is even a point at which the farmer may achieve higher productivity by using his own labour to turn the soil and to sow the seed by dibbling, rather than by maintaining a hungry plough ox and sowing seed broadcast.

Intensive farming of this sort involves growing a wide range of crops, not specialising in one crop, and growing each of those crops in as varied locations as are available on a single land-holding, so as to exploit to the full such variety of ecological conditions as is available. Growing the same crop in varied conditions and growing a number of different crops are both ways of ensuring that the scarce resource of human labour (see below, pp. 31–4) is fully exploited: crops sown over a period and in different conditions ripen at different times; tree crops and vines require labour at times when cereals do not; and so on. In addition, gardening of perishable vegetables for home consumption, particularly if assisted by irrigation, can absorb, and reward, almost any amount of labour most of the year round. Such intensive farming regimes both maximise self-sufficiency and minimise risk.

The origins of such an intensive farming regime are lost in the twilight of the Dark Age. Sufficient archaeological evidence, such as model granaries, survives from before 800 BC to make it unlikely that the Dark Age agricultural regime was significantly more heavily based in pastoralism than the regime of subsequent centuries. When communities are small it is possible for intensive family farming to be carried out from a village basis, rather than from an isolated farm, and the absence of evidence for isolated farms from the archaeology of most of Greece in the archaic period (see below, p. 188) have few implications for agricultural practice, although it does imply that not all the land that could be farmed was farmed. We should imagine basically similar farming practices to have prevailed over much of the Greek world for most of the period under discussion, although there is little doubt that the distribution of landed property varied considerably from city to city, and the availability of non-family labour in some cities and at some times will have significantly affected the nature of farming life, if not the actual agricultural processes. (See below, p. 213, on possible changes in farming regime at Athens during the archaic period.) In general land was more abundant in the case of settlements abroad, and farming practices there came to be more extensive, whereas in the Greek mainland and Aegean islands an intensive farming regime continued through Greek antiquity.

Changing crops

Many crops familiar in Greece today were not to be seen in the archaic Greek landscape. Such basic crops as citrus fruit, maize, tomatoes, potatoes, red carrots, broad beans, cotton, and tobacco were entirely absent from the archaic and classical Greek landscape; currant vines were known but not exploited, and the carob seems to have been limited to Ionia and some Aegean islands. Melon (in a rather undeveloped and not very sweet form), peach, apricot, lucerne, and taro all seem to have entered Greece only during the first millennium BC and none was established during the archaic period. Even staple grain crops were different; in some parts of Greece, including Attica, barley rather than wheat was the staple grain crop (even if imported wheat was preferred for human consumption), and where wheat was grown it was, as it is today in Attica, probably winter-sown durum wheat (the wheat used for semolina and pasta); bread wheat requires more moisture, thrives in a colder climate, and had to be imported to the Greek mainland from the Black Sea area.

Although many of the crops new to Greece during or since the first millennium BC are relatively 'exotic', they serve two very important functions: they are readily marketable, and they spread agricultural labour across the year. Crops such as currants, cotton, and tobacco are durable cash crops, which can be stored relatively easily for quite long periods. They function as olive oil and wine have traditionally done: they enable the farmer not only to insert himself into a wider market economy, but to do so at a low risk. The labour demands of these new crops, like the labour demands of the labour-intensive, and relatively unmarketable, pulse crops, tend to come at different times in the year from those of the traditional triad of cereals, vines, and olives. They thus enable the extensive farmer to use labour power as efficiently as the intensive farmer.

The growing environmental fitness of traditional crops has improved their reliability, as well as increased their productivity. This is significant because the farmer, and particularly the farmer who is not heavily invested in cash crops, needs always to plan for the worst. Increased crop reliability means that a smaller farm area has to be devoted to staples, and that the farmer can survive on a smaller plot of land, or use a larger plot to enter the cash crop market. Such diversification further enables better use of different local ecological niches and more effective spreading of the farmer's labour over the whole year.

The importance of transport

It is improved possibilities for crop transport, however, which have had the greatest effect even on 'traditional' agriculture, for better crop transport alters the place of animal herding within the overall agrarian economy. One of the traditional advantages of cattle, large and small, has been that they can be moved about. As a result, the productive capacity of marginal land can be maximised, by moving animals from pasture to pasture on a daily or seasonal basis, and animals be fattened in one area and marketed in another. Arable crops do not move themselves in this way, and the relationship between bulk and value of unprocessed staple crops was such as severely to limit the distance over land which they moved, given the rudimentary nature of all but the main arterial roads, and the failure to develop efficient harnessing for horses.

Poor transport facilities affect some crops more than others. Grain producers may be prevented by slow communications from exploiting to the full temporary shortages in particular places, but in other ways the slowness of transport has little effect on the movement of cereal crops, just as it has little effect on pulses. Crops that can be turned into something which stores well are equally unaffected: both olives, which could be pickled or turned into oil, and grapes, which could be dried as raisins or fermented as wine, do not require rapid transportation. But soft fruits and leafy vegetables were another matter: only in the immediate vicinity of sizeable towns could farmers expect to be able to grow such crops for the market. Only improved transport possibilities would enable farmers to abandon entirely playing safe by cultivating those varieties of staples which yield most reliably and/or store best, but few farmers will not have kept at least half an eye upon demand for their more readily transportable produce, looking both for the chance to profit from crop failure elsewhere and to make good their own occasional shortfalls.

The combined effect of much more restricted crop variety and relatively high transport costs was to make local events, whether god-sent or man-made, a large feature in the farmer's life and necessarily an active interest. But they did not mean that there was no movement of crops at all. The Athenians who grew barley preferred themselves to eat bread made from wheat. Upland areas could not produce olive oil, and even in areas where oil was produced wealthy men displayed their taste by preferences for oils (and wines) produced elsewhere. There is evidence for oil exportation from Athens back into the eighth century. Those producing oils and wines with specialist reputations certainly kept an eye on the wider world, even if that world could not generally compel the farmer's attention in the same way as local crises. If the development of the Greek city has to be seen against an agricultural background shorter on variety, and more limited in its interactions than even that of 'traditional' small farmers in nineteenth-century Greece, we are not dealing with a world of self-sufficiency. But the shared dependence upon human labour, and upon similar technologies, does mean that ancient agriculture, like that practised everywhere in Greece until the last hundred years or so, was heavily subject to human constraints, and it is these to which we must now turn.

HUMAN CONSTRAINTS

Demography

What people could achieve in archaic Greece was constrained by the natural environment in which they lived, but also by purely human limitations. Ancient authors give no more than an impressionistic picture of mortality and fertility in archaic Greece, and even the considerable bulk of medical writings, which include detailed 'case histories', do not go very far to reveal the nature or extent of risks to health. But comparative data from preindustrial populations, and from modern third-world countries, can give some guidance as to the likely mortality rates, even if fertility rates, and hence potential population change, are very much more society-specific and difficult to reconstruct with any confidence.

It is very likely that only a little over half of those born survived to the age of 18. Perinatal mortality will have been very high, and infant mortality only marginally less so. Even at a time when the population was static, more than 40 per cent of the population will have been under the age of 18; in times of population growth the proportion might reach two-thirds or more. Given what ancient sources tell us about the high age of male marriage, a large proportion of children will have lost one or both parents before the age of 18: comparative figures suggest a third will have lost a father by the age of 11 and upwards of 50 per cent will have lost a father by 18. Any social organisation had to be able to cope with very large numbers of orphans. On the other hand, although there are some well-attested cases of men living on into their nineties, and although being cared for in one's old age is a repeated concern in Greek literary texts, it is highly probable that less than a quarter of the population was over the age of 40 and only some 5 per cent were over the age of 60. The elders of the community were chosen by the lottery of survival. Our understanding of major community decisions such as to encourage members of the community to go and settle elsewhere, or simply decisions to go to war, have to allow for the heavy encumbrance of children.

Everyone dies, but the age at which they die is not wholly unaffected by the nature of the society in which they live. Factors such as the density of the population may have enormous effects on mortality, because epidemic diseases can thrive only when people are in constant contact with others. Residential choices may therefore increase or decrease vulnerability to disease, and, because the residential choices and preferences of different social groups may be different, different mortality rates may be found among different members of the same society. It is highly likely that eighth-century Greece was sparsely enough populated to be largely innocent of infectious epidemics. On the other hand, resistance to disease is reduced by malnutrition, so that periods of food shortage tend to be periods of higher mortality for the poor. Resistance is also reduced in the latter stages of pregnancy, so that women carrying children are particularly vulnerable. Several Greek myths, from book 1 of the *Iliad* on, record the gods sending plague or famine, and often some versions of a particular myth will record famine and some plague. This may be partly a product of the similarity of the two Greek words involved (*loimos* for plague, *limos* for famine), but it is likely also to reflect the fact that periods of frequent death by disease were generally periods of food shortage. Death was frequent, childhood death as likely as not, but only in times of food shortage did it come in waves.

Fertility is even more heavily determined by social rules than is mortality. Changing customary ages of marriage for men, and more particularly for women, can radically alter fertility rates, and so, in combination with mortality rates, alter the rate of change of a population, upward or downward. Decisions about nursing and weaning, which will generally also be social rather than individual decisions, similarly have a direct effect on fertility. Such changing lifestyles may be consequent upon decisions about social organisation undertaken for reasons which are not directly connected with population, or they may be consciously undertaken in order to produce a desired demographic effect in the light of perceived over- or under-population. It is unclear exactly what the upper limit of human fertility in the ancient world was. The highest fertility rates reliably recorded in the modern world have been among the Hutterite religious community in the United States of America, who have an average completed family size of about ten.

Fertility rates are most significant in combination with mortality rates, since rate of change of population is a product of both. On the probable ancient age structure, if we suppose a life expectancy *at birth* of about 25, it will have required some five live births per woman simply to keep the population constant. To achieve a population growth of 1 per cent per annum would require an average of almost seven live births per woman. Fertility of the order found among the Hutterites, which gave them a growth rate of over 4 per cent, would, in this mortality regime, give a growth rate of a little over 2 per cent per annum. On the other hand, if a life expectancy at birth of 30 is assumed, then just under 4.5 live births per woman are required to keep the population stable, and seven live births per woman would produce a population growing by just under 1.5 per cent per annum. Increasing life expectancy at birth to 35 reduces the number of live births per woman required to keep the population stable to just under four, but only with a life expectancy at birth of around 37 do seven live births produce a growth rate of 2 per cent per annum.

Discovering actual fertility rates and mortality rates from surviving archaeological remains is fraught with difficulties, but the constraints indicated by this comparative evidence are extremely important. What they reveal is that, even on the most optimistic estimates of life expectancy, a growth rate of 2 per cent per annum (which means the population doubling every 35 years) would demand families which were consistently very large, and would produce a population in which children very significantly outnumbered adults. Rampant population growth is far less likely to have been a problem than inadequate reproduction, for, given that the factors affecting mortality are unlikely to have been subject to sudden change, any social changes that reduced fertility would have a marked effect on population growth.

Agricultural labour

In modern western economies family size has only limited effects on economic prosperity or on a family's economic strategy. In economies like those of archaic and classical Greece family size had a major impact. Family size is important because it affects what, in a subsistence economy, are the two crucial variables: consumption and production. More mouths to feed mean that more food has to be produced; more hands to labour mean that more land can be cultivated, or that existing land-holdings can be more intensively cultivated. Because of the 'lumpy' labour demands of the agricultural year, with peak demands at harvest times, availability of labour can crucially determine which crops are grown; because the food needs and labour capabilities of a family vary through its life-cycle, those agricultural strategies need to be constantly rethought.

The problems which the labour-intensity of traditional Mediterranean agriculture, and particularly of the cultivation of staple cereal crops, brings, are best seen by examining crop harvesting. Recent work on the Greek islands of Karpathos and Amorgos, where traditional agricultural practices can still be found in operation, has shown that the harvesting of cereals – reaping with a sickle, threshing, winnowing – demands about thirty man-days per hectare, half of which is reaping time. And a hectare of cereals is reckoned to be required *per head* for subsistence. Winnowing and threshing can be spread out over some weeks, but the reaping itself has to take place within the month or so when the crop is ripe but the grain is not yet falling from the ear. At the rates recorded in these communities, one man's labour in reaping can bring in enough grain to feed two or at most three adult mouths. Even in a situation where abundant land is available, the amount of land that a family can cultivate with staple cereal crops will be crucially limited by the labour demands of reaping.

Three consequences of the intensity of the cereal harvest are to be noted. The first is that the family life-cycle has marked effects on a family's ability to survive. A family with several young mouths, or old and decrepit mouths, to feed is going to be under very serious labour pressure, even allowing for a significant input of female labour (which may unavailable in the event of pregnancy or reduced when there are unweaned children). By contrast a family with mature, unmarried children (and men seem generally not to have married until about the age of 30), and no unproductive mouths to feed, would be in a position, if land were available, to harvest a substantial surplus and produce double its subsistence needs or more (see Figure 3). The second consequence is that any distractions – labour obligations to others, political or military obligations – were an extremely serious matter. The third consequence follows from the first two: there is a very high premium on labourers who have only themselves to support; the advantages to all, rich or poor, of access to the labour of those who have no family, are clear. The benefits of slavery are manifest.

Slaves dominated the agricultural workforce in only a few states, but may have become increasingly significant in many during the period discussed here. Once Sparta had conquered Messenia (below, p. 166), and established her own political élite as a leisured military class living off the labour of a subservient population, the agricultural production of Messenia and much of that of Lakonia, the territory immediately around Sparta, was in the hands of the servile helots. Helots seem to have lived in family groups although, perhaps because of their extreme material impoverishment, archaeology has yet to throw much light on where they lived or the size of the lands for which each family was responsible. Neither among these helots nor among the similar servile populations recorded elsewhere in Greece, in Thessaly, the Argolid, or Crete, was the organisation or method of farming distinct. And the same seems to be true in those states, such as Athens, which used chattel slaves; here too the slaves seem to have been joined to the existing family labour force and to have become skilled agricultural labourers rather than being exploited in unskilled gangs.

Even when they were able to supplement their labour with that of a slave, the pressures on agricultural families in archaic and classical Greece were severe. Continuing the family line was not simply a sentimental requirement, but was vital to ensure care in old age. But continuing the family line meant that for more than a decade a family would be hard-pressed to harvest the cereals needed to survive, unless it could count on labour from aged but fit

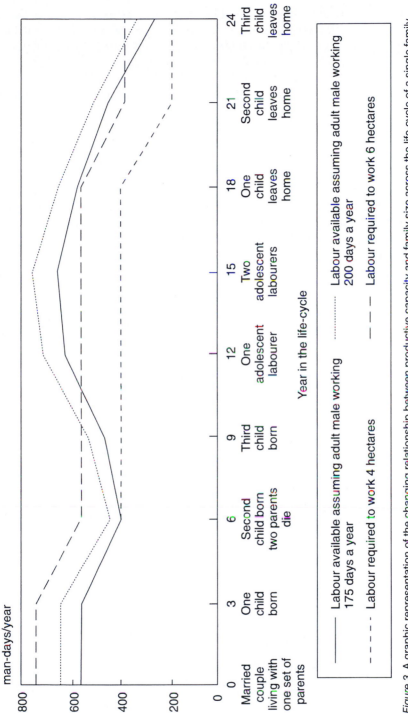

man-days/year

3	6	9	12	15
One child born	Second child born two parents die	Third child born	One adolescent labourer	Two adolescent labourers

18	21	24
One child leaves home	Second child leaves home	Third child leaves home

0

Married couple living with one set of parents

Year in the life-cycle

—— Labour available assuming adult male working 175 days a year

········ Labour available assuming adult male working 200 days a year

– – – Labour required to work 4 hectares

– – Labour required to work 6 hectares

Figure 3 A graphic representation of the changing relationship between productive capacity and family size across the life-cycle of a single family.

parents, unmarried siblings, or the like. Aids such as oxen would make it possible to plough larger areas of land, if larger areas of land were available. But oxen were potentially a mixed blessing: they consume large quantities of grain, and, although oxen can help with threshing, grain has to be harvested by unaided human labour. The farmer's need to devise strategies to cope with the crop failure which variable rainfall rendered common has often been stressed, but human accidents were almost equally likely and rather more difficult to plan for. Unfitness (it has been reckoned that some 20 per cent of adult males were unfit for military service, and such unfitness would reduce their labour input to harvesting too), or the untimely mortality of a husband or son, would cause serious distress.

Family crisis was never far away in the ancient world: death, food shortage, disease, crops withering unharvested. Modern scholars have stressed the way in which the routine occurrence of death, particularly child death, affected popular attitudes to it. But these other threats to normal life will also have affected how people thought and how they reacted to political events.

3

THE PROBLEM OF BEGINNINGS

A SLATE RUBBED CLEAN? THE ONSET OF THE DARK AGE

The end of the Mycenaean world

The Mycenaean world ended with a bang *and* a whimper. Around 1200 BC several of the major Mycenaean centres in the Peloponnese and in central Crete show signs of violent destruction, fire, or abandonment. Most were reoccupied, but the reoccupation frequently took a new form, and was marked by the use of a pottery distinct in style from that which had been in use before, although clearly closely related to the earlier pottery. The great round beehive-shaped tombs, known as tholos tombs, were built no more, except in Thessaly; burial in individual tombs lined with flat stones, known as cist graves, became normal, although chamber tombs, in which more than one corpse was buried, also remained in use. People moved to live in new places, and areas earlier used for habitation were sometimes used for burials. In place of a pottery style in which local variations were few and relatively slight, the new pottery style, known as Late Helladic IIIC, developed in rather different directions in different areas, as different potters picked up and developed different selections of Mycenaean motifs, and combined them in different ways. But although change is manifest in numerous areas of the material record, the element of continuity is very strong. There was no wide-scale abandonment of any area of the Greek peninsula, although the number of sites which have yielded material of this period is smaller than the number which has yielded material of the immediately preceding period (Figures 4 and 5).

Greece in the first half of the twelfth century BC was not cut off or impoverished. This is most clearly seen in a site newly occupied in this period, the cemetery at Perati on the eastern coast of Attica. More than 200 graves are known from this site, the vast majority of them chamber tombs, and the standard Mycenaean practice of inhumation dominates, although some eighteen bodies were cremated. The quality of pottery found in these tombs is high, and the quantity large (some 800 vessels). In addition, beads, seals, and two gold rings were found, along with a number of figurines and eight fibulae

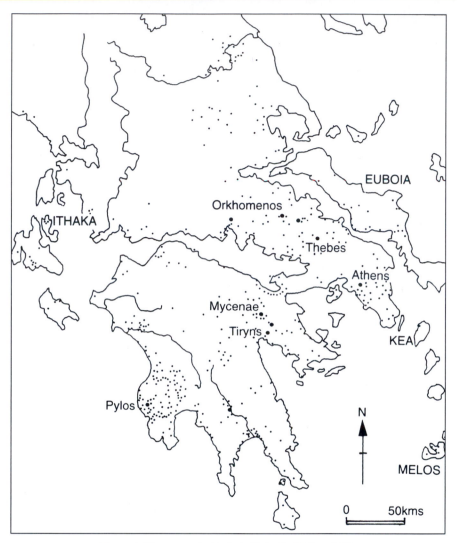

Figure 4 Sites occupied in Late Helladic IIIA2 and IIIB.

(safety pins). Imported objects show that, directly or indirectly, Greece was still in contact with a large part of the near east: there are scarabs and glass from Egypt, seals and an iron knife from Syria, seals from Cyprus, and even an amber bead from the Baltic.

Perati is by no means an isolated phenomenon: Ialysos on Rhodes shows close similarities in its burial practices (particularly identical cremations), its pottery, and its range of imported goods. If anything, the links across the Aegean seem to be stronger in the first half of the twelfth century BC than they were earlier: in this period for the first time a 'Mycenaean' presence can be detected in the north Aegean, at the settlement of Emborio on Khios.

36

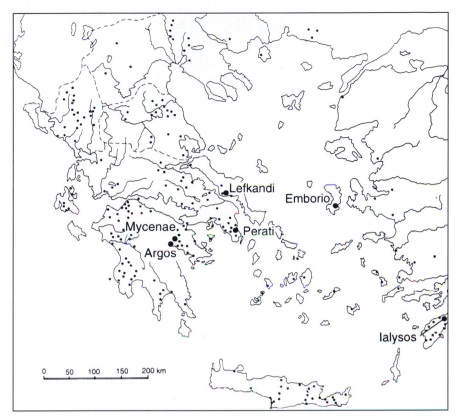

Figure 5 Sites occupied in Late Helladic IIIC.

What is more, Late Helladic IIIC pottery is found in quantity in Cyprus, accompanied by building in a monumental style employing regular masonry of squared stones, known as ashlar, which is familiar from mainland Greece but previously unknown on Cyprus. Even more remarkably, twelfth-century Philistine pottery has been thought to show the influence of Late Helladic IIIC pottery. The mainland palaces may have gone in the twelfth century, but the inhabitants of the mainland continue to show very considerable vigour, artistic energy, and some sophistication.

But if the material circumstances of the early twelfth century BC seem tolerably clear, the forces which produced them are very much debated. Any explanation has to take into account both the marked changes that have occurred, and the very high degree of continuity. Although different regions of Greece proceed to develop in different directions during the twelfth century, as is seen most clearly in new regional pottery styles, almost none of these developments can be shown to be the result of the intrusion of some element not previously present in the material culture of the previous century. To invoke invasion to explain the changes creates as many problems as it solves,

Figure 6 Late Helladic IIIC Lefkandian-style pyxis from Lefkandi.

and explanation in terms of disintegration caused by pressure from within the system seems more satisfactory.

In as far as there are movements of people at this period, the movements seem to be of Mycenaeans eastwards; they appear at Perati in Attica, at Lefkandi on Euboia, at Emborio, Ialysos, and other places in the east Aegean, at Mende (modern Kelendras) in the north Aegean Khalkidike, and on Cyprus. Movement of pottery can, of course, take place without the movement of those who made the pottery, but the presence in Cyprus of characteristic building techniques, as well as characteristic pottery, strongly suggests that migration was involved, and not simply trade. This idea is further supported by the first appearance of the Greek language in Cyprus: a bronze spit from the Skales cemetery at Palaipaphos, which can be dated to the eleventh century, is inscribed with a Greek name, in Arcadian dialect, written in Cypro-syllabic script. That it is Greeks who had moved east, permanently, is further supported by the absence of any continuing influence from the Aegean on immediately subsequent developments in Cyprus: the Skales cemetery itself, which is abundantly supplied with pottery from the near east, has very little Greek material.

In the last phase of its occupation, around the end of the twelfth century BC, the cemetery at Perati became distinctly more impoverished, particularly in terms of the number of imported goods. Similarly, at the important site of Lefkandi in Euboia, the pottery of the final Late Helladic IIIC phase is markedly inferior to that present earlier (Figure 6). Then both sites are abandoned. Further north, it is not abandonment but impoverishment that is marked at the end of Late Helladic IIIC: the cemetery at Elateia in Phokis,

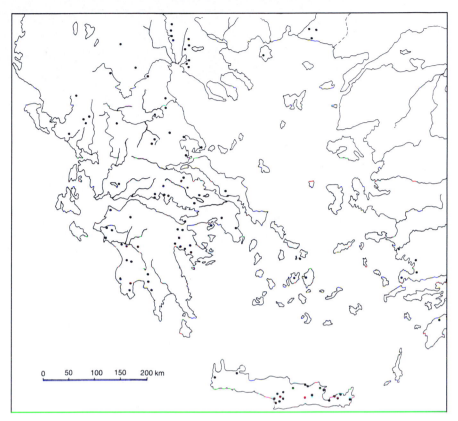

Figure 7 Sites occupied in the period 1125–1050 BC.

which is extremely rich in pottery and bronze in Late Helladic IIIC, sees a change in tomb design and a distinct impoverishment at the end of that period, with hand-made pottery appearing, although the cemetery continues in use into the early protogeometric period. Nearby at the sanctuary of Kalapodi, the earliest occupation in Late Helladic IIIC is also extremely rich: some 20,000 pottery sherds from this period have been excavated at this site. Kalapodi seems to have been only a local sanctuary, but contacts evidently did continue in this period with some movement to places elsewhere in the Aegean: the earliest evidence from Torone on the Khalkidike peninsula in the northern Aegean is a sub-mycenaean ash-urn from the end of the twelfth century. Nevertheless, for all these signs of life, whereas the number of sites known to have been occupied during the first half of the twelfth century is some 220, for the period 1125–1050 BC it is less than half that number, perhaps reducing further still in the second half of the eleventh century (Figures 7 and 8). Yet these changes occur without any associated signs of violent destruction, and with marked continuities in the material record that are only slightly masked by declining quality.

Figure 8 Sites occupied in the period 1050–1000 BC.

We should not overdo the emphasis on the contraction of occupation of the countryside of southern Greece in the late twelfth and eleventh centuries BC, not least because more thorough archaeological investigation is likely to modify the picture to some extent. Rather, we should note the striking characteristic of the material remains: their suggestion of local cultural independence. The regionalisation of pottery styles, apparent already in Late Helladic IIIC pottery, becomes even more marked in the succeeding pottery phase. In western Attica a particular sub-mycenaean style develops which is distinct from that of any other area: it is marked by potting frequently incompetent enough to produce asymmetrical pots, and by a very limited repertory of shapes, all of which derive from Mycenaean predecessors (Figure 9). The decoration on these pots is eclectic, but unambitious in range and poorly executed. Outside Attica a version of Late Helladic IIIC pottery

40

Figure 9 Attic sub-mycenaean amphora from the Kerameikos cemetery at Athens.

seems to have continued into the eleventh century, with little development to distinguish the ceramic products of 1075 from those of 1125. The ceramic isolation of the different areas of Greece is such that it is rarely possible to demonstrate the contemporaneity of the different regional styles, but in almost all cases it is clear that at the regional level the degree of continuity between the last Late Helladic IIIC pottery and the earliest Iron Age pottery is high.

Contact with Cyprus

The communities of late twelfth- and early eleventh-century BC Greece may have gone their own way in their cultural products, unaffected by what was happening elsewhere in the Greek mainland, but, far from being cut off, they were receptive to important innovations elsewhere. Contact with the outside world was certainly reduced, by comparison with the situation in Late Helladic IIIC, but imported goods continue to appear in the graves which provide almost all our evidence. This is true both in central Greece, at the cemetery at Elateia, and in southern Greece: tombs from Argos and from Tiryns suggest that metal goods were reaching Greece from Italy and from the Urnfield culture of central Europe. More important, the apparent debt of the mainland to Cyprus in iron-working demonstrates that there was contact between the Aegean coast of the Greek mainland and Cyprus.

Extensive archaeological work on Cyprus in recent years has revealed evidence which suggests that it was there that important pioneering work in iron metallurgy went on during the twelfth and eleventh centuries BC; by the middle of the eleventh century Cyprus had become the first place in the Mediterranean where iron came to predominate over bronze as the working metal, and hence the first place to make the transition from a 'Bronze Age' to an 'Iron Age'. The independent development of iron technology on the Greek mainland is possible, but, until further evidence is discovered there, it seems likely that both the technology and the types (all-iron knives replacing bronze-riveted knives) of iron knives found in mainland Greece from the end of the twelfth century BC onwards, together with the earliest working iron objects, were derived from Cyprus.

Iron had been known in the Bronze Age, but only as a precious commodity used for prestigious gifts and in some ritual contexts. The transformation which turned iron into the dominant working metal demanded developing complicated technology and also securing regular supply. Cyprus is rich in copper sources and some of the copper ores are also rich in iron. It is at least possible that it was through exploiting the waste products of copper metallurgy, initially as a supplement to bronze manufacture, that the Cypriot iron industry became established. If that is the case, it would explain how Cyprus might slip from the Bronze Age to the Iron Age with relatively little disruption: no changes in supply systems were necessary. But as iron-working rapidly spread, and as iron ores came to be discovered elsewhere and exploited in their own right, the consequences of the coming of the Iron Age would be rather different.

By the year 1000 BC the Iron Age had come to Crete and to the Greek mainland: from Athens between 1050 and 900 BC all eight of the known swords, all four knives, all three axes, and both daggers are made of iron; iron even predominates over bronze in dress pins (by 47 to 13) and fibulae (by 12 to 9); only in spearheads (4 of each) does bronze hold its own. Comparison between metal finds from the Skales cemetery near Palaipaphos on Cyprus and metal finds from Lefkandi shows just how vigorous a metallurgical tradition was established on the mainland. Once the technology had been acquired, the search for new iron sources began; dependence upon Cyprus was short-lived.

Contact with Cyprus is apparent and important in another area too in the middle of the eleventh century BC: pottery. Cypriot pottery of the eleventh century suddenly pictures male warriors and hunters who seem to be inspired by similar figures on the Late Helladic IIIC pottery of mainland Greece; one of the figures even holds a shield of a type long obsolete as a weapon and obsolete even as a symbol in mainland Greece, and it has been suggested that it is deliberately adopted to define a particular section of the Cypriot population eager to set themselves apart as people whose past was in Greece. At the same time, pottery from Athens and from Lefkandi also exhibits previously unknown shapes and systems of decoration, and these can be closely paralleled in the pottery from Cyprus which is known as Cypriot IIIB. Just as Cypriot imports and influence seem to have acted as a catalyst stimulating a mainland iron industry, so the result of the influence of late

Cypriot IIIB seems to have been something of a revolution in pottery, the formation of a very distinct style known as protogeometric. Protogeometric pottery is marked by two technical developments: the use of the fast wheel, and the use of dividers with a multiple brush on one end to draw concentric semi-circles and circles; it is also marked by much higher quality of potting, and by a new simplicity seen in both shape and decoration (Figure 10). Its invention also should be seen as part of emerging group definition in mainland Greek settlements.

The special case of Crete

In the second half of the eleventh and during the tenth century BC Greek communities became increasingly isolated. The new Attic pottery style did influence pottery styles in the Peloponnese, some of the Cyclades, in Thessaly, and at Miletos in Asia Minor, but no near-eastern objects have been found in Greek contexts, and no Greek objects in the near east. Only Crete shows continued links with the non-Greek world, and Crete seems to have been cut off from the Greek mainland. At the old palatial centre at Knossos occupation had not been interrupted and continued on a considerable scale through the eleventh century. Crete's debased pottery style, termed sub-minoan, continues for a very long period with little change, and Cretan regional developments in pottery have no wider influence. Some places in Crete eventually developed

Figure 10 Attic protogeometric amphora from the Kerameikos cemetary at Athens.

a protogeometric style under the influence of mainland protogeometric, but this occurred only towards the end of the development of protogeometric on the mainland. But the contacts between Crete and Cyprus, manifest in the twelfth century BC in both pottery and metalwork, appear to have been maintained; and remarkably some fibulae suggest links between Crete and Sicily and/or Italy.

Systems collapse?

Describing what archaeology currently indicates about the changing material culture of Greece between 1200 and 950 BC is a lot easier than assessing what was happening in human terms. To make such an assessment, it is as important to look at what the material record does not reveal as it is to look at what it does show, although such a procedure runs the risk of being confuted by future archaeological finds. Changes in pottery may be perfectly explicable in terms of continuous development, but to concentrate on such development can crucially obscure the discontinuities. One such break is in settlement. We have very little evidence about where most people were living in the twelfth and eleventh centuries BC, because the vast majority of the material on which we base our account of the development of the pottery, and of the extent of contact with a wider world, comes from graves. But there can be little doubt that all over the Greek world, and in Cyprus too, earlier settlements were abandoned, and where we can trace later settlements they are often not long-lived. The absence of permanent settlements correlates with the absence of monumental architecture: the Mycenaean tradition of high-quality building in ashlar masonry, though still active enough to be exported to Cyprus in the early twelfth century BC, was rapidly lost, and the relatively permanent buildings which are found, such as those in the settlement at Karphi on Crete (Figure 11), owe little or nothing to earlier building traditions. When monumental building re-emerges on the Greek mainland, first in the isolated 'heröon' built at Lefkandi around 1000 BC (p. 55) and then in the temple buildings of the eighth century (pp. 83–4), its form is different from anything seen in the Mycenaean world.

Along with the end of palatial buildings went the end of the administrative traditions which those buildings both depended on and housed. The ability to write records in the Linear B syllabary (above, p. 5) was entirely lost: not only do we have no records from this period, either in the form of clay tablets or as signs painted or scratched on pottery, but when writing comes back, in the eighth century BC, the system is no longer a syllabic one, with one sign for each combination of consonant and vowel, but an alphabetic one with separate signs for consonants and vowels. Clearly the necessity for having written records disappeared at some stage, and it is reasonable to suppose that it disappeared along with the other manifestations of the loss of centralised power structures.

Figure 11 The site of Karphi on the north side of the Lasithi plateau in Crete.

More interestingly still, other forms of impersonal communication seem to have withered away. The vigorous tradition of figurative art, known from the pottery and wall paintings of the Mycenaean period, had no successor in the period after 1200 BC, or at least after the end of the so-called 'Octopus style' and related styles of central Aegean pottery of the early twelfth century (cf. Figure 6). The figurines, thought to be of goddesses, found everywhere, in both sanctuaries and tombs, down into the twelfth century BC disappear thereafter from the mainland, and no more than the occasional find of a clay animal has been made between then and the end of the tenth century BC. Only on Crete does the separate Minoan tradition of bell-skirted female cult idols continue, with a rich series of such figures recovered from the settlement at Karphi.

This raises the further question of whether attempts to communicate with the gods in general died away on the mainland. The decipherment of Linear B has made it clear that the gods receiving cult in the Mycenaean world were, by and large, addressed by the names used for the gods of the classical Greek world. Even Dionysos, depicted in archaic and classical Greek poetry as a newcomer, often from the east, was already worshipped in the late Bronze Age. But how far does the continuity in the pantheon actually imply continuity of cult, either in general or at any particular site? Several important classical sanctuaries, such as Olympia, the Argive Heraion, and the Samian Heraion, were also sanctuaries in Mycenaean times, but that does not demonstrate continuity of cult at these sites. In Crete continuity of cultic activity is demonstrable at the sanctuary at Kato Syme Viannou, where, although the nature of the buildings and of the finds varies from period to period, there is much that seems uninterrupted. Restudy of old material from excavations at the Polis cave on Ithaka suggests that there was no break in its tradition (although definite cult is a little harder to prove). It becomes increasingly likely that occupation at Delphi was uninterrupted through the Dark Age, but we are very far from being able to demonstrate continuous cult activity there. Particularly interesting is the case of Kalapodi: cult activity there seems to be continuous through the Dark Age, but bone remains suggest that there was a marked change in cult practice in the middle of the tenth century: until that time deer dominate the bone assemblage, afterwards the more normal sacrificial mix of domesticated animals. Cultic communications were certainly not insulated from the changes which mark other modes of communication and social relations during this period, but it seems likely that in some places at least change was continuous, and cult activity not seriously disrupted.

The area in which the evidence for continuity and for change is richest is that of burials. As we have already seen, the individual cist tomb, not an uncommon form of poor burial in southern Greece (but not in Crete) in the late Bronze Age, becomes the most common form of burial. After about 1100 BC, cremation becomes something more than just an occasional method of disposal of the dead, and it becomes clearly the most popular in Athens and other parts of mainland Greece from the beginning of protogeometric in the later eleventh century. The grave goods of this period are distinctly impoverished, and, in particular, between about 1200 and 1050 BC burial with arms is nowhere found. After that date early protogeometric graves again show the presence of work-associated objects, for men and women, just as they also show more regular animal sacrifice at graves.

How do all these features fit together? The general impression that we get is of contracted horizons: no big buildings, no multiple graves, no impersonal communication, limited contact with a wider world. After the collapse of the Mycenaean system, things seem to be reduced to an individual level. The picture is coherent enough to make it possible to suggest that, with the end of the palaces, not only the political units, but also the whole social and economic organisation, broke up; individuals' livelihood came to depend solely on their own efforts, and no dominant individual or group extracted a surplus from the rest of the population. In these circumstances, craft specialisms could be maintained only for a limited time, since they depended on community-wide support at a time when community bonds seem to have been growing ever weaker. Bronze-working depended upon access to tin and copper, which seems to have been in the control of the élite. Whether near-eastern problems (see below, pp. 52–3) undermined the ability of the élite to acquire the essential metals, or whether the collapse of the élite itself ended the supply system, it seems likely that the weakness of the bronze industry made the development of iron technology hard to resist. By the eleventh century everything which depended directly or indirectly on organisation at more than an individual level seems to have become impossible to sustain. Hence the gloom: the slate was rubbed all but clear of the traces of earlier organisation and the products of that organisation. It is precisely this that makes the Dark Age so important for the historian of archaic, and indeed of classical, Greece.

MIGRATION, INVASION, AND DECLINE: EXPLAINING THE VOID

Ancient explanations

None of our earliest literary records from archaic Greece, the Homeric epics, the *Iliad* and the *Odyssey*, and the two extant long poems by Hesiod, the *Theogony* and the *Works and Days*, knows anything about, or shows any concern with, the Dark Age (for more on these poems see Chapter 5). The heroic society depicted in the *Iliad* and the *Odyssey* is set in the past, but the contrasts which are drawn between that society and the society contemporary with the performance of these oral poems are conventional, and the poems show no interest in the way in which that world was lost, or in the nature of the world which replaced it. The heroic world of the past is exploited in these poems, not in a spirit of plangency or nostalgia, a desire to turn the clock back, but for the way in which it can, as a purely fictional world also can, cast light upon the structures of the present world.

Nostalgia is more at issue in the poems of Hesiod, with their repeated stress on what has been lost, and how much harder life is now than it was in the past. But Hesiod's myth of the past ages of man, beginning with an age of gold and succeeding through ages of silver and bronze to an age of heroes, and then the current age of iron, is demonstrably a poetic construction for defining the contemporary world, not a serious memory of, or a product of serious interest in, past events. We can no more take as a historical memory his third race of bronze, which has bronze armour and bronze houses and destroys itself in warfare, than we can take as historical the succeeding, contrasting, age of just heroes, some of whom are preserved for ever in the islands of the blest ruled over by Kronos (*Works and Days* 142–69).

By the fifth century BC, however, we find a fully developed explanation of the transition from the age of heroes to the later Greek world. This tradition, which effectively passes over what we would call the Dark Age without comment, is most conveniently expressed by Thucydides in the section of his history of the Peloponnesian war known as the 'Archaeology', in which he tries to prove that no earlier war had been on the scale of this conflict between Athens, Sparta, and their allies at the end of the fifth century BC, during Thucydides' own lifetime. Thucydides records (Text 5) two movements of people which he connects with unrest in the aftermath of the return from Troy: the movement of men from Thessaly to Boiotia, and the movement of Dorians, identified in the fifth century by a common 'tribal structure' and a common dialect of Greek, into the Peloponnese. And he records two further

Even after the Trojan war, Greece was still involved in the movement and settlement of people, so that, not being undisturbed, she failed to grow. The belated return of the Greeks from Troy caused many changes, and strife was quite general in the cities. Those expelled in such strife founded cities. Those who are now Boiotians were expelled from Arne by the Thessalians in the sixtieth year after the capture of Troy, and settled in what is now Boiotia but was formerly called the Kadmeian land (there was a division of Boiotians in this territory previously, too, from whom those who campaigned at Troy came). The Dorians, led by the children of Herakles, got hold of the Peloponnese in the eightieth year [after the capture of Troy]. After a long time, Greece gained peace with difficulty, and, since it was no longer disrupted, sent out settlements abroad: the Athenians settled the Ionians and many of the islanders; the Peloponnesians colonised most of Italy and Sicily and parts of the rest of Greece. All these were founded later than the Trojan war.

Text 5: Thucydides 1.12. Part of Thucydides' account of the weakness of Greece before his own day.

movements of people, which he associates with the arrival of more settled conditions: the movement of Athenians to Ionia and the Aegean islands, and the movement of Peloponnesians to Italy and Sicily. There is no doubt that the last of these movements of peoples is a historical fact, which can be dated to the latter part of the eighth and the seventh centuries BC. But what of the other movements?

No other ancient source has an account identical to that of Thucydides, but we find references to the 'coming of the children of Herakles' to the Peloponnese as early as the mid-seventh century BC, in the works of the Spartan poet Tyrtaios (frg. 2.12–15 West), reference to the coming of Dorians to the island of Aigina in the poetry of Pindar in the early fifth century BC (*Isthmian Odes* 9.1–4), and reference to descendants of Neleus from Pylos in Messenia settling at Kolophon in Ionia as early as the poetry of Mimnermos in the late seventh century BC (Text 6). In the fifth century BC, writing about the origins of the Ionians, identified as a group through common dialect and common cults, seems, perhaps for reasons of contemporary politics, to have been particularly popular. Panyassis, the uncle of the historian Herodotos, is said to have written an elegiac poem 'about Kodros and Neleus and the Ionian colonies', presumably in the first half of the fifth century. At about the same time, or a little earlier, Pherekydes of Athens wrote about the 'colonisation' of Ionia under the leadership of Androklos, son of Kodros king of Athens. Ion of Khios, born at about the time of the Persian wars, wrote a highly influential *Foundation of Khios*

We left steep Pylos, the town of Neleus, and arrived in ships in the Asia we longed for; with insolent force we settled at lovely Kolophon, leaders of trouble and violence. Setting out from the river there we took Smyrna in Aiolis, by the plan of the gods.

Text 6: Mimnermos frg. 9 (West).

which gave it mixed origins – the Athenian hero Theseus' son Oinopion, from Crete, Carians, who were later expelled, and two separate contingents from Euboia.

What are we to make of these traditions? It is clear that there was no single tradition about either Dorian invasion or Ionian migration; the more closely we examine the individual versions, the more various, and indeed often contradictory, they become. Thucydides seems to invent the existence of a group of Boiotians in Boiotia prior to the main invasion in order to square the tradition of an invasion after the Trojan war with the presence of Boiotians from Boiotia in the expeditionary force to Troy detailed in the Catalogue of Ships in *Iliad* 2. These traditions show beyond doubt that, from at least the seventh century BC onwards, which is as early as we could hope to have this sort of evidence, some Greeks found it helpful to think of their past history in terms of movements of people from one area to another. What made them think in this way? Are we dealing with historical memories, or should the traditions be explained in some other way?

The archaeological and philological evidence

The idea of an Ionian migration from Athens has some archaeological support. Indeed, the archaeological record might be held to support not one but two migrations from Athens to Asia Minor: first in Late Helladic IIIC, when there is so marked a common culture at Perati and at Ialysos, and second in the early protogeometric period when Greek settlement seems to have been refounded, after a break, at Miletos, and to employ a ceramic style which some have thought to be Athenian in inspiration. Are we, then, dealing with a tradition which may have conflated two separate occasions but which, at root, is a genuine historical memory? If we are, does this genuine historical memory also guarantee the historicity of the Dorian invasion with which it becomes so closely associated, but for which there is no comparable archaeological support?

The answer to both these questions must be 'no' – and 'no' for important methodological reasons. The first of these is that broad compatibility between tradition and the archaeological record is not enough: we should not be at all surprised that stories that were handed down accorded with observed material realities. The second, related, reason is that if we are going to squeeze out of tradition more than we can squeeze out of our own observations of cultural similarities or dissimilarities, the tradition must be found to be compatible with the archaeology in detail, not in broad outline only, and we must be able to suggest some sort of plausible mechanism by which some genuine memory of the historical reality might have been preserved.

By the end of the archaic period, and perhaps already by the seventh century, there were plenty of features in the observed customs and linguistic patterns of the day to suggest that Athens, or at least Attica, and Ionia had once been closely linked. In the first place, the Attic and Ionic dialects shared important characteristics which set them apart from other Greek dialects; second, Athens, the Cyclades, and Ionia shared certain institutions – in particular, as Herodotos himself observes (1.147.2), the celebration of the festival of the Apatouria, which was the festival at which young men were admitted into phratries (pseudo-kinship groups). In addition, there was a lot of overlap, if by no means total identity, in the names of months and the names that were employed for tribal divisions in these areas.

In a similar way, the distribution of dialects and of institutions in the archaic and classical period could be held to support the tradition of the return of the children of Herakles and the arrival of the Dorians. Not only was the dialect spoken in the Peloponnese and Boiotia distinct from that of Attica and Ionia, but within the non-Ionian speaking south of Greece there were further dialect variations. Only the coastal states of the Peloponnese spoke Doric; Elis (like Phokis and Lokris) spoke North-West Greek, in Arkadia the dialect is what is known today as Arcado-Cypriot, and in Boiotia the dialect was Aeolic. Arcado-Cypriot and Aeolic both have features which cause them to be grouped with Ionic as 'East Greek Dialects', as opposed to the 'West Greek dialects', Doric and North-West Greek. Philologists suggest that many of the distinct features of Doric may have developed in the period after 1200 BC, but there is no doubt that the picture perceived by the Greeks themselves in the archaic and classical period supported the idea that the Dorians were intrusive. And the presence in Dorian-speaking regions of three Dorian tribes (already present as a distinct Dorian feature in *Odyssey* 19.177, perhaps) reinforced this impression.

The function of migration traditions

The Dorian invasion may have provided a neat explanation of the observed linguistic and institutional map of archaic and classical Greece, but this does not of itself mean that the tradition of Ionian migration and Dorian invasion was invented. If, however, we look at the context in which the stories of the Ionian migration, the Dorian invasion, and the coming of the children of Herakles were told in the archaic and early classical period, then further very relevant factors appear. Our earliest source for the coming of the children of Herakles is Tyrtaios, who wrote at Sparta at a time when Sparta was emerging from a long and difficult struggle to subdue the Messenians, and was in the process of establishing a stable constitution headed by two kings (below, p. 167). The identification of these kings as descendants of the children of Herakles, who were *returning* to their land, gave the Spartans a justification for their claim to Messenia, and also established Herakles as apical ancestor for the Spartan kings. In precisely similar but entirely separate ways, apical heroic ancestors were later created for the ordinary Spartiate citizens from the names for the Dorian tribes, and these ancestors were also used, even by Arkadians, in attempts to establish precedents for what they now regarded as desirable current arrangements (Herodotos 9.26).

Once the claims of the Dorians to have returned to the Peloponnese at some stage in the past became generally accepted, identification of the Ionians with the descendants of those expelled by the Dorians was straightforward, and perhaps inevitable. Is it by chance that the earliest surviving claims should record that the Ionians hailed precisely from Pylos, in Messenia? Is it by chance that the first manifestation of a crucially important role for the Athenians, and the first Athens-centred account of the Ionian migration, appear in sources that date to the years immediately before and after the Persian war, when first the Ionians were in desperate need of support against the Persians from Greeks on the mainland, and received it only from Athens and Eretria (below, p. 306), and when subsequently the Athenians were keen to find every justification for their own burgeoning hegemony over the whole Aegean?

It is perfectly possible, therefore, to explain how there could come to be traditions of Dorian invasion and Ionian migration when there were no such historical events. What is more, when the archaeological record is examined in detail it does not in fact support claims that those events occurred. Archaeology is not good at distinguishing movement of goods from movement of people, but it *is* distinctly sensitive to the nature of the social organisation. As we have already seen, material remains suggest that after the end of the Mycenaean palaces the whole social and economic organisation broke up, not just on the mainland but in Attica and in Ionia too. The presence of exotic goods in some twelfth-century BC tombs may suggest that some social distinctions were maintained for a while, but the way in which such goods subsequently disappear makes it likely that any social distinctions had no secure base in prevailing social organisation. But the stories of Ionian migration and of the return of the children of Herakles are stories of movements headed by kings, of strong leadership, and of the setting up in Ionia of political organisations essentially similar to those which had prevailed in the mainland before the supposed arrival of the Dorians. Archaeological information securely refutes this: the Mycenaean political set-up was not transferred from the mainland eastwards, but disappeared without trace. Once we accept that not just the names of the individual leaders but the very concept of a led migration is a product of the needs of archaic Greeks, and not of Dark Age history, it is difficult to see what historical information the tradition contains which is not dependent on inference from the observed realities of the archaic period.

In the face of this, and of the silence of Homer and Hesiod, we are obliged to conclude that the Greeks of the archaic period *knew* nothing about the Dark Age. Indeed, one might say that for them ignorance was bliss, for upon the clean slate they could, and did, write their own beginnings, creating for themselves the past for which contemporary realities and desires for the future made them wish. They could, and did, invent themselves.

THE EASTERN MEDITERRANEAN WORLD

The late thirteenth century BC saw the collapse of the major political powers in the middle east, as well as the collapse of Mycenaean power in Greece (*ANE* 385–400). The reasons for the collapse of the middle-eastern empires are far from clear: there certainly do seem to have been movements of peoples, notably of Aramaeans in the area of Babylonia and Assyria, and of the so-called 'Sea Peoples' all along the eastern Mediterranean coast from Egypt to Cilicia, but it is probably wrong to see such movements of people as the sole, or even the crucial, cause of the collapse of the major political powers.

The Neo-Assyrian empire

What follows in the middle east is not a Dark Age, in the same way that the period is dark in Greece itself, for written records continue, notably in Assyria, and we can still reconstruct at least an outline political history. In the middle east what the following three centuries display is a much greater separateness of the various political units in the area, and an absence of any single dominating power or group of powers. The scale of organisation was not as reduced as it was in Greece, but, compared to what it had been, it was very considerably reduced indeed.

Signs of new, larger scale organisations appear again only in the late tenth century BC, when the Assyrian rulers, Ashur-Dan II and his successor Adad-Nirari II, carried out extensive campaigns which laid the foundations for what is known as the Neo-Assyrian empire (*ANE* 473–537). These campaigns extended the area of Assyrian rule in virtually every direction, and made the borders more secure. Then, in the middle of the ninth century BC, first Ashurnasirp II and then Shalmaneser III ferociously subjugated the various Aramaean peoples. During the late ninth century BC, and even more in the course of the eighth century, Assyria put an end to the independent existence of small states, as is well seen in the Hebrew scriptures' account of David and Solomon (eleventh–tenth century BC), and established a strong control over the whole area, a control which extended into Anatolia (on David and Solomon see *ANE* 449–56).

The Phoenicians

In one important respect, the Neo-Assyrian empire did not simply undo the effects of the collapse of the major middle-eastern powers at the end of the thirteenth century. The retreat of the great powers at that time had left the Canaanite cities of the coast free of domination, and in the years following 1200 BC these cities first became distinct, and acquired a sense of their own unity – even though the name by which we know them, Phoenicians, is a name imposed from outside and often used rather loosely (*ANE* 401–10). The Phoenicians did not form a single political whole, but comprised a group

At the end of twenty years, in which Solomon had built the two houses, the house of the Lord and the king's house, and Hiram king of Tyre had supplied Solomon with cedar and cypress timber and gold, as much as he desired, King Solomon gave to Hiram twenty cities in the land of Galilee. But when Hiram came from Tyre to see the cities which Solomon had given him, they did not please him. Therefore he said, 'What kind of cities are these which you have given me, my brother?' So they are called the land of Cabul to this day. Hiram had sent to the king one hundred and twenty talents of gold.

Text 7: 1 Kings 9: 10–14 (RSV).

of cities, from Ugarit in the north to Jaffa in the south, which governed themselves but shared a distinct, if eclectic, culture. As the Hebrew Book of Kings (1 Kings 9 and 10) shows, the Phoenicians, or at least their most powerful king, Hiram of Tyre, were already in possession of a fleet, and known for their seamanship, in the tenth century BC (Text 7), when there is evidence for their presence at Kommos on the south coast of Crete. Hiram I pursued an expansionist policy, entering into a commercial treaty with Solomon of Israel whereby Israelite agricultural products were exchanged for Tyrian skills and luxury goods, and making profitable joint excursions into the Red Sea area. That it was agricultural products which the Tyrians obtained from Israel may reflect Israel's shortage of other goods for exchange, but is likely also to reflect the inadequate agricultural base on which the populous Phoenician cities were built.

The ninth century BC saw the kings of Tyre, and in particular Ithobaal I, pursuing a policy of territorial expansion, and there are clear traces of Phoenician influence extending into Israel and up through Syria into Cilicia. A mid-ninth-century BC stele inscribed in the Phoenician language has even been found in the neo-Hittite kingdom of Sam'al. But the price of securing access to raw materials from an ever wider area was having to pay tribute to the Assyrians. Shalmaneser III (858–824 BC) publicly boasted of this tribute by having the Phoenician ships bringing him gold, silver, bronze, and purple cloth represented on the great bronze gates at Balawat (and see *ANE* 483–90). In the late ninth century BC the Assyrians extended their territory towards the Mediterranean, and by doing so both cut the Phoenicians off from access to the goods of the north-east and increased the pressure for tribute: Adad-Nirari III (810–783 BC) received twenty times more tribute from the Phoenician cities than had Shalmaneser III. In consequence, the Phoenicians turned, of necessity, more and more to the sea. Phoenician settlements on Cyprus can be shown, archaeologically, to date from the middle of the ninth century, and the traditional date of 814/813 BC for the Phoenician foundation of Carthage, although not yet supported by the finds made at the site, is not impossible, although it must be noted that most literary dates for Phoenician settlements abroad are demonstrably worthless.

The consequences for Greece

These conditions in the eastern Mediterranean are important for developments in Greece for two reasons, one negative and one positive. The collapse of the major middle-eastern empires, and their slow resurgence, meant that there was no major power in the middle east which was seriously attempting to acquire political control over territories further west. Even Assyria was, for most of the three centuries after 1200 BC, more interested in preserving its own borders than in making substantial new conquests. On the other hand, the administrative and bureaucratic collapse of Assyria, Babylon, and Egypt at the end of the thirteenth century did reduce the scale and scope of exchange from the eastern Mediterranean coastlands, east and south. The same events which left the Phoenicians high and dry on their coastal territory, free of political interference, also resulted in their growing need to form contacts in a wider world; but it was to the east that they looked at first. Only the re-emergence of Assyria as a major political power in the area created an urgent need to look west.

Mainland Greece was not under any political threat from the east in the years down to 800 BC, or indeed for another 200 years and more afterwards; but it was increasingly an object of interest to the Phoenicians, and perhaps to other Levantines, as a place from which goods might be acquired, and in which deposited. It is very difficult to distinguish between the Greek discovery of the near east and the Phoenician and Levantine discovery of the Greek world at this time (see below, pp. 98–101). Although we should note that some Greeks acknowledged Phoenician priority in the settlement and exploitation of a number of places in Greece (Herodotos 2.44, cf. 54–6, 4.147, 5.57–8), this was often only one tradition among several.

The first active interchange which the Greeks had with any near-eastern people was with people who were politically unimportant – Phoenicians and Levantines. The Phoenicians were extremely eclectic. They were more often the intermediaries than the originators of cultural exchange. Theirs was the script that formed the basis not only of Greek, as we shall see (pp. 101–5), but also of Aramaic, but they have left little in the way of literature or written records. In coming into contact with the world of the Phoenicians, the Greeks came into contact with a whole range of middle-eastern material culture, and not simply with one national culture. Moreover, one of the fields in which the Phoenicians particularly excelled was in the production of jewellery, objects whose intrinsic value made them sure to be closely scrutinised, but whose small size meant that they might travel easily. The fact that the Phoenicians not infrequently borrowed motifs, without borrowing the setting from the donor culture, meant that those motifs were made particularly readily available for reuse in a new context, and so encouraged the eclectic use of an already eclectic art.

GETTING ORGANISED

In Greece fewer places have revealed material signs of human presence in 1000 BC than at any turn of a century from 1500 BC to the change of era. Even in the areas of central Greece which flourished in Late Helladic IIIC (above, p. 38–9) the subsequent century has revealed occupation at markedly fewer sites. Pottery made at Athens improved markedly in quality around 1050 BC with the invention of the protogeometric style, and that pottery rapidly influenced pottery production in other parts of Greece, but this does not mean that the overall pattern of social, political, and economic organisation changed dramatically. Indeed, the picture we get from the material evidence for the two centuries after 1050 BC is one of successive failures to establish any extensive political, economic, or social organisation. Those failures are the measure of how clean the slate had been wiped.

Life at Lefkandi

Although evidence for human activity in the period from about 950 BC onwards is growing all the time, particularly from Thessaly and northern Greece, the site which provides the most graphic picture of the difficulties of getting organised is Lefkandi on Euboia. On current evidence this is the richest, if not the most progressive, site in Greece at this time. Excavations since the 1960s, although uncovering only a small part of the site, have revealed both settlement and cemetery evidence for Dark Age occupation, followed by abandonment at the end of the eighth century. Here, as at Athens, the middle of the eleventh century BC seems to have been a period of innovation and of foreign contacts: as well as signs of contact with Cyprus, tombs have yielded a necklace of faience beads and a Syro-Palestinian juglet. But for another century after that such exotic goods virtually vanish, and even contact with Athens seems to be weak. Although contact seems never to have been broken off completely, no stable, regular relationship with the wider world had been established, let alone any recognition of the possibility of a mutually productive dependent relationship to that world.

In the middle of this period of greatest isolation, however, just after 1000 BC, the people of Lefkandi were organised to construct a most remarkable building (Figure 12). Some 45 m long and 10 m wide, with one apsidal end, this building anticipates by two centuries any similar building known from elsewhere in the Greek mainland. Its construction has nothing in common with the construction of the Mycenaean palaces, and employs a totally different technique, with walls of mud brick upon a stone socle (foundation), and an exterior peristyle ('colonnade') of wooden posts. The use to which this building was put is no more Mycenaean. In its centre was a tomb in two compartments: one compartment contained a bronze vessel with figures of hunters and animals on the rim and with the cremated bones of a man wrapped in cloth inside, a spear and sword of iron, and the burial of a

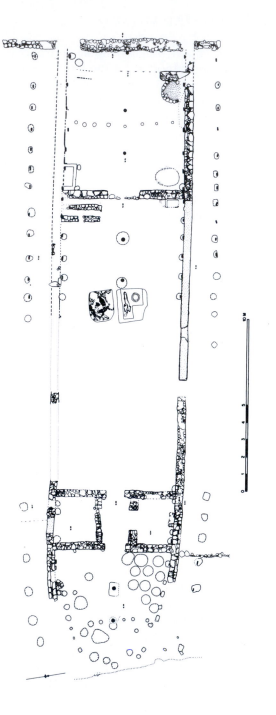

Figure 12 Plan of the monumental apsidal building at Lefkandi.

woman, with gilt hair coils, embossed gold discs over each breast, and bronze, bone, and gilt iron pins by her left thigh; the other compartment contained the skeletons of four horses, two with iron bits in their mouths.

The social implications of this building are thought-provoking, even though there is some doubt as to whether it was ever completed. At a time when, elsewhere in Greece, burials distinguish themselves from one another only by the presence or absence of spears and swords, female jewellery, and the use of different shapes of the closed pottery vessels, known as amphorae, for the ashes of men and women, this burial sets itself apart in a flamboyant way. The identity of the man and woman buried here is impossible to establish; what is important is the social power which this building manifests. Someone was able to command the labour and the skills to construct a building on a scale that must surely have been unheard of within the community, and probably within the whole Greek world, utilising construction methods that may have been well enough known on a small domestic scale, but which are here magnified virtually beyond recognition. That person was also in possession of metal goods with the like of which native smiths had no familiarity, and of enough horses, surely useless except as a display of conspicuous expenditure, to be able to sacrifice four of them at once. All of this implies a hierarchical organisation within the community, and a mode of communal organisation such that one family, or some other very small group, were able to exploit the rest of the local society, and to extract from them such a surplus as to be able to afford a display such as this. More remarkably still, this occurs at a time when other evidence for contact with the outside world is exiguous, and when there is no trace as yet of any goods from Lefkandi being exchanged outside the community.

The great building, even if it was finished, was not maintained for long, and no successor is so far known. Until this building was discovered in 1981 nothing in the remains from the rest of the tenth century BC suggested that anyone at Lefkandi had the sort of social power which this building displays. Continuing work at Lefkandi, which is very far from fully investigated, has yet to reveal any other evidence comparable to this monumental structure. It is clear from comparison with the other Lefkandi cemetery areas that the cemetery area which the building adjoins was reserved for an élite which came to command a wealth of imports from the near east, but that élite appears not to have been subsequently dominated by any single individual. This is perhaps not surprising: without being able to command some special resource, through the possession of a large territory, through the presence of mineral wealth of some description, or through strong links with a centre of production elsewhere with which beneficial exchange relations could be maintained, it is difficult to see how a community could produce the sort of surplus which would allow continued display by the community leader on the scale of that great building and its burials. On current evidence, the social power behind the great building, like the building itself, which seems soon

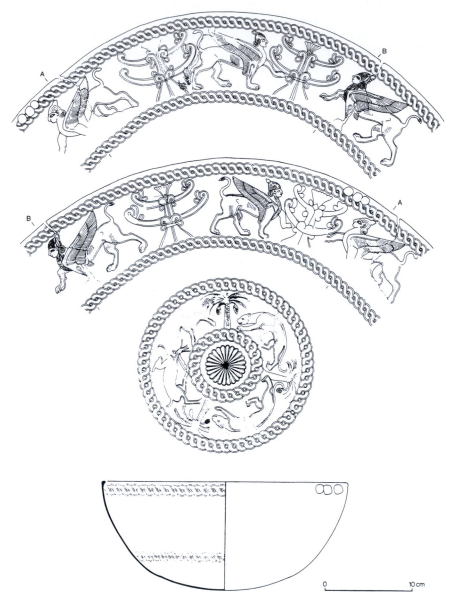

Figure 13 Engraved near-eastern bronze bowl from the Lefkandi Toumba
cemetery, c. 900 BC.

partially to have collapsed in one section, was insufficiently well-founded to
last.

The next sign of the community at Lefkandi getting organised takes a
very different form. Towards the end of the tenth century BC, in the last
phase of the protogeometric pottery style, the cemeteries at Lefkandi again

begin to yield considerable evidence of contact with a wider world, the hill-top site of Xeropolis shows evidence of settlement once more, and a late protogeometric skyphos and cup, that may well come from Lefkandi, appear at Amathous on Cyprus. Pots are imported from Athens in greater numbers, there are Athenian-style cremations with weapons, clear signs appear of contact with northern Greece (with Thessaly and with southern Macedonia), and jewellery, including some 10,000 faience beads, reappears in the tombs along with bronze bowls and other near-eastern products (Figure 13). Much of the gold seems to be of local workmanship, although the raw material is likely to have come from the east, and there are certainly indications that bronze and iron were being worked in the Xeropolis settlement at this time. The possibility of supporting skilled craftsmen points to some degree of social organisation, but the distribution of rich objects in tombs suggests that no single individual or single family dominated that organisation. Not all members of the community were equally wealthy; it is very likely that the wealthy buried themselves separately, and that the burials of the poor have not been recovered, but the burials we know do suggest that wealth was not narrowly distributed, and also that prestige was, in some degree at least, connected with the ability to fight.

During the early ninth century BC, contact with Athens seems to have been reduced once more, but contact with the east was maintained. Athens pioneered a new pottery style, known as early geometric, marked by the rejection of circular ornament and the movement of the decoration from the shoulder to the neck and body of the pot, but the people of Lefkandi continue with a style derived from protogeometric, known as sub-protogeometric. This pottery finds its way around the Aegean to such sites as Torone in Khalkidike. But there were also eastern contacts which certainly included Cyprus: Cypriot ceramic imports have been identified, and Cypriot influence has been suspected to account for a unique terracotta centaur. That centaur should also remind us of the existence and circulation of oral stories whose precise content is now irrecoverable (see below, p. 131–3).

The prosperity and wide but selective contacts of early ninth-century BC Lefkandi raise a number of questions, none of them easy to answer. Were the eastern goods the products of visits by Greeks from Lefkandi to the east? Or of visitors from the Levant to Euboia? (It is, after all, only in the middle of the ninth century BC that the Phoenicians established themselves at Kition in Cyprus.) What were the people of Lefkandi giving in exchange for the goods from the east? Was the lack of contact with Athens a product of conscious rivalry, or simply of interests looking in different directions? What we can be more certain of is the stability of relations between Lefkandi and the wider world at this time. No longer are we dealing with isolated contacts, but rather with contacts which, whatever their nature, could be replicated more or less at will. When Athenian pottery reappears at Lefkandi, in the later part of the ninth century, the Lefkandi potters continued to develop their own range of shapes and decoration, and did not simply turn to imitating the vases from

Athens. And it is in this period that Greek pottery begins to reach the near east in some sort of regular way, first with isolated finds from Megiddo in western Jordan and Tell Abu Hawam in the bay of Haifa, and then, from 825 BC, with a steady stream of Greek finds from Al Mina at the mouth of the river Orontes in the north-east corner of the Mediterranean. Both Attic pottery of the middle geometric style, in which decoration gradually spreads to the whole of the pot, and the drinking bowls known as skyphoi and large shallow plates (Figure 14), both decorated with concentric pendent semi-circles, which are characteristic of Lefkandi and to some extent of the rest of Euboia and the Cyclades, are found on near-eastern sites, sometimes together and sometimes separately. Ironically it is just at this time that we cease to be able to trace developments at Lefkandi itself, for, while its pottery continues to appear abroad, the cemeteries that have been excavated go out of use, and remains from the settlement are scrappy. Firmly established as a community with a clear identity, and a stable and prosperous internal organisation sufficient to sustain contacts with far-away places over a long period and to support an élite of some prosperity and number, Lefkandi was nevertheless not yet firmly rooted to a single site or a single locus of burial display.

Athens

In the present state of our knowledge, we cannot trace the process of social organisation as closely in any other community as we can at Lefkandi. But the greater number of graves known from Athens does allow patterns of behaviour to emerge more clearly, and what is lost in perception of the impact

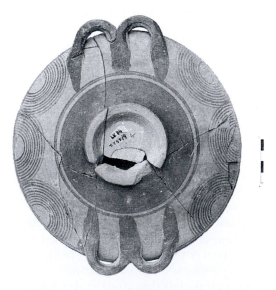

Figure 14 Euboian plate from Lefkandi decorated with pendent semicircles.

of individuals is made up for by a better sense of the community shaping itself within a space which it defines for itself. Athens emerges as a community where competition is both less intense and emerges less quickly than at Lefkandi, perhaps because the population was less densely concentrated.

As we have already seen, the adoption of the protogeometric pottery style at Athens around 1050 BC coincided with a change in burial practice: cremation became universal, men were consistently buried in neck-handled amphorae, women in belly-handled amphorae. What is more, the cemeteries changed: sub-mycenaean cemeteries had served large communities and had plots for eight or nine burials; protogeometric cemeteries seem to have served much smaller communities and to have had small plots with only three or four graves over two generations. At Athens in the sub-mycenaean period children had been buried separately from adults; this pattern continues in protogeometric, but children are now less well represented. Certain areas which had been used for burial in sub-mycenaean times, and in particular the Athenian Acropolis, cease to be so used. In the latter part of the tenth century BC some protogeometric cemeteries appear outside the central Athens/Peiraieus/Salamis area, inland at Nea Ionia and also on the east coast of Attica.

These changes in burial patterns suggest that the family units within the community became more aware of their independence and of their own status. As at Lefkandi, the signs of wealth present in early protogeometric (1050–1025 BC) disappear thereafter, and grave goods and burial practices are more suggestive of equality than of hierarchy. The non-cemetery traces support this picture: in particular in late protogeometric, for the first time, we find sanctuary deposits – at the Academy 2 km north-west of the Acropolis, and on Mount Hymettos. We cannot know what groups were responsible for these, but they suggest a heightened consciousness of place, of existing within a space which needed to be under one's control.

Around 900 BC Athenian pottery again shows a marked change of style, and further changes of burial practice seem to correlate with this. In the pottery, the changes are in both shape and decoration: in shape the high conical foot particularly characteristic of protogeometric open vessels virtually disappears; in decoration the dominance of circular motifs is ended and rectilinear motifs take over exclusively, being featured in small panels between handles and narrow strips on the body and neck. In burials, there is a marked increase in the wealth of grave goods: for the first time for more than a century gold objects are found, in the form of two finger rings, perhaps from Cyprus, in a female grave. At the same time, child burials disappear entirely from the archaeological record: however the large number of infants and young children who died were disposed of, they have left no archaeological trace. Cemeteries of adult burials continue to represent small groups of around ten adults, and there are now clear signs of a desire to establish separate burial plots within cemeteries, with the construction during the ninth century BC of an oval grave enclosure around a group of graves in the Kerameikos cemetery.

For the first time too, there is evidence for kraters (bowls for mixing wine and water) being used as markers on male graves, and deliberately pierced at the bottom so that liquid offerings placed in them could seep down to the cremation urn below.

This burial evidence strongly suggests a marked increase in consciousness of rank and role within society, and of the family as a social unit in which present generations benefit from the achieved position of past members, and make possible the achievement of similar rank in the next generation. The increase in wealth becomes even more notable in the middle of the century: elaborate gold jewellery appears, which displays an ability to form and work with strings of tiny gold beads, known as granulation, and to make the openwork patterns of gold wire known as filigree. These techniques must have been learnt from the east, but they are employed in ways not closely paralleled in material from the east. Eastern material does appear, however, including a Phoenician bronze bowl, faience discs, and ivory seals. These rich finds suggest an increasing element of exploitation within the community, both to sustain the expenditure, and to require, or at least encourage, the display of that expenditure in order to maintain the status hierarchy.

The changes in social organisation, or at least in priorities in social display, which are seen in the burials coincide with changes in pottery style, and this invites closer analysis of the pottery. Two features are of particular interest here: the basic decision to have decoration on more than one area of the pot, a decision which raises the question of the relationship between the two areas of decoration, and the rapid increase, during the ninth century BC, of the complexity of the decoration as geometric decoration spreads to more of the pot, and animal figures are introduced. There seems to be a strong correlation here with an increasingly ranked society in need of ever more subtle and sophisticated means of communication.

Developments elsewhere

Elsewhere in the Greek world the material evidence is rather more scrappy than for Lefkandi and Athens, but there are some scattered signs of similar processes at work during the tenth and ninth centuries. We have seen that at Kalapodi (above, p. 46) cult was substantially reorganised in c.950 BC, and at Tegea in Arkadia the first evidence for cult at the sanctuary of Alea also dates to the middle of the tenth century. At Old Smyrna, in Asia Minor, a city wall was constructed in the middle of the ninth century BC, a clear sign of community organisation. From the late tenth century BC on, there are strong signs of contact with the east in the Dodecanese islands in the south-east Aegean, and the production of imitation Phoenician black-on-red unguent flasks there suggests Phoenician presence on a temporary or permanent basis. Similar social developments can, of course, manifest themselves in a variety of material forms, and one nice example of this at this period seems to be afforded by the site of Tsikalario on Naxos, where funerary display takes the

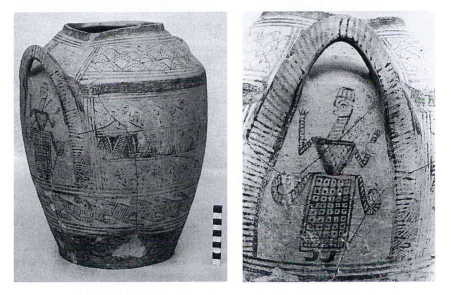

Figure 15 Late ninth-century pithos from the Fortetsa cemetery at Knossos in the style known as Cretan protogeometric B.

form of great tumuli, 10 m across, whose covering layers of stones and sand are held in place by a carefully laid kerb. These tumuli may be influenced by practices in northern Greece, but the associated pottery imitates Attic.

One area with a distinct history in this period is Crete. The refuge site of Karphi (see Figure 11), on the northern rim of the Lasithi plateau, seems to have been abandoned around 1000 BC, and for the next two centuries we have detailed knowledge only about the area close to the Minoan palace at Knossos, where several separate cemeteries have been excavated. What is known of eastern and western Crete suggests that communications between those areas and Knossos were not lively in either the tenth or ninth centuries BC, but it is apparent from the Knossos cemeteries that Knossos itself was in contact with Cyprus. The iron spits or pikes found there are certainly of Cypriot origin, and a number of objects more or less certainly from the near east – a bronze tripod and stand, a lead lion, an ivory pendant, and faience necklaces – may well have come via Cyprus. One tomb yielded both a hemispherical bronze bowl, of Cypriot type but with a Phoenician inscription giving the original Phoenician owner's name, and also no fewer than twenty-eight Attic protogeometric vessels, all but two of them drinking vessels. These pots are but one sign of a close link between Knossos and Athens, a link which is unbroken between the tenth and eighth centuries BC and brought to Knossos even Attic early geometric pottery, which is not at all widely found outside Attica. Pots from other parts of the Greek world, from Euboia, Corinth, east Greece, perhaps Thessaly, also appear occasionally in tombs at Knossos, but this Greek pottery had only slight influence at this time on the local pottery, which remains within the sub-minoan tradition until it takes up ideas not from Athens but from the east and from the Minoan past. The presence of plenty of exotic objects, and in the ninth century BC perhaps of immigrant Phoenician goldsmiths, along with the finding of decorated larnakes (coffins) in newly uncovered Late Minoan tombs, seem to have encouraged in the mid-ninth century a highly distinctive pottery style, known as protogeometric B. This style combines local shapes and motifs with shapes derived from Cyprus, motifs derived from oriental metalwork (particularly the cable pattern) and even human figures whose closest parallels seem to be Minoan (Figure 15).

The relics of past social organisation also seem to have survived at Knossos much more strongly than anywhere else. Burials continued to be made in chamber tombs (sometimes, perhaps often, reused Bronze Age chamber tombs) which receive family groups over several generations, even when inhumation was largely succeeded by cremation. A number of cemeteries, scattered around the Knossos area, seem to have been in use at the same time, and there are interesting distinctions between the burial practices found in the different cemeteries. It is not clear how far this is the result of different social groups keeping themselves more or less consciously apart. Signs of social change during the period are few, and when the Agios Ioannis cemetery goes out of use around 850 BC, and other cemeteries more remote from Knossos come into use, the basic burial practices are sufficiently unchanged to make it seem likely that we are dealing with a change in locational preference rather than any social revolution. A feature of many burials in the North Cemetery is the presence of large numbers of drinking vessels in the tombs: one tomb (KMF T.285.82) contained a middle protogeometric mixing bowl with thirteen cups and six jugs inside, suggesting substantial farewell parties held for more than just the narrow family group. With the exception of the burial of the raw material and products of an oriental goldsmith in a reused Minoan tholos tomb at Khaniale Teke in the late ninth century BC, the amount of precious metal in tombs is not large. The Knossos area seems to have continued through the tenth and ninth centuries BC to be stable both in its family-based social groupings and in its wider contacts, with enough cultural confidence to pick and mix artistic ideas encountered in imported goods. So far, there is little trace of reciprocal influence. No Cretan goods are known either from the Greek mainland or from Cyprus and the east. That it is the Phoenician goldsmith's tomb, and that alone, which has yielded the only sign of contact with the western Mediterranean, in the form of a small bronze vessel from Sardinia, suggests that Phoenician rather than Cretan carriers were responsible for at least some of the Mediterranean links.

Towards the end of the ninth century BC, therefore, there are signs that communities on the Greek mainland were beginning to get organised. Cemeteries show more order and regulation in their placing, in whom they admit, in their family divisions, and in their displays of material distinction. Contacts between different parts of the mainland increase in strength and frequency, and contacts between Greece and the east seem to be established on a regular, though not necessarily frequent, basis. These developments depend upon something more than simple determination to achieve something more than independent subsistence. As yet, however, there is little sign of what that determination would come to involve; to understand that, it is necessary to understand something of the background against which it had to be achieved, in terms of the physical environment of the Greek mainland and islands.

4

FORMING COMMUNITIES

The Eighth Century BC

At the end of Chapter 3 I left the communities of Dark Age Greece showing more signs of internal structure and establishing more systematic contact with eastern communities; I left the Phoenicians, a new colony established at Kition and probably another at Carthage, showing, as they had not a century earlier, an interest in tapping the resources of parts west, as well as parts east. The story of eighth-century BC Greece is a story of a world rapidly changing, and changing in part under the influence of increasingly dense contacts with the world outside. In the first three sections of this chapter I will look in turn at the evidence from settlements, cemeteries, and sanctuaries, before turning to Greek contact with the non-Greek world and to artistic developments.

GROWING PEOPLE

The map of sites of human presence in Greece shows a far more dense distribution for the eighth century BC than for the ninth or tenth. A brief survey of just three different areas will give a flavour of the increased quantity and variety of the archaeological evidence.

Crete

See Figure 16. In north-western Crete, in the area around Khania, during the tenth and ninth centuries there is evidence only of two cemetery sites (at Pelekapina and Modhi) and of occupation of a refuge site at Vrysses. From the eighth century comes evidence for burial at five sites, for settlement at three, for a sanctuary, and for occupation of three cave sites. In central Crete, at Knossos, whose relatively flourishing tenth- and ninth-century community and its cemeteries have been described above (p. 64), the sinking of wells implies extension of the area of settlement, a sanctuary of Demeter was founded, outlying tombs appear, and chamber tombs become so full that niches have to be dug in the passages leading to the chamber to accommodate further burials.

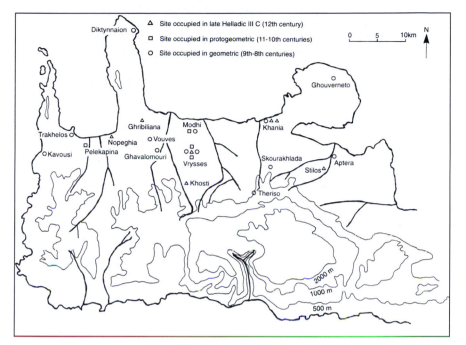

Figure 16 The pattern of occupation in the Khania area of Crete in the ninth and eighth centuries.

The Peloponnese

In Arkadia the only sanctuary which has yielded material from before 800 BC is that of Athene Alea at Tegea; during the eighth century BC there are clear signs of activity also at sanctuaries at Bassai, Kretea, Gortsouli, Gortys, Lousoi, Mavriki, and Orkhomenos (Figure 17a), as also at Rakita in western Akhaia. In the Argive Plain (Figure 17b), where only seven sites show signs of human presence in protogeometric, in geometric (900–700 BC) sixteen sites are in use. Not all these sites have a closely specifiable date of reoccupation, in terms of pottery style, but of those that do, six sites (all of them occupied in protogeometric) were occupied in the early geometric period (900–825 BC), eight in the middle geometric period (825–750 BC), and all sixteen sites have evidence of use in the late geometric period (750–700 BC). Similarly, 94 tombs are known from the Argolid for early geometric, 77 for middle geometric, and 141 for late geometric. While only seven Argolid sites show evidence of religious cult activity in protogeometric, or early or middle geometric, 24 sites show evidence of religious cult activity in late geometric. In the southern Argolid (Figure 17c) where only one site is known to have been occupied in protogeometric, twenty-one are occupied in late geometric. All this seems to indicate that it is the later eighth century BC, rather than the ninth century BC, that sees substantial increase in evidence for human activity.

67

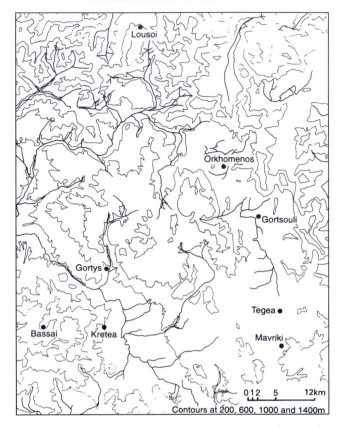

Figure 17a Sites in Arkadia occupied in the tenth to eighth centuries.

Attica

The number of sites known in Attica increases from 15 in the ninth century BC to 50 by the end of the eighth (see Figure 18), and the number of known adult burials from a steady rate of something under one a year virtually throughout the ninth century to a peak of 2.5 a year in the late eighth century BC.

The question of population growth

The change witnessed in all these areas is dramatic, but what caused it? The most obvious explanation is that there was a marked increase in population. The larger number of villages suggests population has outgrown the old settlements, the larger number of sanctuaries suggests that the old points of contact with the gods are no longer adequate, the larger number of graves suggests more people have died, and hence that more people were once alive. Hypothesising population increase not only explains these greater material

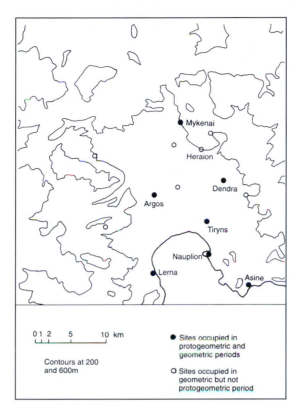

Figure 17b Sites in and around the Argive plain, tenth to eighth centuries BC.

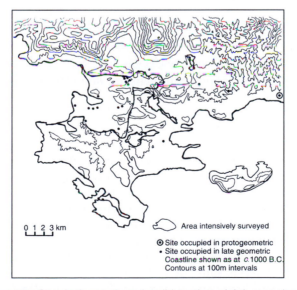

Figure 17c Sites in the southern Argolid, tenth to eighth centuries BC.

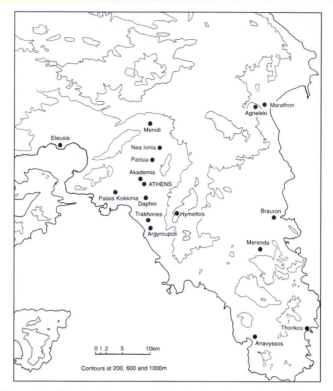

Figure 18a Sites in Attica occupied in the Dark Age prior to 800 BC.

reflections of human presence, but also offers a ready internal explanation for further changes: more people means pressure on resources, with all the consequences that that implies for agricultural innovation, economic prosperity, social relations, competition between groups, relations to, and need for, the gods and for outsiders. But are there actually good independent reasons to believe that population increased in a marked way in the eighth century BC?

There are two independent ways of approaching the question of whether the population increased dramatically in the eighth century BC. One is to show that the historical or archaeological record gives good evidence for changes in human life that might have brought about population growth, either by increasing human fertility or by decreasing human mortality. If we can show that fertility increased or mortality decreased then we can be satisfied that population did increase because it must have done so. The other approach is to demonstrate that the details of the archaeological record of the changed pattern of human presence which we are seeking to explain are exactly those which demographic change would bring about. If we could, for example, show that sites which already existed in the ninth century BC did not decrease in size, and measuring size is problematic,

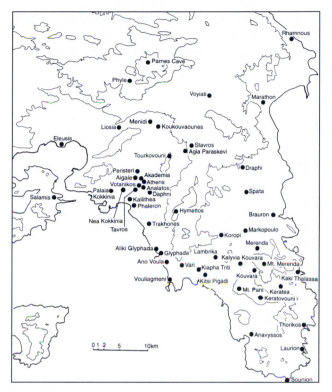

Figure 18b Sites in Attica occupied during the eighth century BC.

while other sites, which were culturally indistinguishable, were occupied on certainly virgin territory, then we would have good reason to think that only increased population could explain the phenomena. I will take each of these approaches in turn.

Is there historical or archaeological evidence for increased fertility or decreased mortality? Some archaeological signs look promising. The greater number of archaeological artefacts preserved from the eighth century BC, and the wider contacts which they suggest (see further below), seem to presuppose increased prosperity; increased prosperity might be expected to correlate with better nutrition, which would reduce both infertility and mortality, particularly perinatal and infant mortality. This argument is dangerously circular, however, and to avoid that danger it is necessary to try to get outside the purely archaeological record.

The issue of age-classes

Among candidates for social changes which will plausibly have increased fertility the most attractive is the age-class. Both classical Sparta and some Cretan cities organised their citizen population in part according to 'age-classes'; that is, they regulated the life, obligations, and opportunities of citizens according to their age (see further below, pp. 169–72). In these societies it was not simply that the education of boys was via age-graded tasks, but that in adult life too the expectations and possibilities varied with age: one could not serve on the Council of Elders (Gerousia) at Sparta, until one was 60 years old. Age-class systems regularly segregate boys and girls; this may encourage, formally, as in Sparta, or informally, the formation of homosexual bonds, and in any case it regularly restricts the opportunity to marry.

The firmer the grip of an age-class system over the population, the more the sexual access of men to women is restricted to certain age groups. Restrictions on sexual access clearly have consequences for fertility, consequences which are likely to be even greater if the age-class system also controls the lives of women and delays the age of first sexual intercourse: 'Age class systems have the effect of a birth control plan.' Classical Sparta suffered a decline in the number of adult male citizens, and it is likely that the age-class system was indeed a factor in this demographic trend. Either the introduction or the abandonment of an age-class system is likely to have marked demographic effect. If the eighth century BC saw a general move in Greece away from age-class organisation, leaving only conservative Sparta and 'backward' Crete with age-classes, then the breakdown of formal restrictions on sexual access would be likely to release a flood of fertility, transforming the demographic structure.

There are two questions to answer here. Were Greek societies generally ever organized into age-classes? And was there a move away from such an organization in the eighth century? Classical Athens, like many other cities, limited political participation by age: one had to be 18 to attend the Assembly, 30 to serve on the Council of Five Hundred or hear court cases, 40 to look after festival choruses, 50 to hear some judicial appeals, 59 to be a public arbitrator. Formally many, if not all, of these age restrictions are fifth- or fourth-century BC inventions, but this does not prevent them being applications to political life of some earlier age-class system. Rites of passage certainly existed in most Greek cities, for both girls and boys, and the comic dramatist Aristophanes (*Lysistrata* 639–47) can jokingly string these out in a way that suggests that girls in Athens might pass through a whole series of rituals as they grew up. The vocabulary available in Greek for describing young men, in particular, is rich, but scholars do not agree as to how precisely the terms were applied. Burial practices in many Dark Age societies show markedly distinct treatment of children (under-12s) and adults, and this is something equally true of later practice. For much of the archaic period some young men and women were singled out for particularly elaborate burial and commemoration, but there is no reason to connect this to their precise age at death. More than a broad distinction between how children and adults were treated in death, a set of rites of maturation which select young women undergo, and a set of different terms for young men are required if we are to prove the existence of a formal age-class system.

Nor do those who emphasise the evidence for age-classes in the ancient Greek world agree as to when the system was operative. The relevance of age-classes to the eighth-century demography depends on the sudden disappearance of age-classes from most of the Greek world in the early years of the eighth century BC. But such a disappearance is hard to posit on the basis of there being *later* evidence for such classes, and other scholars see age-classes as something that develops during the archaic period, emphasising indeed that Athenian 'democracy must also have led to an enormous expansion in the number of subjects of the helicocritical gaze and the number of those baring themselves before it'.

In the current state of the argument, age-classes offer no basis for believing that fertility increased, or indeed that mortality decreased, in these years. If there was an eighth-century BC population explosion the reasons for it would remain unclear. But does the archaeological evidence support the idea of massive population increase in any case?

Burials and demography

The case for population explosion has been most precisely and most strongly argued on the basis of the increase in the number of graves at Athens, in Attica, and at Argos (Figures 19a and b). Far more excavated graves in all these areas can be dated to the eighth century BC than to the ninth, and there is no significant supply of undated graves with which to supplement the earlier burial record. An increase in the numbers dying ought to correspond to an increase in the numbers who have lived. The question is, was the relationship between numbers dying and numbers being buried constant? Two features of the burial record in Attica suggest that it was not: the changing proportion of child graves, and the relationship between changing numbers of child graves and changing numbers of adult graves.

The eighth-century BC population of Attica would be remarkable among pre-industrial populations if the proportion dying in childhood was not high: one would expect to find almost as many child deaths as adult deaths (see above, p. 29). In fact, the proportion of child burials known during the Dark Age and the early part of the eighth century BC is tiny, and a very significant part of the total increase in the numbers of known burials in the second half of the eighth century at Athens and in Attica is an increase in child graves: for a brief period at the end of the century child graves are indeed as numerous as adult graves.

More puzzlingly, the number of adult graves begins to increase significantly earlier than the number of child graves. If increases in grave numbers were brought about by increased fertility, then one would expect numbers of child graves to increase first, as the same proportion of the newly enlarged families died, and numbers of adult graves to rise only later. Similarly, if a sudden decrease in mortality were responsible for the increase in grave numbers one would also expect infant mortality to decrease as early as, or earlier than,

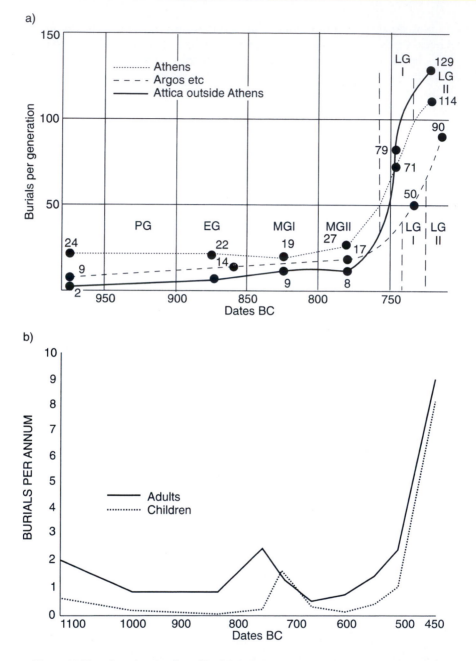

Figure 19 The changing number of burials in Attica: graph a) distinguishes town and country, but not children and adults, and stops at 700 BC; graph. b) divides adult and child burials, and continues to 500 BC.

adult mortality. In fact, numbers of adult graves begin to increase in the late ninth century BC, reach a peak in the middle of the eighth century BC, and then rapidly fall again; numbers of child graves begin to rise in the middle of the century, peak around 720 BC, and then fall again steeply. During the seventh century BC and first half of the sixth, levels of both child and adult burial are much the same as they had been in the tenth and ninth centuries BC. No change in fertility or mortality would seem apt to explain this pattern, certainly no single one-off change. If there was demographic change in the eighth century BC we are certainly not seeing its unmediated effect directly reflected in the burial record. At least part of the change to be seen in the increasing numbers of graves must be a change in who gets buried in an archaeologically visible way. The burial record thus contributes to the evidence for social change in the eighth century BC, but it does not itself offer an explanation for that change.

It is less easy to determine whether the increase in the number of sites which show signs of human occupation in the eighth century BC (Figure 20) is evidence for population growth. The nature of the evidence from sites, not all of which are residential, does not make it easy to determine the size of the group using or occupying them. The steady increase shown in site numbers in areas other than Attica suggests the operation of long-term factors, not merely short-term fashions. Even in Attica, where the site numbers do, rather suspiciously, match the pattern of graves in the eighth century BC, the number of sites does not, as that of graves does, return to the ninth-century level, and it picks up again immediately as the number of graves does not. Site numbers cannot be taken infallibly to attest demographic growth, and certainly cannot offer any sure guidance as to its scale, but they are suggestive. What they suggest is slow and steady population growth, continuously from the tenth century BC on, not a sudden explosion in the eighth century.

Changing numbers of excavated burials do not directly reveal a growing population, but that does not mean that they have no historical significance. Similarly, while changing numbers of archaeological sites may indicate demographic growth, that is certainly not the limit of their historical importance. It is time to examine the place of the dead and the place of the living in more detail.

THE CHANGING WORLD OF THE DEAD

The archaeological remains of the human dead undoubtedly tell us something about the society to which those dead belonged. But exactly how should we reconstruct the priorities and organisation of the living from the way in which the dead are disposed of? There seems good reason to think that distinctions made among the dead should reflect distinctions among the living; but there is no reason to think that different societies, or the same society at different times, will express the same distinctions among the living in the same

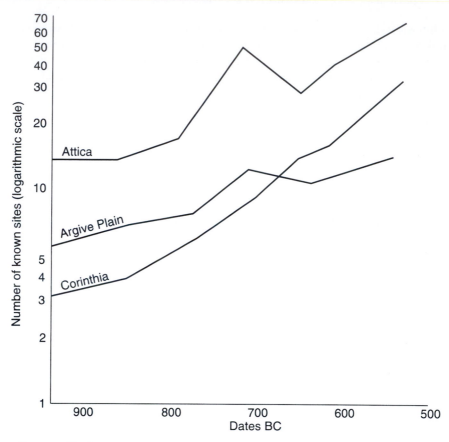

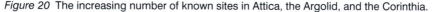

Figure 20 The increasing number of known sites in Attica, the Argolid, and the Corinthia.

distinctions among the dead. Particularly problematic are changes in funerary ritual, where it is difficult to tell whether practicality, changing beliefs about the after-life, or social revolution are to be held responsible.

The eighth century BC sees major changes in burial practices in many areas of the Greek world. Indeed, it has long been noted that the eighth century brings a marked increase in the diversity of burial practices in Greece. I will look first at the situation in Athens, where the data are fullest and analysis has been taken furthest, and then look very much more briefly at how Athenian developments compare with those elsewhere.

Burial practices at Athens

During most of the Dark Age adults in Athens had been cremated, and their bones gathered from the pyre and placed in a pottery vessel whose shape varied depending on the sex of the deceased. The pot was deposited, along with pyre refuse and other, increasingly rich, pottery and metal objects, in a hole which was then filled, and a stone and a pot marker were placed above it. Shortly after 800 BC, along with the increasing number of burials discussed above, various changes in practice occur: inhumation takes the places of cremation as the normal way of disposing of the adult dead, and grave goods decrease in number and quality: gold is now limited to a few graves, and the pots display a more limited range of shapes, with no further evidence for special commissions. At the same time, in at least one Athens cemetery, the Dipylon cemetery, the pots used as grave markers become more elaborate and grow to monumental size. There can be no doubt that these pots, some commemorating women, some men, were manufactured specially for the grave; their figurative scenes show mourning over the corpse (see below, pp. 126–8 and Figure 35) and sometimes ships and communal endeavours.

In the last third of the century the pattern changes. Children, previously inhumed in separate cemeteries, begin to be buried in adult cemeteries. Grave goods gradually disappear entirely from the grave itself, and offering trenches begin to be dug nearby. The pottery offerings deposited there cease to be everyday objects, and instead constitute distinct types made specially for the grave. Pots cease to be used as grave markers. Then, around 700 BC, inhumation of adults is replaced by cremation, but now this involves burning the corpse in the grave ('primary cremation'), a distinctly more elaborate matter than burning the body on a separate pyre and then gathering the bones for deposition in a container in a grave. All funerary offerings are now placed in separate offering trenches. At the same date burial in places not specifically reserved for the dead disappears; with almost no adult exceptions, burials are not now found within the settlement but rather in cemeteries that ring the settled area.

Burial practices outside Athens

To interpret this wealth of change at Athens it is valuable to compare what is happening elsewhere. To what extent are the changes at Athens changes that are happening everywhere? To what extent are they unique? To start from the end, the move to burial only in specially reserved cemeteries outside the urban area is found in other places too, though not at exactly the same moment. In Argos, as at Athens, the change happens about 700 BC; in Corinth it seems to occur fifty years earlier. Athens' practice of secondary cremation during the Dark Age had not been shared universally elsewhere: the people of Boiotia, of Lefkandi, and eighth-century-BC Eretria, and of Crete (where cremation is associated with chamber tombs), regularly cremated, but in Argos inhumation in cists dominated throughout until pithos inhumation is found for poorer burials from the middle of the eighth century and then replaces cists c.700 BC. At Argos children shared adult cemeteries at all periods, although in the seventh century BC some children were buried within the settlement, and pots were not used as grave markers, there were no sex-specific grave goods, and indeed no manufacture of pots specifically for the grave at all. Metal offerings fade out sharply at Athens soon after 750 BC, but in Argos the practice of including arms and jewellery in graves reaches a height in the second half of the eighth century, and decline in offerings is found only *c.*700 BC, coinciding with an increase in the proportion of child burials. At Corinth, which also never cremates, the decline in grave goods dates to the middle of the eighth century BC, and for the next 200 years differentiation between graves is minimal. Other areas of Greece show no similar pattern: Crete and many Aegean islands, including Euboia, seem never to have practised burial within the community, and their detailed burial practices are extremely diverse and rarely show any dramatic change around 700 BC, although on Rhodes a form of primary cremation does seem to have been adopted around this time.

It appears from this comparison that there was a general move among those communities which had previously practised burial within the settlement to cease from such practices, and that at least some mainland cities not far from Athens witnessed a similar, if not exactly contemporary, reduction in wealth of grave goods. These changes demand, therefore, some explanation that will hold valid across a number of different communities between which there is no other reason to believe that there were particularly close ties. The changes in funerary ritual, and in the ways gender difference is signalled, changes which might be thought to relate to social features which would be deeply conservative and common to various communities, seem, by contrast, to be peculiar to Athens and to require explanation in local terms.

Explaining the changes

The decision to exclude adult burials from the residential area presupposes both a recognition of certain areas as residential and a degree of community will and community enforcement. It is unclear what land 'ownership' will have meant in the Dark Age, but insistence on burying only in cemeteries reserved for that purpose implies communal recognition that people cannot simply do anything they like on the land which they control; it also involves the community setting aside land for community use, though the conditions of use are not clear: there are certainly grave groups, and probably family grave plots, in these cemeteries. What motivated this communal action? In Athens it is tempting to associate it with changing attitudes to the corpse, signalled by placing offerings apart from the grave and by cremating the body in the grave itself, where it did not need to be handled subsequently. But there is no such move to cremation at Argos or Corinth, and no such popularity of offering trenches. If a common factor is to be found it must be at the level of community organisation, not of belief, and it is tempting to see the exclusion of burials from central and prominent areas as a control on one aspect of display by the élite.

The decline in grave goods, which happens at different times in different places, also seems to invite explanation in social terms. At both Argos and Athens the decline is rapid, and follows a period notable for its exceptional deposition of wealth in graves. The late ninth century and first half of the eighth century BC at Athens sees a peak first in the number of weapons and then in the number of items of gold and silver placed in graves; shortly after 750 BC, during late geometric Ia, the Dipylon cemetery received its remarkable series of monumental marker vases; at Argos the peak in deposition of weapons, gold and silver, and also obeloi (spits) and bronze, comes in the late eighth century, with its remarkable warrior graves (see below, p. 162). What is happening in other parts of the archaeological record (see below, pp. 86–8) suggests that the decline in grave goods cannot be attributed to impoverishment, and the question arises whether there was some communal resistance to display of this sort, or whether those who had previously so indulged simply now decided to deploy their wealth in other ways.

The possibility of communal resistance to certain sorts of display is raised in a particularly sharp way by developments in figurative art (see further below, pp. 124–9). The painted pots which stood upon the wealthy graves in the Dipylon cemetery carry figurative scenes which evoke both the lying-in-state of a corpse and sometimes also warfare or processions (Figure 35). The figures in these scenes are heavily geometric, and standardised rather than individualised, but the lying-in-state scenes seem unequivocally to refer to the deceased and to the observed world of contemporary Athens. By showing the assembled mourners along with scenes of communal action these pots seem to insert the deceased into his or her wider community, and to stress membership of that community. The approach of the geometric figure scenes, in which no figure is emphasised, is an approach which owes everything to the Attic ceramic tradition and nothing to any outside influence. But some of these same graves contained within them objects which come out of a very different artistic tradition. The gold bands, which are one of the marks of the wealth of these burials, were certainly made in Attica, but they include some animal friezes which draw their inspiration directly from near-eastern art (Figure 21a). These friezes are uneventful but packed with life, the animals are lithe and move easily, and relate to one another. Little is made on these bands of the possibilities which this approach to figurative representation gives, but the contrast with the geometric animal friezes of some other gold bands (Figure 21b) and of the associated pottery is fundamental (Figure 22). (Only in the seventh century will Athenian potters take up this way of representing the world; compare below, pp. 124–8.) How is it that the same person could both choose pottery with geometric scenes, and gold bands with these very different friezes? How are we to explain such cultural schizophrenia?

It is not enough to explain the difference between pottery and goldwork simply in terms of artisans working in different traditions. Some gold bands are heavily geometric, and it is clear that goldsmiths could produce to demand. It is tempting to see the private taste of the rich for goods which carried with them a whiff of an exotic world, competing against public pressure to conform to native traditions. A style war. What it was acceptable for rich Athenians to wear in private, and how the rich presented themselves in public, might

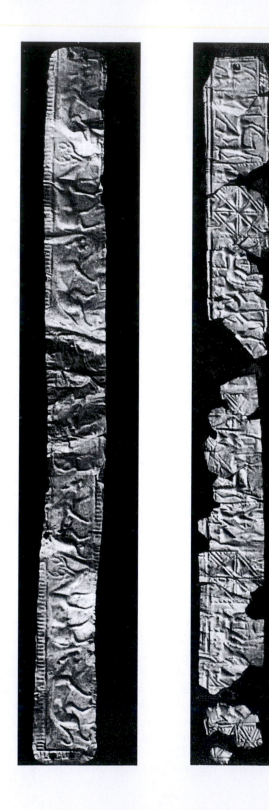

Figure 21a and b Two Attic gold bands of contrasting styles.

be two different things. It may be that the scenes on the great marker vases, busily insisting that the deceased was just another member of the community, protest too much. Are these the (unsuccessful) attempts by the rich to deny their difference while they also parade it? If they are, then eighth-century BC Athens witnessed the first debate in Greek history to which we are privy over the role of the wealthy in society. It would be the first of many.

By the last decades of the eighth century BC at Athens, metal goods are one of the few features which mark out rich from poor graves. Cemeteries seem generally to have become places where status distinctions are no longer marked, as first more adult graves and then child graves invade cemeteries previously restricted to adults of probably high status. Being buried in a highly visible way had clearly ceased to imply élite status, and those who wanted to mark their high status needed to do so in some different way. The decline in numbers of graves at Athens may reflect the impoverishment of the tomb as a status symbol, leading to its abandonment by status-seeking groups. The new burial method, primary cremation, is expensive in resources – tombs have to be more carefully constructed in order to cremate the body inside them, and more fuel is required – and the use of offering trenches made possible the extension of the ceremonial over some period after the actual cremation. Were these ways in which the élite sought to escape the constraints which

Figure 22 Late geometric amphora from Kerameikos cemetery at Athens.

non-élite competition placed upon them in the period 750–700 BC, ways which, because of their intrinsic costs in time and money, were less accessible to emulation?

If we see the disappearance of wealthy graves in Athens, at Corinth, and at Argos as the consequence of the community at large constraining the wealthy, it is not difficult to explain why the precise timing of the changes might be different in the different communities, and why some communities might never be affected. This is surely precisely the sort of development that might start in one community and then spread, but in a haphazard fashion. It is quite possible that the particular factors which encouraged such constraining of the rich may have varied greatly from community to community. The peculiar features of the Athenian case need to be seen in terms of the contrasts in the earlier development of Athens. Athens had developed a tradition, not shared in Argos or Corinth, of specially commissioned vases for graves, and of distinct funerary symbolism and funerary markers for men and women; that tradition had developed as a way of marking out individuals, and it was as vulnerable to pressures to conform as were the Argive warrior graves. That the ritual of lying-in-state, and perhaps the events that followed, are figured on Attic vases may indicate that these were peculiarly elaborated in Athens. The new funerary ritual which primary cremation and offering trenches must have involved, whatever the pretext for them, will have eliminated an opportunity for the display of distinction that had not been curbed by making cemeteries less exclusive by introducing more of the dead and child dead into the visible rituals of the cemetery.

The plausibility of these speculations needs to be assessed in the light of further eighth-century developments.

THE CHANGING WORLD OF THE GODS

Cult in the Dark Age

There is, as was noted above (p. 46), reason to think that, although the pantheon of Greek gods was preserved from the Mycenaean period through the Dark Age, the radical discontinuity in human settlement also affected continuing cult activity. That there was Dark Age cult activity in association with human settlement is, however, in no doubt. There are clear signs of sacrificial activity at Asine in the Argolid and at the so-called 'chieftain's house' at Nikhoria in Messenia in the protogeometric period. By the tenth century BC, if not before, there are signs of cult activity at the sanctuaries of Artemis at Mounykhia and Brauron in Attica and Kombothekra in Elis, at the sanctuaries of Apollo at Amyklai near Sparta and Kalapodi in Phokis, at the sanctuaries of Zeus at Olympia and on Mount Hymettos in Attica, at the sanctuaries of Hera at Samos and Prosymna (the 'Argive' Heraion), at the sanctuary of Athene Alea at Tegea, and at the sanctuary of Poseidon at Isthmia. Part of the interest of these signs of Dark Age cult activity is the variety of the cult places: some are in the midst of settlements, others on the edge of settlements, others isolated from settlement entirely or even removed to a high mountain peak. The drastic changes which followed the end of the Mycenaean palaces evidently did not reduce the complexity of the Greek pantheon, and there is no reason to believe that they impoverished the variety of ways of relating to the gods.

Eighth-century temples and dedications

But in the eighth century BC the world of the gods changed. It changed most markedly in the development of the temple, the monumental building set aside to house the god and the dedications made to her or him. There had almost certainly been buildings specially set aside for cult purposes during the Dark Age, not just in Crete, which develops a very distinct tradition in temples, but elsewhere; but it is in the eighth century BC that a permanent cult building, sometimes of monumental size, begins to be a regular feature of the increasing number of sanctuary sites. Along with the building of temples goes a massive increase in the number of dedications, large and small, made to the deity, and this increase represents not only a quantitative but also a qualitative change: some sanctuaries now clearly attract dedicants from outside just the local area. Archaeology is not very helpful in revealing why dedicants might come from outside, but here the historical tradition may help: the first Olympic games were traditionally dated to the end of the first quarter of the eighth century BC, and in that case some dedicants at Olympia, at least, may have come in order to compete in some form of athletic competition (see further below, pp. 90–3).

Temples

Examination of particular individual sanctuaries will give some idea of how the building which took place during the eighth century transformed them. At Kalapodi in Phokis there had been some construction work in the sanctuary soon after the middle of the ninth century BC: a new hearth altar was constructed and monumental dedications, in particular the first large bronze cauldrons supported on a tripod framework, appear. Late in the eighth or early in the seventh century BC the sanctuary seems to have received two mud-brick temple buildings, although later building on the site has made it difficult to recover their precise form. Then at the very end of the eighth century BC rich jewellery dedications increase and the first dedications of iron weapons are found. At the sanctuary of Alea at Tegea in Arkadia two successive eighth-century temples seem to have succeeded an even earlier structure or structures, and there were further constructions in the sanctuary which may have been designed to display the exceptionally varied dedications which this sanctuary was receiving. Among these dedications representations of the human figure were unusually prominent. At the Samian Heraion a temple 100 feet (c.33 m) long (a 'hekatompedon') was built around 800 BC: this building was put up west of an existing altar, had an east porch, and was 20 feet (c.6 m) wide, with a row of columns down the centre to support the roof, and a base for a statue of the deity at its west end, where it would seem to be the focus of cult activity. It either had an external colonnade from the beginning or was given one in the course of the eighth century BC. By the end of that century the sanctuary had also received a small treasury building.

The importance of the cult statue within the temple is further emphasised by one of the most revealing eighth-century cult buildings, that at the sanctuary of Artemis at Ephesos. The early phases of temple building in this sanctuary, which is now known to have been in use continuously from the sub-mycenaean period onwards, have only recently become apparent. It is now clear that a temple building with an external and internal colonnade was constructed during the eighth century BC, and it is tolerably likely, from a find of tear-drop-shaped amber beads, that it was built to house a cult statue of Artemis, whose curious breast jewellery, well known from later antiquity, would thus date back at least to the geometric period. The temple, with eight columns on the flanks and four on the façades, and with a double colonnade internally, comes rather closer in form and proportions to canonical archaic and classical temples (see below, pp. 253–5) than does the long, thin Samian hekatompedon.

Not all old-established sanctuaries got temple buildings in the eighth century BC, and a good number of archaic and classical sanctuaries never had temples, but some newly established sanctuaries did acquire a temple. Notable among these are the late eighth-century apsidal temple at the remote site of Ano Mazaraki Rakita in Akhaia, and the temple of Apollo at Eretria. Eretria seems to have been settled c.800 BC, and much of the earliest pottery, including the very earliest isolated fragment of perhaps tenth-century date, comes from the sanctuary of Apollo, where, before the middle of the eighth century, a small cult building, known as the 'Bay Hut', was put up, about 9 × 6 m with an apsidal end. Then, close by, around the middle of the eighth century BC, a hekatompedon was constructed, similar in scale and proportions (35 × c.8 m) to the Samian temple, but with an apsidal end, in the tradition of the much earlier and even larger building at Lefkandi. The 'Bay Hut' at Eretria seems to have been somewhat similar in form to the early eighth-century clay building models which have been found as dedications at the 'Argive Heraion' and at the sanctuary of Hera at Perakhora (and which may be house models rather than temples). The sanctuary at Perakhora is another from which the earliest evidence dates to the first half of the eighth century, and it soon received a temple building, c.8 m × 5 m, similar in plan to the models.

On Hektor's command, his mother went to the halls and instructed the attendants, and they gathered together the matrons from all over the town. But she went down to the fragrant chamber where the embroidered garments were, the work of women of Sidon whom Alexandros (Paris) himself had brought from Sidon, sailing across the wide ocean on the journey on which he brought home noble Helen. Hekabe chose one of the garments and brought it as a gift for Athene – the largest and most beautifully embroidered, it gleamed like a star, and lay at the bottom of the pile. Hekabe went on her way, and many matrons streamed after her. When they came to the temple of Athene on the Acropolis, fair-faced Theano, daughter of Kisseus and wife of horse-taming Antenor, opened the doors for them, for the Trojans had made her Athene's priestess. All the women raised their hands to Athene with a ritual cry, and fair-faced Theano took the garment and placed it on the knees of Athene. She invoked the daughter of great Zeus in prayer, saying 'Mistress Athene, saviour of the city, glorious among goddesses, break the sword of Diomede and grant that he falls on his face in front of the Skaian Gates. We will straightway now sacrifice in your temple twelve yearling heifers, not yet accustomed to the goad, if you take pity on the town and the wives of the Trojans and their infant children.'

Text 8: Iliad 6. 286–310. An offering is made to Athene's cult statue by the Trojan women.

Cult statues

The evidence for statues of deities which served as the focus of cult within these temple buildings is not great, but it is vitally important. At Samos there is a base that may have supported a cult statue, at Ephesos jewellery probably from the cult statue, and the temple of Apollo at Dreros on Crete, which is architecturally rather different, has yielded a number of hammered bronze figures, which seem likely to be cult statues rather than simply votive offerings. Despite the paucity of evidence, there seems little reason to dispute that the major purpose of building a temple was in order to house the god. There may have been a continuous tradition of cult statues on Crete, where the refuge site at Karphi (above, pp. 44–5) included a building with goddess statuettes, but in mainland Greece Dark Age cult seems to have been centred on sacrifice and to have used no cult images. The importance of adding images to the repertoire of cult activities is considerable: communication with the gods could now happen not merely through prayers, which might or might not be accompanied by votive offerings, and through the sacrifice of an animal's life, but also through literally face-to-face contact with the divine and through contemplation of the divine image. What is more, the image made the god permanently present within the temple and so within the community, whether summoned to share in a sacrifice or not. Adding the image of the god to a sanctuary both gave the individual the chance to face up to the god, and gave the community a potentially powerful ally offering and demanding protection.

Two incidents which form part of the Trojan legend illustrate the importance of the presence of a divine image. When in the *Iliad* Diomede is waging a particularly successful onslaught against the Trojans, the seer Helenos sends his brother Hektor back to the city to get their mother to organise a procession of ladies to take a new and special robe to the statue of Athene in its temple (6.73–102, 237–310; Text 8), to lay it on the statue's knees, and, promising sacrifices, to ask Athene to have pity on the Trojans. Again, when Troy is sacked, it is to the statue of Athene that Kassandra goes for refuge, and from that statue that she is mercilessly dragged by the Lesser Aias (Proklos' epitome of Arktinos of Miletos, *Sack of Troy*). In both these stories the cult statue is the focus of the divine presence within the community, and being in contact with it puts people most directly in touch with divine power.

Dedications

The growth of sanctuaries during the eighth century BC can also be seen in much more modest features than monumental buildings or cult statues. Take the humble pin, for example. Pins were not infrequently dedicated in sanctuaries, both sanctuaries of female deities such as Artemis, to whom dedications of clothing were made, and sanctuaries of male deities. Fashions for the shape of pins changed over time, and so it is possible to use pins to reveal the increasing frequency of dedications at sanctuaries more generally. The pattern which Imma Kilian-Dirlmeier's work on pins from the Peloponnese reveals (Table 3) is replicated outside the Peloponnese and for items other than pins (Table 4).

These crude statistics are only a very imperfect reflection of dedicatory practice, because of the hazards of survival and of excavation, but they reveal very clearly that different sanctuaries experienced increased dedicatory activity during the eighth century BC, although both the form and the timing of the changes varies from place to place. The tables reveal less well the full extent of the variety in dedicatory practice in different sanctuaries.

The sanctuary at Pherai in Thessaly, where more than 3,500 objects were dedicated during the eighth and early seventh centuries BC, shows one end of the spectrum of the sanctuary experience. Only 77 objects from that sanctuary (that is, 2 per cent of the total number of dedications) can be identified as of non-Thessalian origin, and 38 of these come from nearby Macedonia or the Balkans. Pherai was a large community, and the frequent dedicatory activities here seem to be a product of that community alone and to reflect an absence of wider interest in the sanctuary or stimulus from foreign contacts.

Quite different is the pattern at the sanctuary at Perakhora, which received no fewer than 273 Phoenician scarabs along with significant quantities of metalwork from Italy and the east Greek world (but nothing from nearby Athens). Perakhora is a harbour sanctuary; its commanding position on the Corinthian Gulf may have attracted those engaged in shipping and certainly made it essential for any Corinthian community which had an interest in the sea to control it (Figure 23). Perakhora rapidly came to outstrip the other major Corinthian sanctuary at Isthmia in wealth, and is particularly notable

Table 3 Changing numbers of pins recovered from Peloponnesian sanctuaries, c.1050–c.500 BC.

Sanctuary	Sub-mycenaean and protogeometric (c.1050–850)	Early to late geometric (c.850–700)	Late eighth and early seventh centuries (c.725–650)	Archaic (c.700–500)
Perakhora	0	38	9	78
'Argive' Heraion	2	699	279	388
Lousoi	0	3	5	23
Olympia	7	58	29	225
Tegea	0	273	243	50
Artemis Orthia	0	133	926	403
Menelaion	0	2	17	41

Table 4 Increasing numbers of dedications in sanctuaries across the Greek world, eleventh to seventh centuries.

Sanctuary: item/date	Eleventh/tenth centuries	Ninth and early eighth centuries	Later eighth and seventh centuries
Lindos: fibulae	0	52	1540
Lindos: pins	0	0	42
Pherai: fibulae	0	2	1783
Pherai: pins	1	4	37
Hymettos: vases	69	116	965
Kombothekra: terracottas	0	18	21
Tegea: vases	0	21	75

for purpose-made votives of thin sheet gold. The presence of Phoenician and east Greek dedications there suggests that it does not simply reflect Corinth's contacts in the Corinthian Gulf itself and in parts west. Rather it seems to attract those with an interest in displaying their exotic contacts and tastes.

Such exotic tastes seem even more in evidence at the Samian Heraion, where votive objects come from Egypt, Cyprus, north Syria, Phoenicia, Phrygia, and Assyria in quantities significantly greater than those of objects from mainland Greece, Crete, or even other parts of Ionia. The variety of eastern objects found at the Heraion must reflect widespread Samian contacts, whether those contacts were initiated from the east or from Samos itself. On the same basis the Samian Heraion, despite its precocious monumentalisation, would seem not to be attracting other Greeks, either Ionians or others, in any numbers at this period.

At the sanctuary of Zeus at Olympia the longer history of dedications shows enlarged contacts, but little sign of the pull of the exotic. The earliest dedications belong to the tenth century BC and take the form of bronze and terracotta votive figurines, which are closely parallel to those from the nearby sanctuary of Artemis Limnatis at Kombothekra, simple jewellery, and, perhaps from the early ninth century, bronze tripods. The number of dedications of all kinds increased during the ninth century BC, and even more so during the eighth (18 animal figurines are known from the tenth century BC, 160 from the ninth, 1,461 from the eighth), and the tripods increased in elaboration as well as in number: a new hammered style of tripod was introduced in the middle of the eighth century, and tripods as well as jewellery suggest a widening source of dedications. The presence of miscast bronze figurines shows that these were being manufactured at the sanctuary itself by itinerant craftsmen coming from a variety of metalworking traditions, but the tripods seem to have been manufactured elsewhere, and were perhaps brought to the sanctuary by the dedicant. About half the non-local objects dedicated at Olympia seem to have come from or to have been made by craftsmen from other parts of the Peloponnese, a significant proportion (about one in six) come from Attica, and about one in twelve from either Italy or the eastern Mediterranean.

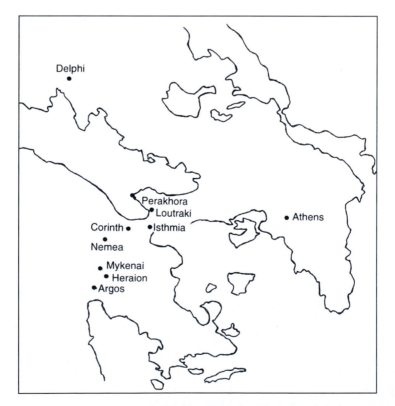

Figure 23 The Perakhora sanctuary and its region.

This glance at just four sanctuaries suggests that there are two separate questions which need to be answered. The first is why this great increase in investment in the divine occurred. The second is why there was so much variation from sanctuary to sanctuary in the way in which this investment was made. I turn to that second question first.

Varieties of sanctuaries

The range of origins of items dedicated at sanctuaries reveals something of the range of contacts which the community local to the sanctuary enjoyed, but the selection of goods dedicated was not determined by those contacts. This is most clearly demonstrable in the contrast between the significant presence of Attic material at Olympia and its complete absence at Perakhora. It is impossible to believe that Attic goods were not available to the community which made dedications at Perakhora, particularly since Attic pottery and terracottas are present at the Isthmia sanctuary from the late protogeometric period onwards. Objects dedicated at sanctuaries were not selected at random, but in order to carry certain messages.

If we ask what message the dedications at any particular sanctuary were intended to convey, the answer has to take into account the particular nature of the sanctuary as well as the whole range of dedications. The sanctuary of Hera at Perakhora makes a particularly interesting case study. This sanctuary was founded around 800 BC on a site which, despite its rugged nature and lack of fresh water supply, was bound to be prominent as soon as shipping in the Corinthian Gulf became important, because it was closely linked by sea to the settlement at Corinth. But in terms of communications by land the sanctuary at Perakhora is remote from Corinth, and tradition suggests that Corinthian possession of it became a sensitive issue as soon as territoriality became significant. The dedications at Perakhora do not suggest that defence of territory or establishment of a territorial outpost was in fact an issue in cultic terms: there is nothing martial about the dedications – the clay model *koulouria* (bread-rings) and the links with female adornment rather bring out Hera's domestic side. the contrast with the sanctuary of Poseidon at Isthmia, established earlier, is informative; Poseidon's sanctuary has a very different range of dedications, including tripods and arms and armour. Isthmia seems to stress male contributions to civic life, Perakhora to bring women's contribution much more to the fore and to rejoice in access to exotic adornments.

The cultic priorities at Perakhora can be seen in a very traditional light. Sanctuaries whose cult and dedications are linked to the lives of women are consistently found on the margins of a territory, and are often found on the coast. The old-established sanctuaries of Artemis at Mounykhia and at Brauron in Attica, and the harbour sanctuary at Emborio on Khios founded in the ninth century BC, conform to this pattern. Whatever developments are marked by the increase in sanctuary activity in the eighth century BC, they did not involve a break in traditional assumptions about the significance of space or the way in which the human community could map itself on to the divine community through the medium of natural geographical boundaries. That the Corinthian community felt a need *c.*800 for such a sanctuary, when it had had no such need previously, might be connected with the development of seaborne communications, which turned Perakhora into an important site, or it might be connected with internal developments within the community. The effect of establishing the Perakhora sanctuary was certainly to make this marginal site, and hence the margin to which it belonged, the focus of community activity in a new way: exploiting associations involved also staking a claim, although we cannot be sure whether the associations or the claim played the more important causal role.

The tripods and arms at Isthmia also stake a claim. Tripods seem to have been a prominent mark of wealth during the Dark Age. Dark Age tripod dedications are known from the Polis Cave on Ithaka, and tripod fragments have also been found at the rich Dark Age site of Nikhoria in Messenia. Tripod cauldrons are objects of high prestige, for their workmanship and as gifts and prizes, in the *Iliad* (23.264) and *Odyssey* (13.13). By the end of the archaic period there is no doubt that tripods were particularly associated with victory in competition and were the most prestigious of all competition prizes. How far tripods had acquired competitive overtones by the eighth century is less clear, but a scene showing two helmeted figures struggling for possession of a tripod on the leg of a tripod from Olympia is suggestive (Figure 24). The enormous rise in the number of tripod dedications at Olympia in the eighth century BC seems to coincide with the establishment of the Olympic games as a major event, but it is doubtful whether there was any major competition associated with the Isthmia sanctuary until the early sixth century BC, and even at Olympia there seem to be more tripods than there will have been victors. The variety of places of manufacture of the Olympia tripods suggest that people brought them with them when they came to the games, and in those circumstances they can be expected to have dedicated them whether victorious or not. Rather than seeing tripod dedications as occasioned by athletic victories we should perhaps see tripods and victories as parallel phenomena, both offering men ways of displaying status.

The developments at Olympia and at Isthmia raise questions about the parallelism between their situations. Both sanctuaries seem until the eighth century BC primarily to have served a local community, and in neither case does that community seem to have been politically defined: there is no reason to suppose that the Isthmia sanctuary was exclusively 'Corinthian'. In the eighth century BC changes occur in both sanctuaries: at Olympia these changes enormously *enlarge* the community which the sanctuary serves; at Isthmia the changes are more difficult to interpret, since they involve both the construction of a terrace, which appears to have accommodated ritual dining, and also distinct changes in the characteristic votives – as well as the tripods and arms mentioned above there is a new variety of cup forms and a wider range of terracotta figurines. Olympia might seem much more remote than Isthmia, but its situation at the confluence of the major rivers Alpheios and Kladeos puts it at the junction of two communication routes of major local importance. The Isthmia sanctuary lies at the dramatic narrowing of the isthmus and on the main artery of land communication into and out of the Peloponnese. Dedications made at both these sanctuaries will have attracted the attention of more than just a local community as they displayed the dedicants' status to a constant flow of passers-by. In both cases, therefore, the sanctuary provides an attractive site for dedications for those, and in both cases these are evidently men, not women, who wish to display their wealth and prestige to a wider community. Both bear witness, as the sanctuary

Figure 24 Leg of a Cretan tripod of late eighth-century date from Olympia, showing a struggle for a tripod between naked figures wearing helmets.

at Perakhora cannot, to the presence within Greek communities of men ambitious to be known to a wider world.

The parallelism between Olympia and Isthmia must not be overstated. Although there is much that is alike in the nature of the dedications, the quantity and quality of dedications at Olympia are very markedly higher. Given that Isthmia commands the busier communications route, the greater wealth of Olympia demands a further explanation. That explanation must surely lie with the Olympic festival. Isthmia offered a site where men could display their achieved status, but Olympia offered a site where men could not only display their status but also enhance it, and enhance it in a peculiarly prominent way.

The Olympic games

There is little reason to doubt that games had been a feature of Dark Age life, but the Olympic games offered something distinct. Funeral games are deeply embedded in the *Iliad* where, as well as the games held by Akhilleus at the funeral of Patroklos (*Iliad* 23.297–897), funeral games for one Amarynkeus are recalled by Nestor (Text 9; *Iliad* 23.629–45). Hesiod says he performed at the funeral games of Amphidamas at Khalkis. Funeral games are, by definition, events which occur at random and at short notice. They are also entirely in the hands of the person giving them: it is Akhilleus who makes up all the rules, decides what the prizes are to be, and arbitrates in disputes in Patroklos' funeral games. The giver of funeral games, as well as the competitors, enhances his status. Games at a religious festival are different: they occur regularly and predictably, preparation is possible, and indeed at Olympia came to be enforced: competitors had to swear that they had been in training for ten months (Pausanias 5.24.9) and, later in antiquity at least, had to come and reside at the sanctuary for thirty days before the competition. The rules were decided by a committee, not by an individual. And at Olympia, though not at all festival games, the prizes were nominal. Victory at Olympia could not

I wish I was in my prime and my strength was firm, as at the time when the Epeians buried their ruler Amarynkeus at Bouprasion and his sons set up games in honour of the king. There was no man like me then, not among the Epeians, not among the Pylians, not among the Aitolians. I beat Klytomedes, son of Enops, in boxing, Ankaios of Pleuron, who stood up to me, at wrestling. I outran Iphiklos, who was good at running, and I threw further than Pyleus and Polydoros. With horses alone did the two sons of Aktor drive past me: they forged ahead through their superior number, jealously eager for victory, because the greatest prizes were reserved for this contest. These two were twins, and the one kept a firm hold on the reins, always a firm hold on the reins, while the other urged with the goad. Ah, that's how I was! Now let younger men face up to such tasks. I have to follow the dictates of hateful old age, but then I was like the heroes.

Text 9: Iliad *23.629–45. Nestor tells of his prowess at the funeral games of Amarynkeus.*

First Olympiad: from the capture of Troy up to the first Olympiad 405 years. The first Olympiad took place in the second year of Aeschylus as judge of the Athenians, and Coroebus of Elis was victorious. . . . Iphitus son of Praxonides or of Haemon set up the first Olympiad. From this time Greek history is believed accurate in the matter of chronology. For before this, as anyone can see, they hand down various opinions.

Text 10: Jerome's edition of Eusebios' chronological work (late fourth century AD) under 776 BC.

be ascribed to greed for the prize, to the favouritism of the giver of the games, to arbitrary judgements, or to happening to be in the right place at the right time: conditions were equal for all, and even to be in a position to compete demanded the conspicuous display of time and energy on preparation.

Later tradition held that the Olympic games were started by Herakles, fell into desuetude and were renewed in 776 BC. The claim that Herakles began the games, like the claim of the second-century AD writer Pausanias that events which were added to the games after 776 BC were added when they were 'remembered', is likely to have been made to enhance the standing of the games rather than to be a 'real' folk memory. By late antiquity, the Olympic games of 776 BC had become the beginning of Greek history proper (Text 10). Although the dating of historical events by Olympiads did not in fact start before the fourth century BC, the adoption of Olympic victors as having universal significance itself demonstrates the continued high status which Olympic victory offered. That status is also manifest in the tradition that cities, when they welcomed back victors, invited them to throw down part of the city wall, on the grounds that a city with such men had no need of walls (Plutarch, *Quaestiones conviviales* 2.5.2), and in a large number of stories about the power of victors for good, or, if crossed, for ill: Pausanias (7.17.13–14) tells how Oibotas of Dyme cursed the Akhaians for not honouring him adequately for his Olympic victory, so that no Akhaian was victorious again at Olympia until an image of Oibotas was dedicated there (see further below, p. 292 and Text 48).

It is likely that in the eighth century BC the Olympic games were rather less elaborately regulated than they later became, and that the prestige of victory was less: one tradition held that the first victor, Koroibos, was not only a local man from Elis but a cook. But the increased number and quality of dedications in the sanctuary at Olympia in the eighth century BC seem to require the development of the Olympic games. Both dedications and games alike require that there were wealthy individuals keen to compete with each other outside their own local community, men who wanted to belong to, and to be distinguished in, a wider Greek world. The Christian chronicle tradition, which registers 776 BC as the start of Greek history (above, p. xvii), no doubt makes too dramatic a divide between prehistory and history, but that the growth of the Olympics marks a significant development there can be no doubt.

Worship and self-definition

To return to the questions posed earlier, it would seem that there is so much variety between sanctuaries because different sanctuaries were doing different things, performing different functions within the local community or within a wider Greek world. But the greater investment in the divine is a widespread phenomenon because those different things have something in common, and that is the greater interest in the definition and advertisement of different roles. Whether it is a local élite using the publicity advantage of a much-frequented road to show themselves off, as at Isthmia, a Peloponnesian élite concerned to achieve and display status in each other's eyes, as at Olympia, or Corinthian élite women using the geographical position of the sanctuary of Hera at Perakhora, made newly significant with the development of more regular shipping, to register their own place within the community, the increased number and variety of dedications at all these sanctuaries reflect an increased concern with developing and marking different statuses and differences of status.

It has long been observed that in some communities there was a broad correlation between the decline of grave goods, particularly of the practice of depositing arms in graves, and the rise in dedications. In discussing the burial evidence from Athens (pp. 79–82) I suggested that we might be seeing communal pressure on the élite to conform in the ways in which they commemorated an experience shared by all. Such pressure may also explain the failure of ceramic art to take up the possibilities of individualised scenes which metalworkers were exploiting, and the end of the practice of depositing rich goods in graves at all. We lack well-dated sanctuary evidence from Athens by which we can distinguish exactly when in the eighth century BC the numbers of dedications rise (though the Hymettos sanctuary shows that Attica was no exception to the rule), but at Corinth the removal of graves from the settlement area, another form of control of élite display in death, takes place about 750 BC, and shortly afterwards changes in dedicatory patterns can be detected at Isthmia. The suggestion that the focus of élite display shifted from the cemetery to the sanctuary is attractive, but we might see a carrot as well as a stick operating: sanctuaries gave scope for marking personal status during one's own life, rather than just family status at the time of a convenient death; they also gave scope for depositing wealth in a way which would continue to be visible for some time, not visible largely at the moment of burial alone. More important still, to make a display in burial was to make a display to a local community; to make a display in some sanctuaries, if not all, was to make a display to a wider Greek world.

To focus on dedications is to focus on individuals, but cult activity was not an individual but a group activity. It was not individuals but groups that consumed the meat from sacrifices, not individuals but groups that enjoyed the facilities for ritual dining which soon developed at Isthmia and Perakhora, and it is likely to have been not individuals but groups who were responsible

94

Athene went to the people and city of the Phaiakians. They used to live in the broad lands of Hypereie, near the Cyclopes, but these were overbearing men who harmed them and were stronger in might. Godlike Nausithoos uprooted the Phaiakians, led them away from there, and settled them on Skherie, far off the routes of traders. He had a wall constructed around the city, and houses built, and he made temples of the gods and divided up the farmland.

Text 11: Odyssey 6.2–10. *Nausithoos transplants the Phaiakians and establishes a new city.*

for housing the god in a temple. The sanctuary at Perakhora did not develop because of what one woman or man did, but because the community felt the need to express certain aspects of its identity by instituting cult activity at a new significant location. It is as part of his foundation of a new base on Skherie for the community of Phaiakians that Nausithoos is described as constructing temples for the gods (*Odyssey* 6.10; see Text 11).

Because the community both occasioned the investment in sanctuaries and is reflected in it, religious developments have a political importance. If people act in concert for cult purposes what does that imply about the way the rest of their lives are ordered? If members of the élite are constrained in their funerary display, by whom are they constrained? If they use sanctuaries as places of self-advertisement, what do they aim to achieve, in whose eyes and by whose support, through that advertisement? If eighth-century-BC sanctuaries reflect differentiation of roles, that differentiation has to occur within a context which must be the context of a community. And if the sanctuary is the place where those roles are reflected, it must be in the community that those differentiated roles are functional.

Communal involvement in cult activity at a sanctuary acquires a new dimension and a new significance when that cult activity takes place at a distance. For those who share a settlement to worship the gods together within the settlement reflects their corporate tie but need imply little more. For people to invest in a sanctuary distant from their own settlement demands that they recognise that sanctuary as in some sense belonging to them. Such an act of appropriation may occur in a variety of circumstances: people may feel that a sanctuary belongs to them because it belongs to all – and I have suggested above that there is some reason to believe that the Isthmia sanctuary may have been somewhat like that during the Dark Age. But the greater the investment made in a sanctuary the less likely it is that that investment is made on so casual a basis.

Part of the importance of eighth-century-BC developments is that some sanctuaries distant from settlements acquired temples which cannot have been casually constructed by those who happened to pass by adding a mud brick. The building of the temple at Perakhora, or the building of the Heraion on Samos, have to mark an appropriation, even if not an exclusive appropriation, of a sanctuary by a community sufficiently close-knit to be able to finance, regulate, and reckon to maintain communal projects, and by that appropriation they claim to be a community with a territory which includes the sanctuary. The Samian Heraion displays a claim by those resident in the settlement at modern Pythagorio to the whole coastal plain extending west to, and just beyond, the Heraion (Figure 25); at Perakhora it is a claim to a territory which includes the land north of modern Loutraki (above, Figure 23).

It is not always easy to judge when the investment at a particular sanctuary has become so great as to signify some kind of appropriation of a sanctuary by a community, but the building of a temple should perhaps be considered unlikely to occur without appropriation. If temples were introduced to house cult statues, we need to ask whether it was such religious developments that stimulated the crystallising of a political community, and whether the availability of larger, communal, investment in cult made possible a religious development which had probably, on the Cretan evidence, long been conceivable. That the increased investment does not always take the form of temple building discourages the view that the initiative was primarily religious.

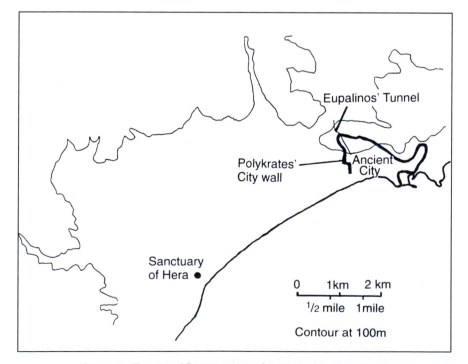

Figure 25 The city of Samos and the Samian Heraion sanctuary.

Tomb cult

There is one other form of religious activity which shows an enormous increase in the eighth century BC: tomb cult. Old graves, usually Mycenaean 'beehive' (tholos) or chamber tombs, became places where ritual deposits were made. The earliest, rather uncertain signs of cult at tombs come from a tiny handful of scattered sites of the tenth and ninth centuries BC, but from the eighth century, and largely from 750–700 BC, some forty instances are known. The tombs involved are various, and their distribution through mainland Greece uneven (no instances in Crete, the north-west Peloponnese, or Thessaly). Some of the deposits are short-lived and it is not clear whether the inhabitant of the grave in question was thought of as special at all; others go on for centuries, and the particular assemblage of objects dedicated suggests that the occupant was characterised in a particular way and thought to possess particular powers. There were certainly cults of heroes at places other than tombs (as of Helen and Menelaos at the Bronze Age palace site of the Menelaion near Sparta), and from the classical period on we know that some occupants of old tombs were thought of as 'heroes', but there is a lively debate as to whether in the geometric period heroes were associated with old tombs at all. If the figures cultivated were indeed thought of as heroes, that might lend some support to the view that cult at tombs was stimulated by the Homeric epics, but the uncertainty about mainland knowledge of the epic tradition in the eighth century, and the absence of tomb or hero cult from Ionia, where the epic tradition was certainly alive, make the hypothesis of epic influence rather unlikely.

Cult at tombs is cult that makes contact with a power from the past and contact with a particular place. Establishing a link with the past is one possible strategy of legitimation. It is the strategy implicit in every appeal to tradition (see above pp. 4–8), and it is a strategy which we will see being employed on a large scale by the Spartans (pp. 273–4). The complex ethnic situation in the Argolid, where there were a number of independent communities in competition continuously from the eighth century BC, when Argos conquered Asine, to the fifth century BC, when Argos finally took Mykenai, makes it possible that claiming links with the past was strategically important there. The same may be true of Messenia, where the threat of Spartan conquest may have anticipated the actual conquest. On what we know currently, that seems less likely to have been important in Attica, where there is little sign of ethnic differences or struggles between groups advertising different myths of descent. In Attica the links with a particular place may be more significant: if the eighth century BC sees sanctuaries outside the main settlement increasingly incorporated as part of the life of all the community, it is credible that residents of a particular locality, or particular groups in a place, might want to express their own peculiar links with a visible past which they can regard as exclusively their own. In Attica it seems likely from the nature of the votives that some tomb cults became part of the regular cycle of cultic activity of the whole local community (as at Thorikos), while others were perhaps rather more exclusively worshipped by a particular small élite group (as at the Menidi tholos).

THE WORLD OUTSIDE

The increased number of settlements, the wider clientele manifest at such sanctuaries as Olympia, the presence of exotic votives at many sanctuaries – all of these suggest that Greeks were moving about more in the eighth century BC, and that they enjoyed much more diverse contacts. More than that, the changes in grave goods and the developments at sanctuaries suggest that individuals and groups within communities were competing in a way not manifest in the Dark Age, that social organisation and personal status were subject to question. In what follows I will explore the way in which internal vulnerability and external mobility were linked.

Greeks and Phoenicians in east and west

Before the end of the ninth century BC there are signs of Phoenician presence in Crete and the Aegean, and of Greek goods getting to the near east. The Phoenician colony at Kition in Cyprus, founded c.820 BC, was joined by further Phoenician settlement on that island during the eighth century BC. By the end of the eighth century, both Greeks and Phoenicians were moving themselves and goods about the whole Mediterranean east of Corsica and Sardinia, and the Phoenicians were present in the western Mediterranean too. It is in the eighth century BC that the great Phoenician expansion into the western Mediterranean becomes archaeologically visible (Figure 26) with

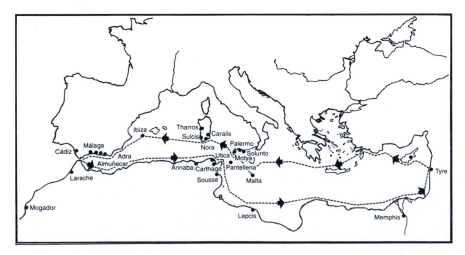

Figure 26 Phoenician settlements and shipping routes in the Mediterranean.

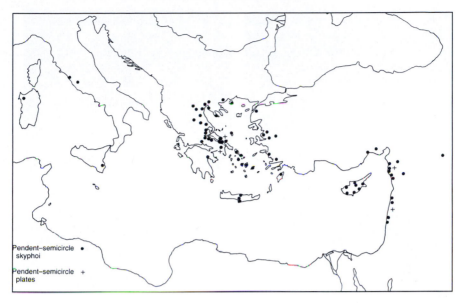

Figure 27 The distribution of Euboian pendent-semicircle skyphoi and plates.

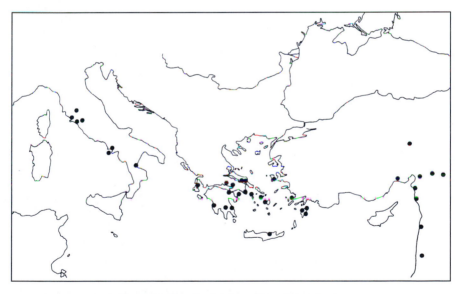

Figure 28 The distribution of Lyre Player Seals.

signs of settlements early in the century at Malaga, Almuñécar, and Adra in Spain, and in the middle or later part of the century at Utica in north Africa, Motya in Sicily, at Sulcis and Tharros on Sardinia, and on Malta. An Attic middle geometric II krater found at Huelva was surely carried there by Phoenicians, but it is in the eighth century BC too that Greek settlement in

99

Figure 29 Exceptionally large Lyre-Player Seal from Francavilla Marittima (a and b) and more typical examples from Pithekoussai (c and d).

Italy and Sicily both begins and becomes established on a large scale, first with the settlement at Pithekoussai, on the island of Ischia off the bay of Naples, shortly before 750 BC, and then with a string of settlements in eastern Sicily and rather more scattered settlements around the foot of Italy and as far north as Campania.

Whoever took the earliest Greek pottery to the Levant, there is not much doubt that Greeks became familiar visitors in at least some coastal settlements in the eastern Mediterranean during the eighth century BC. One of the nicest demonstrations of this derives from the distribution of one particular kind of near-eastern artefact, the so-called 'Lyre Player Seals', objects almost certainly originating in North Syria, but found widely dispersed through the Mediterranean in the years *c.*740–720 BC (Figure 29, compare Figures 26 and 28). These seals have been found in North Syria itself and at some sites on the Levantine coast, but otherwise they are restricted to areas where Greeks were present or with which (Etruria) they are known to have been in contact in the third quarter of the eighth century BC. They are completely lacking from Phoenician settlements and contact areas in the western Mediterranean (Figure 26), but found in just the same areas and on just the same sites as Euboian pendent-semicircle skyphoi and plates (Figures 12 and 27). The most economical explanation would seem to be that Lyre Player Seals caught the eye of Greeks who were in contact with North Syria and were moved by Greek hands.

The alphabet

The single most important borrowing by Greeks from their eastern neighbours was the alphabet. Objects with Phoenician writing on them were brought to Greece at least as early as the ninth century BC, but adapting and adopting the Phoenician alphabet seems to demand close mixing of Greeks and Phoenicians in an eastern Mediterranean milieu, whether in the Levant itself or in Cyprus. As far as we can tell from extant remains, mainland Greece had lost all knowledge of writing with the demise of the Mycenaean palaces which had sustained a limited scribal literacy primarily for record-keeping purposes. Then around the middle of the eighth century writing in what is recognisably a Greek alphabet begins to occur scratched on pottery. The Greek alphabet, or rather alphabets, for there are marked local variations in letter forms among the earliest inscriptions, manifestly take over the forms of their letters from the Semitic scripts used by the Phoenicians, and their names from the names of the Phoenician letters. A Cretan official of the sixth century with scribal duties has the title 'poinikastas', the Greeks called their alphabet 'phoinikeia grammata' (which may mean 'red-dyed letters' or may mean 'Phoenician letters'), and Herodotos (5.58–61) deduced a Phoenician origin from that, although others explained the name by claiming that the alphabet had been invented by Phoenix, the tutor to Akhilleus, or by Phoinike daughter of Aktaion, or that the name came from the use of the leaves of the phoinix (palm-tree) as a writing material. These last explanations seem to be part of a conscious Greek attempt to distance themselves from the east.

Curiously, and importantly, the Greek alphabet functions differently from the Phoenician alphabet: whereas the Phoenician used letters as symbols for consonantal sounds, and not normally for vowels, Greek alphabets from the beginning indicated both consonants and vowels. This is true of all early Greek alphabets, despite their considerable differences (Figure 30) in number of letters used, letter forms, and which letters stand for what. It is unclear whether this innovation occurred because one simply could not write Greek without representing vowels – vowel changes are crucial in showing how the grammar works in Greek, but not in Phoenician – or because there was a single 'inventor' of the Greek alphabet, or at least a particular moment of 'invention'. The representation of vowel sounds makes the Greek alphabet

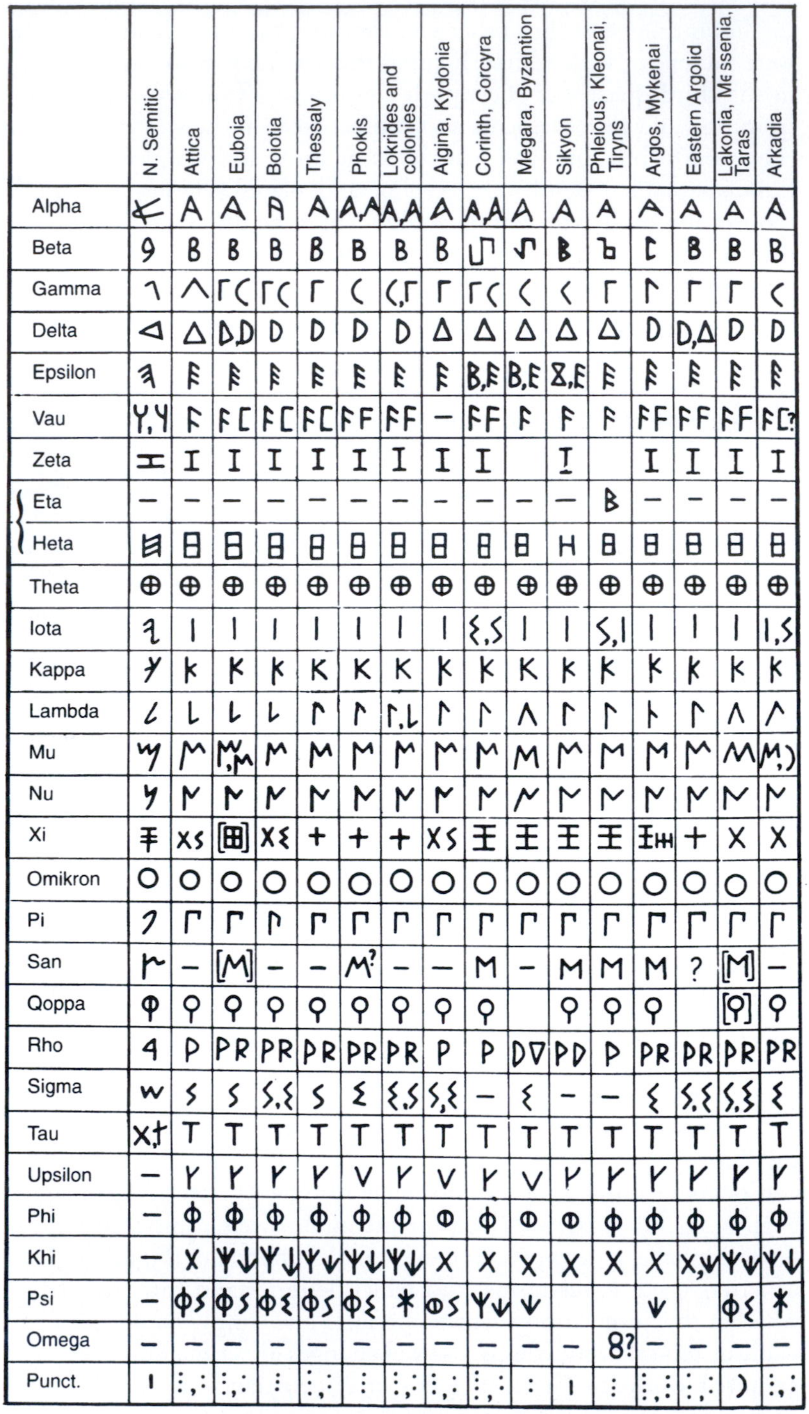

	N. Semitic	Attica	Euboia	Boiotia	Thessaly	Phokis	Lokrides and colonies	Aigina, Kydonia	Corinth, Corcyra	Megara, Byzantion	Sikyon	Phleious, Kleonai, Tiryns	Argos, Mykenai	Eastern Argolid	Lakonia, Messenia, Taras	Arkadia
Alpha	⊬	A	A	ꓤ	A	A	AΛΛ	A	A	AΛA	A	A	A	A	A	A
Beta	9	B	B	B	B	B	B	B	⊔	ᔍ	B	Ꮟ	C	B	B	B
Gamma	⌐	Λ	ᒥC	ᒥC	Γ	C	C,Γ	Γ	ᒥC	C	C	Γ	ᒥ	Γ	Γ	C
Delta	◁	Δ	ÐÐ	D	D	D	D	D	Δ	Δ	Δ	Δ	D	D,Δ	D	D
Epsilon	ᴣ	E	E	E	E	E	E	E	B,E	B,E	Ɛ,E	E	E	E	E	E
Vau	Y,Ч	F	FC	FC	FC	FF	FF	–	FF	F	F	F	FF	FF	FF	FC?
Zeta	ꓝ	I	I	I	I	I	I	I	I		I		I	I	I	I
Eta	–	–	–	–	–	–	–	–	–	–	–	ᗷ	–	–	–	–
Heta	ᖰ	⊟	⊟	⊟	⊟	⊟	⊟	⊟	⊟	⊟	H	⊟	⊟	⊟	⊟
Theta	⊕	⊕	⊕	⊕	⊕	⊕	⊕	⊕	⊕	⊕	⊕	⊕	⊕	⊕	⊕	⊕
Iota	ᘰ	I	I	I	I	I	I	I	ᔑ,ᔑ	I	I	ᔑ,I	I	I	I	I,ᔑ
Kappa	⋎	k	K	K	K	K	K	K	K	K	k	k	K	k	k	k
Lambda	⌿	L	L	L	Γ	Γ	Γ,L	Γ	Γ	Λ	Γ	Γ	⌐	Γ	Λ	Λ
Mu	⋎	M	M,M	M	M	M	M	M	M	M	M	M	M	M	MM	M,)
Nu	⋎	ᑒ	ᑒ	ᑒ	ᑒ	ᑒ	ᑒ	ᑒ	ᑒ	ᑒ	ᑒ	ᑒ	ᑒ	ᑒ	ᑒ	ᑒ
Xi	⊧	xs	⊞	xɛ	+	+	+	xs	王	王	王	王	⊧нн	+	X	X
Omikron	O	O	O	O	O	O	O	O	O	O	O	O	O	O	O	O
Pi	ᒧ	Γ	Γ	Γ	Γ	Γ	Γ	Γ	Γ	Γ	Γ	Γ	Γ	Γ	Γ	Γ
San	ᖆ	–	[M]	–	–	M?	–	–	M	–	M	M	M	?	[M]	–
Qoppa	Φ	φ	φ	φ	φ	φ	φ	φ	φ		φ	φ	φ		[φ]	φ
Rho	4	P	PR	PR	PR	PR	PR	P	P	DᐁPD	P	P	PR	PR	PR	PR
Sigma	w	ᔑ	ᔑ	ᔑ,ᔍ	ᔑ	Σ	ɛ,ᔑ	ᔑ,ᔑ	–	ɛ	–	–	ɛ	ᔑ,ɛ	ᔑ,ᔑ	ɛ
Tau	x,ꓕ	T	T	T	T	T	T	T	T	T	T	T	T	T	T	T
Upsilon	–	Y	Y	Y	Y	V	Y	V	Y	V	Y	Y	Y	Y	Y	Y
Phi	–	φ	φ	φ	φ	φ	φ	Φ	φ	Φ	Φ	φ	φ	φ	φ	φ
Khi	–	X	Y↓	Y↓	Yv	Y↓	Y↓	X	X	X	X	X	X	X,v	Y↓	Y↓
Psi	–	φs	φs	φɛ	φs	φɛ	✳	φs	Yv	v			v		φɛ	✳
Omega	–	–	–	–	–	–	–	–	–	–	–	8?	–	–	–	–
Punct.	⋮	⋮,⋮	⋮,⋮	⋮	⋮,⋮	⋮	⋮,⋮	⋮,⋮	⋮,⋮	⋮	⋮	⋮	⋮,⋮	⋮,⋮	)	⋮,⋮

Figure 30 The variety of early Greek alphabets.

102

Table of local (epichoric) Greek alphabets by region:

Elis	Akhaia and colonies	Aitolia, Epeiros	Ithaka, Kephallenia	Euboic W. colonies	Syracuse and colonies	Megara Hyblaia, Selinous	Naxos, Amorgos	Paros, Thasos	Delos, Keos, Syros	Crete	Thera, Cyrene	Melos, Sikinos, Anaphe	Ionic Dodekapolis and colonies	Rhodes, Gela, Akragas	Knidos	Aiolis

a rather more flexible and user-friendly tool than the Semitic one, for it removes much possible ambiguity, and enables the consonantal sounds to be confidently voiced even by a reader not yet able fully to comprehend what is being said. But there is still by no means an identity of symbol and sound in the Greek alphabet: for example, most early scripts use the same sign for both long and short 'e', and the same sign for long and short 'o'. This limitation is important for the question of what the alphabet was invented for.

Writing enables communication between individuals separated by space or time. It has obvious advantages for record-keeping and for marking the claims of an absent owner, no less advantage in communications with powers unseen, whether they be Olympian gods or the powers invoked in curse tablets. The earliest extant writing includes no record-keeping as such: there are several names and ownership inscriptions (what has been thought to be the earliest known Greek writing of all, on a jug found in the cemetery at Osteria dell' Osa in Latium in Italy and dating to the middle of the first half of the eighth century, may, if Greek at all, record an owner's name), several claims to responsibility for making or writing something, and, from 700 BC or shortly afterwards, both dedications and curses. Striking among early inscriptions are the numbers of abecedarian and of 'X wrote this' inscriptions scratched on pots dedicated to gods; these suggest that writing was seen as powerful in itself. A high proportion of early graffiti are metrical and essentially frivolous: an Athenian late geometric jug declares itself in hexameter verse to be a prize '[for the one] who of the dancers dances most friskily' (*CEG* 432; and compare below, pp. 108–10 on 'Nestor's cup'). From the island of Thera comes a set of early inscriptions, some of them verse, in which named men record admiration for, and sexual activity with, other men. The frequency of metrical inscriptions among longer inscriptions has led to the suggestion that the Greek alphabet was invented, and takes the form it does, in order to write down verse, and perhaps particularly epic verse. But the failure of early scripts to symbolise vowel length, when it is upon syllable length that Greek metre depends, must surely weigh against this attractively romantic claim. It is clear that writing rapidly came to be used for different purposes in different Greek cities and it looks as if, whatever the 'inventor' of the Greek alphabet had in mind, contemporaries saw a wide variety of opportunities opened up by this new system of communication.

If we cannot say what writing was invented *for*, nor is it easy to say what effect it had. It was once fashionable to see literacy as the mother of rationality, and to claim that writing enabled new ways of organising men, and thus the birth of the state, and new ways of thinking, and thus the birth of philosophy. Writing may both influence and make more manifest the ordering and classification of human activities and of objects associated with them, but it is well attested that 'illiterate' cultures also order and classify, without needing literacy in order to do so. The wide variety of uses of literacy in different societies strongly suggests that the implications of literacy are crucially affected by the existing habits and beliefs in the society which becomes literate. Writing remained for centuries marginal to the organisation of Greek cities and the lives of individual Greeks, and it was oral communication that was of the essence in both public and private life; much inscribed material served a symbolic function rather than being there to be read. The use of writing transforms *our* knowledge of the Greeks, but we should be cautious about believing that it transformed the Greeks themselves. To be illiterate in modern western societies is to be politically disempowered, but throughout the archaic period in Greece the contexts in which literacy was functionally required of a political actor were extremely few, though in some circles social pressure might be a different matter.

Al Mina

It seems most likely that the Greeks acquired their alphabet through living side by side with the Phoenicians, but the question of how far Greeks ever established a *settlement* in the eastern Mediterranean is a fraught one. Debate centres on the nature and importance of the site of Al Mina, at the mouth of the river Orontes, excavated in the 1930s (see also above, p. 6). Was this site simply a port of trade, a convenient dropping-off point for Greek goods brought back from the Aegean by Phoenicians, or was it a Greek settlement and the base through which Greeks acquired near-eastern goods? It was not the only site in the Levant to receive Greek pottery: eighth-century BC Greek pottery is known from a number of coastal sites, including Tyre (which even has tenth-century BC Greek sherds), and from major inland sites too, and there is little reason to believe that Greeks were resident in any of these towns. The site on this coast to which a Greek name was given was not Al Mina but Ras-el-Bassit, a little further to the south, which was called Poseideion. But the quantities of Greek pottery at Al Mina in the eighth century BC significantly exceed the quantities recovered from other near-eastern sites, both in absolute terms and in terms of sherds per cubic metre excavated. This does not require that we take Al Mina to be a Greek settlement: it seems that the quantity of non-Greek (both local and also Cypriot) pottery excavated at Al Mina was as great as the quantity of Greek pottery, and the similarity of assemblages encourages the view that Al Mina had a particularly close connection with the settlement at Tell Tainat 50 km away, also a ninth-century foundation, to which it may have served as a port. But, particularly in the light of the Greek-centred distribution of such North Syrian objects as Lyre Player Seals, it does suggest that Al Mina was not simply another port at which Phoenicians dropped off Greek goods.

If Greeks did establish a 'special relationship' with Al Mina, why? What was it that got exchanged? There is some evidence that Greek goods functioned in the near east as exotic goods, rather as Phoenician and other near-eastern goods functioned in Greece: Greek pottery is largely limited to major sites, and the shapes found are largely drinking vessels, objects displayed in company rather than objects of domestic use. But it is no more likely that

Greeks came bringing only pottery than that they went home taking only Lyre Player Seals. Such objects might be attractive gifts to lubricate exchange, but they can hardly have been the basic substance of that exchange. Nor can the undoubted periodic demands for agricultural goods of all sorts have motivated cultivating this particular link. The importance of such perishable goods as (fine) textiles must not be underestimated but, despite the lack of direct archaeological evidence, the most likely commodity involved in the exchange is metals.

Trade in metals

An extensive exchange network for the purposes of securing metal supplies can be traced in the near east far back into the Bronze Age. Assyrians seem to have established settlements in Anatolia in the Middle Bronze Age through which they acquired silver in exchange for tin. In the Late Bronze Age the scale of exchange in metals can be judged by the development of standard *c.*30 kg copper ingots, known as 'oxhide' ingots from their shape and found from Sardinia to Babylon, and from the fact that some 200 such ingots, 6 tonnes of copper, have been recovered from the Ulu Burun wreck off southern Turkey. Oxhide ingots are known from lead isotope analysis to have been exchanged between Cyprus and Sardinia during Late Cypriot III (1200–1050 BC), and some Cypriot bronzesmiths established themselves in Sardinia. Sardinia has a little copper and tin of its own but is extremely rich in lead and rich in iron, and it may have been the lure of iron which brought the Cypriot ingots to Sardinia.

Both the coming of the age of iron from the twelfth century BC on (above, pp. 41–2), and political disruption in the near east itself, which led to a hiatus in inter-regional trade in the eleventh century BC, modified the pattern of supply and demand for metals, but hardly lessened their importance, for although iron is much more ubiquitous than tin it is not found everywhere, and notably occurs only as a by-product of copper ores in the cradle of the Iron Age, Cyprus, an island outstandingly rich in copper resources (see above, p. 42). Iron and lead were being traded by the ship wrecked off Cape Giglio in Tuscany in the sixth century, and iron, copper, and tin were all in continual demand throughout both the Dark Age and the whole archaic period; silver was easily convertible even before the invention of coinage, and must also be included amongst ever-desirable metals. Metals were so important for practical purposes, and not least for weaponry, that any élite, or would-be élite, group needed to secure their supply, exchanging for them whatever raw materials or finished products were in demand.

Greek settlement at Pithekoussai

It is unlikely to be a coincidence that the Phoenician settlements on Sardinia and in Spain were in the vicinity of rich metal resources, or that one of the earliest signs of Phoenician presence in Spain, the Attic middle geometric mixing bowl found at Huelva, was found at the native port for the Rio Tinto mines, the richest Spanish mines of all. Metal ores must also have been responsible for drawing the Greeks to Pithekoussai to settle, and to Etruria to trade.

The island of Ischia to the north of the bay of Naples, although far from barren, has little of its own to offer to any settlers, and yet the evidence from the cemetery at Pithekoussai has been thought to indicate that the population of the settlement had reached between 5,000 and 10,000 within a generation of the first Greek presence there. Simply bringing that number of people to Pithekoussai will have involved a very large number of ship journeys, and to sustain that population, which must have been well in excess of what agricultural activity on the island itself could support, will have further demanded constant movement of goods back and forth to the Greek world. The evidence for ironworking at Pithekoussai is so far limited, but sufficient to demonstrate that the inhabitants were exploiting the resources of the island of Elba just off the coast of Tuscany.

Whether Pithekoussai was also a base from which the rich Etruscan metal-fields were exploited is less certain. Greek pottery begins to appear in Etruria, at the Quattro Fontanili cemetery at Veii, probably around 775 BC; by 750 there is evidence for a Greek potter at work at Veii. By about 750 BC Greek pottery appears in or near Rome, and there were also native potters in Latium who had adopted the new technology of the potter's wheel specifically for making imitation Greek pottery. The Greek pottery assemblages in Etruria and Latium are different from those at Pithekoussai, and Etruscan metals seem to have been exchanged with a different group of Greeks from that established on Pithekoussai.

The primacy of Pithekoussai among Greek settlements in the west suggests that it was demand for metals, and particularly for iron, which brought Greeks to the western Mediterranean, very much at the same time that the Phoenicians were also further opening up the western Mediterranean in a similar quest. Pottery from Pithekoussai finds its way both to Carthage and to Phoenician settlements in Spain, pottery from Euboia to Carthage, but not to the Phoenician west. Greek and Phoenician quests seem to have overlapped or clashed surprisingly little: Sardinia, as well as Spain, lacks signs of early Greek presence, and there is no sign of Phoenician presence in eighth-century BC Etruria, although oriental goods are prominent there in the early seventh century BC, and from the second half of the seventh century onward large quantities of Etruscan bucchero pottery reached Carthage from Cerveteri. At Pithekoussai evidence for Levantine contacts is plentiful, and there are signs of possible Levantine settlers: a Greek amphora has three Semitic inscriptions, one of them related to its secondary use in a burial; and a locally made drinking vessel has two probably North Semitic letters. It is not clear whether this evidence points to Phoenicians or to North Syrians, and in general it looks as if, by whatever process, Greeks and Phoenicians pursued metal resources in essentially separate areas.

In the above discussion I have talked of 'Greeks' abroad in the eastern and western Mediterranean, but exactly who were these Greeks? The earliest pottery in the Levant is made up of pottery from Euboia/the Cyclades and pottery from Attica in 2:1 proportions. Attic pottery then disappears, but by the end of the eighth century BC both east Greek pottery and protocorinthian pottery are appearing in significant quantities alongside the Euboian/Cycladic pottery, which itself disappears after c.700 BC. The place of origin of the pottery is not necessarily the place of origin of those who carried the pottery: Attic late geometric pottery very rarely finds its way outside Attica at all, whereas middle geometric was quite widely distributed, and its lack in the east may simply reflect this parochial distribution. That Euboians had a role in Al Mina is suggested by the presence in the west also of their pottery, and plausibly their potters, along with literary traditions of their involvement; but there is little reason to believe that only Euboians were involved. East Greek pottery is found in the west as well as the east, and by the end of the century there is evidence for Corinthian potters in the west too, as well as plenty of Corinthian pots. In the current state of our knowledge, in which Lefkandi is the best known of all Dark Age sites (above, pp. 55–60), there seems a strong case for Euboians being the pioneers in both east and west, but it is clear that other Greeks quickly joined in these overseas adventures.

The only ancient sources to mention Greek occupation of Pithekoussai associate it with Euboians: Strabo (5.4.9), writing at the end of the first century BC, says that it was once inhabited by Eretrians and Khalkidians who later left the island because of internal dissent and earthquakes; Strabo's contemporary, Livy (8.22.5–6), says that the Greek settlers at Cumae came from Khalkis in Euboia via Pithekoussai and Aenaria, another nearby island. These two accounts probably derive from fourth-century BC writings, themselves drawing on Greek oral tradition, but like all traditions that tradition is likely to have told rather less than the full story. As we have already seen, the cemetery evidence suggests both that the population of Pithekoussai in the later eighth century BC was remarkably large, and also that there may have been at least some Levantine presence. Eighth-century BC Khalkis is ill-known from archaeology, but unless the archaeological evidence at Eretria is highly misleading it is exceedingly improbable that Khalkis and Eretria could have had 5,000–10,000 inhabitants willing and able to seek their fortunes abroad.

One of the most famous finds from late eighth-century Pithekoussai, the so-called 'Cup of Nestor', may stand as a symbol of the mixed society of the island and of its consequences (Figure 31). A Rhodian late geometric kotyle, deposited in the rich cremation grave of a 10-year-old boy along with early protocorinthian globular aryballoi, and other globular aryballoi which appear to have been made at Ialysos on Rhodes but by Phoenicians, bears an inscription, at least partly in verse, scratched in Euboian script by a rather regular and accomplished hand. The graffito has the cup identify itself with the cup of Nestor and wish the joys of Aphrodite on the person who drinks from it. This is a sophisticated piece, which uses parody of the formula for curses to wish what would ordinarily be regarded as a blessing, and makes reference to the epic tradition. The cup of Nestor almost certainly refers to the tradition on which *Iliad* 11.632–7 draws in its set-piece description of a gold-studded cup belonging to the old Nestor which only he can lift when full. It is far from clear (see below, pp. 131–2) how widely the Ionian epic tradition, from which the *Iliad* was created, had spread in the eighth century BC, and it is tempting to see in this cup an image of the unique society of Pithekoussai: East Greeks, bringing their own pots, join in a settlement with Euboians, and familiarise their fellow settlers with their own epic traditions to such an extent that a Euboian can pick up a Rhodian cup at a party (see further below, p. 158) and write on it a witty verse. The people who settled, briefly or permanently, at Pithekoussai formed a cosmopolitan society

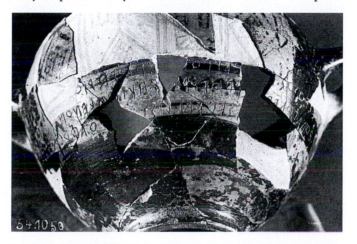

Figure 31a Inscribed Rhodian cup (kotyle) from Pithekoussai cremation.

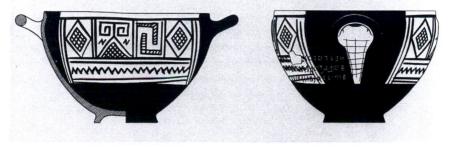

Figure 31b Rhodian cup deposited in a cremation at Pithekoussai around 720 BC, and inscribed 'I am the cup of Nestor, good to drink from. Whoever drinks from this cup, may desire of fair-crowned Aphrodite seize him'.

where fortunes were made and diverse cultural traditions were enjoyed. It is not hard to see why many who heard of this place might want to share its wealth and excitement.

It is unlikely to be chance, or increasing technical skill on the part of artists, that produces a large number of pictures of ships on eighth-century pottery, particularly from Athens but also at Pithekoussai itself. The references in the Homeric poems to ships (note especially *Odyssey* 9.322–3 of a merchant vessel) betray the existence of a large and precise epic vocabulary to describe sea-going vessels, and this too is good evidence for widespread familiarity with shipping on a considerable scale. For Hesiod (below, p. 138) going off to make a profit by sea-trade is an option which is generally available. Both broad merchant galleys, with from twenty to fifty oars, and pure sailing vessels seem to have been available, although the latter are rarely clearly pictured by artists until the sixth century. These vessels were rarely very small (by the fifth century vessels of 80 tons seem to have been the minimum), and some reached several hundred tons' capacity.

A settlement like Pithekoussai could be founded only if those who settled there could be confident that they could keep in more or less continuous contact with the sources for the goods they exchanged. For although the volcanic soil of Ischia is more fertile, especially for vines, than the soil of much of mainland Greece, neither the numbers who came, nor the subsequent decline of the settlement, can be accounted for by the pull of the land. Those who came and settled at Pithekoussai must have been drawn primarily by the possibilities which the site offered for improving their material lot by trade. The foundation, spectacular growth, and particular finds from Pithekoussai require constant activity at its port, involving the regular movement of a very large tonnage of goods by a large number of sailors – in some cases up to fifty on a single merchant galley.

It cannot be stressed too strongly that the evidence from eighth-century Pithekoussai requires an economic organization quite different from that required to explain the movement of goods in the tenth or ninth centuries. Occasional opportunistic travels by small ships carrying attractive prestige goods will account for the archaeological evidence prior to the middle of the eighth century. But the large settlement at Pithekoussai can only have been made once staple goods were being reliably and regularly moved in quantity around the central Mediterranean, and once a significant number of producers of both agricultural and craft products had begun to ear-mark some of their production for sale to markets overseas. Pithekoussai not only shows the expanding of horizons, it shows that the horizon had already expanded.

Greek settlements abroad

For two decades and more Pithekoussai was a unique Greek settlement in the west, but in the last third of the eighth century BC Greeks settled at numerous sites in Sicily and South Italy. Already in antiquity these settlements seem to have been regarded as different in kind from the settlement at Pithekoussai, and modern scholars have included them, but normally not Pithekoussai (or Al Mina), in what they call 'Greek colonization'. In using the term 'colonization' scholars have aligned what the Greeks were doing with the settlements made by European nations around the globe. Those settlements were not independent but controlled and exploited by the nations that founded them, who provided governance and took the profits of their enterprise. These modern colonies were ways of making contact with a foreign world which had resources of various sorts which the colonising powers were keen to access and control. Although there was much room for individual enterprise, there was never any question but that the activities were done on behalf of those who remained in the colonising country. But were the settlements founded by Greeks around the Mediterranean and the Black Sea like that?

An understanding of Greek settlement abroad in the late eighth century BC, for which the Greek term was *apoikia*, meaning a 'home away from home', requires that it be seen in the context of what had been happening during the Dark Age and what was happening on the Greek mainland too in the eighth century BC. Many new settlements were established in mainland Greece and the Aegean islands during these centuries, and continued to be established in subsequent centuries. As conditions changed so did the best places to live. Settlements abroad were part of this more general settlement mobility, and Greeks would go on establishing settlements abroad throughout their history. But the common quality of being established abroad does not mean that all these settlements were established in the same way or for the same reason. We will have occasion to revisit Greek settlements abroad at a number of points in this book, and precisely because those settlements play different roles at different points in history. But we will also treat those settlements abroad as just more Greek settlements, as integral to the history of Greece as long-established settlements in the southern Greek mainland.

Earlier in this chapter I discussed the evidence for new settlements in Greece itself during the eighth century BC, pointing out that it was unlikely that population growth was the only factor which caused people to move out to new places. The expansion of settlement in Greece has to be seen in the light of the social changes which changing burial practices and developments in the sanctuaries of the gods also suggest. Those changes and developments certainly seem more dramatic in the eighth than in earlier centuries, but many can be seen to grow out of trends already visible in at least some parts of the Greek world in earlier years. Settlement abroad is another such development (Figure 32).

Table 5 gives a very inadequate and incomplete account of the growth of the Greek world, but it does something to indicate the long history of settlement abroad. It is heavily biased towards settlements about which there is some literary tradition (it is largely ordered by literary dates), it neglects many sites which are known, often very imperfectly, from archaeological evidence alone, and it makes a tendentious distinction between settlement in Greece (not recorded) and settlement 'abroad'. Much of the archaeological

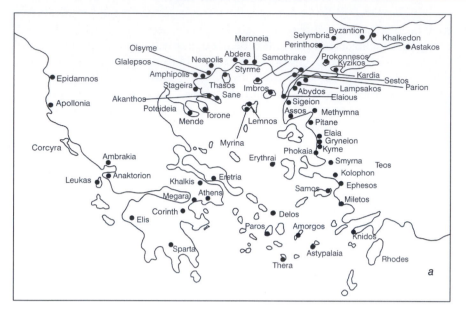

Greece and Asia Minor.

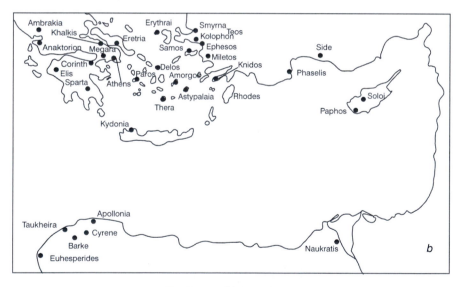

The Eastern Mediterranean.

Figure 32 Greek settlements abroad (compare Table 5).

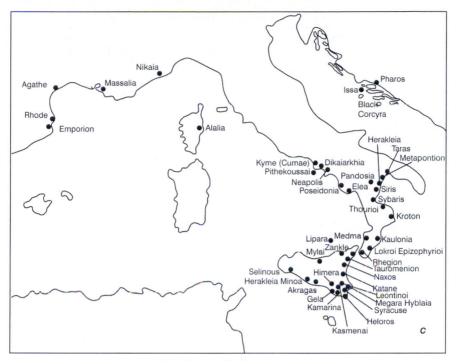

The Western Mediterranean.

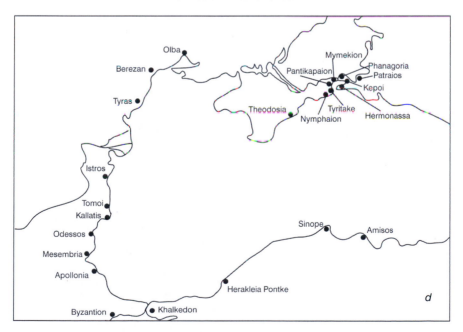

The Black Sea.

Table 5 Greek settlements abroad.

Settlement	Mother-city/cities	Literary date(s) for foundation	Earliest archaeological material	Earlier indigenous occupation?
Sestos	Lesbos	pre-Trojan War		
Paphos	?	c.Trojan War		
Elaia	Athens	c.Trojan War		
Klazomenai	Ionians	c.Trojan War		
Kolophon	Ionians	c.Trojan War		
Kyme	Aiolians	c.Trojan War		
Pitane	Aiolians		LBA, then PG	
Torone	Khalkis		late C12	Yes
Erythrai	Athens	same generation at Ephesos		
Ephesos	Athens	1087 (Eusebios)		
	Athens	1087 (Eusebios)		
Miletos				
Samos	Ionians	1087 (Eusebios)		
Thera	Sparta	c.1000?		
Smyrna	Aiolians		C11/10	
Mende	Eretria		C11? (LH, Sub-myc, PG)	
Phokaia	Phokaia and Athens		C9	
Astypalaia	Megara		C9	
Rhode	Rhodes	C9/8	late seventh century	
Soloi (Cyprus)	Athens		C9/8	
Metapontion	Akhaia	775/4 (Eusebios)	last quarter of C8	Yes
Pandosia	Akhaians/Elis	775/4 (Eusebios)		
Cyrene	Thera	762/1 and 632/1 (Eusebios)	late seventh century	
Sinope	Miletos	pre-757 (Skymnos) 631/0 (Eusebios)	last third of C7	
Trapezous	Sinope	757/6 (Eusebios)		
Kyzikos	Miletos	756/5 and 676/5 (Eusebios)		
Pithekoussai	Eretria/Khalkis	before Cumae (Livy)	pre-750	Sort of
Naxos	Khalkis	shortly before 733 (Thuc.) 737 (Eusebios)	3rd quarter of C8 (LGI)	Yes
Syracuse	Corinth (Tenea)	759 Marm.Par.; 736/5 Eusebios; shortly before 732 (Thuc.)	3rd quarter of C8 (LGI)	Yes
Corcyra	Corinth (earlier Eretrian colony, Plutarch)	same date as Syracuse (Strabo); 707/6 (Eusebios)	second half of C8	Yes
Katane	Khalkis	737/6 (Eusebios) c.728 (Thuc.)	second half of C8	Yes

Settlement	Mother-city/cities	Literary date(s) for foundation	Earliest archaeological material	Earlier indigenous occupation?
Leontinoi	Khalkis	shortly before 728 (Thuc.)	3rd quarter of C8 (LGI)	Yes
Kyme (Cumae)	Khalkis	1050 (Eusebios)	some pre-750 material in pre-Hellenic context first colonial pottery after 725	Yes
Zankle	Cumae/Khalkis	C8	3rd quarter of C8 (LGI)	No
Rhegion	Khalkis (and Zankle)	C8	720s	
Megara Hyblaia	Megara	728 (Th.) before Syracuse (Ephoros ap. Strabo)	3rd quarter of C8 (LGI)	No
Sybaris	Akhaia	720s (ps.-Skymnos) 710/9 (Eusebios)	720s	No
Mylai	Zankle	716 (Eusebios)	last quarter of C8	No
Astakos	Megara and Athens	711 (Eusebios)		
Parion	Paros/Miletos/Erythrai	709		
Kroton	Akhaia	709 (Eusebios)	C7	No
Taras	Sparta	706 (Eusebios)	c.700	Yes
Satyrion	Sparta	Same time as Taras, Strabo	c.700	Yes
Heloros	Syracuse		c.700	
Kaulonia	Kroton	–	c.700	No
Samothrake	Samos	600–500	c.700	Yes
Gela	Crete/Rhodes	692/1 (Eusebios) shortly before 688 (Thuc.)	c.700	Yes
Prokonnesos	Miletos		before c.690	
Phaselis	Rhodes	? 688		
Khalkedon	Megara	685 and 679 (Eusebios)		
Siris	Kolophon	c.680–652	c.700	
Thasos	Paros	1425 Eusebios mid-C7 (Arkhilokhos)	700 non-Gk material 650 for Cycladic material 700–650	Yes
Metauros	Zankle			
Kyzikos	Miletos	756/5 and 676/5 (Eusebios)		

Continued…

Table 5 continued

Settlement	Mother-city/cities	Literary date(s) for foundation	Earliest archaeological material	Earlier indigenous occupation?
Lokroi Epizephyrioi	Lokroi	679 (Eusebios) time of Messenian war (Aristotle)	c.700	Yes
Abydos	Miletos	670 (Str.)		
Akrai	Syracuse	shortly before 662 (Thuc.)	second quarter of C7	
Selymbria	Megara	before Byzantion		
Parthenope	Cumae/Rhodes	C12 (Strabo)	675–650	
Byzantion	Megara	659 (Eusebios)	650–625	
Istros/Histria	Miletos	657 (Eusebios)	perhaps second half of C8/early C7; certainly by 630	
Stageira	Andros or Khalkidians	656 (Eusebios)		
Sane	Andros	655		
Naukratis		c.655 (Strabo)	last quarter of C7	
Akanthos	Andros	655 (Eusebios)	?C6	
Abdera	Klazomenai, then Teos	654 (Eusebios)	2nd half of C7	No
Lampsakos	Miletos	654 (Eusebios)		
Selinous	Megara Hyblaia	651 (Diodoros Siculus) 650 (Eusebios) 628 (Thuc.)	mid-C7	Nearby
Maroneia	Khios	before 650		
Stryme	Thasos	c.650		
Leukas	Corinth	mid-C7		
Neapolis (Thrace)	Athens		mid-C7	
Himera	Zankle/Mylai	650/49 (Eusebios) 648 (Ptolemy & Diodoros)	c.625	
Olbia/ Borysthenes	Miletos	647	575–550 675–650 at nearby Berezan	
Kasmenai	Syracuse	shortly before c.642 (Thuc.)	c.600	
Cyrene	Thera	762/1 and 632/1 (Eusebios)	late seventh century	
Sinope	Miletos	pre-757 (Skymnos) 631/0 (Eusebios)	last third of C7	
Taukheira (Tocra)	Cyrene		c.630	
Lipara	Knidos	630 (Eusebios)	575–550	
Prusias	Miletos	627 (Eusebios)		

Settlement	Mother-city/cities	Literary date(s) for foundation	Earliest archaeological material	Earlier indigenous occupation?
Epidamnos	Corcyra	627 (Eusebios)		
Oisyme	Thasos		650–625	
Galepsos	Thasos		c.625	
Sigeion	Athens	620–10		
Hipponion	Lokroi Epizephyrioi		c.620	
Elaious	Athens	c.610		
Amorgos	Samos	c.609 (Souda)	C9	
Apollonia (Sozopolis)	Miletos	c.609 (Ps.-Skymnos)	late C7	
Assos	Methymna	?C7	C6	
Euboia	Leontinoi		C7	
Anaktorion	Corinth/Akarnanians	C7	late C7	
Ambrakia	Corinth	C7		
Hyria	Crete	?C7	C6	
Leros	Miletos		C7	
Amisos	Phokaia/Miletos		late C7	?Yes
Kardia	Miletos and Klazomenai	late C7		
Perinthos	Samos	602 (Eusebios)		
Kamarina	Syracuse	601 Eusebios shortly before c.597 (Th.)	late C7	No
Apollonia (Libya)	Thera		c.600	
Medma	Lokroi		c.600	
Poseidonia (Paestum)	Akhaia		c.600	No
Pantikapaion	Miletos		c.600	
Poteidaia	Corinth	625–585	c.600	
Side	Kyme	C7/6		
Massalia	Phokaia	598 (Eusebios)	c.600	
Agathe (Agde)	Phokaia	shortly after Massalia c.600	third quarter of C7	
Apollonia (Illyria)	Corinth and Corcyra		c.600	
Odessos	Miletos	585–539	c.560	
Akragas	Gela	shortly before c.580 (Th.)	early C6	Yes
Emporion	Massalia and Phokaia	early C6		
Tomoi	Miletos	early C6		
Euhesperides	Cyrene		610–575	
Black Corcyra	Knidos	C6	600–575	
Nymphaion	Miletos		580–570	
Thracian Khersonesos	Athens	561–556		
Barke	Cyrene	560–550		
Herakleia Pontika	Megara and Boiotians or Miletos	554 (Ps.-Skymnos) (Strabo)		

Continued…

Table 5 continued

Settlement	Mother-city/cities	Literary date(s) for foundation	Earliest archaeological material	Earlier indigenous occupation?
Hermonassa	Miletos and Mytilene		575–550	
Myrmekion	Miletos		575–550	
Tyritake	Miletos		575–550	
Kepoi	Miletos	mid-C6	575–550	
Tyras	Miletos	mid-C6		
Herakleia Minoa	Selinous	before 510	mid-C6	No
Theodosia	Miletos	550–500	580–570	
Patraios	Miletos	550–500	mid-C6	
Alalia (Corsica)	Phokaia/ Massalia	c.545	C6	
Dioskourias	Miletos		540	
Elea/Velia	Phokaia and Massalia	c.540	1st half of C6	
Phanagoria	Teos	c.545	c.540	
Puteoli (Dikaiarkhia)	Samos	531 (Eusebios)		
Kydonia	Samos (then Aigina)	c.520 (Hdt.)		
Gryneion	Myrina		by 500	
Kallatis	Herakleia Pontika	late C6	C4	
Lemnos	Athens	c.500	c.500	Yes
Imbros	Athens	c.500		
Mesembria	Megara/ Khalkedon/ Byzantion	493	c.500	
Neapolis	Cumae		c.470	
Brea	Athens	444/3		
Thourioi	Athens	443		
Amphipolis	Athens	437		
Herakleia on the Siris	Taras	433–2	late C5	
Tauric Khersonesos	Delos and Herakleia Pontika	421	525–500	
Issa	Syracuse	390		
Pharos	Paros	385		
Tauromenion	Hybla, Zankle, Khalkidians	358		
Nikaia	Massalia	C4		
Amastris	Miletos	C4		

information summarised here is subject to debate and new discoveries may radically change the picture in any particular case. Nevertheless, it gives an indication of the importance of the phenomenon of settlement abroad and of the massive variety of places chosen for settlement and of origins of those claiming a special role in making those settlements.

Individuals were highly mobile in the Greek world of the early Iron Age. In the *Iliad* and the *Odyssey* we meet numerous wandering individuals who have been forced from their homeland, most frequently because they had killed someone. Hesiod, in *Works and Days* (630–40) tells of his own father moving from Kyme in Asia Minor back to the Greek mainland and to Askra in Boiotia 'fleeing miserable poverty', a reminder that it is not always easy to distinguish being pushed from jumping, and also that men moved back from settlements abroad as well as out to them. Trade motivates a number of these wanderers, and may entice men under no obligation to leave their homeland: Dionysios of Halikarnassos, who wrote in Rome at the time of Augustus, tells the story (*Roman Antiquities* 3.46–7) of one Demaratos of Corinth who 'chose to engage in commerce', made a fortune trading Greek goods to Etruria and Etruscan goods to Greece, and ended up marrying and settling in Etruria, rather than in a Corinth where Kypselos had established himself as tyrant (below, p. 182–3). Demaratos, like most of these mobile individuals, moves between established settlements. For whole groups to move, and for them to move into areas not previously settled by Greeks, demanded peculiar conditions.

Dark Age Greece had low population densities, new agricultural land was readily available to those who had the labour available to make use of it, and communities increasingly needed to keep up their size in order to maintain status in a world where competition between individuals and groups was becoming regular. In these circumstances, the fact that people left their home community to settle abroad is not a measure of state power but a measure of the limits to the control rulers could exert. Making a new settlement abroad required not simply isolated, individual hopes or crises, but some common expectation of a better life elsewhere, some common threat to be escaped, or common goal to be acquired. The stories the Greeks themselves told about groups moving tended to focus on common threats: in the *Odyssey* (6.2–10; Text 11) Nausithoos moves the Phaiakians from Hypereie to Skherie because of the threat posed by the Cyclopes; later tradition thought of the Greek cities of Ionia as the product of changed conditions in mainland Greece upon the arrival of the Dorians (see above, p. 48). Even as an account of Dark Age movements this latter tradition leaves something to be desired: the settlements in the north Aegean can hardly have been the product of hostile Dorian threats. As a mirror of eighth-century settlement the threat model is even less satisfactory, for it cannot account for where it was that those who left their home communities chose to settle.

What distinguishes the settlement mobility of the later eighth century BC is that it involves not simply filling up the settlement map of the Aegean but striking out into a new world. The settlement of, for example, Thasos, Thracian Neapolis, and Perinthos in the seventh century BC, Lemnos in the sixth century, and Amphipolis in the fifth century shows that the north Aegean retained scope for further settlement. The north Aegean offered a distinctly more reliable climate (even in dry years cereal crops get enough water) and rich natural resources of both timber and metals, and these advantages must have been known, particularly to the Euboians who had links with the area established already in the Dark Age (above, p. 59). Although fashion no doubt played its part, and we should not expect total rationality, the decision to look to the west implies that even more was expected from the west. The settlers were people who jumped without being pushed, and their departure may have been tolerated by those who were left behind, not only because preventing it was impractical but because to do so would be to forgo the possibility of sharing the profits of the enterprise.

The settlement at Pithekoussai, and the evidence of Greek interests in Etruria, suggest that the attractions of the west were linked in with metals and the growth of a dense exchange network. As we have already seen in our discussion of the arrival of iron technologies in Cyprus and the Aegean, the spread of ironworking made obsolete old networks which were geared up to provide tin and copper and make bronze, and challenged the élite to corner the supplies of working iron. Any rich new ironworking area had to be investigated for fear that others might profit first from its exploitation. The opening up of the North Italian iron fields following the coming of the Iron Age to Etruria created a challenge which could not be refused, even if the consequences of pursuing this new source of minerals could not be foreseen.

Contact with Etruria did not mean simply access to desirable minerals, but also contact with a different people, differently organised and offering a model for emulation. A radical change in Etruscan settlement pattern had already taken place in the ninth century, as the dispersed villages of the Protovillanovan culture were replaced by clusters of villages forming rival proto-urban units (*BR* 55, 92). In the eighth century these proto-urban units, which were increasingly dominated by competing aristocrats, seem to have wielded considerable power, reflected in the way in which imported Greek goods are concentrated at the single site of Veii. Similar, but distinct, changes happened in neighbouring Latium, where the earlier settlement pattern had already been clustered, and where the later ninth and eighth centuries BC saw further centralisation; with reference to the discussion of Greek burial practices above it is worth noting that the separation of settlement and cemetery areas occurs in Latium *c.*800 BC, a hundred years before it occurs in Attica. The developments in southern Etruria and in Latium were almost certainly linked: it may well be the proximity and importance of Veii which encouraged the development of Rome as a centre, and through Veii that Rome became included in the network of inter-regional exchange, including exchange with Greeks.

There is no doubt that Greeks were a channel by which the Etruscan élite acquired the means by which to distinguish itself. Writing appears in Etruria around the end of the eighth century and in Latium shortly afterwards (*BR* 103–4): the alphabetic means for this are borrowed from the Greeks (according to the Roman historian Tacitus (*Annals* 11.14), taught by Demaratos of Corinth). Elite burials in Etruria, Latium, and at the southern Villanovan site of Pontecagnano in Campania are so like those at the Greek settlement at Cumae, opposite Ischia, and the series of exceptional burials at the West Gate at Eretria as to suggest that the princely burials in Italy drew their inspiration from those in Euboia (*BR* 89–92). But the Eretria burials (of *c.*700 BC) are no earlier in date than the Cumae grave or the earliest of those at Pontecagnano, and, although the Lefkandi burial more than two centuries earlier might point to a Euboian tradition, the independent development of such burials in Italy is as easy to comprehend as their appearance at Eretria. Did the centralised structures of Etruscan society stimulate social developments among Greeks?

The case of Cumae

Strabo (C243) says Cumae in Campania was the oldest of all Sicilian and Italian foundations, and, as we have seen, Livy (8.22.5–6) says it was founded from Pithekoussai and Aenaria. Archaeological evidence suggests that Greeks were present by *c.*730 BC, while Pithekoussai was still flourishing. For Cumae, as not for Pithekoussai, we have full-blown foundation legends of the sort which typically surround overseas settlements. Strabo tells that 'those who led the expedition were Hippokles of Kyme and Megasthenes of Khalkis, and they agreed amongst themselves that the colony should be named after the one community and considered a settlement of the other; that is why it is called Cumae but the Khalkidians seem to have founded it'. Other ancient sources have different explanations in order to cope with the link of the name to Kyme and the people to Khalkis, such as making the Khalkidians settle the place first and Aiolians from Kyme come later, and one source associates Eretrians as well as Khalkidians with the foundation. What all the stories share is the desire to make Cumae an 'official' foundation, set up by the deliberate act of a city or cities who send out a founder. The determination to give the settlement a pedigree comes out most clearly of all in the account of the Roman writer of the first century AD, Velleius Paterculus (Text 12).

The Athenians occupied Chalkis and Eretria in Euboea with colonies, the Spartans occupied Magnesia in Asia Minor. A little later the Chalkidians, who were sprung, as we said before, from Athens, under the leadership of Hippocles and Megasthenes, founded Cumae in Italy. Some say that the route of this fleet was directed by the flight of a dove which went in front, others hold that it was directed by the sounding of bronze at night – the sort of noise which often arises from the rites of Demeter. A long time later part of the citizen body of Cumae founded Naples.

Text 12: Velleius Paterculus 1.4.1 on the foundation of Cumae.

121

His account both treats the foundation of Cumae as like the foundation of a Roman colony, in which, typically, veteran soldiers were settled both to reward them with land and as a bastion of Roman civilization, and manages to suggest that the settlers were of noble descent and the site supernaturally selected.

As the variant versions of the foundation of Cumae suggest, neither the nobility of the settlers, nor the supernatural selection, have much to commend them as historical. Both were claims which it will have been advantageous for the settlers to make, disguises for a mixed and perhaps rather rough origin, and for opportunistic stealing of land from the native population. Both were claims, too, that cities back at home could latch on to, in order to encourage further departures for foreign lands and to establish some sort of claim on any future prosperity. Pithekoussai may have no such foundation legend simply because it did not flourish for long enough to acquire one, and we should beware of believing that the settlement at Cumae, or of any other early settlement abroad, was established in circumstances that were significantly different from those in which Pithekoussai was established: both are likely to have been opportunistic settlements made for the purpose of immediate gain by a mixed group of adventurous souls to whom the grass of Campania looked greener than that back home, wherever home might be considered to be.

Emphasising the limited extent to which early settlement abroad can be regarded as 'official', and stressing the mixed nature of the settlers, has important historical implications. Settlements abroad cease to be great political events for cities organising a great expedition: for there is no reason to believe that cities in Greece did do much organisation. Rather, we should see settlements abroad as a manifestation of an exceptional degree of restlessness and ambition among individual Greeks. Some settlers will have been pushed by poverty, unpopularity, crime, or scandal; some will have jumped to get land, a foothold in foreign mineral resources, or just a new life free of irksome relatives.

Whatever the individual motives, the scale of Greek settlement abroad in the later eighth century is startling. During the last third of the eighth century BC a new town was founded in south Italy or Sicily about every other year. And those who formed these communities certainly did not all come from Euboia: Corinthians, Megarians, Akhaians, and Spartans would all claim special connections with one or more of these towns, and even if such claims grew with the telling they are unlikely to have been based on nothing. Getting people of diverse origins to venture and settle abroad will indeed have demanded organisation and a high degree of cooperation, but that cooperation should be seen as informal, rather than formal, motivated by desire to secure a better life and inspired by the enthusiasm of a charismatic leader, rather than dictated by obedience to a political decision by a mainland Greek city. Those who went will rarely have wanted, or been able to afford, to cut off links with the community they left, and they, above all those who took

Figure 33 Argive late geometric II high-handled krater dating to c.725 BC.

the lead, will have looked back to that community both for practical help and for models of how to run city life. There was mutual economic benefit for both settlers and the communities from which they came in maintaining links, but those links were opportunistic.

One of the clearest demonstrations of the nature of the links between settlers and the communities from which they came comes once more from the burial record. Large numbers of burials have been excavated at the sites of the earliest Greek colonies in Sicily, above all at Syracuse, Megara Hyblaia, and Gela. Although certain burial practices are common across these communities, in each case we find a different pattern of burial practices, with very different frequencies of different methods of interment (e.g. the extent to which stone sarcophagi are used). Not only is there no single 'Sicilian' pattern, however, but the correlation between burial practices in the Sicilian settlement and burial practices in that settlement's supposed 'mother city' or 'mother cities' is at best loose. Even in this area, where conservatism can be assumed to be strong, the settlers established practices by which they asserted their place in the status hierarchy of the local community, not in relation to practices in any city in 'old Greece'.

Such a movement of people from all over southern Greece is incomprehensible unless seen against a background where mobility was easy, and even normal, and where large numbers of ships and people were continuously and familiarly moving around the Mediterranean. And in moving, people acquired more than just the longing to exploit the greener pastures which they observed and more than just the raw materials, agricultural products, captives, and gewgaws, by exchange of which their wandering life was sustained: they also acquired unprecedented wealth, new technologies, and new views of the world.

THE EIGHTH-CENTURY VIEW OF THE WORLD

Figurative art, unknown in the Greek world during the tenth century BC, reappears in the second half of the ninth, and from then on we possess at least glimpses of how some Greeks viewed the world they lived in. From the middle of the eighth century BC not just isolated figures but multiple figure scenes of various kinds are found on pottery made in a wide range of different places. In addition, bronze figurines of men, animals, and birds (mainly single figures but sometimes more complicated scenes) were being made in large quantities (cf. pp. 87–8 above) and figure scenes appear in low relief on gold bands, and in relief or engraved on some bronze fibulae (safety pins) and other accoutrements. From these figures and scenes we are able to form some idea of the eighth-century picture of the world.

Eighth-century figurative art from all over the Greek world, and in various media, has much in common, but it also displays striking variations. Most regional styles of pottery incorporate figures into the overall geometric schemes of decoration either as friezes (Figure 22) forming a complete decorative band, often at a point where the shape of the pot would prevent a continuous band of geometric pattern, or as panels side-by-side with panels consisting of geometric motifs (Figure 33). Friezes tend to be made up of the repetition of a single figure or group of figures, and panels may be filled with repeated figures or comprise a single figure or group of figures engaged in a less than perfectly symmetrical activity. In most cases the space between and around figures contains a scatter of geometric motifs.

Figurative imagery outside Athens

Pots from ceramic traditions other than the Athenian seem to use figure scenes to carry extremely general reference. Argive pots of a wide variety of shapes and uses bear panels with similar scenes of horses, often associated with men, fish, or birds, and with stylised shapes which seem to be used to put the horses and men into a context in which water is stressed and yokes for harnessing the horses may be indicated (Figure 33). Scenes of action are rare, although women who may be dancing and men who are certainly wrestling do occur. Boiotian geometric pottery similarly uses scenes of men and horses and of women dancers, Euboian has the horses, including a remarkable scene of opposed horses flanking a 'tree of life', but no human figures. Corinthian geometric pottery does not go in for large vessels, and the figures on it are virtually exclusively smaller birds, but before the end of the eighth century BC the protocorinthian style, which develops out of geometric pottery, experiments with figure scenes involving warriors, various animals, and stylised fish, and even occasionally allows the figures to dominate a small pot. On Crete, protogeometric B pottery, in the late ninth century BC, had been precocious in its use of the human figure (Figure 13), with female figures with upraised arms plausibly identified as goddesses and owing something at

124

Figure 34 Late geometric bronze figure of a seated man. The nature of the object which the figure holds to his mouth (flask? musical instrument? conch shell?) is uncertain.

least to Minoan iconography; Cretan late geometric pottery, by contrast, is as unadventurous in imagery as in other respects.

The world of these figure scenes on pots overlaps strongly with the world evoked by figurative bronzes and by engraved decoration on fibula (safety-pin) catch plates, bronze belts, and the like. Among the figurines, horses and birds are prominent along with deer, sheep, oxen, and birds (but not fish). On engraved bronzework, fish, horses, and birds are all found in various combinations. Figurines of men and women differ from the human figures on the pots we have been discussing by virtue of being normally single figures shown in some action, although what action is intended is not always clear. Some figurines have an articulation of form which is so fluent as to be positively sensuous, and evoke emotion, as well as action, with great economy of means (Figure 34).

The world of this imagery is a world dominated by gendered individuals and their encounters with the natural world. The images with which people surrounded themselves seem to be images from everyday reality, and that reality seems scarcely shaped at all by any rituals (except perhaps the women dancers). Of fantasy there is less sign – only a bronze of a man fighting a centaur and some centaurs on clay storage vessels from the Cyclades with relief decoration suggest that the fabulous had gripped the visual imagination

Figure 35 Attic late geometric I krater used as a grave marker and with a scene of funerary ritual.

(note also the earlier centaur from Lefkandi, above, p. 59). There is no interest in hierarchy, or in corporate activity, and the imagery does not seem to be sensitive to the particular shape or use of the object which carries it. The stylised figures carry no more than a message about presence or absence, and do nothing to indicate the quality of the object shown. But with the expressive plastic forms of some of the bronze figures we begin to glimpse a world where emotion plays a part, and where the quality of life is either important or subject to change.

The Athenian figurative tradition

The world of Athenian ceramic imagery is different. As we have mentioned (p. 77) one series of Attic geometric pots of large size which are the product of a small number of workshops, mostly from the middle of the century, carries images clearly related to the pot's use. These are pots associated with graves, often as grave markers: mixing bowls mark men's graves, belly-handled amphorae women's. They bear scenes of the laying out of the corpse: the corpse is shown on a bier with a stylised shroud above, and is

126

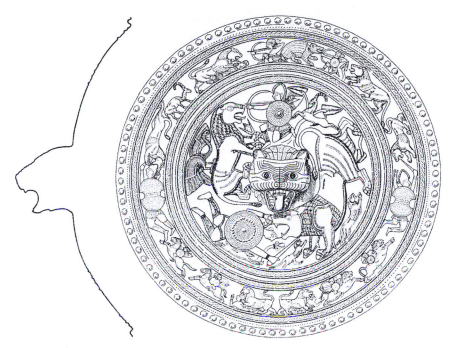

Figure 36 The so-called Hunt shield from the Idaian cave.

surrounded by male and female mourners, their hand or hands to their heads tearing their hair (Figure 35). Other Attic pots, of various shapes, seem also to refer to funerary ritual; in particular there are scenes of men and women seated, sometimes at what appear to be tombs, with what are conventionally known as rattles in their hands. Scenes that are identifiably funerary are virtually unknown outside Attic art, and there seems no such straightforward connection between iconography and non-funerary use on any other geometric pots.

Whether the further scenes found on these Attic funerary vases have any connection with the use of the pot is not clear. Associated scenes sometimes show processions of chariots (as Figure 35), sometimes scenes of fighting – including scenes involving both soldiers and ships. Are these to be taken as scenes from the life of the deceased? Some of the scenes certainly include apparently careful detail (such as the strings of fish and dead birds carried by some mourners on Figure 35), and very occasionally exceptional figures (for example, the presence of a woman in a military scene). The lack of a focus to the composition and comparison with the way imagery on pots made outside Attica works, however, suggests that we should think in terms of generic scenes, and not any specific story, whether of life or myth. The figures which have attracted most scholarly attention are the 'twin' warriors, two bodies emerging from behind one shield; they have been associated with the two Moliones, sons of Aktor, twins who appear fleetingly in epic literature (*Iliad*

127

11.709–10, 750–2; 23.637–42 (Text 9); Hesiod, *Catalogue* 17–18), but the context in which they are shown is not consistent and there is no sign of any attempt to allude to a particular story.

Whatever precise reading we give to these scenes, it is abundantly clear that the world evoked by Athenian ceramic imagery is different from that evoked on any other eighth-century-BC pottery. Rituals, communal actions, and cultural artefacts figure large. The different roles of men and women are distinguished and their relationship displayed and explored. Warfare is quite as prominent as struggles with beasts, although animal friezes and encounters of men with animals remain an important feature. Athenian imagery is social in a way no other imagery is. But does Athenian imagery also reveal a fantasy life? Our answer to this question will depend in part on whether we think that 'myths' are being evoked in some of the multi-figure scenes. But the presence of the occasional fabulous creature, such as a centaur, certainly encourages the belief that what was told in story may have inspired Athenian artists as well as what was seen in life.

If Athenian pottery shows different, wider, and more corporate interests than either pottery or bronzes do elsewhere, other Athenian artistic products promise an even more marked change in the view of the world. The gold bands with their 'orientalising' animal friezes have been mentioned above (Figure 21), but there are other ways too in which late eighth-century Athenian jewellery stands in a world of its own: diadems show sphinxes as well as centaurs, girls bearing waterpots as well as acrobats. Among Athenian late geometric bronze figurines there is one of a bull-headed man, certainly fantastic and perhaps a mythical Cretan minotaur slain by the Athenian hero Theseus. Appropriately enough, perhaps, the only other area of the Greek world whose products can in any way parallel this Athenian imagery is Crete.

Although Cretan pottery is conservative in the eighth century, Crete has produced bronzes that are distinctly avant-garde. Not only are there the cult figures mentioned above, but there is a whole series of bronze objects, in particular shields, with relief decoration, which stand apart from the geometric tradition both in style and content (Figure 36). Heavily influenced by near-eastern metalworking traditions, and incorporating elements of near-eastern iconography, these bronze reliefs introduce a whole medley of fantastic eastern winged creatures. The expanding range of this imagery, the desire to take on oriental imagery, and the signs that the ear as well as the eye is beginning to shape the visual imagination, herald the coming of a new vision of the world.

FROM COMMUNITIES TO *POLEIS*?

The changes described in this chapter were momentous. There can be no doubt at all that the intensity of interactions both within and between communities in 700 was of a quite different order from that in 800. The material available to those who lived in the late eighth century for negotiating their position both in the local community and in the wider world was in every way more varied. Pottery had acquired a figurative tradition which enabled allusion to be made both to the events of life and the incidents of story. Small and not quite so small-scale sculptures explored the three-dimensional and sensuous forms of the observed and imagined world and of real life and story-book interpersonal interactions. Awareness of other cultures might be signalled by form or decoration. The range of quantity and quality of goods whose deposition in cemetery or sanctuary stated a claim to status was much expanded, and the range of sites at which such depositions might be made was much increased. All of this spells a quite new sophistication of social relations.

But what sort of change in the nature of the community did these newly sophisticated social relations occasion? Scholars have often talked of 'the rise of the *polis*' as a phenomenon of this period. *Polis* was the Greek word for a town or city. Applied originally to the physical site, *polis* came to have a distinct political meaning with reference not simply to the town but to the town and surrounding countryside united as a single political entity, the so-called 'city-state'. The term *polis* has come to be invested with a technical sense which it did not possess in antiquity. The *polis* is seen as a peculiar synthesis of place, people, and political independence, a political unit embracing city and country as equal partners. The *polis* is distinguished from the *ethnos* (plural *ethne*), which is thought of as a grouping of people who identify together through a common myth of descent but do not focus on a single city community. Maps are even produced distinguishing parts of mainland Greece which have the *polis* from those which are organised by *ethnos*.

The range of political arrangements in the classical Greek world defies such straightforward divisions between *poleis* and *ethne*. Many political communities which were effectively independent chose nevertheless to collaborate in various ways (military, religious) with others whom they regarded as related to them by descent. They might do this within a political league or under the umbrella of their 'ethnic' links. More or less the full range of relationships between political units, from total independence to total subservience of one community to another, can be found in classical Greece. So too some political units took great pains to ensure that rural communities were incorporated into the political structure, while others effectively ignored the countryside and its inhabitants.

In the second century AD Pausanias (10.4.1) famously sneered at the city of Panopeus in Phokis, noting with amazement that one could call a place a *polis* when it had no gymnasium, theatre, agora, public water supply, or administrative offices. Even at that late date a check-list approach, which grants or withholds the title *polis* according to the presence or absence of certain features, proved unhelpful. Whether in dealing with questions of whether Greek cities were urban (the *polis* as city) or questions of whether cities were states (*poleis* as state), the check-list approach is even less illuminating for the archaic period, let alone for the eighth century.

The ways in which cities organised themselves both on the ground (see further below pp. 220–30) and in terms of their political arrangements and institutions was immensely varied throughout the archaic period. What happens in the eighth century is not a matter of the arrival of particular political arrangements, particular buildings, or a particular relationship between town and country. Held up against criteria-led definitions of what it is to be urban or what it is to be a state, some Greek cities will qualify, others will fail to qualify. What marks the eighth-century Greek communities out from those of the ninth century is not the achievement of some threshold but the degree of change over a wide range of aspects of community life. Just as in discussions of 'urbanisation' particular criteria, whether in terms of density of population, absolute population level, or particular cultural features, produce clear but practically meaningless classifications and it is relative size and density of population which mark the creation of different sorts of settlement, so in discussions of community organization, it is comparisons with what went before that demand our attention. We will not understand the changes of the eighth century any better for claiming to see there the 'rise of the *polis*'; indeed the application of terms familiar from the very different classical world will only cloud our view.

One of the best illustrations of the irrelevance of the *polis* to the existence of sophisticated political understanding comes from the poetry of Hesiod and Homer. Once more here scholars have debated whether or not Homer knows the *polis*. What close reading of his poetry shows is that issues of political power and its operation within the community are a central issue in both *Iliad* and *Odyssey*. Those discussions, however, are carried out primarily in terms of the leader and the people, not in terms of the *polis*. That this is if very far from making those poems irrelevant to the social and political conditions of the Greek world around 700 BC is something that I explore in the next chapter.

5

THE WORLD OF
HESIOD AND HOMER

The most obvious way in which the advent of writing changes our ability to study ancient Greece is through the survival of extensive texts. The earliest such texts to survive seem to have been handed down to us substantially in the form they acquired around 700 BC or a little after (see below, pp. 149–52), and take the form of long poems: the *Iliad* and the *Odyssey* ascribed to Homer and the *Theogony* and *Works and Days* of Hesiod. None of these poems offers much in the way of direct narrative history of the Greek world, but all of them presuppose certain interests and experiences on the part of the audience of the poems. And because those poems were preserved in more or less their early seventh-century form, they had a formative effect on the later archaic and classical world which was arguably more powerful and fundamental than the effect that any constantly changing tradition of oral poetry could have had. In this chapter I want to explore what can, and what cannot, be learnt of the Greek world *c.*700 BC from these monumental poems.

THE TRADITION OF ORAL POETRY

Composing poetry and handing on the poems that have been composed do not require writing. Peculiar word-forms and metrical assumptions present in the Homeric and Hesiodic poems reveal that these poems are only the end-products of a poetic tradition which certainly stretches back continuously to a stage of linguistic usage earlier than that represented by the Linear B tablets that survive from the last century of Mycenaean Greece. Linguistic and metrical evidence of a similar sort suggests that that poetic tradition was not one shared by the whole Greek world, but one that had particular antecedents in Thessaly and then in Lesbos and the other Aiolian settlements of Asia Minor, before being taken up by the Ionian Greeks of Asia Minor and reimported to mainland Greece, perhaps through Euboia. The tradition of the Homeric epics shows less Ionian influence on its language than does the tradition of the Hesiodic poems, and this may suggest that poetry of the sort we know from Hesiod had a slightly shorter history.

Formulaic composition and its historical significance

This tradition of poetry in dactylic hexameter metre was preserved through 1,000 years or more of oral existence not by the memorisation of earlier compositions but by constant recomposition. Composing within this tradition was not a matter of stringing individual words together, but of telling and retelling stories through set phrases and set scenes. The set phrases, or 'formulae', often combine a noun and an epithet and introduce characters or situations in a way that satisfies the metrical demands of part or all of a hexameter line; the set scenes, which might be several lines long, cover standard events – feasts, sacrifices, and, also, in the *Iliad* such martial activities as arming and death. Speeches of Odysseus in the *Odyssey* are standardly introduced with the phrase 'In answer to him [or her], cunning Odysseus replied', and a new day in the *Odyssey* is twenty times brought in with the phrase 'when early-born rosy-fingered dawn appeared'. This way of composing an oral poem by use of 'formulae' has parallels in modern instances of oral poetic composition, and fieldwork among the oral poets of Bosnia has been able to demonstrate that poets can orally recreate poems, preserving themes and varying only in details, on different occasions decades apart.

For the historian, as also for the literary critic, one crucial question is the extent to which such techniques of oral composition constrained the poet simply to reproduce what was essentially the 'same' poem or poems. Epic formulae display a high degree of 'economy', that is, there tend to be only one or two epithets which will combine with a particular noun in a particular metrical position, so that if that noun is to appear in a particular part of the line it is bound to be combined with that epithet. This has suggested to some scholars that the originality of the oral poet was narrowly restricted. The repetition which this economy produces has similarly been considered to render many epithets effectively meaningless. But recent work has emphasised that neither Homeric nor Hesiodic poems are wholly, or even dominantly, formulaic. In both, the number of unique lines heavily outnumbers the number of repeated lines; and it is clear that formulae can be used, or modified, to individual effect, which demonstrates that position in the line is not the *sole* determinant of choice of formulae. In the Homeric poems, which consist very largely of speeches, speakers do not all speak an indistinguishable epic parlance, but are given their own distinctive styles. The oral poet built with some blocks that had been pre-constructed over a considerable number of previous generations, and these blocks made possible the creation of near-identical poems on different occasions, but that does not mean that the poetic creations had to be identical on each occasion, let alone in every generation.

The Greek language changed over time, and particular formulae ensured that the linguistic forms of a given age were preserved for any subsequent generation that continued to exploit that formula in building their poems. As a result, the Homeric and Hesiodic poems reveal at least something of the subject matter, as well as the language, of earlier stages of the tradition.

Glorious Hektor hurled his spear at Aias at a moment when he was turned directly towards him, and he did not miss. He hit him where the two baldrics were stretched across his chest, one for his shield and one for his dagger with silver rivets. These protected the soft flesh. Hektor was angry…

Text 13: Iliad 14. 402–6. Aias is struck by Hektor but comes to no harm (the crossing baldrics imply no cuirass and a body-shield, both early Mycenaean features).

There is thus reason to believe that as far back as the middle of the second millennium BC poetic performances told of war and death, employed direct speech and similes, including lion similes, and featured Asias, his brother Teukros, and Odysseus. Troy can be shown only to have been present somewhat later, during the 'Aeolic' phase and perhaps not far distant from the date (c.1200 BC) at which the late Bronze Age city known as Troy VIIa was destroyed. Nestor, Lokrian Aias, and probably Akhilleus, Agamemnon, and even Thersites, came in at the same date as Troy. But to show that certain broad themes, and certain particular persons or objects, were continuously present in the poetic tradition from a certain date is not to demonstrate that the stories that were told were unchanging: once more it must be emphasised that the building blocks enable, rather than dictate, the telling of a story.

The material world described in the Homeric poems seems closely parallel to the linguistic world. Just as there are Bronze Age linguistic phenomena, which have been continued because they perform a useful function, and perhaps because their archaic overtones are seen by the poet and the audience as part of what an epic poem should contain, so also objects are described which are almost certainly relics of the Bronze Age, and were not to be found in the eighth century BC. Such things as the silver-riveted sword (*Iliad* 2.45), boars' tusk helmet (*Iliad* 10.261–5), and 'shield like a tower' (*Iliad* 7.219, 11.485, 17.128, always carried by Aias), all seem to go back to the Mycenaean world, if not before (Text 13). Some of these objects may have carried particular episodes with them, and have been preserved because of the reuse of those episodes; but just as the presence of some Bronze Age linguistic elements does not mean that the poems simply reproduce the language of the Bronze Age, let alone simply replicate its interest, so the presence of Bronze Age objects does not make the material world of the poems a Bronze Age world.

HESIOD'S WORLD

Of the various poems, extant and lost, ascribed to Hesiod in antiquity, two are of particular importance: the *Theogony* and the *Works and Days*. Both poems are formally hymns, to the Muses in the case of the *Theogony*, and to Zeus in the case of the *Works and Days*, and it is probably right to imagine religious festivals as the original setting for the performances of the poems, although Hesiod (*Works and Days* 653–9) does tell of singing at the funeral games of Amphidamas at Khalkis, and some modern scholars think that it was the *Theogony* that he sang there.

The world of the *Theogony*

After an introduction, in which the Muses are introduced as responsible for singing about all the gods, and where the poet relates his direct encounter with them while shepherding flocks on Mount Helikon, and a brief section celebratory of the Muses themselves, the *Theogony* tells of the creation of the world, the birth of the gods and their struggle for succession, and the battle between gods and Titans. For the historian, the poem has three principal sources of interest: 1) it is an attempt to understand the world as an ordered creation, as a place of which sense can be made; 2) it sets out patterns of moral and immoral, just and unjust behaviour; and 3) it represents a tradition of thinking about the gods which, though not incompatible with the picture found in Homeric epic, is quite separate from that in the *Iliad* and *Odyssey*.

The cosmogony of the *Theogony* gives priority to Earth, Tartaros (what lies under the earth), and Eros (desire), which are the first things to come to exist out of Chaos. The heavens and the waters around the earth are created subsequently. Gods, giants, and other monsters are products of the union of earth and heaven, and the history of the world is a seen as a history of struggles among these creatures for supremacy and to discipline the wild, in order to produce a world in which humans and gods can live in a stable, if unequal, relationship. Hesiod gives various catalogues of names of gods and other non-human creations which serve the function of providing a place in the order of things for those creatures about whom some tale is told.

The most obvious way in which the *Theogony* establishes the relationship between humans and gods is in the story of Prometheus (whose name means Forethought) and the creation of woman. Prometheus is represented as one of four children of the Titan Iapetos, who is himself son of Earth and Heaven and older brother of Kronos. Prometheus' brothers are Atlas, who is made to use his strength to hold up the heavens, Menoitios, a violent person who rejoices too much in his manly strength and against whom Zeus has to use his thunderbolt, and Epimetheus (Afterthought), who is witless. Prometheus himself is wily, and is punished by Zeus for dividing an ox unequally when the human and divine world were separated. Prometheus' division, which gives the gods the bones wrapped in fat and men the flesh of the ox, provides an explanation for sacrificial practice, in which it is the fat and bones which are burnt on the altar for the gods. Zeus retaliates by keeping fire from men, but Prometheus steals fire, too, in a fennel stalk, and gives it to men. At this point Zeus not only punishes Prometheus, but also has the craftsman god Hephaistos create a woman, Pandora, who is loaded with charms and troubles. Her presence on earth ensures that men either labour to support wives and children or have no support themselves in old age. This is a bleak, as well as a misogynist, view of the world, but it is a view which sees the relationship between gods and humans as reasoned and regular, not random or arbitrary. Meat and fire are seen as gifts which put men in the position the gods would enjoy, and for which they pay by their labour to support the family structure which sets them apart from beasts.

The sense of the world of the gods as being a world fundamentally directed by justice is brought out most clearly in the account of the battle between the gods and the Titans. The Titans are portrayed as committed to relentless war against Zeus; their confinement to Tartaros, the dwelling of Night, Sleep, Death, and Hades, and the place of the waters of Styx, through whose terrible properties the Olympian gods are kept from lies, is presented as the prelude to Zeus' rule over a world where gods have different roles given to them and in which Zeus marries Themis (Right) and begets Peace, Justice, and Good Order. Zeus' power is seen as the guarantee that good, rather than evil, should prevail, and it is through the agency of the Muses, daughters of Zeus, that human rulers are held to derive their wisdom and justice (*Theogony* 80–93).

The sense of divine justice which permeates the *Theogony* has much in common with that which permeates the *Iliad* and the *Odyssey*. In all three poems the gods banter with humankind, are capable of tricking men, and make decisions whose morality men might regard as questionable (Poseidon's putting an end to the Phaiakian ship which has carried Odysseus home in the *Odyssey* is one notable instance (*Odyssey* 13.159–87)). But, despite working within a tradition which has much in common with that from which the *Iliad* and *Odyssey* were created, Hesiod's *Theogony* exploits a very different area of myth.

The concerns of the *Theogony* with cosmogony, with divine struggles for supremacy in heaven, and with battles between gods, have rather little in common with the concerns of the Homeric epics, and much more in common with epic poetry known from the near east. Although they were not preserved by any continuous tradition, various epics survive in more or less complete form from the near east, including the beginning of an untitled epic about the struggle for kingship in heaven, an epic of creation and of battles between the gods (the *Enuma Elis*), and an epic concerned with the creation by the gods of humankind to be labourers, dissatisfaction with the noise humans make leading to an attempt by the gods to drown them, and the salvation of humans by a wise man who builds a ship (the *Atrahasis*).

How direct a link should we suppose there to be between these near-eastern texts and Hesiod's *Theogony*? An interest in division of responsibilities between gods, in succession struggles between generations of gods, and in humankind enjoying a privileged position because the gods have been tricked by a wise man, is common to these near-eastern epics and the *Theogony*. There are also some specific parallels: the battle for supremacy in the Hittite text about kingship in heaven involves castration of the top god, from whose genitals other gods are born, one of them in the belly of the castrator; in *Theogony* Kronos castrates Ouranos, Aphrodite is born from Ouranos' genitals (Text 14), and Kronos later swallows, and is then made to regurgitate, his children.

Ouranos (Heaven) came bringing on night, and he embraced Gaia (Earth) desiring to make love, and stretched himself all upon her. But his son from his hiding place stretched out with his left hand and with his right he took the great sickle, long and jagged, and swiftly cut the genitals from his own dear father, and threw them behind him to be carried away. They did not leave his hand without having an effect: all the bloody drops that spurted out Gaia received, and when the seasons of the year had gone round she gave birth to strong spirits of vengeance and great giants, gleaming in armour, with long spears in their hands, and nymphs known throughout the boundless earth as Tree Nymphs. As soon as he had cut off the genitals with the steel he threw them down from the land to the stormy sea, and when they were carried for a long time through the waves white foam appeared from the immortal flesh, and on this a maiden was reared.

Text 14: Hesiod, Theogony *176–92: the castration of Ouranos and the birth of Aphrodite.*

Behind these parallels, however, lie considerable differences. In Hesiod the succession struggle happens within a single family: in the Hittite epic there are two families struggling; in the text on *Kingship in Heaven* (Text 15) the genitals are swallowed because bitten off: in the *Theogony* there is no direct connection between Kronos cutting off Ouranos' genitals with a sickle and his decision to swallow *his own* children. Myths of castration and eating children can be found in cultures with no connections with the Indo-European world, for instance among the native American Hopi. As alternative modes of interfering with natural succession, their presence in stories which are trying to account for the nature of divine power in terms of a succession struggle is hardly surprising. Given the traditional nature of Hesiodic poetry some linkage between near-eastern epics and his poem seems not improbable, but there is little reason to believe that this linkage occurred in the eighth century BC or that the poet himself was conscious of it.

The world of the *Works and Days*

The poets of *Iliad* and *Odyssey* never introduce themselves at all. In the *Theogony* Hesiod introduces himself only in the introduction, when he relates how the Muses inspired him; in the *Works and Days* the poet is present everywhere, and although, as a hymn, the poem is formally addressed to Zeus, it is effectively addressed to Hesiod's brother Perses, with whom he has a quarrel over inheritance. The high degree of self-reference has often been thought to mark out *Works and Days* as a poem less constrained by tradition, in which the poet's own experience plays a major part. In fact we cannot simply assume that references to himself, to his brother, or to his father having come from Kyme, are straightforwardly autobiographical, for such details too may be part of a traditional poetic persona; even Hesiod's name, which means 'he who emits voice', is not beyond suspicion. But if we must be cautious about how much of Hesiod's personal experience we

Nine in number were the years that Anus was king in heaven. In the ninth year Anus gave battle to Kumarbis, and like Alalus [the former king in heaven, just defeated by Anus] Kumarbis gave battle to Anus. When he could no longer withstand Kumarbis' eyes, Anus struggled forth from the hands of Kumarbis. He fled, he Anus; like a bird he moved in the sky. After him rushed Kumarbis, seized Anus by the feet and dragged him down from the sky. Kumarbis bit his 'knees' and his manhood went down into his inside. When it lodged there, and when Kumarbis had swallowed Anus' manhood, he rejoiced and laughed. Anus turned back to him, to Kumarbis he began to speak: 'You rejoice over your inside, because you have swallowed my manhood. Rejoice not over your inside! In your inside I have planted a heavy burden. First, I have impregnated you with the noble Storm-god; second, I have impregnated you with the river Aranzahas, not to be endured; third, I have impregnated you with the noble Tasmisos. Three dreadful gods have I planted in your belly as seed. You will go and end by striking the rocks of your own mountain with your head!'

Text 15: Kingship in Heaven *Col. 1.18–35 (trans. adapted from J. B. Pritchard (ed.),* Ancient Near Eastern Texts relating to the Old Testament *(Princeton, 1969)).*

can recover from *Works and Days*, its concerns with the world of human labour and seasonality, even if they are traditional, illuminate an area of life in many respects quite different from that illuminated by the *Theogony*. Indeed the traditional nature of the poem is one of the things which suggests that, despite its localisation in Boiotia, at 'the miserable village of Askra which is bad in winter, awful in summer, and good at no time of the year' (lines 638–40) (Figure 37), this work is no less relevant to the whole Greek world than is the *Theogony*.

The *Works and Days* falls into three sections. In the first (lines 1–382), an opening celebration of Zeus' power to humble men leads to reflections on good and bad strife among men, and on Perses' injustice, and to a number of stories which explain why it is that men must labour, and that their failure to do so is both predatory on other men and short-sighted. In the second (lines 383–694), a calendar of the farming year, including remarks on the seasons for sailing, sets out the right way of working. In the third (lines 695–828), miscellaneous good advice is given, some of it linked to the calendar. Often described as a 'didactic' poem, the teaching involved in *Works and Days* is not practical but moral: despite the injunctions about when to plough and when to sow, and the long description of how a plough is constructed, one cannot learn how to farm from Hesiod. The sense of a world where justice finally rules, which pervades the *Theogony*, is seen in the *Works and Days* too but at an everyday level.

The concern of *Works and Days* with morality in action could be effective only if the action in question was set in social, economic, and political circumstances familiar to Hesiod's audience. This makes the poem particularly important for the historian.

Politically, the world of *Works and Days* is a world where dispute settlement is in the hands of *basileis*, rulers of some kind but not necessarily hereditary

Figure 37 The site and setting of Hesiod's home village of Askra.

rulers, as the common translation 'kings' would suggest. Hesiod pictures his inheritance dispute with Perses as settled, in Perses' favour, by *basileis* who have been bribed by Perses. He warns that wickedness and unjust judgements may ruin the whole community, but envisages no recourse from such decisions except through final divine intervention: 'the eye of Zeus sees all' (lines 248–73). Hesiod's concern is not with what the rules are, but with whether decisions in cases of dispute are fairly made (Text 16); his dissatisfaction is not with who has power, but with how power is operated, and he advocates keeping clear of meetings at which others' disputes are settled.

Although Hesiod writes as one who neither has nor seeks an active political role, his poem assumes residence in a political community responsible for its own dispute settlement. Similarly, Hesiod assumes that members of that community live by farming and have it in their power to secure their own livelihood, with the failure of one member of the community to do so presenting a burden to the community as a whole. Selling and buying goods abroad is an option which Hesiod discusses (618ff.), and which he recognises to be a possible source of profit, but he presents it as misguided to imagine that it offers an easy way to escape from debt and hunger. Denying that there are short-cuts to prosperity is fundamental to Hesiod's view of the basic fairness of the world, a fairness upset by unfair division of inheritance. Hesiod assumes that wealth gives power, and the important thing is to be one who is in a position to give rather than needing to receive, in order to exploit the resulting possibilities for influence. Although rulers have the power

Perses, pay attention to what is just and do not foster violence. Violence is a bad thing for poor mortals: not even a good man can bear it easily, but it weighs him down and he comes to mischief. Better is the road that goes the other way, to fairness. In the end justice wins out over violence, as the fool discovers by suffering. Oath comes quickly on the heels of crooked judgements. There is a clamour when justice is dragged around, when men who take bribes lead her on and make judgements about what is right with crooked justice. She follows wailing through the city and the haunts of men, clothed in mist, bringing evil to men who drive her out and do not deal straightly with her.

Text 16: Hesiod, Works and Days *213–27. Hesiod pleads for justice within the community.*

disastrously to upset the just ordering of resources, it is wealth, not birth or official position, which Hesiod sees as giving effective power over others in day-to-day matters.

Hesiod's perceptions of the political importance of economic prosperity give little indication of his own social class. Although it has been argued that Hesiod shares 'the image of the limited good' which some anthropologists have claimed to be general in peasant societies, it is not in fact clear that Hesiod thinks that prosperity itself is achieved at another's expense; rather, he notes that prosperity gives power over those who happen not to be prosperous. There is little value to classifying Hesiod according to modern categories, many of whose defining features – in the case of 'peasants', independent culture and dominance and exploitation by outsiders – are entirely absent. It is more enlightening to observe the absence of social stratification below the level of the *basileis* in Hesiod, and the easy social mobility which he assumes throughout. Such easy mobility is displayed not just in the possibility of transforming poverty to prosperity by work, but in the way in which Hesiod's father is presented as having come in poverty from Kyme and yet been in a position to leave substantial landed wealth to his sons (*Works and Days* 37–41, 633–8, Text 17). The lack of allusion to social stratification makes the *Works and Days* easy to export to communities differently organised, but the reception of the poem elsewhere surely depended upon personal labour in agriculture dominating the life of poor and prosperous alike, and upon the economic and social independence of the bulk of those who worked the land.

The present world, whose logic and morality *Works and Days* explores, is a world without war. It has to be, for the sudden gains and losses which the violence of war bring would upset the plausibility of a direct connection between labour and prosperity. In fact, if we take the autobiographical information seriously, Hesiod's own day may have been marked by serious warfare: Hesiod boasts of achieving a poetic victory in funeral games at Khalkis in Euboia for Amphidamas (*Works and Days* 654–9), and a later writer associates Amphidamas and his death with the Lelantine war (Plutarch, *Moralia* 153e–f). This war held a place in fifth-century BC tradition as exceptional for involving different political communities uniting together on each side (Thucydides 1.15.3). The way in which the outside world fails to

You yourself wait until the season for sailing is come and then drag a swift ship down to the sea. Equip it with a well-fitting cargo so as to bring home a profit. That is how my father and yours, poor Perses, used to sail on ships, because he lacked a good livelihood. And once he came even here, he left Kyme in Aiolis and completed a journey over a great stretch of sea in his black ship. He did not flee riches, wealth, and prosperity, but dreadful poverty which Zeus gives to men. He settled down near Helikon, in a wretched village, Askra, bad in winter, awful in summer, and good at no time of the year.

Text 17: Hesiod, Works and Days *630–40, on sailing, trading, and settling abroad.*

impinge on the Askra of *Works and Days* may therefore have been entirely artificial, and this must stand as a warning of the very severe limits to Hesiod's picture of life in his own day. The distorting effects of Hesiod's particular agenda cannot be ignored, and may be most active precisely where the poem seems most autobiographical.

War in *Works and Days* belongs to a past which is glimpsed largely in the 'myth of the generations' (lines 106–201), in which the past is seen to have featured successive silver, bronze, and heroic generations with a variety of failings which followed a perfect golden race which did not have to labour (Hesiod's Bronze Age is the age of the heroes of Homeric epic). In this succession of races Hesiod characterises the current generation as the race of iron, a race not entirely devoid of good things but one still degenerating morally, and declining into a future which will also be marked by the sacking of cities. How far this scheme of a sequence of races exploits an established trope in near-eastern literature, from which later similar examples are preserved, is not clear, but one of the functions of the 'myth of the races' for Hesiod is to allow an exploration of moral failings which goes beyond those which can be displayed in the context of the quarrel with Perses. This wider view of human nature, like the wider view of the human dilemma embraced by the story of Prometheus and Pandora retold in this poem, establishes the full extent to which the question of the right relationship between men and gods underlies the conduct of life within the narrower community.

THE WORLD OF THE *ILIAD* AND *ODYSSEY*

While the *Works and Days* is set in a war-free present, the *Iliad* is set in a war-torn past. To turn from *Works and Days* to *Iliad* or *Odyssey* is to turn from what seems to be realistic description to what seems to be fantasy and fable. Even though *Iliad* and *Odyssey* seem to be far less heavily laden with 'magical' interventions and devices than were other epic poems, now largely lost, the direct interventions of gods on the battlefield at Troy of the *Iliad*, and the Cyclops and other monstrous creations of the wanderings of *Odyssey* belong to a realm far removed from the earthy reality of the labouring farmer and his oxen. However, just as, even in *Works and Days*, Hesiod tells a story which is shaped by a poetic tradition, so conversely the manifestly traditional stories of *Iliad* and *Odyssey* are retold with a necessarily contemporary agenda in mind.

In assessing the historical importance and use of *Iliad* and *Odyssey*, it is important to realise that different elements in the poems may have very different historical significance. There has always been a strong temptation to take the very vivid descriptions of objects, whether cities, landmarks, or personal possessions, as description of objects which at some stage existed in reality. It was indeed such a conviction which drove the excavations of Heinrich Schliemann and led to the dramatic discovery of Bronze Age remains at Troy, Mycenae, and elsewhere. However, as those discoveries also showed, the places and objects described in the poems will in many cases have been entirely unfamiliar to any audience of the Homeric poems. Such descriptions owe their existence in the poems not to the pleasure of a shock of recognition, but to the ability to conjure up a lost world which stimulated critical thought about the present situation, just as the entirely mythical world of the golden race stimulates critical thought in the context of the *Works and Days*. The demands of the context may allow an object unfamiliar to the audience to be described 'intact', like the boars' tusk helmet which Meriones lends to Odysseus in *Iliad* 10.261–5, which may have survived because the whole episode is an exceptional one, not subject to contemporary parallels. In other circumstances an object may metamorphose in order to serve the current purpose, as the shield which Aias carries in *Iliad* 7 seems to be a leather shield which acquires first an outer layer of bronze and then a central boss, as the audience's changing understanding of how shields worked in battle demanded (*Iliad* 7.219–23, 245–8, 266–7). Or again, and this is particularly true of similes, a description might lose its very purpose if the object described is unfamiliar.

How far is what is true of physical objects equally true of social organisation? That there is a general coherence to the Homeric world there can be no doubt: the expectations about social hierarchies, about how men of the same social rank conduct their relations, and about ethical issues are consistent over both epics. But does this general coherence mean that *Iliad* and *Odyssey* describe a society which belongs to a single point of time? Or do the details of social organisation contain 'fossils' of various dates which have been preserved in passages whose issues have remained live, while the details of the incident through which the issue is explored have changed? Examination of three areas of life – marriage and property, political organisation, and military organisation – will reveal the problems and the issues.

Marriage in *Iliad* and *Odyssey*

Marriage is at the centre of the *Odyssey* (Text 18). Life in Ithaka during Odysseus' long absence has come to be focused on the wooing of Odysseus' wife Penelope by eligible bachelors from far and near, and the poem comes to a climax not just with their rooting out and murder by Odysseus but

So he spoke, and I replied and addressed him: 'Alas, far-sounding Zeus made women from the beginning the instruments of his terrible hatred of the offspring of Atreus. Many of us perished because of Helen, and Klytaimestra arranged this trick for you when you were still far away.' So I spoke, and he replied and straightway addressed me: 'So, you should never be easy with your wife. Don't tell her the whole of what you know, but tell part and keep part concealed. But you will not be murdered by your wife, Odysseus: the daughter of Ikarios, shrewd Penelope, is very discreet and her mind knows clever ploys. She was a young bride when we left her behind and went to war, with an infant son at her breast who must now be counted among the men, happy he. His father will see him when he comes and he will embrace his father, as is right. But my wife did not allow me even to set eyes on my son before she murdered me.

Text 18: Odyssey *11.435–53. Odysseus and Agamemnon on wives.*

with Odysseus' return to the marriage bed. Marriage is central also to the *Iliad*: Paris' seduction of Helen brings about the Greek expedition against Troy on behalf of the cuckolded Menelaos, and marriages are one of the most important means by which networks of alliance have been created on both Greek and Trojan sides.

In the course of both epics a large number of marriage alliances, all of them among the élite, are described in some detail. In many instances the bride is seen as a prize, bought by the personal qualities of the bridegroom, but also by his material gifts to her family. But in other cases the bride appears not to be bought but herself to bring to her new family a wealth of resources: the king of Lycia offers Bellerophon half his kingdom on his marrying his daughter and settling in Lycia (*Iliad* 6.191–5); the polygamous Priam expects to ransom the children of his wife Laothoe out of the resources she herself brought into the family (*Iliad* 22.46–51).

Two things are striking about the existence of gifts moving sometimes in one direction and sometimes in the other direction on marriage: that in no single instance are gifts recorded as passing in both directions, and that no consistent pattern of differential status of bride and groom seems to determine the pattern. For some modern scholars the existence of both patterns of gift-giving is a reflection of a norm that gifts flowed both ways; but there is in the poem itself some sign of regarding gifts from bride's father to groom as something whose unusual nature can be exploited to mark an unusual social situation: part of Agamemnon's attempt to persuade Akhilleus to return to battle (*Iliad* 9.144–57) is an offer of his daughter without receiving gifts from Akhilleus but along with gifts of treasures to Akhilleus. This seems at least to suggest that different social customs have become embedded in the epic tradition, and that an outdated custom has become exploited because it raises critical questions in the context of the poem's plot.

Political organisation in *Iliad* and *Odyssey*

Both *Iliad* and *Odyssey* are intensely political poems, in which the making and enforcing of decisions by individual rulers, by the élite group, and by the larger body of people, bulk very large, and where the fortunes of communities, in particular Troy and Ithaka, are a serious issue. It is notable that the Greek camp at Troy is itself transformed into a community structured politically like any other, and that Odysseus' visit to Phaiakia is made into an opportunity to introduce an exploration of a political order into the fairy-tale landscape of Odysseus' wanderings. The sense of community is highly developed, as we see most strikingly in the separation of communal from private business, and the exclusion of private business from communal discussion, in poems which turn upon conflicts between individual and group interests (Text 19). It is also seen in the stress, as in the whole plot of the *Iliad*, on the way in which the actions of leaders affect the whole community, and the need, emphasised especially by Mentor at *Odyssey* 2.229–41, for the community in turn to take responsibility for making life tolerable for its leaders. At the same time, both poems turn upon the supreme importance of rulers, both those referred to as *wanakes* and the less prestigious *basileis*, around whose individual activities, and on the interweaving of whose public and private lives, the plots of both poems turn. The personalising of the political is highly reminiscent of the real-life situations in the Persia of Herodotos' Xerxes, the Macedon of Philip and Alexander, or the Rome of the Empire – all situations where the supreme power of an individual gave a peculiar significance to familial and personal relations. Yet what is striking about the rulers of *Iliad* and *Odyssey* is their lack of supreme power, indeed their comparative powerlessness.

The powerlessness of rulers in the Homeric poems deserves some more detailed discussion. Agamemnon not only cannot enforce his will over Akhilleus, he cannot enforce it over the army at large. Odysseus' final triumph in Ithaka is achieved by overwhelming violence, not by virtue of his reclaimed political position. Individuals exert political influence according to their social standing, their rhetorical abilities, and their personal charisma, but not according to their holding the office of ruler. Holding the office of ruler gives responsibilities for looking after the people, but those responsibilities appear most clearly when the leader fails to fulfil them. The curiously nebulous political position of the ruler is further reflected in the considerable unclarity about what makes a ruler: Odysseus 'succeeded' his still-living father Laertes, who subsequently seems to have no political role or influence, but Telemakhos does not acquire Odysseus' position in his absence, and is not assured of it if Odysseus dies. This almost systematic unclarity about the powers of the ruler is seen in the important but undefined role of the ruler's consort: Aigisthos both takes Agamemnon's wife Klytaimestra as his own wife and assumes power in Mycenae in the absence of Agamemnon, and it seems taken for granted that whichever suitor marries Penelope will acquire political influence; yet it is equally

'Hear what I say, men of Ithaka. Neither our assembly nor our council has ever met since glorious Odysseus went off in the hollow ships. So which of the young men or the older men has had to call it now? Has he heard some news of an army invading – perhaps he could tell us clearly if he is the first to learn it? Or does he want to declare and tell some other public matter? He seems to be a good man if he will do us some good. May Zeus bring good to completion for him according to his heart's desire.'

Text 19: Odyssey *2.25–34 speech of Aigyptios opening the assembly which Telemakhos has called.*

conceivable that Penelope will be sent back to her father Ikarios (*Odyssey* 1.274–8), and she herself has no constitutional powers. This situation is very much replicated in Phaiakia, where the power of Alkinoos' wife Arete is emphasised on several occasions: Odysseus is told by her daughter Nausikaa that it is to her that he must first go, and she is said to 'resolve quarrels even among men' (*Odyssey* 7.53, 74), yet her role within the palace seems to be purely domestic, and indeed Alkinoos seems to act with more authority in Phaiakia than do rulers elsewhere in the poem.

It is relatively easy to see why rulers are so important, but so insignificant, in the Homeric poems. On the one hand, the figure of the ruler enables the clash between personal and communal values and responsibilities to be highlighted in a dramatic way: personal decisions may have political consequences, and vice versa, for all, but for rulers the results of personal decisions can realistically be expected to be particularly immediate and dramatic. On the other hand, the relevance of the observation that political and personal decisions are interwoven is more readily brought home to a society where power is not in the hands of a single ruler if the official powers of the ruler are removed from the picture. Monarchical rulers too are good to think with, even, perhaps especially, in a community that lacks them. We should see the Homeric poems as retaining such rulers not because they were still a feature of the society of 'Homer's own day', nor indeed because the poems have preserved a fossilised kingship from earlier epic tradition, but because they are integral to the effective exploration of the issues with which the poet wished, as his predecessors within the tradition may long also have wished, to entertain his audience.

Warfare in the *Iliad*

So too with Homeric warfare. Warfare in the *Iliad* features warriors in chariots, and concentrates on the clash between individual heroes on each side. This has often been thought to stand in strong contrast to the massed ranks of heavily armed infantry who fought in wars between Greek states in the historical record (see further below, pp. 163–4). Arguably no ancient author gives a fully comprehensible view of a battle, and it is certainly impossible to gain a coherent overall picture of how a battle works from the

The Trojans pressed forward in a crowd, Hektor leading. As when a great wave roars against the current at the estuary of a swollen river, and the heights of the shore boom around as the sea bellows out, such was the shout of the Trojans as they advanced. But the Akhaians stood around the son of Menoitios with a single resolve, walled in with brazen shields.

Text 20: Iliad *17.262–8. The Trojans advance to try to take the body of Patroklos.*

Iliad. The Myrmidons, who follow Akhilleus, mass close together for battle (e.g. 16.211–17) but become more or less invisible when battle has begun. Champions face each other in what often seems like solitary combat, but when one falls it turns out immediately that other champions are at hand to fight over the body: the narrative of Patroklos' assault on the Trojans and of the battle over Patroklos' body in *Iliad* 16 and 17 is notable in this regard (Text 20). Chariots repeatedly make an appearance in a transport role, roaming over the field of battle as if there were no significant body of warriors there. The presence of items of equipment which seem to belong to different ages has been discussed above (p. 133); but more significant in this context is the fact that that equipment has not been inserted into a tactical framework that is consistent through the poem and so yields little military sense. This lack of military sense guarantees that the *Iliad*'s picture of warfare is not a picture of warfare at any given point in time, but a picture which enables certain features of what it is to fight, and of who must fight, to be stressed: both the role of the individual and the vital necessity of everyone's fighting in an organised mass are brought out, and both these features are essential to the overall plot of the poem. But this does not mean that the description is of no interest or use to the historian. Just as individual items of equipment can be proved to be genuine memories of the past, so also we may speculate, even if we cannot so easily prove, that various tactics which are stressed, such as the insistence on the close-packing of Myrmidon ranks, refer to actual battle tactics at a particular point in time (see below, p. 164 for this particular case).

The conclusion to which this discussion inevitably leads is that *Iliad* and *Odyssey* do not give us a picture of the Greek world at any particular date: successive poets have drawn on the tradition within which they work to create poems which use the past to think about, and to engage, the present. The inclusion of material objects and institutions unrecognisable to a contemporary audience is not a product of blind repetition of lines or sections formulated by earlier poets but the product of critical use of an inheritance to cast light on present concerns. Such features lend to the world portrayed in the poems a distance from the present which precludes the audience from identification with, or identification of, characters in the poem with characters in their own society. That Odysseus can identify and feel for characters in the poems which Demodokos sings in *Odyssey* 8, and cannot stop himself from weeping as he listens, causes shame to him, and makes Alkinoos change the entertainment from song to athletic competition: the distance which the Phaiakians enjoy from the events is surely an image of the distance expected of every epic audience.

Homeric values

There is, however, another side to this picture: if the material world and the institutions described in *Iliad* and *Odyssey* are an unhistorical composite, the values which the poems explore have to be relevant to, and illuminative of, the values of the audience. And, just as a highly localised physical setting for the poems would have condemned them to a parochial future (part of the advantage of a setting at Troy may be widespread Greek interest in the Dardanelles), so a moral setting that was highly localised must have had the same effect. The values of the poems must be values that can be recognised by, and are central for, more than a socially restricted audience. It is a direct product of this situation that scholars have managed to find in the Homeric poems both highly aristocratic and markedly populist sentiments. Both poems are issue-centred, and those issues are created by the possibility of the same behaviour being seen differently by different groups, or according to the values employed in different contexts: individuals clash with each other over the extent to which political factors should interfere with individual rights, or individual grievances with political behaviour, and groups clash with each other over the appropriate behaviour in unprecedented situations.

There has often been a tendency to see the Homeric epics as dominated by a competitive ethos, in which individuals come before the group, and success in competition comes before all else. There can be no question that such competitive values are prominently paraded in both poems, but they are paraded to be questioned. The conflict with which the *Iliad* is concerned, as becomes poignantly clear in the final book when Akhilleus is moved to treat Priam with generosity, is not that between Greeks and Trojans, but between the values which Akhilleus puts to the fore and those which motivate Agamemnon. The quarrel between the heroes highlights the problem of authority: what gives Agamemnon authority over Akhilleus? What are the limits to what Agamemnon can use that authority to do? What are the limits to Akhilleus' requirement of loyalty? What gives a man authority to speak and by virtue of what does he speak with authority?

The heavy emphasis on speech in *Iliad* and *Odyssey*, which seems to have marked these poems out from other Greek epics (though a similar emphasis is found in such near-eastern epics as the epic of Gilgamesh), serves further to emphasise how values may be negotiated, and how advice and adviser interact. Persuasive speech is central to both epics, and between them the speakers deploy a wide range of persuasive strategies and techniques, both directly exploiting well-organised argument and deliberately under-cutting expectations of such organisation of argument for emotional effect. We would, of course, expect a long poetic tradition to have left its practitioners highly skilled in story-telling, and the way in which Odysseus builds up expectations among the Phaiakian audience as he begins the narrative of his wanderings mirrors the skills deployed by the poet in the epic as a whole. But the rhetorical techniques shown in formal public speeches, which anticipate those displayed in classical deliberative oratory, imply a familiarity with political oratory which presupposes an institutional background suited to the development of such skills. Nor are these skills somehow external to the heroic world: the ability to give good advice, and to give it in a persuasive way, is an ability which is expected of the heroic figure: excellence in council is as much expected and admired in a heroic figure as prowess in fighting. Both Akhilleus and Odysseus stand out among heroes for their skill with words (Text 21): Akhilleus is an outsize hero in being better than others at fighting but he is also outsize in his exceptional capacity for verbalising experiences and drawing conclusions from them; Odysseus is cunning of act, but much of that cunning lies in his capacity for deceptive speech – strikingly summed up in his claim to the Cyclops that his name is 'No One' (so that Polyphemos shouts out that 'No one is killing me'), a name which, in one of its forms (*mê tis*), is identical with the word 'cunning' (*mêtis*).

A broader picture of the values to which the audience for these epics is expected to subscribe emerges from the contrasts drawn to distinguish the world of Akhilleus and Odysseus from the world which Odysseus encounters on his wanderings, and indeed from the world of the dead which he also visits. Those contrasts are partly political: the Cyclopes have no laws and no deliberative councils (Text 22), the dead have no power to affect the lot of another. But the contrasts are also more generally in way of life and in priorities: none of the non-human figures whom Odysseus meets, whether benign or malign, practises agriculture or sacrifices to the gods. They have no cooking and no wine: nature is exploited by hunting and gathering but it is never modified. Their relations with others are perverted: Circe's

Odysseus himself came before Atreus' son Agamemnon and took his ancestral sceptre. With it he went through the ships of the Akhaians who wear bronze armour. Whenever he met any ruler or man of rank, he stood beside him and spoke gently to him: 'My friend, it isn't right to terrify you like a coward. But just you sit down and seat the rest of the folk. You haven't realised Agamemnon's intention. He is testing us now, but he will soon threaten the Akhaian lads. Did we not all hear what he said in council? I fear he may harm the Akhaian lads in his anger. Rulers whom the gods nurture have mighty pride, they get their honour from Zeus and Zeus the counsellor loves them.' But when he saw an ordinary man and found him shouting, he struck him with the sceptre and upbraided him: 'My friend, you just sit still and hear what others, who are better than you, say. You are feeble, and not fit for war. You don't count either in war or in council. Not all us Akhaians here are rulers, and it is a bad thing if everybody tries to take charge. Let there be one man in charge, one ruler – the one to whom the son of cunning Kronos has given authority.'

Text 21: Iliad 2. 185–205. *Odysseus demonstrates the variety of methods of persuasion required in a ranked society as he attempts to prevent the Akhaians from abandoning Troy.*

idea of hospitality is to turn her guests into animals; the family of Aiolos is entirely incestuous. By contrast the hospitable Phaiakians, on the look-out for eligible bridegrooms from outside the community, are agriculturalists in an environment which exceptionally favours it, where gardens bear fruit throughout the year, and where sacrifices not only establish communications with the gods but end up with the gods coming to join the feast. In exploring deficiency and excess in this way the *Odyssey* makes clear the fundamentals of civilised life, and by insisting that only Ithaka will do the poem emphasises the unique value of being Greek.

Examination of the values of the Homeric epics in this way reveals how close their world is to the world of Hesiod. Agriculture and sacrifice may not be explicitly moralised or theorised in *Iliad* and *Odyssey*, in the way that they are in *Works and Days* and *Theogony*, but they are fundamental in all the poems. Issues of political authority are explored in *Iliad* and *Odyssey* in settings – a camp of a long-besieging army, the palace of a long-absent ruler – which seem remote from the real-life experience which it is so tempting to see directly reflected in Hesiod's quarrel with his brother Perses, but the issues are not themselves dissimilar. All these poems belong to a world where political authority is being debated and explored, where power is not simply inherited, where social status correlates closely with access to power, but does not fully determine it. Public speaking, and the arguing out of a case in a public forum, are normal in this world, and rhetorical skills are both admired and highly developed. What is more, the place of women is an object of attention in all these poems: Hesiod's Pandora portrays woman as a 'structural problem', impossible to do with or do without; the *Iliad* turns on quarrels over women – Paris' rape/seduction of Helen, Agamemnon's initial refusal to ransom Khryseis and subsequent laying claim to Briseis – and highlights the way treatment of women leads to clashes between individual and community interests; the *Odyssey* parallels the dramatic adventures of wandering Odysseus to the patient resistance of Penelope to the advances of suitors, who have set their aim on the political conquest of Ithaka by sexual conquest of Penelope, and repeatedly makes clear the considerable political role which the sexually desirable woman plays.

All these values emerge not from the building blocks from which these traditional poems are built but from the way those blocks are put together.

We came to the land of the Cyclopes, arrogant, lawless, men who rely on the immortal gods and neither plant with their hands nor sow seed, but everything grows without sowing or ploughing, wheat and barley and vines which produce the wine that comes from fine grapes which rain from Zeus swells. They have no laws and never meet to take counsel, but live on the top of high mountains in hollow caves, each making the rules for his children and wives and taking no notice of each other.

Text 22: Odyssey 9.106–15. *Odysseus describes the life of the Cyclopes, the inversion of the Greek life of farming and political activity.*

Endless alternative epics of warfare or wanderings could have been created, and no doubt were created, in which a very different way of life was valued. Indeed the way in which the emphasis on competitive values in *Iliad* emerges, more from reading between the lines than from how stock formulae describe characters or approve actions, suggests the novelty of that emphasis. The historian, who must exercise the utmost care in assuming that any object or institution described in *Iliad* or *Odyssey* belongs to the world in which the poet lived who was responsible for the poems in the form we have them, need have no qualms about assuming that that poet's world shared the values which those poems explore.

HESIOD, HOMER, AND HISTORY

Rather few of the topics discussed in the preceding chapter are seriously illuminated by the *Theogony, Works and Days, Iliad,* or *Odyssey*. Those poems are rather good on the mobility of individuals and groups, but changes in population, in burial customs, in residential preferences, in the placing of sanctuaries, or in dedicatory practices, have left little mark on the poetic tradition. And when the poems do describe the material world, or particular institutions or practices, we cannot jump to the conclusion that the objects or practices described belong to the world in which the poet lived, or are in any detailed sense familiar to the audience.

The contribution which the Homeric and Hesiodic poems make to the historian rests not with any additional information which they provide on topics illuminated by the archaeologist, but with the evidence they give for ways of seeing the world, ways which archaeology can at best only dimly illuminate. Where archaeology can show something of where and how the gods were worshipped, Hesiod gives us some sense of the rationale for that worship, and the sorts of explanation which might appropriately be invoked to explain the material traces familiar from archaeology. Where archaeology gives us evidence for Greeks moving from place to place and establishing contact with non-Greeks, the *Odyssey* can show something of how Greeks used the different customs and priorities of others to clarify what it was to be Greek; and the *Theogony*, in particular, can add to the evidence which art history and the development of the alphabet provide for how the encounter with foreign practices and objects was rendered productive within Greek communities.

The Hesiodic and Homeric poems reveal a highly developed self-consciousness about moral and political values. The sophistication of political rhetoric, most notably in the *Iliad*, the eager attempt to ground moral values in an overall view of the world, gods included, in the Hesiodic poems, and the scrutiny of the sources, nature, and limitations of claims to authority, which dominates all the poems, give evidence without parallel for the maturity of self-analysis to be found in the communities which formed the audience for these poems. Any attempt to make sense of the material traces of Greek life at the time these poems were first heard must take account of this evidence.

The context of poetic composition

The poems themselves must also be treated as artefacts whose existence and nature need to be explained. The world of Hesiod and Homer has to have been a world in which conditions were such that epic poems of this sort could be created. The songs which feature in the *Iliad* and *Odyssey* seem, like the poems of Hesiod, to be relatively short – part of an evening's entertainment, to be switched on and off more or less at will. It is easy to see that such poems, which are not necessarily in hexameters, might be created in a more or less domestic context, and were easy to adapt to such occasions as the funeral games of Amphidamas at which Hesiod says he performed. But *Iliad* and *Odyssey* are different, for their scale (the *Iliad* is almost 16,000 lines long, the *Odyssey* 12,000) makes them entirely inappropriate for any domestic setting. What is more, neither poem seems designed for a particular local audience, neither concentrates on features particularly familiar in a given area, and, although some broad geographical focusing of references has been suspected, any context of performance would seem to have to be one in which local loyalties and interests were expected to play little part. There is good evidence for later performance of the poems at religious festivals, and it is tempting to think that only a religious festival drawing in people from a fairly wide variety of different cities could provide the time, or the panhellenic focus of interest, which the *Iliad* and *Odyssey* presuppose. Such festivals can be traced archaeologically in the number and varied origin of dedications found at certain sanctuaries, most notably Olympia, in the second half of the eighth century BC, but evidence for the existence of such occasions earlier is entirely lacking. It would seem reasonable therefore to suggest that *Iliad* and *Odyssey*, at least, simply could not have been created before about 750 BC. But this gives, at best, a date after which the poems were composed. The question of when exactly the poems were first heard in substantially the form in which we have them is considerably more complicated.

If *Iliad* and *Odyssey* required specific historical circumstances for their creation, they also demanded specific historical circumstances for their preservation. Successive earlier products of oral epic tradition had for centuries disappeared without any trace except those borne by subsequent creations: so why did the Homeric poems not disappear likewise? The preservation of *Iliad* and *Odyssey* requires that something happened to the oral tradition. The oldest surviving texts of the Homeric poems belong to the third century BC, and the earliest texts of which we hear belonged to the middle of the sixth century BC. At that date the poems were being performed by men known as *rhapsodes*, who recited sections of the poems in competition with one another. When and how did the creative oral tradition that enabled the monumental composition of *Iliad* and *Odyssey* come to be transformed into a non-creative tradition of repeating an existing poem?

Two sorts of explanation offer themselves for the end of the oral tradition and the beginning of the rhapsodic tradition. One explanation builds on the context in which rhapsodic repetition is known to have occurred, the context that can be postulated to have made monumental epic possible, namely the religious festival. Festivals, and particularly competitive festivals (Text 23), it might be argued, created a demand for standard tasks to be performed, and thus occasioned a move from commissioning a song to suit the circumstances, as happens in Phaiakia, to requiring the repeated performance of a single 'test' text. The other explanation appeals to technology: what turned oral composition into repetition of a fixed text was the availability of a fixed text which writing made possible. Indeed some would suggest that it was the possibility of a written record which promoted the idea that there might *be* a fixed text.

The possibility of a written text of the Homeric poems from the beginning is perhaps strengthened by the situation with Hesiod, where the 'autobiographical' elements in the poems, and the possible signs of late insertions into an existing text by the poet, have encouraged the belief that the poet composed with the aid of writing. Whatever the Hesiodic situation, the scale of the Homeric poems makes recording them in writing a very different task. Later ancient tradition had no memory of a definitive early text: in as far as a moment is singled out in tradition, it is the moment when Hipparkhos, son of the Athenian tyrant Peisistratos, is said to have brought the Homeric poems to Athens and had them performed in order at the Panathenaia (Plato, *Hipparkhos* 228b). The superficial colouring of Attic dialect which the poems have acquired does suggest that transmission via Athens was indeed crucial to the text which we have, although there are also orthographic features which are perhaps best explained by the hypothesis that there had been an earlier text written in East Ionic script. In the Hellenistic period there was considerable detailed variation between one text and another, and ever since antiquity some scholars have wanted to excise even whole books as not being by 'Homer'. Few of the detailed variations are of any great significance, and variations are extremely common in all ancient texts, making it clear that even in a text which has been written from the beginning interpolations could occur freely.

The possibility that additions were made to the Homeric poems at some date after their monumental composition makes the dating of that composition

You have many temples and wooded groves, and yours are all the cliff-tops and viewpoints on high mountains and the rivers that run on to the sea. But you especially delight in Delos, Apollo, where the Ionians gather in their long linen garments, with their children and their shy wives. They delight you with boxing and dancing and song, whenever they hold a contest with you in mind.

Text 23: Homeric Hymn to Apollo *143–50.*

extremely problematic. As we have seen above, the Homeric poems describe objects preserved in the poetic tradition from various past ages. It might seem that the poems should date to the period of, or a period later than, the latest objects which they describe, but contemporary objects are among the things most likely to have been added to a substantially existent text. In the light of this, it is striking that very few objects in the poems can in fact be dated to later than *c.*650 BC, whereas a number (such as Agamemnon's Gorgon Shield, *Iliad* 11.32–40) seem datable to the first half of the seventh century BC, an observation which concurs with the likelihood that the reference to the wealth of (Egyptian) Thebes post-dates the destruction of that city in 663 BC (*Iliad* 9. 381–4). The reference to Egyptian Thebes is particularly important, since it comes in a context where its excision would substantially alter the nature of the poem. This concurrence would seem to suggest that the text of the poems *was* fixed by *c.*650, but not substantially before that date, and it seems reasonable to suggest that the *Iliad* and *Odyssey* as we know them were not composed much before that time.

A precise date for Hesiod's poems is equally difficult to arrive at, but a broadly similar or slightly earlier date seems most likely. Hesiod describes no archaeologically datable objects, but his reference to the funeral games of Amphidamas at Khalkis is later linked to traditions of war between Khalkis and Eretria (above, p. 139), and the tactics said to have been employed in this war, together with the possible archaeological consequences of the war, suggest a date around or shortly after 700 BC. More precise dating of the poems is unrealistic, and in view of the nature of the historical evidence which they provide – evidence for values and concerns which are likely to change over the medium rather than the short term – this general early seventh-century BC date is all that is required. In any event both Homeric and Hesiodic poems were composed substantially later than the late ninth-century date which Herodotos surmised (Herodotos 2.53).

6

REFORMING COMMUNITIES

The Seventh Century

The Homeric epics and the poems of Hesiod are products of a long tradition, but in the form we have them they could not have been created in the Greek world of 800 BC. The expansion of horizons during the eighth century BC, and the growing sense of separate communities competing with each other, surveyed in Chapter 4, was necessary to create both the issues upon which those poems focus and the occasions for their performance. But it is arguable that those poems are not really at home in an eighth-century world either, and that it was the further and radical changes in perspective which occurred around 700 BC which those poems most strongly reflect. In this chapter I shall try to explore what changed at the end of the eighth century, and how the world that followed differed.

AN ARTISTIC REVOLUTION

The worldview of the seventh-century-BC artist is distinct from that of the eighth-century artists reviewed in Chapter 4, distinct even from the worldview of those exceptional eighth-century artists of Athens and Crete. Three concerns dominate seventh-century art: exploring the world through myths that are rendered clearly identifiable; facing up to the gods; and communal action. Two icons, both admittedly in many ways exceptional, will illustrate the seventh-century view.

The Chigi vase

The sizeable jug (*olpe*) (26 cm high), found near Veii in Etruria, and shown in Figure 38a and b, takes its shape from east Greek pottery but was almost certainly made in Corinth. Known as the Chigi vase after a former owner, it belongs to a ceramic phase known to scholars as late protocorinthian, dates to the middle of the seventh century BC, and was decorated by an artist whose work can also be detected in a number of other vases and who is known as the Chigi Painter, after this vase, or the Macmillan Painter, after the donor of a much tinier (7 cm high) perfume vase by the same hand, which is now in

Figure 38a The protocorinthian Chigi vase (*olpe*) from around the middle of the seventh century, with scenes of hunting, hoplite warfare, and of the Judgement of Paris.

Figure 38b Detail of central frieze.

the British Museum. The outside of the jug is decorated in bands, with lotus and palmette decoration on the lip and immediately below the neck, and four successive figure scenes on the body, three of them polychrome.

The top, and tallest, figure scene shows the clash of heavily armed troops in battle. The soldiers are shown wearing crested bronze helmets, bronze cuirasses, and greaves, and wielding shields held firm on the left arm by two handles, one at the centre of the shield, through which the forearm passes, and one at the edge of the shield and gripped by the hand. The outsides of the shields bear emblems (compare the Cretan shields discussed above, p. 128), with a probable gorgon, the earliest gorgon shield known from archaeology, clearly displayed. The soldiers advance in serried ranks, with a piper (*auletes*) to keep them in step. This scene is separated from the next polychrome frieze by a dark band on which are painted hounds chasing wild goats.

The middle frieze has a labelled Judgment of Paris scene, with Paris (called by his alternative name Alexandros), Hermes, and the three goddesses, Hera, Athene, and Aphrodite. Behind Paris is a lion hunt, in which the lion has mauled one hunter; behind Aphrodite is a cavalcade, with a boy leading a chariot which is followed by pairs of horses each controlled by one rider. A double-bodied sphinx comes between hunt and chariot. At the bottom is another hunt scene in which young men use dogs to hunt hares and foxes.

Many features of this outstanding pot contrast with geometric art: the polychromy, the concern for detailed depiction of bodily forms, the use of writing and inclusion of an identifiable scene of myth, the sense of compositional focus, and the productive juxtaposition of discrete scenes. While historians debate whether shield-forms in geometric art should be interpreted as descriptive of contemporary reality or as symbolic, there is little doubt here that the painter was concerned not merely to evoke 'warriors' but to evoke soldiers of a particular kind: this is indeed the earliest unequivocal representation of what is known as 'hoplite warfare' (below, pp. 164–5). The artist's decision to show the moment at which the armies meet suggests that he is less concerned with who wins than with the fact that battle takes place and with showing off this new style of battle. The use of writing in the central frieze, by contrast, suggests that the artist regarded the identification of this particular scene as vital: the viewer is not to take this as *any* encounter between men and women, this is a particular man's verdict on women and a verdict which matters. However, nothing is done to make lion hunt, cavalcade, or fox and hare hunt specific. The oriental overtones of the lion hunt, in particular, suggest that display may be intended to be a keynote of the central frieze; the focusing of attention on the boy restraining dogs in the bottom frieze seems similarly to point to timing and prowess.

It seems unlikely that the combination of scenes here is accidental. Judging between exotic goddesses, like hunting exotic animals, is a high-risk matter, and not merely, like the cavalcade, a way to show off. Wild dogs may chase wild goats, but men who hunt need to control wild instincts and to choose their moment. War is a serious matter which should not be entered upon

155

Figure 39 Pithos from Xombourgo on Tenos with a scene of a miraculous head-birth.

lightly. If the guest whose cup is filled from this jug finds the clash of troops as riddling as the sphinx below, the host who pours, who looks upon the scene of the Judgment of Paris below the handle, is reminded that discrimination has its consequences. There is no single way to 'read' these images, but the themes of display, decision, and pursuit that run through the figured decoration here, suggestively open up critical paths for any viewer.

The Xobourgo 'Birth of a deity' *pithos*

My second icon (Figure 39) is also ceramic, but belongs to a very different class of object: large storage vessels (*pithoi*) with relief decoration. Vessels of this sort with non-figurative decoration are found in the geometric period in several different areas of Greece, but in the seventh century BC a tradition of figurative decoration of such vessels seems to thrive particularly in the Cycladic islands and Boiotia. This particular example comes from the site which has been most prolific of relief *pithoi*, Xobourgo on Tenos (see below, p. 188), and it is thought to date to the first quarter of the seventh century BC. The neck of the *pithos* has a scene with a central seated winged figure, with frontal face, profile body, and arms upraised. From the head of this figure springs a further winged figure, with frontal body and profile face, wearing a helmet and carrying weapons in both hands. To the left is a small standing

156

female figure with wings and a sickle or knife; to the right a naked winged figure kneels by a tripod, and a further winged figure stands above. Below, on the body of the pot, are four friezes: on the shoulder horses move briskly to the right; next lions, moving left, attack a running man and a hind; under them three chariots process to the right, and finally a row of half-figures, armed with helmets and round shields, move left.

It is the scene on the neck of this vessel that has provoked most discussion. Who are these winged figures? One god is shown emerging from the head of another in classical iconography when the birth of Athene from Zeus is depicted. There is no doubt that the story of Athene's birth was one familiar in seventh-century BC Greece, and the armed figure emerging from the head suits the martial aspects of Athene, which are stressed in the *Theogony*'s account of the birth. Yet the clean-shaven and rather feminine seated figure here has nothing in common with Zeus in later iconography, wings are no stable attribute of either Zeus or Athene, and the subsidiary figures elude obvious identification. Scholars have suspected oriental influence, but although the wings can be closely paralleled in oriental artefacts the overall composition seems as unexampled outside as inside Greece.

The frontal face and raised arms of the seated figure evoke the frontal figure of the 'Mistress of the Animals' found on other relief *pithoi* of the same period, and it is tempting to suggest that that association is played upon here, particularly in view of the frieze of horses on the neck which is very similar to that found on the 'Mistress of the Animals' *pithos*. What our *pithos* does, however, is to introduce both human craft and violence into the picture. The figures which flank 'Zeus' offer images of man's positive use of craft, and in particular metalworking, skills – the sickle and the tripod. The arms of 'Athene' introduce the more negative side. Athene is balanced in the lowest frieze by similarly helmeted warriors, and in between we see men harnessing nature to their service, in the charioteers, and man pitched against nature, in the lion attacking a man. Taken together, these scenes explore the hierarchy of gods, humans, and beasts, with the possibilities of progression both upwards and downwards that the central position of humanity and the special gifts of gods to humans involve. The ambiguity as to the gender of 'Zeus' and 'Athene' in the scene on the neck is crucial in promoting this wider-ranging exploration of the relationship between gods, humans, and the natural world. The power that is at issue here is certainly not merely male military and political power.

Not all seventh-century BC art is of the quality or complexity of these two vessels, nor is the artistic revolution one which happens overnight. But the sense of art as a way of exploring the world, rather than a way of summarily describing it, and the sense of viewing as a way of thinking, is one very frequently forced on the viewer by the products of the seventh century BC, and from all over the Greek world. Just as the Homeric epics are marked by their awareness of the problems with conventional values, and the possible clashes within accepted value-systems, and just as Hesiod struggles to produce a coherent relationship between the world of the gods and the human world, so the visual arts in the seventh century BC grapple with human relationships and relations between human, animal, and divine worlds in a way not familiar in geometric art. The means with which they do so, large-scale and fully articulated human figures, explicit invocation of a natural setting in the use of decorative motifs derived from the natural world, even certain detailed iconography, do derive from near-eastern examples, but the results are very difficult to parallel in the near east itself.

The uses of the oriental

There have been many occasions already in this book when Greeks have been seen to take over technologies and imageries from parts east. The poetic traditions which must have bulked large in Greek life in at least some areas of the Greek world in the eighth century and before owed something, if only in the rather distant Bronze Age past, to traditional stories circulating in parts east – there are even some grounds for thinking that the *Odyssey* and the Indian *Mahabharata* have a common ancestor. In the poetic tradition the case for conscious exploitation of this eastern legacy is an arguable one (above, pp. 135–6), but there can be no doubt that in other areas the exoticism of recognisably imported devices had been deliberately employed to make a particular kind of communication. Already in the ninth century BC Greek jewellery took advantage of access to eastern crafts, and probably eastern craftsmen, both in articulating very un-eastern forms with granulation and filigree and in producing some very un-Greek forms (above, p. 62). In the eighth century the élite seem to have used both the alphabet and the ways of presenting animal forms which they had learnt from the east to set themselves apart, particularly in the competitive context of private social gatherings (above, pp. 104 and 109). And we should not ignore the evidence from the east that Greek goods functioned as precisely similar exotica, becoming items sufficiently fashionable to acquire a social role which gave them a value well in excess of that which they possessed back in the Greek homeland (cf. above, p. 105).

Down to around 700 BC both Greek use of the eastern and eastern use of the Greek seem to have been limited to the private domain. Public use of Greek motifs in the east would have to wait for several centuries; but from around 700 BC onwards Greek use of eastern motifs occurs in increasingly public contexts. There is little doubt that eastern motifs became the touchstone of the new view of the world which was involved in the scrapping of geometric forms and geometric decoration, not simply in pottery but in metalwork too. This was not because Greeks did not know about such motifs until after 700 BC, but because only after about 700 BC did the mass of people desire to achieve what the eastern tool enabled. We must appreciate both sides of the chicken and egg problem here: that without the means which exotic arts provided, Greek craftsmen would have been unable to forge a new vision of the world; but without the sense that there was a new vision to be seen, the

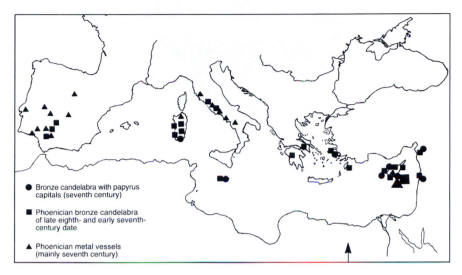

Figure 40 The distribution of eighth-century Phoenician candelabra with that of seventh-century Phoenician metal vessels and 'candelabra' with papyrus leaf capitals.

eastern imagery would lie around unused – as the alphabet had not been used until the eighth century, although some Greeks must have come into contact with it as early as the twelfth century. Once eastern motifs became fashionable the signs are that home production of the exotic actually reduced demand for exotic goods themselves: certainly the distribution of seventh-century Phoenician bronze jugs and bowls misses out Greece in a way that the distribution of eighth-century Phoenician candelabras does not (Figure 40).

One further, rather humble example will serve to illustrate what was happening. There is no doubt that the motif of two facing animals which join in a single frontal head is one which appears in the east before it appears in Greek art (Figure 42). It is but one of the many faces of the monstrous which Greeks in the seventh century took from or developed out of oriental originals. Those monsters, some resembling real animals, others bearing no resemblance at all, invaded objects of all sorts. They came to characterise Corinthian pottery of the second half of the seventh century, and particularly to characterise small Corinthian pots. Many of the pots with animal friezes went with a certain lifestyle, for they were characteristically pots for perfume or jugs for wine (Figure 41). The pots for perfume adapted one of the few Phoenician pottery shapes to make headway in the Greek world, and in the wake of the perfume came the context for its use – the practice of reclining on couches at the small male drinking parties which themselves seem to have been a feature of Greek life by the early eighth century (above, p. 109).

The monsters which cheerfully decorate these Corinthian jugs and jars escaped from the confines of a lifestyle that wanted to advertise itself as eastern. The frontal heads had already migrated to the shields of the soldiers

Figure 41 Seventh-century Corinthian *olpe*, found on Rhodes.

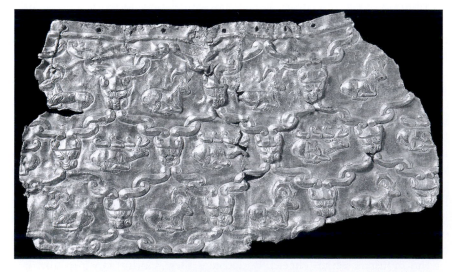

Figure 42 Fragment of gold belt, Iron Age, eighth to seventh century BC, perhaps from Ziwiyeh, north-west Iran.

on the Chigi vase, and to the face of the divinity on the Xobourgo *pithos*, and the extravagant overequipment with two bodies was gradually transformed until the frontal head was provided with wings, arms, the legs of a wild beast, and the tail of a fish in a sixth-century product, perhaps of Greek craftsmen in Italy or Sicily, which seems eclectically to borrow from oriental and Skythian, as well as Greek traditions, rolling together figures of panic and fear in order the better to faze the enemy (Figure 43). As competition between members of the élite within a city developed into competition between cities, and as unstable relations within the human community introduced a new anxiety into the way people pictured the gods, the exotic became more than just a way of setting oneself apart as cosmopolitan; it became a vehicle by which a whole world of exciting but frightening new possibilities could be explored and exploited. And exploring those possibilities itself led to a vision of new problems and new possibilities, and in due course new elements of eastern culture were plundered to deal with this new situation (see below, pp. 195–8 for the next episode in this ongoing story).

A WORLD AT WAR

Arms and armour in the late eighth century BC

The Chigi vase brings us not only into a world viewed differently by its inhabitants, but into a world where wars are differently fought. That there

Figure 43 Bronze shield blazon from Olympia.

Figure 44 Early seventh-century Corinthian-style helmet, made at Corinth or in the Peloponnese, from Olympia.

was both fighting between individuals and warfare between communities throughout the Dark Age is not seriously in question. Dark Age graves frequently received weapons, though not armour, among the grave goods, and the transformation from a Bronze to an Iron Age is seen particularly graphically in the rapid and almost complete change from using bronze to using iron for swords. But of the nature of Dark Age warfare we are almost completely ignorant, beyond the little that can be deduced from the weapons themselves.

The first signs of change appear in the middle of the eighth century BC. Representation of warfare first occurs in late geometric Athenian pottery, where there are processions of armed men in carts or chariots, lines of infantry marching with their spears over their shoulders, and some scenes of rather mixed warfare in which archers and infantry seem both to be involved (cf. Figure 35). In scenes of actual fighting it is the sword which appears as the usual weapon, rather than the spear. Although no attempt seems to be made to show a particular battle scene, or even a particular type of battle, it is abundantly clear that fighting, and fighting in various ways, was both familiar and good to think with in late eighth-century Athens (see above, p. 127). At about the same time, two graves at Argos received heavy armour, in one case a bronze cuirass and a heavy bronze helmet with elaborate crest. These remain isolated finds; deposition of arms in graves generally dies out in the late eighth century, except in less politically developed areas of Greece, but from about the same date it is widely found in both 'state' and panhellenic sanctuaries,

How important was the introduction of the hoplite shield? As we have seen, there is good reason to think (and the *Iliad* does not contradict this; above, pp. 144–5) that fighting in massed infantry ranks was already *the* prime form of fighting in the late eighth century BC. Fighting in massed ranks implies that numbers are important: where mobility is limited the opportunities for the skills of an individual or a small group to outweigh significant inferiority in numbers are small. It seems improbable, therefore, that the hoplite shield seriously changed the priorities of the battle line, or seriously increased the need to mobilise as large a portion of the community as possible. But it may be the case that the introduction of the hoplite shield did do something to enable more to serve. Both the *Iliad* (2.529, 830) and archaic lyric poetry (Alkaios frg. 167 Page) attest to the wearing of corslets of linen, and by the classical period the bronze cuirass was becoming a rarity, and hoplites regularly went in to battle with relatively light body-armour. Arguably this move away from the heavy bronze cuirass was enabled by the introduction of the hoplite shield: for when each individual wielded his own, necessarily light, shield purely for his own protection he might feel the need for a second line of defence; but the protection offered by the heavy hoplite shield, and by the greater rigidity of line which it produced when used in a close-packed phalanx, may well have made heavy body-armour less essential. Scholars stress that either all or none of a line had to carry the hoplite shield, because it was no use some members of the line protecting only half of themselves if others in the line are not protecting the other half of them, but this argument is strongest when heavy body-armour is *not* also worn. It may be as important to note that, if used with close-packed ranks, the hoplite shield is the *only* piece of armour which a hoplite has to have: hoplites could be anything but uniform behind their hoplite shields, as the continuing experimentation with helmet types, breastplates, etc. clearly demonstrates. And unlike body-armour, the hoplite shield did not have to be made precisely to measure, but could be passed on from generation to generation.

How different was warfare in the later seventh century BC from warfare in the earlier part of the eighth century? In appearance the changes were certainly great: it is indeed no exaggeration to suggest that no item of armour was unchanged and that both strategies of warfare (how closely packed infantry ranks were), and tactics (the dominance of the thrusting spear) had been transformed. As to personnel, the changes may have been rather more subtle. The involvement of numbers as large as possible is likely to have been at a premium even before 750 BC, but the scope for the well-armoured to stand out in the line is likely to have been much reduced. Fighting in massed, but still loose, ranks may in reality, as in the *Iliad*, have allowed individuals to determine the overall success of the battle; the close-packed hoplite line was as strong as its weakest part. Arguably the focus of battle was now as much on the weak as on the strong, and community morale important as well as community numbers.

The changing world of war can be seen in the historical and literary traditions as well as in the archaeological and artistic record. It is best examined through scrutiny of the one city about which we are uniquely well informed by near-contemporary writings: Sparta.

SPARTA

Sparta has only a small place in my discussion of the eighth century BC. But excavations at the sanctuary of Artemis Orthia, at the Menelaion sanctuary of Menelaos and Helen, and elsewhere, along with the elegiac and lyric poetry of Tyrtaios and Alkman, mean that there is no city for which we have a richer seventh-century record – even without resorting to the later traditions which were so abundantly generated by this city, which was perceived as exceptional even by other Greeks.

Tyrtaios and Messenia

The exceptional control of another territory, Messenia, and the enserfment of its inhabitants as helots, dominated the history of classical Sparta. When exactly Sparta took control of Messenia, and how far the Messenians were a self-conscious group when conquered, are questions it is impossible to answer. But we have unusually good evidence for what the Spartans believed in the seventh century. The Spartans' need to keep control of a helot population, which they correctly believed to hate them, was not only an important factor in determining both foreign and domestic policy decisions but was made to justify current social arrangements and to explain their historical creation. To sustain these claims about their own past the Spartans seem to have repeatedly recited a selection of the poems by the seventh-century BC poet Tyrtaios in the communal dining groups (*sussitia*) to which all male Spartiates were obliged to belong. These poems enable us to share the Spartans' own picture of their history both immediately before and during Tyrtaios' own time.

Tyrtaios' preserved poems are dominated by war, with several long poems on what it is to be a good soldier (Text 24). And Tyrtaios' past is dominated by war too. He writes of the nineteen years which 'the fathers of our fathers' spent fighting for Messenia 'good to sow and good to plant' before they took it in the twentieth year (frg. 5 West). Tyrtaios emphasises the subjection which the Spartans imposed upon the defeated Messenians, 'like asses ground down by great burdens', who have to give up half their crops to their overlords (frg. 6 West).

Young men, fight keeping steadfastly by one another. Don't start shamefully running away and don't start to panic. Be stout-hearted and great-hearted, and when you are fighting against men don't dwell on how great life is. Don't flee and desert your seniors, the old men, whose knees are not so nimble.

Text 24: Tyrtaios frg. 10 (West) 15–20. Tyrtaios urges bravery in the hoplite phalanx.

In the second century AD, when Pausanias wrote his *Guide to Greece*, there was a whole enormous Messenian tradition about this war, and about a second Messenian war which occurred when the Messenians attempted to revolt and which took many, many years to quell (Pausanias 4.4–24). In the form Pausanias has it, the story was almost certainly heavily elaborated on, if not created, after the people of Messenia were liberated from Sparta in the fourth century BC, and there is some reason to think that the so-called second Messenian war was partly, if not entirely, invented out of Tyrtaios' exhortatory poems. These poems do not, as preserved, mention Messenians at all; it is purely convention that connects them with another Messenian war, rather than with the conflicts with other Peloponnesian cities about which Herodotos was evidently told in the fifth century BC. Pausanias' account offers a fascinating insight into the creation of a distinct community identity in response to political independence bestowed by outside intervention, but is of extremely dubious value for the writing of Spartan history.

The Lykourgan constitution

Tyrtaios himself may already have made the connection between successful war and a well-ordered political constitution which was certainly stressed by fifth-century BC Spartans, as Herodotos' account (1.65) shows. For, in a poem entitled 'Good order' (*Eunomia*), he may have associated the adoption or the adaptation of an agreement about the relative powers of kings, council of elders (*gerousia*), and people, with the reign of the same king, Theopompos, in whose reign Messenia was conquered. This agreement survives not simply in Tyrtaios' paraphrase but in a direct quotation, almost certainly lifted from Aristotle's *Constitution of the Lakedaimonians*, in Plutarch's *Life of Lykourgos* 6 (Text 25). Known as the 'Great Rhetra', this agreement provides, in somewhat obscure language, for regular meeting at a fixed location of an assembly with powers to make decisions, powers which might be set aside by kings and elders. Tyrtaios' paraphrase seems to guarantee that this agreement was already in place before his own time, making it the first certain constitutional regulation to survive from archaic Greece, but in structure and concerns it is closely to parallel to early regulations elsewhere (see below, pp. 174–7).

By the time that Herodotos wrote in the fifth century BC, Spartan tradition held that the constitutional arrangements which then prevailed had been established by a lawgiver named Lykourgos and derived by him either from the Delphic oracle or from Crete (Herodotos 1.65). Lykourgos is not mentioned in the poems of Tyrtaios which survive, and it seems very unlikely that he was mentioned in any poems of Tyrtaios at all. Herodotos quotes a Delphic oracle which expresses uncertainty as to whether Lykourgos was a god or a man, suggesting perhaps a god. This may reflect Sparta asking the oracle whether cult should be paid to Lykourgos, a question that would itself have been part of an attempt to give Lykourgos' laws the most prestigious possible pedigree. The more exalted Lykourgos' status, the stronger the argument against making any changes to them. That argument was involved seems likely from the disagreement between Herodotos, writing in the late fifth century, and Aristotle (*Politics* 1313a25–33), writing a century later, over whether the five annual magistrates known as ephors were created by Lykourgos or were a later creation of Theopompos. Ephors are apparently not alluded to in the 'Great Rhetra', and it may indeed be their absence there that fuelled the case of those who wanted to maintain, almost certainly correctly, that the constitution of Sparta had not remained unchanged from the day it was instituted. How the developed constitution at Sparta worked will be further discussed later (pp. 289 and 316–7).

But if the constitutional settlement at the end of the eighth century BC came to be elaborated on for political purposes, the same is almost certainly true of Spartan settlement abroad at that time. In a fascinating story (Strabo 6.2.2–3), which goes back at least to the fifth-century historian Antiokhos, the settlement of Spartans at Taras (Taranto in the heel of Italy) at the end of the eighth century BC is said to have occurred after children, born to the wives of those fighting the Messenians during the absence of their husbands and hence known as Partheniai (maiden sons), were deprived by the victorious returning soldiers of political rights, and, becoming potentially rebellious, were persuaded to settle abroad (see below Text 31). Lakonian material of this date at Taras confirms that there was a connection, but for the archaic period there is no evidence that Taras had particularly strong links with Sparta, either in political or in material terms, though in the sixth century BC there is more

Lykourgos was so keen on this constitution that he brought an oracle from Delphi about it, which they call a 'rhetra'. It goes like this: 'Having founded a temple of Zeus Skullanios and Athena Skullania, having formed tribes and obes, having established a council of elders numbering thirty together with the leaders of the people, hold regular meetings of the *apella* (feast of Apollo) between Babuka and Knakion, and use this to introduce measures and reject measures. Power and right to speak (?) belong to the people.' In this forming tribes and obes means dividing the people and distributing them into groups, some called tribes and some obes. The 'leaders of the people' are the kings, and the *apella* is the assembly, for the whole motive and organisation are ascribed to the Delphic oracle. They now call Babuka and Knakion Oinous, but Aristotle says that Knakion is a river and Babuka is a bridge. They held the assembly in the middle of these, without any colonnade or other structure. He thought these made no contribution to wise counsel, but rather harmed it, producing a disposition to be talkative and spongy-minded in those who were assembled, whenever they sat in the assembly looking at statues or paintings or theatre scenery or highly decorated council-house roofs. When the people gathered he permitted none of the others to speak, but the people had the power to decide upon the proposals made by the kings and elders. Later the masses changed and transformed decisions by adding and taking away elements, and the kings Polydoros and Theopompos added this to the rhetra: 'If the people make a crooked decision, the oldest in birth and the leaders of the people can be setters-aside.'

Text 25: Plutarch, Lykourgos *6.1–8. Plutarch's exposition of the Great Rhetra.*

Lakonian pottery there than on other south Italian sites. That there were indeed some Spartan settlers is not in question, but the story of how they came to settle may well be an invention in order to claim that the last time Spartan internal relations had been marked by serious conflict was at the time of the Messenian wars, and before 'Lykourgos' had done his work. The value of the story for Taras emerges in the fourth century BC and hellenistic periods when the Tarentines on several occasions asked for and got military commanders from Sparta.

The nature of Spartan society

Can we get behind these later traditions to what was really the situation in early seventh-century Sparta? Crucial is the question of whether the social order of seventh-century Sparta was the result of conscious changes or was a survival of a pattern which was general in the Dark Age, but which died out elsewhere (see above, pp. 71–3). On the one hand, the Great Rhetra does seem good evidence that there was some conscious reform at Sparta on the political front; on the other, nothing in the Rhetra has any significant bearing on the strict organisation of education in year-groups or the communal dining groups, to which full Spartiates had to belong and to contribute dues of food, and which are so striking a feature of classical Spartan life. Those who want to see these features of Spartan life as 'survivals' of primitive social arrangements have sometimes appealed to the presence of similar social organisation in other warlike societies, such as the Zulu. That parallelism might itself be employed in more than one argument, for the association of age-class organisation with military pressure is entirely compatible with the argument that the traumatic experience of fighting the Messenians for twenty years was the catalyst for reorganisation at Sparta. But in any case the parallelism seems essentially superficial: age-class societies in the anthropological record are very strongly associated with stateless societies without leaders. Whatever was invented at the end of the eighth century BC in Sparta, the unique dual kingship was not, neither archaic nor Dark Age Sparta can really be supposed to have been leaderless, and, although important for military training and organisation, year-groups never played more than an indirect and peripheral role in Spartan political life.

The suggestion that the Spartan social, as well as the Spartan political, order was indeed the product of late eighth-century decisions seems, however, to get some support from the archaeological record. As we have seen earlier (p. 87), the Spartan sanctuaries of Orthia, on the west bank of the Eurotas, and of Menelaos and Helen, on a height a short distance east of the Eurotas, are among the many Greek sanctuaries which display an enormous increase in the number of objects dedicated between the late eighth and the seventh century BC. Among the objects first found dedicated at the Orthia sanctuary in the seventh century is a class virtually unique to this sanctuary: terracotta face-masks (Figure 45). These masks, found in significant numbers in the

Figure 45 Mask from Sanctuary of Orthia at Sparta.

seventh century BC and then in very large numbers in the sixth (603 separate noses can be counted in all), present something of an enigma. Although there are some general similarities with masks found in the Phoenician and Punic worlds (but never in large quantities, and in the Punic world in tombs, not sanctuaries), the origin of the masks is uncertain. Some of the masks could be worn, but significant numbers have no pierced holes for eyes or are too small to fit a human face. The masks are quite various in their features, and although they do to some extent fall into types, archaeologists are by no means agreed as to the appropriate typology. In the face of so many uncertainties, speculation as to the significance of the masks can only be tentative. We might expect, however, that the different context in which they are found means that, even if the masks were formally influenced by Phoenician masks, their role was not determined by the model; that even if these are purely votive objects they correspond to some ritual or event in life in which changed appearance was central; and that that ritual or event was one very widely shared within the society. Dramatised changes in life are very clearly involved in organisation by age-classes, which move a child from one category to another, and eventually into full adulthood, in a way which has a more or less arbitrary relationship to gradual physical development. It is attractive, therefore, to see the masks as reflecting, directly or indirectly, the ceremonial involved in moving from one age-class to another, and their first appearance as an indication of the invention, or at least the elaboration, of such ceremonial.

Further support for the idea that ceremonial involving year-groups became increasingly important in the course of the seventh century may come from the poetry of Alkman. His poetry, like that of Tyrtaios, achieved classic status at Sparta and seems to have been continually reperformed; for Aristophanes (*Birds* 251, *Lysistrata* 1296–315), Alkman's lyrics were *the* choral poetry of Sparta. But Alkman's poetry contained no references to contemporary political or military life, and was not easily transferable to societies which lacked the equivalent choral contexts; it was little quoted by later writers. As a result our knowledge of his poetry is largely dependent upon fragments of papyrus excavated in Egypt. The poems preserved in these fragments, and in particular the poems known as *Partheneia* (Maidensongs), although in many ways as enigmatic as the masks, cast a startling light on seventh-century BC Spartan society. The striking thing about the *Partheneia* is not simply that they are songs sung by girls' choruses, but that the girls sing about themselves, identifying and commenting on named individuals (Text 26). The poems reveal the girls in the chorus to be bound together in a relationship that is both competitive and passionate, strongly implying that they do not simply come together for occasional dances but that they live lives intimately bound together. That the young girls who engaged in choral dancing had such a relationship does not necessitate that young men were similarly grouped, but given the social organisation familiar from classical Sparta this evidence about girls seems good evidence that young men were already so organised in the seventh century BC. But what it is even better evidence for is the central importance which Sparta gave to the education of young women. The intensity of association between women which Alkman's poems demonstrate is not compatible with a society in which women were simply breeding machines, which is how classical Sparta is sometimes represented. This is a society which takes seriously female fulfilment, and reckons to integrate women as much as men into the life of the city.

Whether we choose to conceive of a single moment of radical social and political change in Sparta in the late eighth century BC, or of a series of changes which successively elaborate both the political and the social structure, there seems good reason to believe that life in Sparta was transformed between, say, 725 and 625 BC. By the late seventh century it is probable that there was already in place something like the full classical apparatus of military organisation, involving a variety of military units – tribes and obes, *lokhoi*,

---

There is such a thing as the gods' punishment. Prosperous is the man who weaves his days happy at heart and with no cause for mourning. But I sing the radiance of Agido. She seems to me like the sun, which Agido summons to shine upon us. The famous leader of our chorus will not let me praise or blame Agido. For she seems outstanding, as if one were to set in a meadow a sturdy horse which wins contests with its thundering hooves, such a horse as one sees as one dreams in the shade of a rock. Do you not see? The racehorse is from Venice; the hair of my cousin Hagesikhora blooms like undefiled gold, her silver face – why am I telling you so explicitly?

Text 26: Alkman, frg. 1.36–56. An extract from Alkman's Partheneion *in which the singer celebrates the other members of the female chorus.*

Figure 46 Early sixth-century lead model hoplite dedications from the Othia sanctuary.

and *enomotiai* – employing hoplite armour and tactics (from *c*.650 BC at the Orthia sanctuary, and from *c*.600 BC at the Menelaion, model hoplites were dedicated in very large numbers: Figure 46), and also at least the beginnings of the educational organisation referred to in later sources as the *agoge*, in which boys from the age of 7 up underwent a strict military training in year-groups referred to by different names, culminating in the *eirens* at 20. By the same date the full political organisation was probably also in place, with two kings, five annually elected magistrates known as ephors with considerable executive power and also influence, not least because they chaired the Assembly, and the *gerousia*, a council of twenty-eight elected elders which had judicial and perhaps deliberative powers (see below, pp. 289–90).

War and identity at Sparta

Warfare, and the exceptional and uneasy subjection of the population of Messenia, played a big part in this transformation of Sparta. But the conquest of Messenia itself demands explanation, particularly since the mountainous barrier between Lakonia and Messenia which is constituted by the Taÿgetos mountain range is rather more adequate than the physical boundaries between most other Greek cities. Land-hunger seems an extremely unlikely explanation for the conquest, particularly given the already exceptional size of Lakonia and paucity of archaeological evidence for Dark Age occupation there, and we should probably think more in terms of war as a means of community self-definition. This idea is made particularly attractive by the stark 'othering' of the Messenians through the helot status, which they were made visibly to parade with the dog-skin hats they had to wear. On this view of the war, the political and social reforms would be part of the war, rather than consequent upon it. And the evident inclusion of women in the intense group training, which can hardly have been done solely to produce fit mothers of strapping babies, points in the same direction. So too do the probability that Messenia was not the only part of the Peloponnese in which

Sparta interfered in the eighth century BC – there are signs of activity in Triphylia to the north of Messenia – and Sparta's continuing military activity in the seventh century.

Sparta's warlike activity in the seventh century BC is rather shadowy in our evidence. A tradition, found only in Pausanias (2.24.7), held that Sparta had been defeated by Argos in the battle of Hysiai in 669/8 BC. The site of this battle, in the most south-western part of Argive territory, indicates that the Spartans were the aggressors. That there was indeed war with Argos seems confirmed by references in the poetry of Tyrtaios. That there were wars elsewhere also is less clear, but Herodotos certainly was told of a long history of unsuccessful conflict with Tegea, her neighbour directly to the north, and there are other traditions of defeat by Orkhomenos, further north still (Theopompos *FGH* 115 F 69). Sparta's evident lack of success in these conflicts belies the claim made in the classical period that her new constitution brought her from weakness to strength; once more the wars should be seen as parallel to the constitutional changes, not causing them nor caused by them.

The forging of a distinct identity also emerges from the archaeological record. It is not just that mass dedication of masks is a particularly Spartan phenomenon, or that lead figurines are otherwise found only in places probably influenced by Sparta and in nothing like the same quantity (more than 100,000 were excavated from the Orthia sanctuary alone). Sparta readily latched on to fashions from elsewhere in the seventh century BC but then developed them in particular ways. This can be seen in relatively humble developments, such as pottery: moulded *pithoi* show, in shape and decorative scheme, their awareness of traditions in such pottery from the eighth century BC on, but develop in the late seventh and sixth centuries in distinct ways; painted pottery borrows many devices, motifs, and techniques from other Greek styles, particularly Corinthian and east Greek, but employs them in new combinations and on unique shapes. The same can be seen in luxury goods, most notably ivory. Sparta was one of only two places in the Greek world, the other being Ephesos, which imported unworked ivory from the east and developed a school of ivory carving. Relatively few finished imported ivories have been found in Sparta, and there seems to have been a strong preference for importing the raw material and turning it into distinctly Lakonian products, some of which were then re-exported (including perhaps Figure 51).

Sparta certainly stood out in many ways from other cities in the seventh century BC, but, if the definition of the community there took forms not easy to parallel elsewhere in totality or in detail, that does not mean that the desire to define the community, both with regard to other communities and with regard to individuals within it, was unique. The changes in armour and the tactics and strategy of war, discussed above (p. 164), which are apparent in other communities as early as they are apparent in Sparta, can be seen to be part of just such a concern with self-definition. So too, Sparta's constitutional law may be precocious, but it can be widely paralleled by the end of the seventh century BC.

LAW, CONSTITUTIONS, AND EXTRA-CONSTITUTIONAL RULE

In Sparta the community was defined, and so strengthened in the face of war, both through the Great Rhetra and through fighting the wars themselves. In other communities similar community definition was achieved by adopting laws through experiments in new forms of political dominance. Both the making of law and the domination of political life by prominent individuals came to be used to point morals and adorn tales in later Greece, but the survival of some laws on stone, and the existence of some contemporary poetry which is politically involved, enable some picture of the seventh century BC to be recovered even in this area which archaeology does little directly to illuminate.

Limitations on magisterial power

The earliest inscribed law to survive from Greece is probably that from the temple of Apollo at Dreros in east central Crete (for which see above, p. 85) and thought to date to the second half of the seventh century BC. This law (Figure 47; ML 2/Fornara 11) maintains that anyone who has held the (presumably annual) office known as *kosmos* cannot hold that office again for ten years, and that if he makes any judgements they are to be invalid and he is to be fined and deprived of civic rights. The enactment is announced as the decision of the *polis*, and it is sworn to by the *kosmos* and 'the Twenty of the Polis'. This law marks a concern to define the limits of authority in the city, and to declare that granting powers to an officer is not the same as granting them to an individual. It is not what the *kosmos* does when in office that is in question, but the limits to that office.

The concerns of this Cretan law can be paralleled in the rather fragmentary laws discovered at Tiryns in the Argolid, which also seem to date to the late seventh century BC (*SEG* 30.380). These laws reveal a large number of different officers, and concentrate on defining whose job it is to see that another magistrate does his job: so in one enactment the duties of the *platiwoinoi* (perhaps 'Pourers of Libations') are controlled by *platiwoinarkhoi* ('Officers in Charge of the Pourers of Libations') who in turn are controlled by the *hieromnemon* ('Sacred Remembrancer'), who is overseen by the people acting together, who in turn are overseen by an *epignomon* ('Arbiter'). This enactment is one of several, and, although it is clear from the fragments that the enactments together by no means went to make up any systematic code, it is unthinkable that, for instance, this 'back-stop' role was the only one

Figure 47 The law regulating the office of *kosmos*, from the temple of Apollo at Dreros on Crete. The law begins at the top right, and the lower piece originally joined the left-hand edge of the upper piece.

expected of the *hieromnemon*: we must be dealing here with an extensive attempt both to empower and restrict magistrates.

Two points need stressing about these early laws – points also true of laws moved in the sixth century BC which survive on stone. The first is that these laws show little or no interest in the relations between groups, whether status groups or social classes. Although the Tiryns law mentions the people, it treats the people simply as one more source of authority, a source as much to be regulated by another officer as itself a regulator of officers. We are in almost total ignorance about the Tiryns of this time, and do not know what was covered by the term used for the 'people' in this law, but there is no sign of divisions of the people by class or status. Similar treatment of the people appears in a sixth-century law from Olympia, according to which they may alter the law but only as long as the Council of Five Hundred agrees to the changes and that they do not change it more than three times (Buck 64), and in the setting aside of the decisions of the people in the Great Rhetra at Sparta (above, p. 167 and Text 25): in these cases too the people are one source of authority but not the ultimate source.

The second point is that these laws are not concerned with the ultimate regulation of behaviour: frequently they do not decree what may or may not be done – they decree only who is to regulate what may or may not be done. Occasionally a particular offence is stipulated (a woman's wearing a brightly coloured robe in a sixth-century regulation from Arkadia or Akhaia

(*LSCG* 32, Buck 16); sexual intercourse in the sacred precinct in a sixth-century regulation from Olympia (Buck 64)), but even then the focus of the regulation is not on the offence, but on who should see that the appropriate measures are taken.

Together these two aspects of these laws strongly suggest that the purpose of the regulations was not to control the powers of the élite with regard to the people, nor to restrict the arbitrariness of those with authority, but to control the distribution of powers within the élite. This is élite self-regulation, motivated not by any sense of overwhelming injustice but by a concern about which individuals have power.

If we compare the picture conjured up by such laws as those quoted above with the picture we get from *Iliad* and *Odyssey* or *Works and Days* (for which see above, pp. 143 and 137–9) there is a contrast. In both *Iliad* and *Odyssey* the powers of individuals are ill-defined, and titles seem to have little in the way of technical meanings. In *Works and Days* only one magisterial title is in evidence, and that seems to carry vague, but extensive, powers. By contrast the Tiryns of these fragmentary laws have many magisterial titles, and the powers that follow from them are being very strictly regulated. Neither the *Odyssey*'s concern with how power is passed from one man of authority to another, nor the *Works and Days*' concern with how power is operated, are answered by these enactments. These are rather the enactments of an élite for an élite, concerned with how one officer relates to other officers, and that the powers are shared around the élite on terms that all can understand and that can be regulated.

We see another aspect of this élite concern with the behaviour of other members of the élite in the most extensive of all seventh-century-BC laws to come down to us, the homicide law of Drako (ML 86/Fornara 15B). This law has not survived as inscribed in the seventh century, but in an edited version re-enacted in Athens at the end of the fifth century BC as part of a general review and reinscription of Athenian law at that time. We need to be aware that, in the political atmosphere of the late fifth century, there was capital to be made from ascribing a law to Drako, but while it is clear that there has been some editorial intervention, nevertheless we can have some confidence that the re-enacted law on involuntary homicide bore a close relationship to the law enacted in the late seventh century. The opening of the law ('Even if someone kills another without premeditation, he shall be exiled') makes it look as if it is the killing that is regulated, but in fact the emphasis is not on the killing (there is no further definition of 'without premeditation', which is a translation of a word more usually translated 'unwilling'), it is on who has the right to grant pardon and who the right to prevent pardon being granted. This is not a law about homicide as such, but about the extent of the family which can pursue vendetta, and the ways in which conditions can be made safe for the homicide's return to the community. It is a law which aims to end the situation where any killing leads the perpetrator to a life of wandering exile, such as is frequently glimpsed among displaced persons in *Iliad* and

Odyssey. Although this law applies equally to all involuntary homicides, it is easy to see that it is of most importance in cases where the person involved might return to a position of some authority.

Traditions about early lawgivers

Traditions about early lawgivers, including Drako, tend, however, to look rather different. Not only do they regularly involve scenes, which migrate freely from one lawgiver to another, in which the lawgiver gets caught by his own laws, but they put the stress on peculiar things regarded as offences and peculiar punishments meted out. So, Drako was widely remembered for the severity of his penalties for offences, and Aristotle, in his rapid survey of the contribution of various lawgivers at the end of *Politics* 2, records that Pittakos of Mytilene increased the penalty for violence if it was committed when drunk. Scepticism about the existence of some of these lawgivers, as about Lykourgos at Sparta, goes back to antiquity, and we can rarely have any confidence that we can strip away invention from tradition or distinguish genuine from invented elements within a tradition. But two points can be noted. The first is the number of stories in which the lawgiver is made an outsider to the community to which he gives laws: to mention only examples given by Aristotle, Philolaos, reputedly one of the Bakkhiad aristocracy of Corinth, makes laws for Thebes; Androdamas of Rhegion gives laws to the Khalkidians of Thrace. The second point is that, for all the interest in morals and curiosities, two concerns seem particularly prominent in the laws cited as examples: procedure and property. In the case of Kharondas of Katane, for example, Aristotle picks out his procedure for prosecution for false witness as his special contribution, and also mentions his fining the rich if they did not man the courts, but letting the poor off; in the case of Philolaos Aristotle selects his law about adoption, and expressly identifies it as a measure to preserve the number of estates. Nor are these simply Aristotelian concerns: Aristotle's pupil Theophrastos cited laws of both Pittakos and Kharondas on sale, and Aristotle's older contemporary, the historian Ephoros, cited regulations on contracts by Zaleukos.

The consequences of written law

The particular interests and limited scope of early laws are important in one more general debate, the debate over the role of literacy (see p. 104 above). It was already a standard claim in classical Athens (e.g. Euripides, *Suppliant Women* 433–7) that written law protected democracy, and writing became very much associated with the supposed fixity of law, a fixity which is part of the etymology of our 'statute' and was similarly part of the etymology of the Greek term *thesmos*. But fixing the words of a law in writing does nothing to guarantee that those words are operated in a consistent or 'just' way: the very same orators who celebrate the democratic writing of law themselves use appeals to the lawgiver's intention in order persuasively to redefine those laws. Law can regulate only what it is possible for a community to enforce, and whatever their personal interests or wisdom, lawgivers can only bring into effect what those in the community who have power see it as in their interests to support (as the Skythian Anakharsis observes to Solon in the fictional story in Plutarch, *Solon* 5.2).

In as far as extant laws and plausible traditions enable us to gain a picture of what early lawgivers did, that is a picture not of the interests of inspired individuals but of the interests of the élite. Societies could be regulated by custom while they remained homogeneous, but the increasing competition between individuals and groups which is manifest in the eighth century BC had destroyed such homogeneity; if there was to be any effective regulation from this point on it had to be by law, by rules which the competing bodies agreed to enter into. The significance of the making, writing up, and, within limits no doubt, keeping of law lies in the willingness it represents in an élite to regulate their relationships with each other and with the rest of the community. To agree to laws is to accept a degree of homogeneity, to subordinate the separate interests of family or other group to the unity of the community. As law is made, the Agamemnon of the *Iliad* admits defeat.

To see early law as heavily embedded in conflict among the élite not only emphasises the lack of distinction between laws and constitutions – relations of political power being only one of the areas of inter-personal relations in which the whole community took an interest – but also shows up such law as the formal side of the intense and antagonistic relations within the élite which are revealed in surviving seventh-century BC lyric and elegiac poetry. The foremost examples of such antagonism are to be found in the poetry of Alkaios of Mytilene, whose life spans the end of the seventh and beginning of the sixth century BC, and in the lines ascribed to Theognis of Megara, a collection of material, including some also separately preserved under the name of other archaic poets, which seems to include both seventh-century BC and rather later contributions.

Alkaios, Theognis, and quarrels among the élite

The extant remains of Alkaios' poetry and those of Theognis are markedly contrasted. Of Alkaios' work we have but scraps, some literally scraps preserved on fragments of papyrus in Egypt and others scraps quoted by later authors, often in the context of reconstructing Alkaios' life from his poetry. The corpus of Theognis, on the other hand, consists of more than 1,000 lines preserved as continuous in a relatively rich manuscript tradition. As a result, Alkaios' fragments provide fitful, if passionate, illumination of the concerns of the circle for whom he wrote, while Theognis' lines give a good indication of what was generally at issue among the Megarian élite.

Theognis' world is a world of violence and turmoil, where desire for wealth overcomes loyalty to kin and friends, and where even possession of landed property is liable to be under threat. It is a world in which wealth is a prerequisite for social standing: poverty renders even the man who has knowledge voiceless (669–718, cf. 649–52), and the wealthy can command noble marriage partners whatever their own pedigrees (183–92). Competition within this élite is intense, and those who are on the winning side have to be urged to moderation and warned that the consequences of pursuing their superiority by outraging and dishonouring others will be open civil strife, leading to seizure of power by an individual who will dishonour all (39–52, 1081–1082b). Justice, straight actions, and the virtues of listening to the wise can all be appealed to (27–8, 543–6, 563–6, 753–6, 805–10), both as ideals and to get one's own way (337–50), but the wisdom needed for survival encompasses cunning intelligence, the intelligence of the octopus 'which appears to the sight like whatever rock it clings to' (215–16). Individuals are pulled between loyalty and the need to adapt to the way the wind blows; few can be trusted (73–4, 101–12, Text 27), and even the man who steers clear of enemies can find himself betrayed (575–6). In Theognis, as in Alkaios, sailing and the sea provide an extremely rich fund of imagery, which can encompass both the personal circumstances of the intoxicated individual and the reeling of a city where good order is threatened by private interests, where those who have goods on board have overthrown the pilot and give orders themselves (675–80).

Although particular lines are addressed to a certain Kyrnos, the elegiac verses of Theognis are rarely specific in their allusions, making them both hard to date and of little use for constructing a political narrative (the ancient disagreement as to whether Theognis belonged to mainland Megara or Megara Hyblaia in Sicily cannot be resolved). In this they contrast markedly with the fragments of Alkaios, whose involvement in the affairs of his city was surely close, even if not all the biographical deductions made by ancient and modern scholars are to be believed, and who alludes to named individuals. But however particular Alkaios' own situation, the political turmoil to which he alludes is strongly reminiscent of that found in Theognis. He rejoices in the death of one dominant political figure (a certain Myrsilos, frg. 332), laments the way popular support has put in a

May no person persuade you, Kyrnos, to have a worthless man as a friend. What benefit is a coward as a friend? He would not save you from difficulty and calamity, and he would not have any good to give in exchange. There is scant hope of grateful returns for the man who helps cowards: he might as well sow the expanse of the grey salt sea, for neither would the man who sows the sea reap a deep harvest, nor would he who helps worthless men take good in return. Worthless men can never be satisfied, and if you fail in one thing the friendship earned by earlier benefits is all poured away. But worthy men give the greatest reward for being well treated, they remember good deeds done and reciprocate with gratitude.

Text 27: Theognis 101–12. On choosing the right friends.

Father Zeus, the Lydians, indignant at what had happened, gave us two thousand staters to enter the sacred city, even though they had never experienced or even known any good turn from us. But he, like a tricky fox, thought it would be easy, and expected to escape notice…

Text 28: Alkaios 69. The beginning of a poem in which Alkaios boasted of some exploit against Pittakos. The rest of the poem is lost.

dominant political position Pittakos, a man of dubious origin (frg. 348), urges action to stop his outrages (frg. 306), and claims to have entered into a sworn undertaking to bring him down, since he has broken his oaths, and rescue the community from distress, even if the attempt means death (129). Alkaios signals the breakdown of the traditional rules of élite behaviour by striking lapses of decorum in the language of his verse. He paints himself as driven into exile, longing once more for political activity in council and assembly (128), taking money from the Lydians (69; Text 28) to force his way back to his city against the wiles of Pittakos the fox, and keen to stop quarrelling with others in order to make war on Pittakos (117). There is little in Alkaios of the appeal to justice, straightness, and moderation found in Theognis, indeed no sense that anything is at issue except personal rivalries for political power. Alkaios can lament the follies of the community in allowing Pittakos power and regret the trouble which Pittakos' rule brings on them, but there is no sign that his own ambitions are other than to see that power is in the hands of himself and of the comrades whom he addresses and with whom he swears to take vengeance.

Tyranny

The contemporary evidence of Theognis and Alkaios is vital to our understanding of political developments in the seventh century BC. Theognis observes that what civil strife produces is men who rule on their own (*mounarkhoi*, 52); Alkaios refers to the position in which the community has put Pittakos as *tyrannos* (frg. 348). Both clearly associate rule by one man with outraging the whole community (Alkaios frg. 306, Theognis 1181–2). *Tyrannis* (rule by a *tyrannos*), as was already noted in the fifth century BC, was a word first found in the mid-seventh-century poetry of Arkhilokhos of Paros. Arkhilokhos used it in a much-cited poem in which he denied that he yearned for anything – not for the wealth of Gyges, nor for the ability to act like the gods, nor for great *tyrannis*. Whatever the origin of the word, which is obscure, there is no doubt that it was first employed in the seventh century BC and that it was used to refer to a new political phenomenon.

What exactly was the new political phenomenon which merited the name *tyrannis*? The evidence surveyed so far in this chapter suggests that the continuing process of community self-definition led, during the later eighth and the seventh century BC, to changes in the quantity and quality of warfare, which at least weakened the link between the very wealthy élite and success in war, and to more formal regulation and limitation of the powers exercised by individuals. The way in which at least some of the laws are framed strongly suggests that the pressure for regulation came from within the élite, and that it should be seen as the other side of the strife between élite factions to which Alkaios and Theognis attest. The Dreros law illustrates this well: it is holders of other offices who have the key part in enforcing the limits to the powers of the *kosmos*. The definition of powers and their abuse go together; regulations are only as strong as the authority which enforces them, and they actually provide clear markers by which success in the pursuit of personal advantage and personal enmities can be measured. Where there is bitter mutual distrust, a long legacy of resentment, and no traditional source of authority that can summon cautious or sentimental conservatism to its aid, the path to openly ignoring any rules is clear, and the only security comes from establishing personal rule.

Political control in a large number of Greek cities fell, for longer or shorter periods during the seventh and sixth centuries BC, into the hands of a single man. At Mytilene ancient scholars used the poems of Alkaios to reconstruct a series of sole rulers: Melankhros, Myrsilos, Pittakos, three successive coups bringing men who were not related to one another to power. At Corinth, too, there were said to have been three successive tyrants, but from a single family line: Kypselos, Periander, and Periander's nephew, named Psammetikhos by some sources, Kypselos by others. Few cities other than Sparta did not enjoy or endure some period with one man in overall control. It remains exceedingly difficult, however, either to account in detail for the successful coup of any particular tyrant or to characterise his rule. What contemporary evidence there is comes, as in the case of Alkaios, from opponents, who are free with their abuse over parentage, marriages, physique (Alkaios refers to Pittakos as pot-bellied), and so on, but offer little in the way of serious political analysis. Later traditions, the product of men for whom tyranny was politically undesirable and 'tyrant' was increasingly pejorative rather than descriptive, are concerned rather to warn about the ways in which individuals make the option of themselves as rulers plausible than to describe accurately what those historic tyrants did.

The tradition of the bad tyrant

What distorts our image of tyranny is not just that we are reliant upon those who thought one-man rule politically incorrect, but that succumbing to tyranny, allowing some rival to be the last man standing in the competition for power, involved shame. For the élite, the coup by one member was an outrageous act of insolence, which disgraced the rest; for the people, to be thought willingly to have endured arbitrary rule or accepted the breaking of community regulations was to have been guilty of belittling their own capabilities. Not only do tyrants personally have to be painted black, because tyranny is a bad thing, but the accession of one man to political dominance has to be explained away. Thus the shadow of the tyrant falls not only on his own person and deeds but also on the manner of his rise to power and the regime which he replaced.

Two further factors have had a big effect in shaping the traditions. The first is that the threat that one man, or a small group, might take over political control did not die out with the Persian wars. Greek states, both on the mainland and elsewhere, in both east and west, continued to experience periods of rule of a single individual who seized power. As a result tyranny was an important object of attention for those analysing varieties of government. So Aristotle, writing his *Politics* in the second half of the fourth century BC, constructed a typology of government in which there are both good and bad ideal types, and in which tyranny is the 'bad' version of monarchy (*Politics* 1279a32–b10). Aristotle both tried to explain at the theoretical level how and why good constitutions degenerate into bad ones, and chose from the traditions about the past to support his theoretical points (1305a6–28; 1310b12–1311b6). Like the popular use of stories about tyrants as political warnings, Aristotle's use of the traditions in *Politics* is one that encourages noting what can be universalised and discourages historical specificity – not that Aristotle was himself in a position to recover specific historical events from tradition.

The second factor of importance is that *tyrannis* became a concept which could be transferred from individuals who seized power to individuals who enjoyed legitimate rights to rule but ruled in an autocratic manner, and to cities which acted autocratically with regard to other cities. In the fourth century BC both Philip II of Macedon and Alexander the Great were presented as tyrants in speeches at Athens (Demosthenes 1.5, 17.4; Hypereides 2.8). Thucydides has both Athenians and their opponents describe Athens as a tyrant city in the fifth century (1.122.3, 124.3; 2.63.2; 3.37.2), and the Spartan 'empire' of the early fourth century could also be so presented (Demosthenes 20.70). This extension of the use of 'tyranny' ensured the continuing appropriateness of telling stories about archaic tyrants and gave a premium to telling stories that dwelt on illegitimacy, lawlessness, unrestrained power, and arrogance in its exercise.

It is against such a background that we must read even the earliest and fullest tyranny story. This is the story about Corinthian tyranny picked up by Herodotos at a time when Corinthians were already seeing Athens as a tyrannical power, and related by him in two separate elements: the taking and exercise of power by Kypselos and his son Periander, and the relations between Periander and his own sons. The story of the taking of power by Kypselos is put into the mouth of a Corinthian named Sokles (Herodotos 5.92), who tells it in order to dissuade the Spartans and their other allies from restoring Hippias to tyranny at Athens (see below p. 278). Sokles' story is of a Corinth in the hands of one family, the Bakkhiads, who are overthrown by the son of the lame daughter of one of their own number, whom none of the family was prepared to marry. The motif of the defective

Aristippos tells the following story about him, in the first book of his 'On ancient luxury': that his mother Krateia fell in love with him and slept with him secretly; and he enjoyed this. But when it became known he became harsh to all because of his pain at the discovery. But Ephoros records that Periander boasted that, if he were victorious at the Olympics in the four-horse chariot race, he would dedicate a gold statue. When he was victorious he did not have enough gold, and so, seeing the women adorned at some local Corinthian festival, he took their jewellery away and so sent off the statue. Some say that he wished the place of his burial to be unknown and so devised the following scheme. He ordered two young men to go by night along a road he showed them, to slay the man they met and to bury him. Then he told another four men to walk after these, to kill them and to bury them. And again a larger group after these. And so he himself met the first pair and was killed.

Text 29: Diogenes Laertios, Lives and Opinions of the Eminent Philosophers *1.96 on Periander.*

being the source of downfall to those who rejected it, familiar in many other Greek myths, of which the Oidipous myth is only the most famous, is developed through a series of oracles predicting the violent downfall of the Bakkhiads, and through a scene where an attempt to murder the baby Kypselos is foiled, first because the baby's smile unmans the murderers' resolve, and then by the mother cunningly concealing the baby in a beehive. Here we have both the characterisation of the preceding regime as narrow, unjust, and unpleasant, and the identification of the tyrant-to-be as marked out as special by oracles and by divine protection. Sokles then goes on to report briefly on the killings and property confiscations carried out by Kypselos and at length on the continuing murderous rule of his son Periander. Periander interprets the action of a fellow tyrant in cutting down all particularly tall ears in a cornfield as advice to make away with all who were in any way distinguished in the city, and his personal lack of control of his lusts and his greed and general outrageous behaviour extend to using armed men to strip all the women of Corinth of their finery, and to necrophilia with his wife. Ephoros in the fourth century BC explained that Periander stripped the women in order to get gold to make a statue to celebrate an Olympic chariot victory; and Aristippos would add incest with his mother Krateia to his record of sexual abuse (Diogenes Laertios 1.96; Text 29).

Periander's screwed-up relations with his family are at the centre of the other long Herodotean story (Herodotos 3.48–53). This story explains Corinthian enthusiasm to campaign against Samos in the late sixth century BC (see below, p. 263) in terms of the Samians having prevented Corinth from having 300 of the young men of Corcyra castrated by Alyattes king of Lydia because the Corcyreans had murdered Periander's son. The killing of Periander's son comes as the end of a family dispute, in which the son refuses to talk to his father because his father was responsible for his mother's death, is exiled to Corcyra, and is only persuaded to return to Corinth to take over on condition that Periander moves to Corcyra. The impossibility of reconciling the chronology of the story with independent chronological evidence, and the way in which a later author (Plutarch, *Moralia* 860b) was able to attribute the rescue of the boys to Knidos, not Samos, warn that this tale belongs to myth rather than history. This is a myth which not only characterises the tyrant as one who cannot even manage right relations with his own family, but also characterises the difficult relations between Corinth and Corcyra, her 'daughter' settlement, in terms of the difficult relations between tyrant and son, of the 'daughter's' willingness to kill the son to prevent rule by the father, and of the mother-city's willingness to have the future of the daughter settlement undermined by the castration of its young men.

The tradition of the good tyrant

Later writers have different versions both of the rise of Kypselos and of the character of Periander. Kypselos' coup can be painted as the act not of an outsider but of an insider – a man who gets hold of a high magistracy using his judicial powers in such a way as to get widespread support (*FGH* 90 F57, Nikolaos of Damascus from Ephoros). Periander can be portrayed (already by Aristotle, *Politics* 1284a26) as giving, rather than receiving, the cunning silent advice to remove all threats to one's control, his name is regularly to be found on lists of the 'Seven Sages', and he was credited with a poem 2,000 lines long (Diogenes Laertios 1.97: we owe much of our knowledge of traditions about sages to Diogenes' 'superficial and unreliable' *Lives of Eminent Philosophers* probably written in the third century AD).

Such variations in the stories about how tyrants got and operated power are regular. Despite Alkaios' complaints, Pittakos too enjoyed a reputation as a wise man; he was held to have composed songs, 600 lines of elegiac couplets, and a prose work *On Laws* (Diogenes Laertios 1.78–9); Aristotle (*Politics* 1285a29–b1) invokes Alkaios to show that Pittakos was an elected tyrant, an *aisymnetes*, and he was widely held to have resigned his position once he had sorted the political situation out. Already by Herodotos' time one story of cunning wise advice, in which a wise man draws attention to the Ionians' doing something militarily ridiculous in order to make the Lydian Kroisos aware that his own military plans are ridiculous, was attributed both to Pittakos (a chronological impossibility) and to another of the reputed sages, Bias of Priene. Many other such stories of cunning wisdom are attributed to Pittakos, some of them illustrating mildness as well as wisdom – he set free a man who had killed his son, saying 'It is better to pardon now than to repent later.' Nevertheless, more bloody trickery is part of his traditional character too: during a conflict with the Athenians Pittakos agreed to meet an Athenian Olympic champion in single combat, and then used a concealed net to capture and kill him.

Stories about tyranny enabled the critical consideration of basic political issues, not only in the context of the continuing threat of tyranny, not at all dead even in the classical period, and of more general problems of relations within the city, but also in the context of relations between cities. Focusing on one man makes it easier to see the interplay of the personal and the political, and renders visible issues of the violence and insolent behaviour of a ruling class, of what constitutes loyalty and what treachery. Had there been no tyrants, one can see why they might have been invented; even though there were tyrants, that did not stop the invention.

The temptation to pick and mix a selection of more or less plausible incidents chosen from the mass of tyranny stories needs to be resisted. A whole range of explanations for tyranny can be supported in that way: we might stress tyrants as outsiders, newly rich men from outside traditional aristocracies coming to power because of resentment at the narrowness of existing regimes; or we might stress tyrants as insiders, even as men converting hereditary but constitutional power into power contained by no tradition or convention (as with Pheidon of Argos, said by Aristotle to have started as king and become tyrant: *Politics* 1310b26–8); or we might stress popular support for figures who have acquired civil or military repute, particular in the context of changes in the way wars were fought; or we might stress the tyrant as the peace-maker, who puts an end to political infighting. The only firm base on which to build is the contemporary evidence, the direct evidence of Alkaios and Theognis, the indirect evidence of early codes of law. What that suggests is that tyranny stems from the tensions in communities attempting to police their own identity as a community in the face of the desire of those whose family or possessions give them power to act in ways which promote themselves at the expense of others. It was because tyranny challenged the limits of oligarchy that it so often became a move on the road to community self-regulation.

SETTLEMENTS AND MOBILITY

The eighth century BC was a time when communities were spreading themselves across the local landscape, establishing settlements and activity centres through the territory to which they laid increasingly formal claim. It was also a time when those who moved across the Mediterranean in search of desirable goods, and particularly metals, used the knowledge they had acquired to encourage others to join them in settling on coasts where Greeks had not until then been living (above, pp. 110–20). The seventh century saw a continuation of this activity abroad, but both abroad and, even more dramatically, at home, there seems to have been a change in focus.

Although there are literary claims that Greeks settled in the Black Sea, at Sinope and Trapezous, during the eighth century BC, and although Greek knowledge of the Black Sea by *c.*700 BC or shortly afterwards is assured by the Homeric poems, both the literary and the archaeological evidence point strongly towards eighth-century settlement abroad being focused in the west, in southern Italy and Sicily. There was further settlement in the west during the seventh century BC, but that century also saw Greeks settling in Egypt (and not just at Naukratis, *ANE* 641), in North Africa (see Chapter 1 for a discussion of the case of Cyrene), and in the north-east, in the Propontis and Black Sea. New settlements were also made relatively close to home, in the north Aegean.

Settlement in the north Aegean

The settlements in the north Aegean are particularly important for our understanding of continuing Greek settlement abroad. In the case of Thasos we have some contemporary evidence in the form of the poetry of Arkhilokhos. He famously claimed that 'the scum of all Greeks ran together to Thasos' (frg. 102), and portrayed the island as unattractive, 'crowned with bristling wild woodland like the back of an ass' (frg. 21) and not at all as desirable as the lands settled in south Italy (frg. 22; cf. 228). Archaeological evidence does show that the coming of the Greek settlers did disrupt the existing pattern of settlement by Thracians, and Arkhilokhos' own evidence is that the settlement had to be bargained and fought for (frgs 93a; 105, Text 30), and that the fight was carried over to the Thracian mainland opposite (frgs 5; 291). Few traditions about foundations contain allusions to such fighting, and the one tradition where fighting is reported is that about the foundation of nearby Abdera. In the case of Abdera, Herodotos (1.168) reports that the original leader of the settlers from Klazomenai in the middle of the seventh century BC was killed fighting Thracians, and Pindar refers to further fighting on the occasion of the Teian refoundation in the sixth century BC (*Paian* 2.59–70). Given the fighting and the lack of immediate attractions to which Arkhilokhos attests, it seems reasonable to speculate that the mineral resources, for which by the fifth century BC Thasos and this area of Thrace were famous, were the reasons for the seventh-century settlements. (Thasos is further discussed below, pp. 220–4.)

Settlement in south Italy

The settlement of Thasos suggests that the lure of special resources, and in particular metals, was now drawing some Greeks to seek their fortune in places

---

The way of saying one thing and indicating something different from what one says is called allegory. An example is Arkhilokhos, cut off in the Thracian crisis, likening war to the billows of the sea when he says: 'Look Glaukos! The waves of the deep sea are troubled, and a cloud stands around Cape Gyrai, the sign of a storm, and panic comes from unexpected events.'

Text 30: Herakleitos, Homeric Allegories *5.2. Herakleitos, writing perhaps in the first century AD, quotes some lines of Arkhilokhos (frg. 105 (West)).*

where they had to fight for a foothold. Others were beginning to investigate parts to the south and to the north-east, where there may have been stories of wealth but where there were no abundant metals. The implication of these two developments has to be that there were no longer immediate rich and easy pickings to be had from the west. That picture of increased competition in the west seems further supported by the decline of Pithekoussai in the seventh century BC, and by the number of sites in south Italy where Greeks seem to have joined native settlements rather than founding independent sites of their own. Three sites close together in the instep of Italy, Incoronata, Metapontion, and Policoro/Siris, all show Greek and native pottery together in the first half of the seventh century BC along with some 'Greek' building forms and some 'native' burial customs. In the second half of the century occupation at Incoronata ceased, and occupation at the other two sites markedly changed its character to become purely Greek in archaeological terms, and marked by evident public building. Interpretation of what was going on at any of these sites is difficult, and it is unlikely that the literary traditions which exist for Siris and for Metapontion can be made to illuminate the archaeology. It is plausible, however, that after a period of mutually beneficial coexistence Greek communities became more exclusive, and that this led to a showdown with the native population, a showdown with contrasting results in different cases. In the case of Metapontion, evidence for early sixth-century BC division of the land into regular-shaped lots strongly suggests that part of what was at issue may well have been exploitation of territory, as Greek settlers came less and less to rely on links back to Greece, and the exchange of goods with Greek cities, and more and more to rely on local resources. (On Metapontion see further below, pp. 224–7.)

The change of focus in the west from exchange to territory, which is paralleled in the way settlers in Libya in very much this same period started at Aziris but rapidly moved to Cyrene, may well account for the nature of the expansion of Greek settlement in Sicily. Early settlements in Sicily concentrated on the east coast, and were sometimes quite close together; seventh-century BC foundations (Gela, Selinous, Kamarina, and Himera, all with extensive territories) turn the corner and spread west along the south and north coasts. Where the eighth-century BC settlements can be seen still to look back to the Greek mainland, as well as to each other, the new settlements arguably look inwards. Is it by chance that Gela and Selinous, like the seventh-century BC settlement at Paestum in south Italy, rapidly established a monumental presence, in the form of impressive sanctuaries, such as only Syracuse among the older settlements ever seems to have indulged in (see below, pp. 248–50)? Such sanctuaries made the new town a focus for the surrounding countryside and dominated that countryside, and at the same time they made the town the centre for display. Here were towns whose ruling élites were keen to make an impression at home, and whose focus was not on glory, or profits, achieved elsewhere.

Changing settlement patterns in the Greek homeland

The change in focus of settlement at home seems to reflect different issues and different pressures. Although archaeological surface survey has as yet only imperfectly revealed archaic settlement patterns, three contrasting patterns of development seem to be visible: areas where settlement in the countryside increases, areas where it decreases, and areas, such as Boiotia, where it never even begins.

In some parts of the Greek world, and at present the clearest cases are the southern Argolid and some islands in the Cyclades, the seventh century BC seems to have been a period of settlement expansion, a period when occupation is attested for the first time at an increasing number of places in the landscape. This certainly seems to be true of the island of Kea, and is probably true of the island of Melos, where archaeological claims of an eighth-century explosion of settlement may have misdated the material. In the southern Argolid it is not just that the number and size of settlements increase from 700 BC on, but that there appear signs of some sort of settlement hierarchy, with towns, villages, more isolated buildings or clusters of buildings, and also distinct sanctuaries.

In other parts of the Greek world abandonment of some sites in the countryside in the seventh century BC seems certain. This is true, for example, of other islands in the Cyclades. A whole series of large Dark Age and eighth-century sites, such as Zagora on Andros, Xobourgo on Tenos (see above, p. 156), Agios Andreas on Siphnos, and Koukounaries on Paros, are more or less abandoned in the seventh century. These sites are all in easily defensible but not easily accessible positions, and Koukounaries is the only one of them well placed for communication by sea. They cease to be significant residential centres at different times from about 700 BC on, settlement flourishing longest into the seventh century at Koukounaries, but most of them continuing to be important ritual centres even after ceasing to be important settlements. In the absence of intensive survey of the countryside it is impossible to tell where settlement was being relocated, but the history of these sites strongly suggests widespread change in settlement priorities associated with a reduced premium on strong defences and a decline in the dominance of a single major settlement. The dissociation of sites of cult activity from settlement and the continuation of cult activity at abandoned settlements are paralleled in Attica.

In the area round Athens long years of extensive exploration suggest that there was a marked change in the nature of occupation in the countryside in the seventh century BC. Where the eighth-century countryside had attracted numerous small settlements, marked by cemeteries, in the seventh century such settlements contracted or vanished altogether, and it is cult places which show the best evidence of continuing presence in the countryside (Figure 48). This corresponds, of course (see above, p. 73), to a period when archaeologically visible burial was accorded to a rather smaller proportion of the Athenian population than had been the case in the eighth century

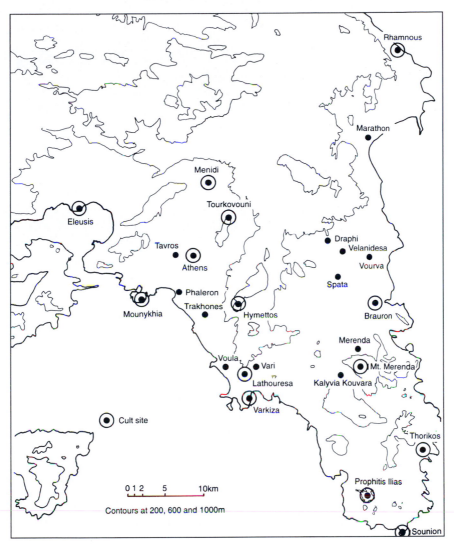

Figure 48 Sites occupied in Attica in the seventh century BC.

BC. It is as if the pressure which had developed in the later eighth century to display one's status at death, even in the case of the death of an infant, had been overcome, and as if competition was now taking place in other areas, in sanctuaries and in areas not archaeologically visible at all – notably politics. If the tradition that the first Athenian archons, as the chief Athenian annual magistracy was called, were chosen in the first quarter of the seventh century has any basis, and it does seem to coincide with the explosion of magisterial office attested for example by the Tiryns laws, then we might suspect that it

Figure 49 The physical setting of the sanctuary at Delphi. The Corinthian Gulf is seen in the foreground, Delphi is in the middle ground to the right of centre, and behind Parnassos the island of Euboia can be seen.

is in the political arena that energies and fortunes were being displayed and dissipated during this period. (On Athens see further below, p. 202.)

A DIVINE REVOLUTION

Religious phenomena have appeared in the discussion already at numerous points in this chapter. We have met officials with religious duties in seventh-century laws, oracular pronouncements supporting seventh-century legal and constitutional arrangements, oracles as part of the justification for settlement abroad, the site and nature of religious display as markers of changing settlement options. It is appropriate at this point to bring together these strands.

The Delphic oracle

The religious phenomenon which makes most impact on traditions about the events of this period is undoubtedly the oracle at the sanctuary of Apollo at Delphi on the southern slopes of Mount Parnassos in central Greece (Figure 49). Consultations of the Delphic oracle litter traditions about tyranny and about settlement abroad (Text 31). The traditions maintain that the oracle gave instruction about where settlements should be placed and indications about their future prosperity and its limits. When initial advice was not understood, repeated consultations eventually brought the right answer. The oracle was also held to foretell the fortunes of individuals and more or less ambiguously to encourage attempts to seize power. Traditions about oracles contain plenty of material that is certainly invented, but what, exactly, are we to make of all these stories?

There had been a substantial settlement at Delphi in the late Bronze Age, and continued occupation can be demonstrated for all but the very last decades of the eleventh century. Certainly by the middle of the ninth century a substantial community was established, which increased steadily thereafter. Ninth-century pottery is dominated by Thessalian/Euboian styles, but after c.800 BC most of the fine pottery is imported from Corinth. The earliest indisputable evidence for a sanctuary is the appearance of bronze votive figurines and bronze tripods in the early eighth century BC, but the scale of votive activity appears to have been relatively limited during the whole of the eighth century – not nearly as extensive, for example, as the activity at Perakhora – and no evidence has yet been recovered of any sanctuary buildings. Only in the last quarter of the eighth century BC is there any marked expansion of sanctuary evidence, in the massive increase in the number of votives (compare the pattern elsewhere, above, pp. 86–7). At this period not only do numbers of votive objects of all sorts increase, but both bronzework and pottery now come from a very wide variety of origins, covering central Greece, Attica, the Peloponnese and Crete. Tripod dedications continue in a steady stream, by contrast to Olympia where the more numerous eighth-century sequence rapidly ceases after c.700 BC. The Corinthian material notably includes 'Thapsos cups', a shape which Corinth seems to have made primarily for use in Sicilian and south Italian settlements. Neither the range of objects nor the presence of prestige dedications *proves* that Delphi was a focus of attention for worshippers of an equally wide range of élite individuals, but the very strong representation of high-value goods, some of which, such as the Cretan tripods and shields, are found in no other mainland sanctuary, certainly encourages that view.

What was drawing Greeks to Delphi in the late eighth century BC? The similarly 'panhellenic' appeal of Olympia to all Greeks from the eighth century BC on can be understood in terms of the rise of the Olympic games, and the consequent importance of Olympia as a site where honour can be disputed in a wider world than the world of the individual community (above, pp. 93–4). In due course, in the early sixth century BC, Delphi developed a tradition of games which attracted competitors from all over the Greek world (see below, p. 232), but no such games can be posited for the eighth century. Yet even for traffic which is otherwise using the Gulf of Corinth the sanctuary at Delphi is an out-of-the-way place. In the *Iliad* Delphi is simply 'rocky Pytho' (2.519–20; 9.404–5), and a place of fabulous wealth, but although the spectacular position which Delphi enjoys may sufficiently account for its becoming the most important sanctuary in the region, it seems less likely that this would

When the Messenian war occurred, those of the Lakedaimonians who did not take part in the campaign were separated off as slaves and were called Helots, and all those children born during the campaign were called Partheniai and were deprived of civic rights. Those unable to tolerate this, and there were a great number, plotted against those in power. Those in authority became aware of the plotting and sent certain men to pretend to be friendly and report back the nature of the plot. Amongst these was Phalanthos, who was apparently their champion, and he was not absolutely satisfied with those named to form a council. It was decided that they should make their attack at the festival of the Hyakinthia at the Amyklaion sanctuary, when the games were celebrated, at the moment when Phalanthos put on his leather cap (you could recognise the citizens by their hair). The spies in Phalanthos' council secretly reported back what had been decided, and when the games were begun the herald came forward and said 'Phalanthos must not put on his hat.' Perceiving that the plot had been betrayed, some ran away and some sought sanctuary. The authorities told them not to fear, and handed them over to guards. They sent Phalanthos to the oracle of the god to ask about settlement abroad, and the god said 'I grant to you Satyrion and the rich region of Taras to live in and to be trouble for the Iapygians.' So the Partheniai with Phalanthos came, and the barbarians and Cretans who occupied the place received them. They say that the Cretans were those who had sailed with Minos to Sicily and after his death at Kamaki, when he was staying with Kokalos, they set sail from Sicily, but as they tried to sail home they were driven off course to Taras.

Text 31: Antiokhos (FGH 555 F13) (late fifth century BC), quoted by Strabo 6.3.2, tells of the foundation of Taras by men expelled from Sparta.

have given it a supra-regional appeal. The oracle which is so important in later traditions, and which is already alluded to at *Odyssey* 8.79–82, must surely have some part to play.

Oracular consultation as such left no material traces at Delphi: late accounts of prophetic ecstasy induced by vapours emerging from a hole in the ground (Diodoros 16.26), or by the chewing of laurel leaves, have no basis in fact. It is therefore impossible to tell when an oracle was first set up at Delphi, how early the elaborate consultation procedure prevalent in the classical period was established, or the nature of the earliest consultations. It is a reasonable guess that the first enquiries at Delphi were on everyday problems with a focus on domestic or parochial matters. Only the hypothetical connection between the oracle and the increase in dedicatory activity at the sanctuary in the late eighth century BC offers any clue as to when the oracle began to be consulted on broadly 'political' questions – questions for which one of the numerous local oracles, for which there is evidence throughout Greece, could not be relied upon to give an unprejudiced response.

Consultations of Delphi in the classical period for which we have good evidence use the oracle to give advice on questions which cannot be resolved by human reason, either because they concern the future or because the nature of the subject is such that no direct human knowledge is possible. Examples would be questions about cult practices and the desires of the gods (cf.

Plutarch, *Moralia* 408C, and Xenophon, *Memorabilia* 1.1.8–10). Questions are asked only by those with the requisite authority to carry through the course of action which the oracle will endorse; so heads of household ask about family matters, the political élite or designated officers about matters of state. Questions to the oracle frequently take forms which offer the god a simple choice, or can be answered by 'yes' or 'no'; it is clear that it was not thought appropriate simply to ask the god to foretell the future: that the Lydian king Kroisos does so at Herodotos 1.47 is a mark of his not knowing how to use oracles. Broadly speaking, oracular consultations seem to have taken place when a community could not decide between options but had no strong view as to which option to take, as in the case of many cult matters, or when a course of action had already been decided upon but required some authority from without the community to make the decision stick. Such a use of oracles can be paralleled widely in the anthropological literature.

In the traditions about early consultations of the oracle, the oracle is given a rather more active role than this picture of its classical activity allows. As we saw in Chapter 1, the story of the foundation of Cyrene involved the oracle giving an answer not connected to the question asked, selecting a particular man as leader of the expedition, and choosing the site to be settled. Many other foundation stories involve Delphic selection of sites, and a number involve sending to found a city a man whose Delphic enquiry has been about something different, thus giving instructions to a man who at the time of receiving them does not have the authority to carry them out. When oracles are quoted they are frequently in verse, and frequently give quite specific directions in a riddling or ambiguous way.

Should we believe that the way the oracle was used or the way it responded changed between the archaic and classical period? Certainly, already in antiquity the difference between the traditions about oracular responses and the responses of the day excited interest; Plutarch wrote a short treatise on *The Oracles at Delphi No Longer Given in Verse* (*Moralia* 394E–409D). But there are strong reasons for thinking that the peculiarities of early responses are a product of tradition, and not of changing practice. One reason lies in the nature of oral tradition, discussed in Chapter 1: what is 'remembered' is determined not by what happens but by what it is most useful to tell of the past. When oracles are themselves sought in order to give authority to a disputed decision, then the more fulsome the oracular response the greater the force of the oracular support. An oracle which simply says 'yes' or 'no' to a question posed will be far less impressive in a story than an oracle which in its answer embraces and elaborates the terms of the question. And the 'otherness' of the god will be better summed up in his use of verse than in mundane prose. But another reason for not believing that archaic practice was different lies in the political embarrassment which Delphic initiative would bring: if a state sends to Delphi to get authority for one set of actions and finds a response compelling some other momentous action this may make a good story in order to absolve the secular authorities of responsibility for the second action, but it will hardly make Delphi popular. Men consult oracles not in order to discover the future, nor in order to get ideas, but in order to get a decision made for them or to get their own way. The traditions about archaic oracles cover up, rather than reveal, the reasons for consulting oracles.

Delphi has sometimes been seen as the great 'information centre' of the Greek world, more or less systematically collecting information from those who came to consult the oracle, and then using that information to advise others. That picture is one that goes closely with the conviction that settlements abroad at this period were 'state' enterprises, initiated and planned centrally and executed by groups selected by the city sending them out and led by a state-designated leader. It is also a picture which demands a very much larger traffic in consultations, and a very much more extensive quizzing of consultants than any evidence, even in the traditions, gives grounds for. The alternative suggested here, where, as in the classical period, those who came to consult the oracle by and large brought with them the information necessary to achieve the desired response, leaves little room for any formal role for the oracle in the information network. Settling abroad did indeed demand information, but that information will have come rather from the dense network of exchange which there is good reason to believe already existed in the late eighth century BC than from any Delphic store of wisdom. Delphi's role was above all a political one.

The 'rise of Delphi' should be seen as a product of political events, not of decisions about settlement. It is the tradition of Lykourgos the Spartan getting a Delphic mandate for legal and constitutional innovations, not the tradition of Battos, that we should see as central to Delphi's prominence. Communities which attempted some permanent settlement of power disputes among the élite by inventing offices and patrolling their powers required some way of enforcing these limitations in the face of resistance from those who suspected that the result would be a lessening of their own influence. Communities whose self-definition through conflict with neighbouring communities ran the risk of being costly in life and property needed a way of preventing any failure undermining the authority of those who had encouraged such activities. Communities in such crises as these, as much as communities which aimed to force a troublesome group to settle in some distant part, had need of oracular sanction. And the more distant and distinguished the oracle the greater the chance that its authority would stand firm against attack. In the case of settlement abroad Delphi became important at the moment that those settlements needed to be turned into 'colonies' and the successful settlement reclaimed for the 'mother-city'. A story of Delphic intervention provided the ideal way of covering up the fact that a group had been thrown out, or of turning a pioneering individual into a state representative. And the more accurate the oracle could be made to seem the greater the authority that could be ascribed to it.

The development of sanctuaries

The case of Delphi nicely illustrates the way in which the changing nature and priorities of Greek communities created new roles for old cult practices. But the dominance of political issues in the traditions about Delphi is a product of what oracle stories were good for, rather than representative of actual consultations, and consideration of other evidence from sanctuaries confirms the range of roles that they played within the Greek city community. The survey of eighth-century BC cult practices in Chapter 4 has already stressed the increasing variety of uses of sanctuaries to which the divergent archaeological facts bear witness (pp. 82–96). In discussing settlement pattern in Attica and in Sicily and South Italy (pp. 186–9) I have suggested some ways in which further differentiation is to be seen in the seventh century BC, and it is to other indications of the developing role of cult that I now turn.

The eighth century BC had seen an enormous increase in activities which left material traces in sanctuaries: sanctuaries were bounded with walls and elaborated with temples, dedications increased greatly in number, the site at which gods were worshipped became also the site of personal and political competition (above, pp. 93–4). For much of the seventh century BC the material evidence from sanctuaries is less dramatic, but it is arguable that the change in material remains marks a further and important change in the place of the gods within Greek societies.

Many fewer dedications survive from the seventh than from the eighth century BC. In particular, small bronze animal figurines strikingly decrease in number. At Olympia, where some 895 surviving animal figurines can be dated to the second half of the eighth century BC, only 143 can be dated to the first half of the seventh century. At some sanctuaries a change in material goes with this decline in numbers: at the sanctuary of Artemis Orthia in Sparta terracotta takes over from bronze as the most popular material for horse figurines. But in other sanctuaries the decline of bronze animal figurines coincides with a change in subject matter: in Thessaly human figurines take over from animals.

Human figures in sculpted dedications

Bronze statuettes of men are known from eighth-century Greece, but the human figure is particularly prominent as a dedication in the seventh century BC. The human figures which take over from wild or sacrificial animals as the appropriate gift to the gods take a variety of forms: musicians, bearers of animals to sacrifice, occasionally craftsmen, charioteers, warriors, or, especially towards the end of the century, figures engaged in no distinctive activity. The focus seems to have shifted from representing to the gods the natural world upon which human life uncertainly depended to representing to the gods human activity or just human existence.

Figure 50 Relief in the so-called Daedalic style from the temple at Gortyn.

Figure 51 Ivory plaque with scene of Perseus and Medusa from Samos.

The importance of the human figure in dedications is further underlined by its use as an adornment of other dedications. Bronze cauldrons, although often ornamented with griffins inspired by eastern art, are also decorated with wholly or partly human forms (compare the bronze vessel dedicated by Kolaios the Samian, above, p. 12); ritual bowls (*perirrhanteria*) are given stands whose legs take the form of human figures; the frame of a lyre may be turned into human form with the 'arms' carved as a jumping youth. Animal forms do not cease to be significant, but the human form is basic to the dedicatory repertory in the seventh century BC as it was not in the eighth.

The human figure seems to have played a particularly important part in Crete, where a distinctive style developed and along with it the earliest widespread use of stone for figured monuments. From about the middle of the seventh century BC figures, including rather large figures of a metre or more in height, are known which are marked by distinctively triangular faces, 'wig' style hair reaching just on to the shoulders with strong horizontal divisions and often divided into three or four thick braids on each side, and a relatively stiff frontality (Figure 50). Found in Crete in clay statuettes and reliefs and also in stone, this style, which has become known as 'Daedalic', came to be very widely distributed over the Greek world. Only in Crete does 'Daedalic' sculpture seem to have been employed to decorate buildings, as in the example here illustrated, which seems to have stood as the lower part of the wall of a temple at Gortyn. Some Cretan 'Daedalic' sculpture seems very heavily influenced from the east, as with the nudity of the figures illustrated or with the Egyptianised seated figures from the temple at Prinias. Those features do not export, but the use of 'Daedalic' reliefs, statues, and statuettes as dedications is found over a wider area of the Greek world and marks the beginning of a revolution in the appearance of Greek sanctuaries (Figure 51).

Towards the end of the seventh century BC the first freestanding stone figures of men and women, of the forms known respectively as the *kouros* and the *kore* appear. *Kouroi* were naked, and faced directly forward, arms to side, one foot slightly advanced. They were life-size or larger, and employed as dedications and perhaps in cemeteries. *Korai* were initially under life-size, clothed, female figures, often holding an offering in one hand. The general form of *kouroi* figures can be paralleled in small bronzes of earlier date, and ancient texts claim that their proportions were directly inspired by Egyptian stone sculpture. But detailed measurements have failed to bear this out, and the Greek *kouroi* differ from the Egyptian in their nakedness and in their contexts of use; where the Egyptian standing male statues seem to mark the power of a specific individual, the Greek *kouroi* seem rather to prompt reflection on what it is to be a man and how men relate to the gods. Nor is there any Egyptian equivalent of *korai*. Although the earliest extant *kouroi* are around life-size (Figure 52), by *c.*600 or shortly afterwards kouroi of 5 m or even 10 m high were being constructed. Power and status were certainly at issue in these dedications, most of which were made by individuals although at least one was made by the Naxians at the sanctuary of Apollo on Delos. But

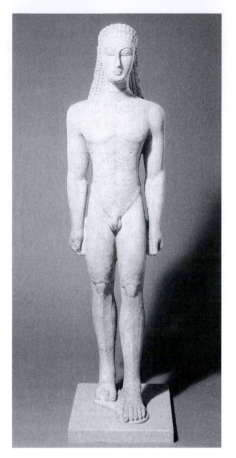

Figure 52 The so-called New York *kouros* dating from around 600 BC.

by comparison to the political statements made by Egyptian statues, these statues do not specifically reference political life. Rather they find the beauty of young male and female lives useful mirrors in which to reflect upon human relations with the gods.

The *kouros* and the *kore* between them transformed the experience of visiting a sanctuary. By the end of the sixth century BC some sanctuaries seem to have displayed very large numbers of such statues: more than a hundred *kouroi* have been recognised in the preserved remains of the sanctuary of Apollo Ptoieus at Akraiphnion in Boiotia, and a large number of *korai* are known from the Athenian Acropolis. The appearance of these Greek sanctuaries had nothing in common with anything in Egypt: if Egypt supplied anything, it was means not ends. Some other uses of Egyptian motifs failed to catch on: the Egyptian tradition of seated stone figures is directly reflected in the sculptures of the late seventh-century-BC temple at Prinias in Crete, but it did not flourish elsewhere.

The development of the Doric temple

The Egyptian contribution to the other great transformation in the appearance of sanctuaries during the seventh century BC is even more open to debate. The monumental stone temples which appear in the Greek world in the second quarter of the seventh century have certain marked similarities with Egyptian buildings: they use large dressed stones, and columns about six diameters high crowned with a square stone abacus and carrying smooth stone beams with a further vertical face above. But not only was the idea of housing a statue of a god in a building not new in the seventh century, as we have seen, but the radically new form of stone temple may appear too early to be encouraged by knowledge of Egypt. The *Iliad* seems to know about the fall of Egyptian Thebes in 663 BC (above, p. 152), and Ionian and Carian mercenaries are credited with helping Psammetikhos I to free Egypt from the Assyrians in *c.*660 BC (Herodotos 2.163, *ANE* 636–8), but for sight of Egypt to have been the inspiration behind the stone temple in Greece would require contact a generation before this. There is nothing Egyptian about either the techniques of using stone or the details of the so-called 'Doric' order of architecture – the frieze of triglyphs and metopes with associated taeniae, regulae, mutules, and guttae (Figure 53). Similarly, it is not from Egypt that the idea or the manner of using terracotta roof tiles was derived, roof tiles which crucially determined what was to be the characteristic shape of the Greek temple because they could only be used on a shallow slope.

The earliest stone temples seem to be those in the north-east Peloponnese. Earliest of all is the temple of Apollo at Corinth, constructed probably in the second quarter of the seventh century BC, which displays a high degree of sophistication in its roof tiles: five different types of tile are used, made from moulds for specific locations. The total weight of tiles must have been some sixteen tons or more. It is uncertain whether this building had an external colonnade at all, though the temple of Poseidon at Isthmia built shortly afterwards seems to have had a wooden colonnade with seven columns across the façade and eighteen columns on the flank, each standing on separate stone blocks. In any case both buildings were still distinct from the classical peripteral temple, where the room housing the cult statue (the cella) is surrounded by a colonnade, and a single roof with gable ends covers both cella and colonnade, in that they had a hipped roof on at least one and possibly both ends, and probably had no triglyphs and metopes. The earliest certain gable-fronted temples (though still with one end hipped) are those at Corcyra and Thermon dating to the last quarter of the seventh century BC, whose roofs, although technically distinct, are certainly inspired by Corinthian developments. The Isthmia temple had walls covered with stucco and painted with a frieze including animals and perhaps human figures, and the temple at Thermon, which had a colonnade with five by fifteen columns, had (terracotta) metopes which were painted, eaves decorated with modelled

199

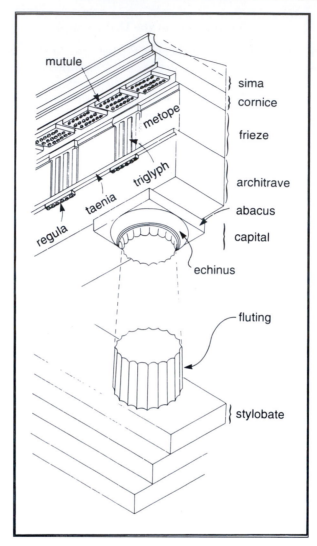

Figure 53 Details of the Doric order, as fully developed.

and painted heads of women and lions, and a large terracotta disc decorating the end of the ridge-pole.

The monumental stone temple seems very quickly to have made its impact. The full Doric order was rapidly exported to Thermon, in a Corinthian 'sphere of influence', late protocorinthian pot painters showed buildings with Doric columns, and tiled roofs deriving from the system used at Corinth and Isthmia were used in the third quarter of the seventh century BC at Sparta (temple of Artemis Orthia), at the Argive Heraion, and at Olympia (perhaps an early temple of Hera and a treasury). The idea of the stone temple seems to have spread to Ionia before the end of the century: the temple of Athene at Smyrna had fluted stone columns and stone walls, although the techniques and detailing were quite different.

Between them the development of the monumental temple and the development of the monumental dedicatory figure began to transform the appearance of Greek sanctuaries. Vessels of bronze and of precious metal which did not involve figurative imagery long continued to be dedicated to the gods, but it was now the human figure which dominated the sacred spaces in which people met to communicate with the gods through sacrifice. The power of the gods, which had been conveyed in terms of the uncertainties of the agricultural world and the threats of the monstrous, was now primarily expressed in ways more closely related to the expression of human power. Individuals continued to make their mark in sanctuaries, but the more colossal *kouroi* and stone temples will have been beyond the means of individuals to produce on their own and so were increasingly the preserve of a community.

7

THE GREEK WORLD
IN 600 BC

The last three chapters have endeavoured to give an impression of how the Greek world changed during the eighth and seventh centuries BC. They have concentrated on areas of life in which things can be seen to be happening which made the world a different place in 600 BC from what it had been in 800 BC. In this chapter I attempt to take stock, and to conjure up a picture of what the experience of living in a Greek city around 600 BC was like. To do so I choose a small number of 'windows' opening on to particular places or particular sections of society, in an attempt to get some idea of the variety of what it was to identify yourself as Greek and to restore some of the particularity lost in the universalising claims inherent in writing diachronic history.

ATHENS

The account of the Athenian constitution ascribed to Aristotle mentioned only the creation of the annual elected office of archon, supposedly in 683/682 BC, between the legendary story of one Hippomenes, whose cruel punishment of a daughter taken in adultery caused the end of the kingship, and the attempted coup of Kylon, probably to be dated around 630 BC. Athenian history effectively began, even in antiquity, with Kylon's conspiracy.

The Kylonian affair

For the story of Kylon's coup we are dependent upon fifth-century BC traditions, interested less in the coup itself than in the consequences of the manner in which it was suppressed. Herodotos (5.71, Text 32) tells us that Kylon, an Athenian Olympic victor, gathered a group of young political supporters around himself, tried to take the Acropolis, failed, sought sanctuary, was dislodged by the authorities in the form of the obscure 'prytaneis of the naukraries', and, together with his followers, was killed by the family known as the Alkmaionidai, who were consequently accursed. Thucydides (1.126) similarly explains the curse, adding various details, including a misinterpreted

The 'accursed' Athenians got their name in this way. Kylon was an Athenian Olympic victor. He proudly thought himself worthy of being tyrant, got himself together a group of contemporaries, and tried to take the Acropolis. He was unable to take it and went and sat at the cult statue as a suppliant. The magistrates in charge of the naukraries, who ran Athens at that time, removed them, undertaking that their punishment should not include death. The blame for murdering them fell on the Alkmaionidai. This happened before the time of Peisistratos.

Text 32: Herodotos 5.71. Herodotos' vague description of what happened to Kylon.

Delphic oracle and the claim that Kylon was son-in-law of Theagenes tyrant of Megara, and disputing both the question of who was in authority – he says it was the nine archons – and whether Kylon himself was killed.

That there was an episode in early Athenian history which led to the Alkmaionidai being regarded as accursed is clear, for that curse was invoked more than once in subsequent history in order to have that family expelled from Athens (see below, p. 278). It seems likely that this episode occurred in the context of political strife. Beyond that, it is difficult to be certain about details; the differences between Herodotos and Thucydides show that even when the story of Kylon was related for the same purpose the details of the account might vary. When Plutarch (*Solon* 12) tells the story he connects it with a Megarian attack on Athens, and the detail that Kylon was related to Theagenes seems likely to stem from traditions of hostility between Athens and Megara in the late seventh century BC. Kylon's Olympic victory is recorded separately by Eusebios for 640 BC, and, although it is hard to know how reliable that tradition is, Thucydides makes his connection with the Olympic games fundamental to his misinterpreting Delphic advice on when to make his bid for power, and this suggests that the victory in the games was a firm part of the tradition from an early date. It is, of course, entirely consonant with other evidence for the *kudos* which atheletic victories could give (above, p. 93) – but that might equally cause it to be invented!

For our understanding of late seventh-century BC Athens the crucial evidence which this story provides is of political struggle. That Kylon should attempt a coup, and that there should be a backlash against a whole family because of the harsh measures taken by one of their number, strongly suggests that political influence was bitterly disputed, and that family ties were taken to be fundamental to political sympathies. Both the importance of the family and the use of reactions to violence to score political points seem confirmed by the homicide legislation held in the late fifth century BC to stem from Drako's late seventh-century laws (above, p. 176), and it may be that the attempt by 'Attic men' (Alkaios frg. 184) to settle at Sigeion at the entry to the Hellespont at this time should also be seen as a product of political point-scoring in domestic Athenian politics.

203

Solon and his poetry

Onto this world, in which bloodshed is a central part of political life, the poems of Solon cast a fitful, oblique, light. The Solon who first appears in our sources (Herodotos 1.29–32) is a wise adviser, preaching to Kroisos king of Lydia the doctrine that happiness is independent of material possessions. Of Solon the Athenian politician Herodotos certainly knows: he introduces him as a man who had made laws for the Athenians on their orders, and later claims that Solon took from Amasis of Egypt the law that each man should reveal to a magistrate annually the source of his livelihood (2.177). But neither Herodotos nor Thucydides, who does not mention Solon at all, found it necessary to explore Solon's life or political acts in any further detail. Solon remained prominent among the sages (Plato, *Timaios* 20d – with another chronologically impossible setting), but his political importance at Athens grew greatly with the constitutional debates brought on by the crisis in confidence in democracy during the Peloponnesian war, and he came to hold an important place in the appeals to ancestral practice which are a central part of fourth-century political discourse. The rich stories which later writers have to tell about Solon and his actions derive either from Solon's own poetry, from laws correctly or incorrectly attributed to Solon, or from traditions written down for the first time in the fourth century BC.

Solon's own poetry is preserved for us only in as far as it is quoted by later writers. Much that is preserved is preserved in the context of discussions of the political actions of the historical Solon: both the Aristotelian *Constitution of the Athenians*, written in the 320s BC, and Plutarch's *Life of Solon*, written in the early second century AD, illustrate their claims about Solon with quite extensive quotation. Other writers quoted Solon for striking poetic comments appropriate to other contexts, and a long elegiac poem (frg. 13, cf. frg. 23) preserved by the fifth-century AD anthologist Stobaeus, which insists that wealth be sought by just means and through the gods' favour and that outrageous behaviour brings destruction, may well have been in the mind of whoever first told the story of Solon and Kroisos.

Some lines are ascribed to both Solon and Theognis, and the mixture of observations of extreme generality with observations which seem to apply to specific circumstances is common to both. Solon's poetry certainly does not supply any systematic commentary on the situation at Athens or on his own actions, but it does flag some particular areas of concern which it will be worthwhile to dwell upon.

Solon's moral strictures single out a number of values which are regarded as not open to dispute. The important positive values are the fatherland, freedom, and fairness; the threat comes from civil strife, and the crucial need is for good leadership. The poems have an intense sense of maintaining the glory of an Athens in which the gods take a concern and which can claim to be the oldest of Ionian cities (frgs 4.1–4, 4a). Solon claims he would rather not be an Athenian than have to bear the shame of letting go of Salamis (frgs 2, 3). The threat to the fatherland is manifested in the lack of commitment to freedom: the rapacity of the few, who even steal what is sacred and what belongs to the community, has caused many poor men to go to other lands as slaves (frgs 4.11–14, 23–5; 36.8–15, Text 33). The very freedom of the city is threatened by the 'open wound' of civil strife, a product of individuals pursuing their own selfish interests (frgs 4.5–20; 34.1–5; 36.20–2; cf. 39). Athens is suffering from 'Dysnomia' (bad regulation) and requires 'Eunomia' (good regulation) to put an end to outrageous behaviour, crooked judgments, and overweening acts (frg. 4.30–9). But it is not solely a matter of conflict between individuals or individual powerful men behaving badly; Solon presents the *esthloi* ('good' = wealthy) as in conflict with the *kakoi* ('bad' = poor). This is a politically interested claim, in as far as it enables him not to side with or against any individual, but it must have rung true to those who read or heard him. Solon puts himself in the middle as one who protects opposing groups from each other (frg. 5.5–6), yet is treated like a wolf amid dogs (frg. 36.27) or like a boundary stone in a border war (37.9–10). In the face of this, the community requires leaders who can moderate their behaviour (frg. 6; 36.21–2; 37.7), and inculcate a sense of fairness: it is important not that all receive the same but that all receive what they deserve (frgs 5.1; 34.8–9; 36.18–20); that it is not the virtuous who are wealthy is no reason for redistribution of wealth (frg. 15). But there is danger that giving power to the wrong individual will itself bring enslavement (frg. 9), and such enslavement could be avoided if more attention was paid to men's acts than to their words (frg. 11). Men are wrong to think that a day of absolute power is worth any consequence (frg. 33), and Solon denies that he himself is seeking the power of the *tyrannos* (frg. 34.7).

Focusing on these issues and treating them in this way highlights not individuals' acts but their attitudes. Through almost all the preserved poetry

Did I stop before achieving any of the aims which made me gather the people together? Black Earth, the greatest mother of the Olympian gods will best bear witness at the tribunal of Time: I took up the boundary-stones, which were fixed all over her, and, once enslaved, she is now free. I brought back to Athens, their fatherland founded by the gods, many who had been sold, some justly, others unjustly, and others who had fled through constraining debt, men who had been wandering the world over and so no longer spoke the Attic dialect. I freed those here who suffered unseemly enslavement and feared the tempers of their masters. I did this by harnessing force and justice together with power, and I carried through my promises. I wrote statutes alike for those of high and of low social status, fitting straight justice to each. If someone other than I had taken the goad, some ill-intentioned and greedy man, he would not have been able to control the people. For had I been willing to do what pleased the opposing party then, or what the others planned for them, this city would have lost many men. That is why I made a stout defence all round, turning like a wolf among many hounds.

Text 33: Solon frg. 36 (quoted by [Aristotle,] Constitution of the Athenians 12.4. Solon boasts of his achievements.

there is stress on the tension between the individual and the community. Solon manages to construct a vision of a community interest which overrides individual or sectional interests. Pursuit of individual interests leads not only to strife, for which there is no remedy since no one can be trusted not to abuse positions of power with which they are entrusted, but to loss of territory and loss of face. The loss of personal freedom by some Athenians is shown up not, as in modern states, as the responsibility of some disembodied economic crisis but as a direct result of the greed of others. But greed is attributed to poor as well as rich – only the poet evidently knows what is fair.

Solon's picture of Athens and of Athenians, and of their response to himself, is bleak. Ironically, despite his own insistence that attention should be paid to deeds and not words, the Athenians apparently both elected him to the archonship, traditionally in 594/593 or 592/591, and on that or possibly on some subsequent occasion agreed to have him implement a large number of disparate laws. It would be ridiculous to claim that Solon invented the crisis he seems to have been empowered to solve – after all, some consciousness of problems lay behind Drako's legislation traditionally dated to 621 BC – but his words may themselves have reduced people's willingness to tolerate conflict as normal and sharpened perceptions of the dangers to the community which the feuding of the late seventh century BC represented. The power of poetic performance, which is something that Plutarch (*Solon* 8) stresses in his *Life*, and which is shown also in the association of other of the Seven Sages with writing poetry (above, p. 184), must not be underestimated. It is highly unlikely that Solon's poetry was composed for or performed at public meetings; some of it was certainly, and all quite probably, composed for élite symposia, where competition was of the essence and where Solon was not above competing directly with famous lines by other poets (frg. 20). But such competition itself depends upon the fact that good verse is memorable, and what is remembered can also nag. Solon may well have done much to create the conditions in which his own appointment was necessary.

The picture of point-scoring by individual against individual accords well with the way in which actions taken to prevent one individual, Kylon, from asserting control were used to undermine the position of those responsible for them. It accords well too with the insistence by men with only a distant kin connection that they should have a share in the decision as to whether a man's accidental killer be let off to which the Drakonian homicide law attests (ML 86/Fornara 15B). And it may not be too fanciful to see Drako's heavy penalties as a measure of desperation in the face of spiralling disputes. But to get a more detailed picture of the sorts of actions which manifested, to Solon at least, the attitudes which his verse condemns, recourse must be had to what we know of Solon's laws.

Solon and his laws

The political importance in the fourth century BC of Solon as *the* lawgiver led to many laws not of his making, including laws made in the fourth century itself, being ascribed to him. This happened even though Solon's own laws seem to have survived, in the form in which they were originally written down, until the hellenistic period. Distinguishing between laws correctly and laws falsely attributed to Solon is a fool's task, for there is no touchstone that can be employed: not even the small number of laws which are cited from the Solonian monuments are beyond question. The archaism of the language of some laws, and the extent to which other laws are deeply embedded in classical legal procedure, encourages the belief that they are truly Solonian, but no firm boundary can be drawn. Nevertheless, the certainty that there was a written text, and that that text could be correctly cited, justifies valour rather than discretion.

The Aristotelian *Constitution of the Athenians* (9, Text 34) says that Solon's most populist laws were the prohibition of borrowing on the security of one's own body, the enabling of a third party to bring a prosecution on behalf of an injured party, and allowing reference back to a court. All three of these measures have a good chance of being genuinely Solonian, and it is noteworthy that two of the three measures are procedural and the other concerns property. The offences against which third-party prosecution was allowed strongly suggest that its purpose was to prevent powerful men from so constraining the less powerful, by physical or other means, that they could not themselves bring a prosecution. Reference to a court seems to represent a constraint upon the decisions of magistrates. In both cases it is élite behaviour which is constrained.

Solonian concern for property can be seen in other laws besides that about enslavement for debt. He seems to have concerned himself with inheritance, including definitions of legitimacy, and with the order of succession, the

These three seem to be the features of Solon's constitution which most favoured the people: first and greatest, forbidding loans on security of a person's body; second, the possibility of a volunteer seeking justice for one who was wronged; third, and they say that this particularly strengthened the people, appeal to the court – for once the people has the decisive vote the people is decisive in the constitution. Also there is the matter of the laws not being written simply and clearly, but like the law on inheritance and heiresses, so that many disputes occur and the court ends up deciding all matters, both public and private. So some think that Solon deliberately made the laws unclear in order to give the people the deciding role. That is not in fact likely, rather it was that he was unable to give a complete definition of what was best. One should not judge Solon's intention from how his laws work now, but from the principles displayed by the rest of his constitution.

Text 34: [Aristotle,] Constitution of the Athenians *9. The Aristotelian view of the way in which Solon increased the powers of the people at Athens.*

conditions of validity of wills, the circumstances in which children could be adopted, heiresses and their fate, behaviour near property boundaries, and rights to water. In all cases it is those who possess significant amounts of property that are affected by the law; even in the case of the prohibition of enslavement for debt the fortunes of the creditor as well as of the debtor are changed. Some of Solon's laws in this area were traditionally held to have been remarkably detailed: he listed the circumstances in which the making of a will would not be valid – if the testator was drunk, drugged, in chains, senile, or under the influence of a woman; he specified that a wall had to be one foot from a property boundary, a building two feet, a tomb as far away as it was deep, an olive or fig tree nine feet but other trees only five feet, and a beehive had to be 300 feet from any previously established hive; he limited the size of the reed mats used in funerals to a cubit long, and the number of garments buried with the deceased to three; he held that an adulterer caught in the act could be killed with impunity only if the woman involved was the punisher's wife, mother, daughter, sister, or concubine kept for the procreation of free children; and he insisted that when next of kin married heiresses, as he obliged them to do, they had sexual intercourse with them three times a month. Such specifications were sometimes ridiculed later in antiquity, and were sometimes held to create disputes ('Was he or wasn't he drunk?' 'Well, it depends what you mean by drunk . . .'), but they are best understood as attempts to make everything absolutely plain and simple, as designed to make obedience easy rather than designed to make enforcement easy.

Solon's crisis

That Solon was concerned to produce a stable and responsible élite emerges too from his treatment of the 'classes', based on property ownership, into which the Athenian citizen body was divided. Far from abolishing these, Solon seems to have extended them, perhaps adding another class and certainly making membership of a particular class a determining criterion for possession of various rights and duties. Not the least striking feature of these classes, however, as has emerged from recent re-examinations, is that they were very heavily weighted towards the richest members of society. Three of the four classes seem to have involved owning very substantial amounts of land. Solon is not here dividing responsibilities across the whole of the population of Attica, he is introducing distinctions among the rights of the rich élite. Solon clearly accepted property ownership as a fundamental divide, something clearly, if vaguely, implied in his poem's denial that all should have equal shares of the land of Attica (frg. 34.8–9). If claims that he regulated against homosexual love affairs between slaves and boys are correct then he was also concerned to assert status differences marked by freedom rather than property.

The realisation that the Solonian 'classes' did not divide up the citizen body into anything like equally sized groups, but rather split the wealthy according to relatively fine property distinctions, is of fundamental significance for understanding what Solon was doing. The traditional understanding has been that Solon took power away from an hereditary aristocracy and distributed it according to wealth. But the basis for believing that Athens or any other archaic city was ever in the grip of an exclusive hereditary aristocracy is fragile. There is no doubt that birth was indeed cited to justify claims to prominence within a city, but as we have seen in the imaginative community of Homer, birth was only one possible criterion. Wealth had never not been significant, not just in its quantity but in its form: being able to give others gifts that were prestigious not simply because expensive but because of their past associations is fundamental to the negotiation of position in Homeric epic. But in real life as in Homer the ability to speak well or give wise judgement counted very significantly. So too did the ability to carry off other prizes offered. We have already seen that *kudos* was to be won from athletic victory, and Solon is indeed said to have introduced top-up awards for victorious Olympic competitors, but whoever took the prize offered for frisky dancing in the eighth-century graffito on a jug from the Dipylon cemetery (above p. 104; *CEG* 432) will also have enhanced their position thereby (notwithstanding the fate of Hippokleides, p. 266 below).

Athenians in the classical period believed that there had been a group of families in archaic Attica known as the 'Eupatridai', and gave these a formal place in the mythical constitutional arrangements they attributed to Theseus and in the highly dubious arrangements that they alleged to have been introduced in the immediately post-Solonian period ([Aristotle,] *Constitution of the Athenians* 13.2; cf. below p. 213). Such claims are not surprising: it was natural to think, as Aristotle indeed suggests in *Politics* 1, that family organisation had preceded community or state organisation. Since in the classical world family alone nowhere determined the distribution of political power, there had to have been a time when families lost that power. To be able to claim that there was such a time suited in particular those who regarded their own families as particularly worthy, giving them an argument that they should be afforded special treatment. In fact, those who regarded themselves as well-born had always complained that others less well-born were infiltrating their ranks or achieving influence in a way that would not have been allowed in the past. To interpret this as evidence for actual social and political change is to mistake argument for description – in just the way the well-born wanted people to.

Solon makes no reference to Eupatrids nor to any other family grouping. He divides between the 'good' and the 'bad', but the criteria for the division are never spelt out. Modern scholars talk of the *aristoi* (the 'best'), of aristocrats and of aristocracy. *Aristokrateia* was coined by classical Greek political philosophers to describe 'rule by the best', but it always referred to the institutional arrangements, not to a set of people, and no term 'aristocrat' was ever derived from it. The idea that there was a set of people who thought that political power was their birthright and who associated only with each other, sharing a single 'aristocratic ideology', is a modern fantasy. Throughout this book I have referred simply to the élite. This is simply shorthand for those who secured the dominant position in society, however they had achieved that position. Indeed the beauty of the term lies in the absence of association with any particular set of qualities (birth, wealth, athletic success) other than that of being recognised to be 'on top'. Position at the top was competitive and those who competed for it employed all the means they had at their disposal.

Solonian concern for the wealthy élite was both for their relations with each other and for their relations with the rest of the community. In antiquity Solon was associated with the slogan 'Shaking off the burdens' (*Seisakhtheia*). Exactly what the burdens were, and how they were shaken off, was already debated in the fourth century BC (Plutarch, *Solon* 15), and it is clear that no direct reference to the slogan was to be found in Solon's poetry. One burden that Solon himself was clearly proud to have removed was the threat of enslavement; he claimed to have brought back to Athens many who had been sold abroad, some of them so long ago that they no longer spoke the Attic dialect of Greek (frg. 36.8–15). Some ancient commentators ([Aristotle,] *Constitution of the Athenians* 12.4) connected the shaking off of burdens with the removal of boundary markers, which, in one poem, he says made the Black Earth free rather than enslaved (frg. 36.3–7). In the classical period such boundary markers were used to record that the property whose boundary they marked had been mortgaged, and the removal of such markers would be tantamount to the abolition of debts. But such markers, which survive in considerable numbers from the late fifth and fourth centuries BC, are not attested archaeologically at an earlier date and, although there is no reason to believe that land could not be used as security on a loan in the seventh century BC, the idea that removing boundary markers *c.*600 BC meant one-off clearance of debt is improbable.

Ancient views of Solon and debt were influenced by the false belief that coinage already existed in Solon's time. In fact the earliest Athenian coins date to the middle of the sixth century, and although the earliest coinage in Asia Minor just might belong to the late seventh century BC, it is certain that coinage was unknown in mainland Greece in Solon's time (see below, p. 237). This not only casts doubt on laws ascribed to Solon which involve fixed monetary fines, such as the claim that he fixed the penalty for rape at a fine of 100 drakhmai, it also requires that debt be conceived in non-monetary terms. To do so is to stress debt as a relationship of obligations rather than a financial matter.

The picture is further complicated by the association of Solon with a group of people who had disappeared by the classical period, share-croppers known as *hektemoroi*, men who probably rented land on the basis of returning one-sixth of its produce to the owner. These people became symbols of the crisis Solon was to solve, but was their crisis an economic one or a social one? Neither claims that the population of Attica was rising rapidly at this time, nor claims that the land was overpopulated and its fertility exhausted can muster either archaeological or textual support. As we have seen in Chapter

3, labour availability is more likely to have been a problem than availability of land: to get the higher returns available from intensive, as opposed to extensive, agriculture required being able to command labour in quantity. Hence indeed the attraction of share-cropping to the large landowner. When Solon talks of the enslaved whom he freed, he talks of men who fear the habits of their masters, and there are some attractions in seeing the burden of masters' behaviour as being what was shaken off, and in associating the return of those enslaved with the restoration of civic rights to all who had lost them (except those properly judicially condemned for major offences). On this view the boundary markers will not have recorded a debt, but the obligation to pay a sixth of the produce, and in uprooting them Solon would have been freeing tenants from landowners, giving them the land they owned, and turning Attica into the land of small farmers which it was in the classical period. Contrary to the view of the Aristotelian *Constitution of the Athenians* (12), there would have been no cancellation of debts, but rather a limited redistribution of land. In this area, as in others, Solon would be chiefly concerned about the behaviour of the élite.

It is not at all clear that any of Solon's laws shed any light on the Athenian economy. Herodotos records that he took over from Egypt the requirement that men annually accounted for their source of livelihood, and Solon claims that he insisted that fathers have their sons taught a trade, but even if these claims are correct their focus may well be social rather than economic. One of the laws for which a precise reference to the inscribed Solonian monument is given is the obligation of the archon to curse any who exported any produce except olive oil. Not only does the coupling of the curse with a fine of 100 drakhmai if the archon does not do this duty cast doubt on the genuineness of the law, but the law as cited is more interested in the behaviour of the archon (compare the seventh-century laws cited at p. 174) than in the exporting of produce.

Solon's world is a world of bitter conflict among the élite, a world in which verbal accusations of cowardice in war or parricide are likely enough to cause conflict that it is worth banning them. This conflict is played out at every opportunity, disputing boundaries, disputing inheritance, fighting over the penalties for offences, putting on competitive displays at funerals (Text 35). At the same time, it is a world in which those who have power over others use that power with favouritism and often without mercy, whether those others be tenants or men who come under the jurisdiction of some magistrate. Solon can be seen to have raised awareness of the danger to the community as a whole which such conflict represented, both by stressing the moral dimension of the conflictual behaviour and by emphasising its effect on Athenian territorial claims and ambitions, perhaps particularly over Salamis. His laws aim to shackle conflicting parties by imposing clear limits on the occasions which are open to dispute, and the extent to which discrepant behaviour can be penalised. They also seem to have tried to confirm a regular framework for Athenian life by encoding

You will realise still more clearly from the following law, men in the court, that Solon the lawgiver had a keen concern for relatives, and not only grants to relatives the property that has been left but also it is for the relatives that he makes all the difficult regulations. Read the law. 'The dead man must be laid out inside as he wants. The dead man must be carried out to burial on the day after he has been laid out, before sunrise. The men are to head the procession, when the body is carried out, the women to follow at the rear. No woman is to enter the dead man's house, or to follow the body when it is taken to the tomb, unless over sixty years old except she be one of the family within the degree of cousin. Nor is any woman to enter the dead man's house when the corpse has been carried out except she be within the degree of cousin.'

Text 35: [Demosthenes] 43.62. The speaker attributes Athenian regulations on funerals to Solon.

religious ritual, through a stated calendar of festivals in which the nature of the sacrifices was specified and thereby the scope and nature of the glory to be achieved on such occasions at least to some extent controlled. Solon may even have invented some festivals: a case has been made for his instituting a commemoration of the dead at public expense for the community as a whole, in competition with, and removing part of the rationale for, private celebrations of the anniversary of death.

It is important not to overstate the importance of Solon. Many aspects of life were left effectively unchanged by him. It is very doubtful if life for the élite, at least, on a daily basis was very different after his activity than before. Nor were relations between men and women changed. Only the accident of fourth-century Athenians' having rhetorical use for Solon has preserved for us his poems and traditions about his laws. The material record from Athens and Attica shows no significant rupture. Indeed, two features apparent in the archaeology may mark a raising of the stakes in the competition among the élite which Solon failed to check. At the very end of the seventh century the custom arose of dedicating to the gods such massive *kouroi* as the New York *kouros* (Figure 52) or the Sounion *kouros* as offerings. At much the same time substantial funerary markers surmounted by a sphinx appeared. Although *kouroi* later become more modest in size, they formed one of the standard dedications for more than a century, and similarly the sphinx stele was the shape of grandiose commemoration of the dead until the middle of the sixth century. Neither of these developments shows any sign of having been checked in the early sixth century, despite the tradition of Solon's interest in curbing funerary extravagance. In the late seventh century BC too, Athenian pot painting underwent a marked change in style, partly under Corinthian influence. The protoattic style gave way to the incised drawing of black-figure, and this development was followed by a virtually constant revolution in terms of pot shapes – both innovative large pots and the beginnings of the very rich cup tradition – and in terms of iconography, which lasted for the next half century. Large display pots are found both before and after Solon, and nothing connects any of the pot iconography with his poems or laws –

despite the fact that the pottery assemblage is increasingly strongly dominated by shapes to be associated, as is Solon's own poetry, with the symposion.

If I stress that Solon's crisis was a political and social crisis, rather than an economic crisis, that is not to say that economic factors were irrelevant. As the developments in Athenian pottery and sculpture show, Athens was very much in touch not only with the rest of the Greek world but with the whole Mediterranean world in the late seventh century. Athenian amphorae of the type known as 'SOS' amphorae because of the decoration on their necks, and which almost certainly transported both olive oil and wine, had been reaching both the eastern and western Mediterranean from around 700 BC on. The distribution of Athenian fine pottery in the first decade of the sixth century strongly suggests that Athens was part of a trading network in which merchants were highly sensitive to market demand and transported commodities which they knew they would be able to sell at the particular destination for which they were headed. Such trading networks brought considerable profit, and may indeed have influenced Athenian foreign policy (as in the clash with Mytilene over Sigeion), but their effect on Athenian society is more likely to have been to increase the competition between members of the élite than to create a new élite. And in as far as increased competition meant pressure to maximise agricultural production, and in particular saleable agricultural production such as olive oil, it may have led to the élite putting more pressure on the poor in order to turn still more land over to intensive agriculture.

Direct archaeological traces of Solon point to the political results of his actions rather than their social or economic roots. In the Athenian agora, the market and civic centre, buildings which do not conform to the pattern of private houses seem to have been constructed around the beginning of the sixth century BC in the corner where the council chamber later stood. But even if these were new community resources for political life, the character of political life seems to have been little changed by Solon: the Aristotelian *Constitution of the Athenians* (13) reports that within a decade of the laws there had been two years without an archon because dispute had prevented an election, followed by a year when one Damasias, elected for a year, held on to office for twenty-six months. Élite conflict had found new channels.

If Solon made a difference it was at a level of society below what is archaeologically visible. The pattern of landownership in classical Athens strongly suggests that relations between propertied élite and the propertyless were transformed by turning tenants into small landowners and removing any obligation to a landlord. This transformation was of fundamental importance for the later history of Athens, for it was upon a population dominated by small landowners, strongly tied to their villages and their land, that the further redistribution of political rights in the reforms of Kleisthenes, reforms which led to the creation of something identifiable as democratic, at the end of the sixth century was based (below, pp. 278 and 286).

WOMEN

Solon's world is a man's world. When he discusses love it is love for boys (frg. 25), and when he describes human life in terms of ten distinct periods of seven years each it is a man's life that he describes (frg. 27). When women appear in Solon's legislation they appear as means for men getting things done – useful to display at funerals, a means of keeping a household together in the absence of male heirs – or as items of male property, damage to whom by rape requires punishment. Only once does a woman appear as an active agent in her own right – when Solon legislates to make invalid a will written by a man under the influence of a woman.

Semonides and Arkhilokhos: the view from the symposion

Such a view of woman is to be found very much more powerfully expressed in the poetry of Semonides of Samos. Semonides was another politically active poet; he was held to have been the leader of an expedition to settle at three sites on the island of Amorgos, probably in the last quarter of the seventh century BC. Only two extensive poems by Semonides have survived, both of them preserved because quoted by the anthologist Stobaeus. Although differing in metre, and thus in occasion, from the poems of Hesiod, the tone of Semonides' poems takes up the pessimism of the Boiotian poet ('ten thousand are mortals' plagues and their misery and trouble defeat expression', frg. 1.20–2). That sense of variation on a Hesiodic theme is very strong in frg. 7, which takes up the reference in *Theogony* 591 to the 'accursed race and tribes of women' descended from Pandora, and describes those 'tribes' in detail, employing animal imagery and imagery from the natural world, in the tradition of animal fable rather than epic, to convey the varying vices of different women (Text 36).

Hesiod's Pandora represented woman as a structural problem to audiences at a more or less public gathering at which both men and women were probably present (above, p. 133); Semonides, writing for men gathered privately to drink together in the symposion, concerns himself with the defects of particular women, the dirty pig, wicked fox, vicious bitch, hungry and insensitive earth, changeable sea, randy and thieving ferret, proud and vain horse (whom only a tyrant or ruler can afford), and ugly and tricky ape. The only woman who attracts no blame is the bee, a faithful mother who takes no pleasure in the company of other women gossiping about sex. Semonides' concern is not only with woman as hungry mouth, unreliable housekeeper, and unfriendly company, but about woman as source of shame to a man in the eyes of male friends and neighbours: 'where there is a woman a man cannot even give well-planned entertainment to a stranger come to his house' (frg. 7.106–7).

Semonides' poem ends, as we have it, somewhat self-reflexively: every man criticises others' wives and praises his own, not recognising that the fate of all is alike because of the bond of desire forged by Zeus which makes men willing even to fight over women (frg. 7.112–18). This ending reflects a striking feature of the poem as a whole: even while offering abuse, the poem parades women's attraction. Indeed it is men's inability to do without women and frustration, in the light of that, at not being able to control them, that gives the poem its force.

A further glimpse into this world of gossiping men dominated by women is given in the poetry of Arkhilokhos, where we find men boasting of their own and ridiculing others' sexual conquests. We do not have to believe, as ancient readers did (cf. frg. 295), that Arkhilokhos always wrote autobiographically to make historical use of his poems celebrating his sexual desire for women, abusing former lovers, and replaying successful seductions (esp. frg. 196a). For these poems belong to a world in which the determination of the father to preserve the chastity of his daughter and the credit of his house is pitted against the young man's determination to make conquests without assuming responsibility, as part of the competition within the élite. This is a world where a man's view of women depends on the relationship of the moment, and where what is said is as important as what is done (Arkhilokhos' abuse was said to have driven the daughters of Lykambes to suicide, *Palatine Anthology* 7.351, cf. 69–71, 352).

That the view from the symposion was not a view that fairly encompassed the world of *c.*600 BC we can fortunately demonstrate from other surviving contemporary poetry. The view of the Semonidean man, bitching with his male friends, that the only good woman was the woman who kept aloof from other women and did not go in for swapping stories about lovers, is complemented by the celebrations of female fellow-feeling which are found, as we have seen (above, pp. 170–1), in Alkman and also in Sappho and in the *Homeric Hymn to Demeter*. Not only do these poems reveal an appreciation amongst men of the positive values of affective bonds between women, in as far as Alkman was a male poet and the hymn to Demeter, whatever its authorship, was surely performed to a mixed festival audience; but the poems

---

God at the first made the mind of a woman variously. He made one from the bristly sow: everything in her home is soiled with mud, lies untidy and rolls around on the ground. She doesn't wash, her clothes are never laundered, and she sits and grows fat on the dung-heap. God made another woman from the wicked vixen who knows everything. She knows about everything that is bad and everything that is good, and often calls the bad good, and the good bad. Her moods change from day to day. Another woman from the dog, good for nothing, the image of her mother, wanting to hear and know everything, she barks as she wanders about looking everywhere, even if she does not see anyone. Men can't even shut her up with threats, by angrily shattering her teeth with a stone, by speaking to her gently, or having her sit with guests; whatever the circumstances she keeps up her useless howling.

Text 36: Semonides 7.1–20. The beginning of Semonides' denunciation of women.

215

of Sappho also reveal the existence in the archaic city, and not just in Sparta, of social space outside the family circle in which women could become intensely attached to one another.

The *Homeric Hymn to Demeter*

The *Homeric Hymn to Demeter* provides an aetiological myth for the cult of the Mysteries at Eleusis. It tells of the rape of Persephone by Hades, of her mother Demeter's grief and search, and of the hospitable treatment she received from the ruling family at Eleusis. It tells of Demeter seeking to make the child of that household, Demophoön, immortal, and of how, when she is prevented from doing that, the action she took in withdrawing fertility from the earth made Zeus insist that Hades give up Persephone for part of the year. In a delicate and touching scene Demeter rejoices in Persephone's return and, as she has promised to do, reveals the rites of the Mysteries to the Eleusinians, so that people initiated into the Mysteries may enjoy a more blessed afterlife than other mortals. But although the *Hymn* is all about Eleusis, and not a general celebration of Demeter, it curiously fails to make as much of the local setting as did other versions of the story, and in particular, by contrast to the Orphic version, Demeter does not teach agriculture to the Eleusinian Triptolemos for him to reveal to the rest of the world.

If the end of the *Hymn* is the establishment of the Eleusinian Mysteries, the focus is on the affective bond of mother and daughter and on the forming of further affective ties, particularly with Demophoön (Text 37). It is the meeting of divine and human worlds that here results in the revelation of the Mysteries – they are not simply a by-product of the divine celebration of the return of Persephone. It is because gods care about humans that Demeter withholds fertility, and it is because gods care about humans that Zeus reacts to that. But the areas of life which manifest that concern are areas of fundamentally female experience.

The *Hymn to Demeter* draws heavily on epic, but it does so to insist that female life, even ordinary female life, involves epic experience. Demeter's journeying search and her lying tale about her identity – she tells the Eleusinians that she is a Cretan woman captured by pirates – evoke Odysseus,

---

Rich-crowned Demeter then addressed her: 'Lady, you must rejoice, the gods give you good. I will willingly take your child as you ask me to, I will rear him. I do not expect him to suffer from a nurse's negligence, and neither a spell nor the Undercutter will harm him. For I know a strong antidote which will get the better of the Woodcutter, and I know a good protection against troublesome charms.' So she spoke, and took the child to her fragrant breast with her immortal hands, and the mother rejoiced in her heart. So she brought up in the house Demophoön, the glorious son of wise Keleus, whom rich-girdled Metaneira bore, and he grew like a god, neither eating food nor suckling…

Text 37: Homeric Hymn to Demeter *224–35. Demeter becomes nursemaid to Demophoön.*

her anger and withdrawal evoke Akhilleus. But Demeter's experience of the loss of a daughter is not a unique loss, like Akhilleus' loss of Briseis, but a loss experienced by every mother whose daughter marries. The *Hymn* does not simply celebrate the necessary fertility of women – it marks the pain and loss which each generation of women must experience to release the fertility of the next generation. There is a depth of human sympathy here for the grief which their 'structural' role involves for women, and this strikingly contrasts with the narrow and unsympathetic view embodied in Hesiod and Semonides. Yet this is a hymn, written not for some private female gathering but for a festival audience of men and women, and taken up and repeated to explain a central event in the religious calendar, the festival of the Eleusinian Mysteries, in which, exceptionally, all could take part, men and women, Athenian and non-Athenian, free and slave.

Of the many moving passages in the *Hymn*, one of the most memorable is Persephone's account of how she came to be snatched by Hades when out with a group of twenty and more other girls and goddesses, whose names fill seven lines of hexameters, picking flowers in the 'longed-for meadow' (416–33). Both the naming of the girls and the sense of sexuality which the passage breathes recall the celebration of girls' choruses in Alkman's *Partheneion*. In Alkman, too, the sensuous delight in young girls is combined with the pathos of imminent loss, as girls leave the chorus to marry. While the *Hymn to Demeter* does not require the particular social setting which Alkman's poetry draws upon, it becomes very much more vivid if we presuppose a social context in which the life of women was marked by intense bonds between mother and daughter and between coeval girls.

Sappho and her setting

Such a social context seems required, too, if we are to come to terms with the poetry of Sappho. Both in antiquity and since, discussion of Sappho's poetry has been dominated by concern to turn it into a window on to Sappho's life. But the historical importance of the poems does not depend on the (unknowable) degree to which the experiences described in the poems are autobiographical, but upon the experience with which the poems require the audience to be familiar and the nature of the audience which the poems presuppose. The poems of Alkaios and Arkhilokhos between them demand an audience experienced and interested in fighting, drinking, and sexual conquests. Sappho's poems demand an audience concerned with relationships, uncertain courtship, passion, and appreciative of the sensuousness of the natural world.

But how far apart is Sappho from her male fellow-poets? When Arkhilokhos says that he couldn't care less about Gyges' wealth, heroic deeds, or lording it over others (frg. 19), or when he or Alkaios claims not to care that they have thrown away their shields (Arkhilokhos frg. 5, Alkaios frg. 184) they challenge accepted values; not so very different is the challenge embodied in Sappho's rejection (frg. 16) of the view that a fine display of military might is the most beautiful thing on earth, in favour of the claims of 'whatsoever a person loves'. In all these cases the poet suggests that the values of an individual may not be the same as the values of the group. In pointing to Helen to exemplify the power of love, Sappho makes positively the point which Semonides (frg. 7) makes grudgingly when he admits that men's desire for women blinds them to their vices and makes them willing even to go to war over them. These later seventh-century BC poets can be seen to take up and explore at the personal level the conflict between individual and group which the *Iliad* explores on an epic level.

But if one of the consistent ploys of all these poets is to prefer personal values, in a group setting which could be expected to affirm the values of the group, it is hard to see the same group as equally receptive to Arkhilokhos' finally rather callous boasting of dumping one girl and seducing another (frg. 196a) and to Sappho's plaintive evocation of the pain of losing a woman friend to whom she was passionately attached (frg. 94). Alkman and the *Homeric Hymn to Demeter* show that men could be sensitive to the strength and importance of female affective bonds, but if we suppose that the primary performance context of archaic lyric poetry was all-male, we cannot explain either the existence of a female poet or the subject matter of her poetry. Women's place in this society can hardly be limited to neighbourly gatherings in the house or at the fountain.

That Alkman is Spartan, the *Homeric Hymn to Demeter* Athenian, and Sappho from Lesbos, suggests that women and their concerns were prominent not just in a single community or small group of communities, but across the later seventh-century Greek world in general. We should see Semonides' allusion to women gathering and talking about sex as confirming that gathering to share personal experiences was as possible and as important for women in his community as it was for the men whom he himself was addressing. The routines of daily life and the need to fetch water from well or fountain will have provided one setting for such meetings, but even more important, because less fleeting, will have been the religious festival. The festival of Demeter known as the Thesmophoria, which was regularly limited to women, is the single festival most widely celebrated over the whole Greek world. It is also women who come to be figured as the archetypal worshippers of Dionysos as soon as religious devotees make their appearance on Greek pottery, early in the sixth century (Figure 54). Men's poetry, created for the male symposion, often smacks of the camaraderie of the camp; but in many of Sappho's lyrics (Text 38) it is worship of the gods, of Artemis, Hera, Zeus, and above all of Aphrodite, that is close to the surface. Female society rarely makes its appearance in political narrative, but in the delicate process of creating communities which left space for the individual the self-scrutiny of the values of the individual woman as well as those of the individual man had scope to play a part.

218

Figure 54 Attic black-figure amphora of mid-sixth-century date showing worshippers of Dionysos.

The evidence of painted pottery is important in this context. As we have seen (pp. 153–61), seventh-century BC pottery had been invaded by mythology. A wide range of stories attract artists' attention. Herakles makes his appearance rescuing Deianeira from the centaur Nessos, Odysseus blinds the Cyclops Polyphemos, Perseus, assisted by Athene, beheads the gorgon Medusa, Paris judges the beauty of Hera, Athene, and Aphrodite. At the end of the seventh century Athenian potters and painters, influenced by the potters and painters of Corinth, adopted a new technique and with it developed a new range of pot shapes and subjects for painting. Initially many of the subjects reflect strongly the repertoire of Corinthian pot painting, but Athenian artists gradually add a new range of scenes. One scene that features prominently on a number of particularly large and elaborate Athenian pots is

...you like one of the well-known goddesses, and particularly enjoyed your song. But now she stands out among Lydian women, like the rosy-fingered moon at sunset outshining all the stars; its light spreads out over the salty sea and the flower-strewn meadows alike, and the beautiful dew falls; roses, delicate chervil and flowerlike honey-bloom thrive. As often as she visits here she remembers gentle Atthis, and her heart is eaten with desire...

Text 38: Sappho frg. 96. Lines of Sappho which survive only on a scrap of papyrus.

the marriage of Peleus and Thetis. This scene gave the artist the opportunity to show a parade of gods and goddesses, but does not otherwise offer obvious pictorial attractions. The attractions must lie in the subject itself, a glamorous wedding between a sea-nymph and a mortal, and in what it presages – the birth of a son, Akhilleus, who will live a short but exceptionally glorious life. When such a scene is painted on mixing bowls employed at symposia there can be little doubt how strongly those gathered on such occasions appreciated the centrality of women in the formation and fortunes of the social group.

NEW CITIES

Extant poetry goes some way to enabling us to conjure up the mind-set of Greeks at the end of the seventh century BC, but it is to archaeological evidence that we have to turn to get any impression of the physical setting. Three brief sketches will give a picture of both the consistency and the variety of habitational environment which shaped Greek lives. All these settlements are outside the core area of the Greek world, and were themselves established only in the eighth or seventh centuries, but although some scholars would class them as 'colonies' they were independent cities whose development and social dynamics were in all essentials parallel to those of settlements throughout the Greek world.

Thasos

Arkhilokhos' poetry (above, p. 186) gives us some impression of the rugged natural state of the Thasos to which he went from his native Paros, and of the fighting with previous occupants which he and those with him engaged in as they attempted to establish their claim to the island and to the mainland opposite. It gives little impression, however, of the settlement on Thasos itself or of its advantages.

During the eighth century BC the centre of human occupation on Thasos seems to have been a hill-top site inland in southern Thasos, known as Kastri, but this site was abandoned at the end of the eighth or early in the seventh century BC, at very much the same time as settlement is first attested on the coast at the north-east tip of the island. This site (Figures 55 and 56), which was to be the main Greek site, has tremendous natural advantages, particularly for anyone for whom communication by sea is important. It faces the mainland, which protects it from the north, and its natural, if shallow, harbour is further protected from the east by a rocky, but not dangerous, headland. Immediately south of the harbour a small area of coastal plain quickly rises some 150 m to a defensible acropolis, while further west the plain widens into a quite extensive area of good alluvial land. Furthermore there were rich mineral resources to be mined elsewhere on the island, on the mainland opposite, and even on the acropolis hill itself, where they included gold.

Figure 55 The acropolis of Thasos seen across the agora.

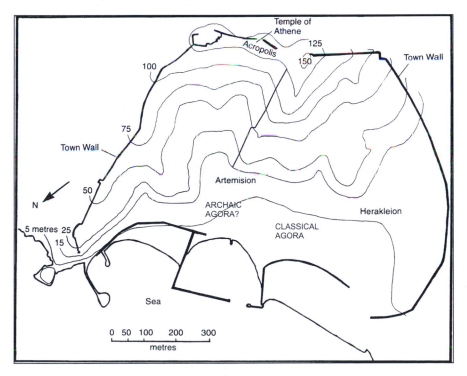

Figure 56 Plan of town of Thasos.

221

Figure 57 Seventh-century plate with polychrome decoration from the Artemision at Thasos. The plate was made in the Cyclades and shows the young hero Bellerophon riding on the winged horse Pegasos and aiming his spear at the monstrous khimaira.

There has been much dispute as to whether the Greeks were the first to settle at this site, or whether the first occupants were natives who were subsequently displaced by Greeks. The earliest material is abundant pottery from an apsidal house. The form of the house does not clearly indicate whether the builders were Greeks or Thracians, but the pottery includes nothing Greek, and in particular nothing Cycladic; rather there is local pottery, Thraco-Macedonian pottery, and Aiolian/Lemnian pottery (found also at Kastri). All of this would point clearly towards native settlement, were it not that a small quantity of the same Aiolian/Lemnian pottery has also been found in a deposit at the undoubtedly Greek sanctuary of Artemis, along with some Greek pottery and votives, particularly two oriental lions in ivory, which would normally be reckoned to date to the early seventh century BC. This has led to the suggestion that what we have is early Greek settlers who made use of local pottery. However, the marked change in the material assemblage around the middle of the seventh century BC, after which point Greek pottery alone is employed, together with the evidence furnished by the poems of Arkhilokhos – who is himself securely dated – make it most probably that Greek settlers arrived only in the middle of the century and that they joined a small but flourishing native settlement.

Early Greek occupation concentrated on the rising land at the foot of the acropolis hill, above the 5-metre contour. Here sanctuaries of Artemis, known from some very high-quality pottery dedications (Figure 57), and of Herakles, where the earliest sanctuary building seems to be c.620 BC, were quickly established, and residences were built on virgin soil well west of earlier occupation. We need to think away the later circuit wall and envisage two discrete clusters of settlement, which, in the sixth century seem even to have been separated by a wall. Traces at the sanctuary of Artemis suggest that metallurgical activity may have begun by 600 BC. On the acropolis seventh-century Daedalic figurines have been recovered from the sanctuary of Athene, and some relief sculpture, showing a lion and a panther, which marked the entrance to the sanctuary of Athene, may also date to the seventh century. Elsewhere in the island the important sanctuary at Aliki (Figure 58) on the south-east tip was established, and Greek occupation at Neapolis (modern Kavala) and Oisyme on the mainland opposite also dates back to the seventh century BC.

Around the end of the century there are signs of a new degree of planning being introduced into the settlement. Whereas earlier the orientation of buildings and streets seems anarchic, parallel streets were now established in the area of the Herakleion, almost parallel streets in the area of the Artemision. Earlier houses seem to have been rebuilt and enlarged, and it becomes possible to distinguish various different types of house, sometimes occurring side by side – urban houses built round courts and more 'rural' types with attached yards. A memorial to Glaukos (ML 3, Text 39), almost certainly the Glaukos referred to by Arkhilokhos in connection with the settlement on Thasos (frgs 96, 105 (above Text 30), 117, 131), was established that probably marked an important crossroads at the entrance to the public space of the agora on the flat land north-west of the Artemision. A second building in polygonal

Figure 58 The two archaic Doric temples in the sanctuary at Aliki at Thasos.

I am the memorial of Glaukos son of Leptines. The children of Brentes set me up.

Text 39: ML 3. Late seventh-century memorial from the agora at Thasos.

masonry at the Herakleion and a small temple to Athene on the acropolis were probably built shortly after 600 BC, and at about the same time the sanctuary of Artemis was extended and a massive marble statue, 3.5 m high, of a *kouros* carrying a lamb was dedicated to Apollo. But the community seems to have remained throughout the sixth century a bi-polar one, and in the middle of the century there was even a wall built dividing the two poles.

The overall picture afforded by Thasos around 600 BC is of a prosperous but complex community in whose life the sanctuaries of the gods, both in the settlement and outside it, play a most important part, and which is beginning to regulate its own activities but which places no premium on visible or physical unity. Regularity is conspicuously absent from the earliest settlement, and there is no sign of equal division of urban or rural land being an issue. The establishment of the sanctuary at Aliki suggests that the territory, rich in metals and marble as well as in agricultural potential, was important from the early years of Greek occupation, but there is no doubt that Thasians also looked very much to and across the sea.

Metapontion

Italian Metapontion provides an even more complex case of interaction and integration between varied Greek settlers and indigenous population. Ancient tradition, as handed down by Strabo (6.1.4), told that Metapontion had been founded by men from Pylos in Messenia under Nestor, their ruler in the *Iliad*, and had then been destroyed by Samnites, but refounded by the Akhaians who had settled at Sybaris. Although there are Bronze Age Greek remains in the area, the story of permanent Greek settlement in the area begins at the end of the eighth century BC.

It has become clear that understanding what happened at Metapontion depends on understanding the pattern of settlement in the whole area. Indeed, the earliest evidence for Greek presence comes not from Metapontion but from a site eight kilometres further inland, on the other side of the river Basento (Figure 59). Here at Incoronata, on the slopes and subsequently the top of a naturally fortified plateau, there are traces of settlement from the ninth century BC. There is one piece of Greek pottery of the middle geometric style (first half of eighth century), but Greek pottery appears in quantity only after 700 BC, and only at the site on the top of the plateau. That Greek pottery includes large numbers of Attic and Corinthian storage amphorae as well as fine protocorinthian pottery, Greek 'colonial' pottery, and native geometric and sub-geometric pottery. Around 700 BC a road was built through the site on the slopes, and the round huts there seem to have been abandoned. On

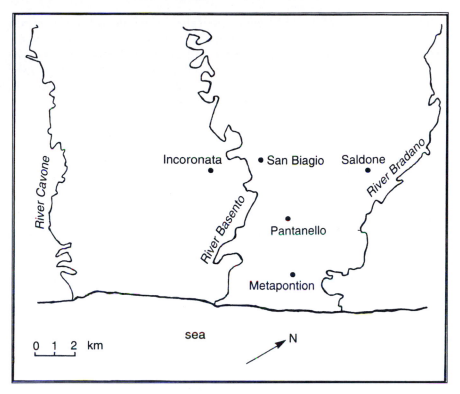

Figure 59 The Metapontion area.

the hill-top there is some building of more rectilinear structures in the early seventh century BC; these retain the characteristic local sunken floors, and both the mix of native and Greek pottery, and the twenty-seven seventh-century burials in 'native' style, with the bodies flexed, in the nearby cemetery suggest that the settlement changes do not indicate a change of population, but rather an assimilation of some aspects of Greek material culture by the indigenous people. Somewhere in the third quarter of the seventh century BC all occupation of the site seems to have ceased, except for cult activity at a small sanctuary site datable to the sixth century BC.

The earliest signs of settlement at Metapontion date to the early seventh century BC, and take the form of structures similar in form to those at Incoronata, and accompanied by a similar mix of indigenous and native pottery. This settlement continues throughout the seventh century, but around 600 BC there are widespread signs of destruction by fire, followed immediately by new building. The new building included an identifiable sanctuary building ('Sacellum C') and, most remarkably, a large wooden structure which may well have served the same purpose as the stone theatral structure (the 'ekklesiasterion') which replaced it on the same site around 550 BC and which seated some 8,000. Archaeologically it is impossible to tell whether the signs of fire at different parts of the site belong to a single episode or several, but there are signs of continuity between the old settlement and the new, both in functional division of space and in cultural links. Votives in the area of Sacellum C date to the late seventh century BC, and the Sacellum itself may have had a wooden predecessor. Links with Sybaris are to be detected in the pottery from Incoronata. In the countryside around, too, there is evidence of cult activity beginning just before 600 BC at the sanctuary of Artemis and Zeus at San Biagio and perhaps also at Saldone.

No single 'colonising' episode is thus to be detected in the history of settlement in this area. Greeks and natives seem to have shared goods, shared ideas, and, in the end, shared settlement. When manifestly Greek structures, including the vast wooden meeting place, were established in the early sixth century BC, we can be certain that there was conscious reorganisation of the community going on, but there is no reason to believe that this reorganisation excluded natives. That reorganisation certainly involved the countryside as well as the town: a considerable number of further rural sanctuary sites are attested from the first half of the sixth century. But it is as unclear in the countryside as in the town whether natives were displaced: a number of sites with indigenous pottery are known from the territory, and a small number have both indigenous and Greek pottery, but unfortunately the indigenous pottery cannot be closely enough dated to tell whether Greek and indigenous pottery was being used at the same time or whether the Greek pottery succeeded the native. A similar problem occurs in the country at Pantanello: here 'native' burials occur, where the knees of the corpse are bent, and these may be earlier than or contemporary with the Greek sarcophagi in the same cemetery, and may mark the continuation of native settlement beside Greek settlement, the replacement of native by Greek settlement, or the subjection of natives to new Greek settlers. In settlement terms, the revolution in the countryside comes in the second half of the sixth century BC, when the number of known farm sites in that part of the territory which has been subjected to intensive archaeological survey increases from five to sixty-six. This increase may be the result of extending civic organisation to the countryside: certainly by c.500 BC it is clear that the territory of Metapontion had been subjected to regular land division in parallel lines. Pollen and seed evidence suggests that the more intensive agricultural exploitation was associated with the introduction and spread of olive cultivation.

The Metapontion evidence strongly suggests that Greek settlers came in dribs and drabs from the end of the eighth century BC on, joined natives and encouraged a material culture which was ever more Greek in form. Whether or not there was a new influx of Greek settlers about 600 BC, there was certainly here, as, less dramatically, also at Thasos at about the same time, a taking in hand of the civic community and its facilities which implies a determined assertion of identity by the community. That urban assertion seems to have been accompanied by extended incorporation of the territory into the life of the community through the foundation or enlargement of a number of sanctuary sites more or less distant from the town. But only some years later, when civic participation in political life had demanded the monumentalising of the space where citizens met in the form of the stone 'ekklesiasterion', does the town seem to have interfered actively in the productive capacity of the territory, with a reorganisation that seems to map citizen equality onto the natural face of the landscape and that must surely have affected land-holding, landownership, and residential patterns.

Megara Hyblaia

The Greek settlement at Megara Hyblaia was established in the eighth century BC, apparently on a site not previously inhabited; it offers an example of a town with a long history of uninterrupted settlement development by 600 BC. Although Thucydides' story (6.1.4) of the initial settlers tells of successive negotiations with pre-existing Greek settlers at Leontinoi and with the indigenous ruler Hyblon, once Megara Hyblaia was founded its settlement history in the archaic period is remarkably uneventful. The settlers seem to have cooperated from the beginning, not only to leave a central space in the settlement for corporate activities, but also to allow individual residences sizeable and more or less equal plots of land arranged on a grid (Figure 60). In marked contrast to eighth-century BC practice in mainland Greek cities like Athens, the inhabitants of Megara Hyblaia from the very start disposed of their dead, by cremation or inhumation, at a very considerable distance

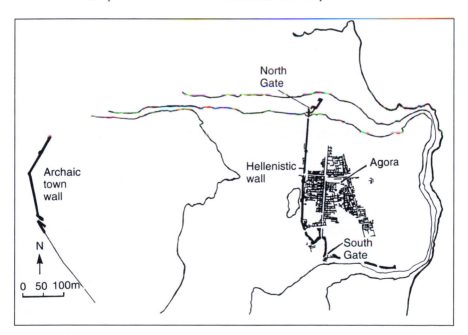

Figure 60 Megara Hyblaia.

from the residential area. This is one manifestation of the degree to which this is a settlement turned outwards, rather than inwards. The peculiarities of the plan are well explained by the desire to provide access out of the site – to the cemeteries, to a band of sanctuaries, and to the port.

The evidence of early planning at Megara Hyblaia has excited a great deal of attention. In fact there is evidence for not one but several, perhaps even five, separate grids of eighth-century origin in different parts of the site, suggesting that the early settlers clustered in groups and that there was a high degree of cooperation within the group, rather less cooperation between the groups. The eighth-century houses are remarkably small, single rooms of sides of 4–5 m, that get rebuilt and variously extended and elaborated during the course of the seventh century BC, and somewhere around the middle of the century seem to have walled off their separate plots. This demarcation of private property more or less coincides both with a marked growth in the number of houses and with the first securely public buildings in the agora: stoas, the earliest known with civic rather than sacred functions, were built on the east and north sides, temples towards the south, and two private houses just south of the agora were converted into a public building. A building just across a street from the agora has been identified as a heröon, presumably offering cult to the founder; it also seems to date to the last third of the seventh century BC, again implying the bolstering of community identity and self-consciousness at this period.

The forging of a community identity at Megara can be seen not simply in the pattern of building, which is distinctive in domestic building techniques and in the precise form and function of the new monumental public buildings, but also in the development of a separate pottery style. Just as at Thasos and in the area of Metapontion, so at Megara Hyblaia the seventh century BC is marked by local pot production which, although deriving inspiration from other pottery traditions, is essentially independent. In the case of Megara, where the eighth century BC had seen local imitations of Corinthian cups, seventh-century pottery is in the form of large figured vases, mainly of closed shapes with polychrome decoration and some mythological scenes (Figure 61). Neither in shape nor in decoration are these pots close to the Corinthian tradition; some of the shapes are much closer to Cycladic seventh-century products, some of the imagery best paralleled in earlier Cretan products. There is lively observation of the natural world (a wonderful bristling boar on one oinochoe) and more distinctive characterisation of human characters than found in Corinthian painting (as in one fragment with a group of men pulling on a cable, possibly part of a scene with the Trojan horse). The wide contacts, and probably mixed origins, of the first settlers, which are manifested in the presence of Corinthian, Attic, Euboian, Argive, and Rhodian pottery at Megara Hyblaia in the eighth century, has been here exploited to produce a self-confident art, eclectic but beholden to no one. This contrasts with the Corinthian-dominated pottery found in mainland Megara.

Figure 61 An example of the polychrome pottery made in Megara Hyblaia. This vessel is notable for its characterful animal frieze and for the fantastic creatures (centaurs and animal-headed man) in the panels of the main picture zone.

At all three of these sites the later seventh century BC saw physical transformation of urban settlement which began to turn a community with a priority on survival into a community with a distinct civic identity, willing to invest in communal facilities, to render its civic face visible by monumental constructions, and to map its political self out in visible terms. If the simple and spaced-out houses of eighth-century Megara Hyblaia offered an undifferentiated space in which a variety of familial arrangements could be accommodated, the elaboration of house forms and the enclosure of surrounding spaces in the middle of the seventh century BC suggest both functional differentiation and the establishment of symbolic statements appropriate to a community in which individual status has succeeded mere survival or material profit as a major driving force. If new settlers inevitably think of themselves in relation to the world they have left, late seventh-century residents at all these sites seem to have come to see themselves more particularly in relation to the community in which they lived.

But it is a mistake to treat these cities as if they were isolated communities, turned in on themselves. Just as what happens in late seventh-century Athens cannot be understood without an awareness of the degree to which Athenians were engaged with and dependent upon a wider world, so all three of these cities were only in a position to invest in their own physical plant because of the place they occupied in the wider world. We are not in a position to detail, let alone to quantify, the nature of that engagement. In the case of Thasos the mineral wealth of the island itself and of the neighbouring mainland must already be important. In the case of Metapontion the rural reorganisation of the sixth century can only have occurred because of a prehistory of agricultural

229

exploitation at a level in excess of that needed to meet local demand. But for neither Metapontion nor Megara Hyblaia are we likely to be dealing with an economy founded on particular specialisation. Rather both enjoyed geographical positions which guaranteed that shipping passing from Greece to southern and western Italy or from Greece to the Greek cities of southern Sicily would find occasion to call in and engage in at least low levels of trade.

The planned and differentiated civic space, the increasingly monumentalised sanctuaries of the gods, and the clear material marking of personal or familial status revealed at these three sites are also to be found at other sites throughout the Greek world within a generation of the year 600 BC. Even at the settlements by the Black Sea, at places like Berezan or Histria, such developments can be observed. Greeks, wherever they lived, had by around 600 BC ceased to belong to a world whose priorities were the priorities of Hesiod, narrowly focused on survival and on the morality of individual relationships. Rather they belonged to a world whose priorities were the priorities of Solon, Sappho, and the *Homeric Hymn to Demeter*, concerned with the articulation of the community through civic leadership and religious gatherings, where the family was no longer the sole, or even major, focus of attention for individuals, and where the tension between family ties and links with, and role within, the wider group absorbed personal emotional energies and created civic issues. It is the creative power of such a tension that we see manifested in the physical transformation of sanctuary and city in the years around 600 BC and that created the sixth-century world of the city.

8

INTER-RELATING CITIES

The short Sixth Century (600–520 BC)

In Chapter 4 I offered an interpretation of the archaeological evidence which suggested that during the eighth century BC there was an increasing sense within Greece of belonging to a particular community and that this went together with an awareness on the part of individuals that they could use achievements outside their community to enhance their status within it. In Chapter 6 I stressed the development of structures of relating within the community, the increasingly political ends to which links with men and communities outside the home city were put, and the cultural competition between communities. The tension between city particularism, the sense of belonging to one Greek community rather than another, and panhellenism, the sense of being part of a wider Greek world, informs early Greek history; Greek cities compete in one sphere as they collaborate in another, keen to assert difference but always within the framework of broader distinction between themselves and the non-Greek world. During the sixth century BC some forms of city particularism reach a height, while, first culturally and then in response to burgeoning political threats from the non-Greek world through actual political collaboration, Greek cities increasingly link up for common action as political issues cease to be merely parochial and come to be seen as belonging to a wider agenda. In this chapter I will explore the height of city particularism and the beginnings of new political cooperation.

COMPETING IN A PANHELLENIC WORLD

A circuit of festivals

From well before the end of the eighth century BC, Greeks had come from various cities to compete and to display their prowess and wealth at Olympia. They left behind valuable dedications and took away intangible glory which could nevertheless be cashed in for political power at home (above, p. 93). There is little doubt that the circle of those competing grew ever larger, just as, according to tradition, the range of events was also increased. Early in the sixth century BC the Olympic model was copied at Nemea (traditionally *c*.573

BC), Delphi (traditionally *c.* 582 BC), and Isthmia (traditionally *c.* 582 BC), and a 'circuit' was formed in which the festivals at these sites took place in a fixed four-year sequence. Delphi, Isthmia, and Nemea in this way asserted a claim to be a focus of attention for all Greek cities and a source of glory for all Greek competitors, and they seem to have bolstered this claim by advertising their links with the struggles of Herakles. Tradition held Herakles to be the founder of the Olympic games. His labours provided a model for athletic competition and were to adorn the metopes of the fifth-century temple of Zeus there; although Herakles' struggle with the Nemean lion is already celebrated in the *Theogony*, scenes of Herakles struggling with Apollo for the tripod at Delphi first appear in the early sixth century BC (see below, p. 247).

Such a multiplication of the sites and occasions on which glory could be won in an arena which all Greeks cared about needs to be understood not just from the point of view of the sanctuaries at Nemea, Isthmia, and Delphi promoting themselves, but as a response to an increasing demand. The increasing competition for power and influence within the political community, which we have seen in the seventh century BC to have been behind both the formalisation of constitutions and the rise of the tyrant, meant that there was a greater need for occasions on which symbolic capital could be earned. Kylon the Olympic victor was unsuccessful in his coup at Athens (above, p. 202), but his was a route others also wished, if less dramatically, to emulate.

The demand for symbolic capital could be fed from within as well as from outside the city. We saw in the last chapter how Solon devoted attention to the festival calendar at Athens. Within twenty years of the three new panhellenic competitions being created, the Athenians had revamped the festival of the Panathenaia as a civic festival on a grand scale (Figure 62) (Marcellinos, *Life of Thucydides* 3/Fornara 26). They now celebrated the goddess of the city with competitions which were not merely local but made claims on the attention of all Greeks, particularly in the musical competitions and the rhapsodic competition which led to what may have been the first fixed texts of the *Iliad* and *Odyssey*. Curiously, from a modern viewpoint, musical and rhapsodic performers never themselves earned the fame of athletes; the Panathenaic promotion of music and poetry made capital for Athens rather than for individual Athenians. But there is a curious correlation between years of unrest at Athens and years in which the Great Panathenaia was celebrated, and the story which the Athenians came to tell (Herodotos 1.60; [Aristotle,] *Constitution of the Athenians* 14) about Peisistratos gaining a grip on power by having a strapping girl, in the guise of Athene, accompany him into the city in a chariot, shows clearly the opportunities which the festival pageant gave for both achieving glory and cashing it in (see further below, p. 267).

The politics of poetic myth

The tension between city particularism and panhellenism is well seen in the public literature of the period, and particularly in the Homeric hymns, which

Figure 62 Panathenaic amphora of the so-called Burgon Group which perhaps dates to *c.*560BC and so to one of the earliest Panathenaic festivals.

seem to have mainly reached their present form between 650 and 500, and the Hesiodic *Catalogue of Women*. In discussing the *Hymn to Demeter* in the last chapter I noted that local Eleusinian colour was little stressed, that claims of Athens and Eleusis having an exclusive role in the origins of agriculture were not emphasised, and that broader issues, such as hospitality, were underlined. This insertion of local events and celebrations into a wider frame is in fact found repeatedly in the Homeric hymns. The strategy is particularly marked in the *Hymn to Apollo*, which conflates what were originally two separate hymns to celebrate into a single complex whole both Apollo as experienced at Delos and Apollo as experienced at Delphi. In doing so it makes clear that full appreciation of Apollo as a god pre-eminent in the spheres of the bow, the lyre, and of prophecy cannot be attained at either Delos or Delphi alone. Three times in the poem there are elaborate geographical catalogues – one as Apollo's mother Leto seeks a place in which to give birth to the god, a second as Apollo seeks a site for an oracle, and a third as he seeks servants for the sanctuary at Delphi – and these catalogues manage to incorporate reference to much of the mainland Greek world and to the Ionian and Aegean islands. The poem does indeed also include much local detail, including a charming description of the dancing and other competitions which were part of Apollo's festival on Delos (lines 146–64), but it is as a gathering of Ionians, not just of inhabitants of Delos, that that festival is celebrated. Both in the case of Delos and in the case of Delphi the *Hymn* insists that Apollo came to sites with no previous tradition – Delphian claims to autochthony, which are in evidence elsewhere, are tacitly contradicted, as Apollo has to import priests from Crete.

The *Catalogue of Women* attributed to Hesiod, which does not survive complete, continued the *Theogony* by exploring the genealogy not of the gods but of heroes, and its five books seem to have contained genealogies covering the whole heroic age. Like the *Theogony* itself, this poem was the product of a tradition, or in this case of a number of traditions which have been tied together by the plot line of the irresistible attraction of beautiful women. These traditions probably began as local genealogies, told in order to justify the political structures and political claims of separate cities and communities, and were put together into a more comprehensive whole during the seventh and sixth centuries BC. The form of the poem, which starts by going through unions between gods and mortal women, has been thought to suggest an origin in north-west Greece, which is particularly fertile in genealogies of that sort, but the signs of manipulation of the genealogies for political purposes at a late date come mainly in genealogies pertaining to cities in south-east Greece; the section of Attic genealogies is notably parochial, a feature which supports some slight linguistic evidence that the poem reached its final form in Athens. The significance of the poem rests, however, not on where it was composed, but in the fact that it was composed at all. That the poem entered popular circulation (it was very widely read later in antiquity) shows that desire for a comprehensive overview, bringing together encyclopedically all the heroic traditions of the Greek world and relating them to each other, had won out over, and despite, the political manipulation of a heroic past to justify institutions within the city or claims to control over other cities.

The decline of archaeological regionalism

The gradual triumph of the panhellenic, of that which could be taken as equally relevant to all Greece, over the local, can be well illustrated from the visual arts too. In the eighth century regionalism had been alive and well in traditions of bronzework (in tripods as well as in small bronze animal figurines) as well as in painted pottery, in which numerous regional styles may be distinguished. In the seventh century, although common developments are not difficult to discover, pottery traditions remain separate and become, in some ways at least, even more disparate; but the Daedalic style of sculpture was very widely adopted, and when *korai* and *kouroi* appeared they were taken up as offerings, and indeed produced, over a very large area of the Greek world. Like the forms of temple architecture (above, p. 199), the forms of sculptural dedication to be found in sanctuaries in the sixth century BC were heavily standardised, with quite as much variation apparent between the sanctuaries of different deities within a city as was to be seen between sanctuaries of the same deity in different cities. Only in the subject matter of the architectural sculpture on their temples (see below) did cities occasionally promote subjects and themes particular to their city alone. But even more striking than this high degree of sculptural uniformity is the way in which in the sixth-century regional pottery traditions went into a distinct decline, as Athenian pottery became more and more widely used as the fine pottery. In the seventh century a large number of Aegean islands, many mainland cities, and a number of Greek settlements abroad produced their own distinctive fine pottery; in the sixth century even Corinth, whose pottery had been so widely distributed and copied in the seventh century, ceased producing figured pottery around 550 BC, and by the early fifth century the little fine pottery made outside Athens imitated Athenian pottery. Athenian potters adapted their output, in iconography and even in shape, to at least some of their non-Attic markets, notably the non-Greek Etruscan market (Figures 63 and 64), but those non-Attic markets were also happy to import pottery whose imagery was intimately connected with Athens.

A foray into two essentially new, and very different, forms of cultural expression, architectural sculpture and coinage, makes particularly clear both the extent of, and the limits to, cultural panhellenism in the sixth century BC. If the triumph of panhellenism is required to explain the rampant spread of Doric architectural forms, the tensions between panhellenism and city particularism seem essential if we are to understand why, although the first stamped tokens of regular weight seem to have been minted in Lydia, it was the Greek world which took up, improved upon, and extended the whole concept of coinage.

Figure 63 So-called 'Tyrrhenian' amphora, made in Athens for the Etruscan market. This example: Courtesy of Boston Museum of Fine Arts, H.L. Pierce Fund.

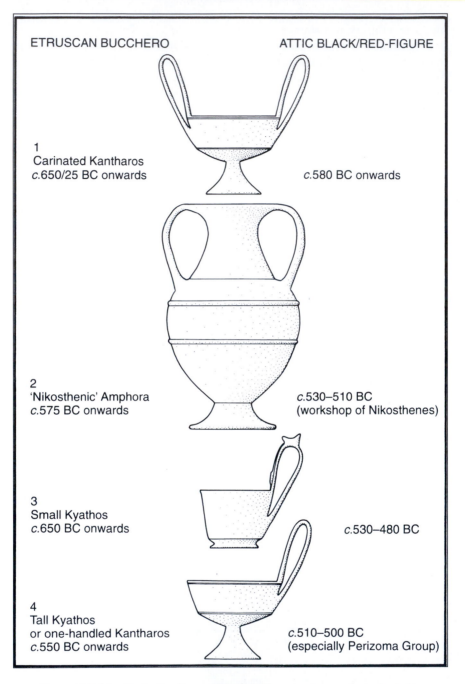

ETRUSCAN BUCCHERO   ATTIC BLACK/RED-FIGURE

1
Carinated Kantharos
c.650/25 BC onwards   c.580 BC onwards

2
'Nikosthenic' Amphora
c.575 BC onwards   c.530–510 BC
                                     (workshop of Nikosthenes)

3
Small Kyathos
c.650 BC onwards   c.530–480 BC

4
Tall Kyathos
or one-handled Kantharos
c.550 BC onwards   c.510–500 BC
                                     (especially Perizoma Group)

Figure 64 Table of indicating the way in which Etruscan shapes were adopted by Athenian potters.

The origin and development of coinage

The date at which the first coins were struck is much disputed, for lack of good archaeological evidence. Argument turns entirely around the interpretation of finds of a large number of coins of electrum (a naturally occurring alloy of gold and silver) found at the Artemision at Ephesos, in a deposit which must date to before 560 BC and in the company of other objects which are unlikely to be later than the early sixth century. The Artemision deposit includes lumps of electrum of standard weights, but without any marks, lumps with just a square punchmark (a so-called incuse square) on the reverse, and lumps with an incuse square on the reverse and striations on the obverse, as well as coins with incuse square reverse, striations, and type on the obverse, or simply incuse square reverse and type on the obverse. It is tempting to see here a developmental sequence where the introduction of standard weights of precious metals is rapidly followed by the marking of those weights to indicate that they are indeed standard, and to indicate their origin or issuing authority; but any development must have occurred very rapidly: one of the lumps without a type was stamped with the same punch used to stamp a coin with a type. It is striking that as soon as there are obverse types those types seem to originate from a number of different Ionian cities, and to be used to mark out the city of origin. So, although the largest number of coins among the Artemision finds have types which seem most probably to be associated with Lydia (lion heads and lion paws), there are also types with the head of a seal which seem to anticipate the city of Phokaia's later punning references to its own name (Greek *phôkê* = seal) (Figure 65).

The rapid diffusion of the idea of coinage, to which the Artemision finds seem to bear witness, continued throughout the sixth century. By the end of our period the vast majority of major, and many minor, Greek cities, not only in Ionia but in the Greek mainland, along with the Greek cities of Italy and Sicily, had begun producing their own distinctive coinages, each with one or a limited range of obverse types (Figure 66). These coinages were mainly now in silver, but on a number of weight standards and in a varying range of denominations (Table 6).

Figure 65 Early Phokaian electrum stater with 'seal' (*phôkê*) punning on the name of the issuing city.

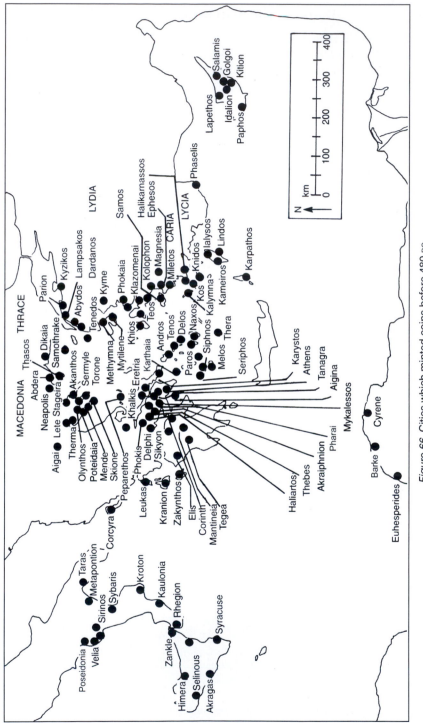

Figure 66 Cities which minted coins before 480 BC.

Table 6 Cities minting their own coins by 480 BC.

Name of city	Date*	Material of earliest coins	Earliest weight standard
Abdera	500	silver	Thraco-Macedonian
Abydos	480	silver	
Caria	500	silver	
Dardanos	480	silver	
Ephesos	550	electrum	Milesian
	A	silver	
Erythrai	A	electrum	Phokaian
	A	silver	Khian
Ialysos	500	silver	own standard
Idyma	480	silver	
Kalymna	480	silver	Euboeic
Kameiros	480	silver	Aiginetan
Karpathos	A	silver	Milesian
Khios	A	electrum	Milesian, later Khian
	500	silver	
Klazomenai	A	electrum	Milesian
	480	silver	
Knidos	A	electrum	Milesian, later
	A	silver	Aiginetan
Kolophon	480	silver	Persian
Kos	500	silver	Persian
Kyme	480	silver	
Kyzikos	A	electrum	Phokaian
	480	silver	
Lampsakos	A	electrum	Phokaian
	A	silver	
Lesbos	A	billon	Lesbian
Lindos	500	silver	Milesian, then Aeginetan
Lycia	500	silver	Lycian
Magnesia	480	silver	
Miletos	550	electrum	Milesian
	500	silver	
Mytilene	A	electrum	Phokaian
Parion	480	silver	
Phaselis	500	silver	
Phokaia	550	electrum	Phokaian
	480	silver	
Priene	480	silver	
Samos	A	electrum	Euboeic, later
	500	silver	Milesian

*550/500/480 = coins of this city found in boards before these dates A = archaic on grounds of style

Name of city	Date*	Material of earliest coins	Earliest weight standard
Selge	500	silver	
Sinope	480	silver	Aiginetan
Tenedos	A	silver	Thraco-Macedonian
Teos	550	electrum	Milesian
	500	silver	
Termera	A	silver	Milesian
Thracian Khersonesos	500	silver	Attic
Aigina	500	silver	Aiginetan
Andros	500	silver	Aiginetan
Argos	480	silver	Aiginetan
Athens	480	silver	Attic
Boiotian cities (Akraiphnion, Haliartos, Mykalessos, Orkhomenos, Pharai, Tanagra, Thebes)	A	silver	Aiginetan
Corcyra	480	silver	Corcyran
Corinth	500	silver	Corinthian
Delos	500	silver	Attic
Delphi	480	silver	Aiginetan
Eretria	480	silver	Euboeic
Karthaia	480	silver	Aiginetan
Karystos	480	silver	Euboeic
Khalkis	480	silver	Euboeic
Leukas	480	silver	Corinthian
Mantineia	480	silver	Aiginetan
Melos	480	silver	Milesian
Naxos	500	silver	Aiginetan
Paros	500	silver	Aiginetan
Sikyon	480	silver	Aiginetan
Siphnos	A	silver	Aiginetan
Tegea	480	silver	Aiginetan
Tenos	480	silver	Aiginetan
Thera	480	silver	Aiginetan
Golgoi	480	silver	Persian
Idalion	480	silver	Persian
Kition	500	silver	Persian
Lapethos	480	silver	Persian
Paphos	500	silver	Persian
Salamis	500	silver	Persian
Barke	500	silver	Attic
Cyrene	500	silver	Attic
Euhesperides	480	silver	Attic
Oreskioi (Macedonian tribe)	480	silver	Thraco-Macedonian

Continued…

Table 6 continued…

Name of city	Date*	Material of earliest coins	Earliest weight standard
Laiai (Macedonian tribe)	480	silver	Thraco-Macedonian
Derrones (Macedonian tribe)	480	silver	Thraco-Macedonian
Lete (Macedonia)	500	silver	Thraco-Macedonian
Dikaia (Macedonia)	500	silver	Thraco-Macedonian
Edonoi (Macedonian tribe)	480	silver	Thraco-Macedonian
Ikhnaioi (Macedonian tribe)	480	silver	Thraco-Macedonian
Bisaltai (Macedonian tribe)	A	silver	Thraco-Macedonian
Aigai (Macedonia)	480	silver	Thraco-Macedonian
Aeneia	480	silver	Euboeic
Akanthos	480	silver	Attic
Mende	480	silver	Euboeic
Neapolis	500	silver	Thraco-Macedonian
Olynthos	480	silver	Euboeic
Peparethos	480	silver	Attic
Poteidaia	500	silver	Euboeic
Samothrake	A	silver	Thraco-Macedonian
Sermyle	480	silver	Attic
Skione	500	silver	Euboeic
Skyros	480	silver	
Stageira	500	silver	Euboeic
Thasos	500	silver	Thraco-Macedonian
Therma	480	silver	Thraco-Macedonian
Torone	480	silver	Euboeic and local
Akragas	480	silver	Attic
Gela	480	silver	Attic
Himera	500	silver	Euboeic
Messana	A	silver	Euboeic
Naxos (Sicily)	A	silver	Euboeic
Samians at Zankle	480	silver	Attic
Selinous	500	silver	?Attic
Syracuse	480	silver	Attic
Zankle	480	silver	Euboeic
Kaulonia	480	silver	Akhaian
Kroton	480	silver	Akhaian
Metapontion	500	silver	Akhaian
Poseidonia	500	silver	Campanian
Rhegion	480	silver	Euboeic
Serdaioi	A	silver	Akhaian
Siri-	480	silver	Akhaian
Sybaris	500	silver	Akhaian
Taras	A	silver	Akhaian
Velia	480	silver	Campanian

Why was coinage invented, and why did it catch on so quickly in Greek cities? Any answer to the first of these questions has to account also for why the earliest coins are of electrum rather than of a pure metal. Electrum had the advantage of being of ten times higher value than silver but only two-thirds as high as gold; it had the disadvantage that its value depended upon the proportion of gold to silver in the alloy: this varies in naturally occurring electrum and therefore varies in early electrum coins, and, since colour changes are not an entirely reliable guide, the variation is hard to detect without an Archimedean grasp of specific gravity. It is difficult to believe that the high value was itself seen as an advantage of electrum: from the first not only high-value units, staters, but fractions of staters were employed: the unmarked lumps at Ephesos weigh an eighth and a twenty-fourth of a stater, and the coins vary from half staters to ninety-sixths of a stater (0.14g). What is more, when silver coinage began to be employed in Ionia around 550 BC it was immediately employed in small fractions, tiny in both size and value.

Early Ionian coinages all work on the stater system: that is, coins are described as fractions of some large standard weight (stater means 'weigher'). But exactly what that standard weight is very quickly comes to be different in different communities or groups of communities: most of the coins at the Ephesian Artemision are on what modern scholars refer to as the Milesian or Lydian standard (stater = c.14.1g), but Samos minted on the Euboeic standard (stater = 17.5g), Phokaia on one between the two (stater = c.16.5g). If one is dealing with a coinage which is not token, but worth its face value, different weight standards are not difficult to cope with, provided one has a pair of accurate scales, but the eagerness to use local weight standards for coinage strongly suggests that facilitating easy exchange over a distance was not the prime motivation for these Greek cities adopting coinage.

The primarily local coin use which the variety of weight standards suggests offers a clue not merely to the origins of coinage, and to why it catches on in the Greek world but not in the Persian empire (outside Asia Minor coins were simply treated as bullion), but also to the attractions of electrum. Because of its variable gold content, electrum is actually not obviously well suited to a 'real-value' coinage. Use of electrum would seem to require an issuing authority prepared artificially to declare that tokens of equal weight, but different gold content, will be treated as of the same value. In consequence circulation will be limited more or less to the area where that authority would be recognised. Rather than think that electrum is curiously ill-suited as a medium for a universal coinage, we should think of it as an ideal medium for localised exchange. Unlike gold or silver, electrum was likely to be of most value in the area politically under the influence or control of the issuing authority. Electrum coinage would provide a means of making standard payments to a large number of individuals, whilst also guaranteeing that those individuals reinserted themselves into the local economy. On this analysis it is attractive to see the Lydian need to pay mercenary soldiers as one important context for early use of coin.

Figure 67 Early Aiginetan stater with turtle device.

This view of early coinage would explain the rapid spread of the idea in Ionia: separate cities would see the convenience of standard units of exchange, but would need to produce these themselves for their own political realms. It would also explain the lack of concern to have a single weight standard, and how it was that on Lesbos a successful coinage was produced in debased (billon) silver. When silver coinages began to be minted, from about 550 BC onwards, some cities produced fractional coinages on a very large scale indeed. This argues for the continued importance of the use of coin within the issuing city (tiny coins are hardly a good medium for international exchange), although it also suggests that coinage had ceased to be primarily for making standardised payments. Silver could cross city boundaries more easily than electrum, at least until there was general confidence that a city could produce electrum with a consistent gold content (Kyzikos did manage to establish such confidence in her electrum staters, which were about 45 per cent gold, in the fifth century).

That silver coinage largely replaced electrum is probably to be understood both in terms of the more plentiful supply of silver in the Greek world, and especially in mainland Greece, and in the advantages of having coins that could be treated simply as bullion in areas to which the political authority of the minting city did not extend. It is uncertain whether Lydia replaced its electrum coinage by silver (and gold) before or after its incorporation into the Persian empire *c*.545 BC, but if before then incorporation seems to have had no direct effect on the issuing of coin; only under the rule of the Persian king Darius, at the end of the sixth century BC, were Lydian coins discontinued in favour of Persian darics and sigloi.

Mainland Greek silver coinages seem to begin about the same time as the Lydian abandonment of electrum. Although many mainland and western Greek cities rapidly began to mint silver coins, not all cities did, and the distribution of minting cities suggests that coinage was seen as serving different purposes in different places. The earliest of all mainland coinages is perhaps that of Aigina (Figure 67), which was not a city which had silver resources

Figure 68 Dodekadrachm (weighing 40.45g) issued by the Thraco-Macedonian Derrones around the end of the sixth century. It shows a bearded man, wearing chiton and kausia and holding a whip, who sits on a wheeled seat with lattice sides, drawn by two oxen. Above is a crested Corinthian helmet, and below a flower.

of her own, nor a city which in the mid-sixth century BC had its political independence seriously threatened; it was, however, a city unusually deeply implicated in trade. The way in which Aigina alone among mainland Greek cities was party to the settlement at Naukratis in Egypt (Herodotos 2.178), and alone among mainland Greek cities received Khian pottery, is symbolic of this, as is its enormous prosperity, displayed, for example, in its temple building (see below). But the way in which many Macedonian tribes and cities, not at all so involved in exchange relations, also began minting coins before the end of the sixth century suggests that coinage offered cities which had local silver resources a convenient way to realise the value of their bullion. This different motivation for coining is reflected in the denominations minted: Aigina minted didrachms/staters (12.2g) and divisions; the Macedonian cities and tribes (Figure 68) minted in unusually high denominations, from staters (9.2g or more) upwards to dodekadrachms (*c.*40.5g).

Trading connections seem to have played a part both in Aigina's decision to mint coins and in its ability to acquire silver – probably both from the island of Siphnos and from Attica. Coinage in turn played a significant role in Aigina's sixth-century trade. Hoards containing early Aiginetan coins have been found locally, in Crete, whose cities minted no coins of their own, and the Cyclades, where the influence of Aiginetan coinage is also manifested in the adoption of the Aiginetan weight standard and Aiginetan-influenced types. Hoarded Aiginetan coins have also been found both west and east through the Mediterranean, in Asia Minor, in Egypt, in Taras, and in Selinous. Politics as well as trade seems to have played its part even in the use and influence of Aiginetan coins: the Delians (politically under pressure from Athens) and Melians (who traced their descent from Sparta) stood out from their Cycladic neighbours and did not adopt the Aiginetan standard, and this suggests that outside Ionia coinage was seen from the beginning as a way of marking identity and staking claims to independence or to friendship.

How revolutionary was coinage? In some ways coinage should not be seen as revolutionary at all. Coinage did not transform the archaic Greek economy. There is no doubt that the existence of standard payments which commanded widespread confidence facilitated trade across the Greek and indeed the wider Mediterranean world. But coinage is more powerful as evidence for the pre-existence of economic networks and economic demand than because it created such networks. So large denomination coins were a convenient way of distributing silver, but silver distribution did not demand their existence. At the other end of the scale, small change was a convenient way of making small transactions locally, but such transactions could be made in other ways. What the minting of large denomination coins and of small change show is the level of demand for more convenient ways of making the various transactions. The rapid development of coinage is yet one more sign that both locally and across the Greek and Mediterranean world the level of exchange of goods was extremely high, and the prosperity of communities depended upon maintaining and enhancing this level.

Similarly, coinage did not substantially alter the way in which value was conceived. Standardised measures certainly antedate coinage, and the frequent ambiguity as to whether an ancient text is using stater, drachma, etc. as an indication of weight or a reference to coin shows how unimportant it was to make a distinction between the two. Nor did evaluation in monetary terms have to await coinage, whether for purposes of assessing punishment or in other contexts. Coinage long remained only one way of rewarding success (for example, in games) or meeting obligations (for example, dowries), and was by no means necessarily the preferred means. This was the case both for transactions within a city and for transactions which crossed city boundaries. On the one hand cities preferred to have local services performed directly by the rich, rather than paid for by taxation: that is how classical Athens financed plays and other elements of festivals, the equipping of triremes, and so on. On the other hand the local connotations of coinage might mean that pretensions to international status were best embodied in other goods.

Where coinage may have had a more revolutionary effect is in a more intangible area. The Ionian philosopher Herakleitos (see p. 299) claimed that 'all things are an exchange for fire and fire for all things, like goods for gold and gold for goods' (frg. B30). The way in which money put into everyone's hands something that could be exchanged for anything else rendered all things commensurable. Animals, crops, manufactured items, labour, services – all these now had a precise equivalent. That there might be one thing to which all others could be reduced was the central idea of the earliest philosophers (p. 298), and it is an intriguing thought that thinking in these terms might have been occasioned by reflecting on coined money.

Coinage was by its nature caught between the universal and the particular. One aspect of this is the tension between city particularism and panhellenism, particularly illustrated by two curious episodes in Ionian coinage. The first of these is the minting on Samos of lead coins, apparently originally covered with electrum foil. By the time of Herodotos these coins were being explained as minted to trick and bribe the Spartans to lift their siege of the island (see below, p. 263). Herodotos does not believe that story, and we should probably not believe it either. The more plausible alternative explanation, that they were minted for internal use when there was a crisis shortage of precious metal for minting, presumably because of the siege, is very significant: it implies both a heavy demand for coinage to meet internal Samian transactions, and a sufficiently strong political authority to make such a token coinage possible. The second episode is the final manifestation of electrum coinage in Ionia. A series of staters, on the Milesian weight standard, of similar fabric, and with similar reverse punches, were minted at some point late in the sixth century BC at a number of Ionian mints (Klazomenai certainly, probably also Khios, Lampsakos, and Phokaia). These coins bear ten different obverse types, several of which closely echo the types regularly used by Ionian cities. The occasion and motivations for these staters are uncertain – dating makes the traditional association with the Ionian Revolt (below, p. 304) unlikely – but it would appear that here we have a common coinage which nevertheless also respects the separate identities of the different participating cities. Was this common coinage a political gesture, in the face of Persian pressure, or was the motivation economic – a way of providing a guarantee of uniform gold content in a widely distributed coinage? Whichever is the case, the unwillingness to go for complete monetary union is striking. (For a further illustration see below, p. 269, on Athens.)

The development of architectural sculpture

Similar tensions between uniformity and particularity can be seen in the very different medium of architectural sculpture. Architectural sculpture effectively begins with the two, apparently identical, pediments of the temple of Artemis on Corcyra (Corfu). Carved in the first quarter of the sixth century BC, the pediments were dominated by the frontal-faced running figure of Medusa and by two lions/leopards, also with frontal faces, lying heraldically head-inwards. Medusa seems to have been accompanied at the centre by much smaller figures of her children, Pegasos and Khrysaor, and at the corners of the pediments these are very much smaller figures again, perhaps showing gods and titans (the children and one of the titans are also *en face*). The stress here on coming face-to-face with the gods, and on struggling with monsters and/or animals as a way of figuring the gods' relations with humans, is shared by many subsequent sixth-century temple sculptures. A similar gorgon, but in terracotta and much smaller, certainly featured on the pediment of the temple of Athene at Syracuse before 550 BC, both gorgon (at the corner) and lion featured on the architrave of the Ionic temple of Apollo at Didyma (*c.*540–520 BC), and Medusa may also have been central to the pediment of the Athene temple of the same period on the Athenian Acropolis. Certainly the latter featured facing lions, on this occasion savaging a bull. That motif

Figure 69 Metope from Temple C at Selinous showing Perseus and gorgon.

of a lion attack, already familiar enough in painted pottery of the seventh century BC, would still find a prominent place in the east pediment of the temple of Apollo at Delphi when it was rebuilt around the last decade of the sixth century. The centre of the Delphi pediment was taken up with a frontal view of the chariot of Apollo, a composition also essayed slightly earlier at Delphi in the west pediment of the Siphnian treasury and in the middle of the century on the metopes of Temple C at Selinous in Sicily. The metopes at Selinous also featured Medusa (being beheaded by a Perseus assisted by Athene, Figure 69) as well as Herakles carrying off the Kerkopes (Herakles, like Perseus and Athene, with frontal face), and that latter scene in turn featured in the metopes from the Heraion of Foce del Sele in Italy, of roughly the same date, where other deeds of Herakles, including the struggle with Apollo for the tripod, also appeared. That struggle for the tripod made its appearance at Delphi in sculptural form some quarter of a century later in the east pediment of the Siphnian treasury.

This brief tour of sixth-century-BC temple sculpture brings out, I hope, how far sculptors in the Greek mainland, the Ionian islands, in Sicily, in Italy, and to at least some extent in Ionia, were largely working with the same body of imagery, and employing the same sorts of artistic devices to impress the power of the gods on the worshippers at a sanctuary. Bold, broadly symmetrical compositions, frequent use of frontality, and highly legible actions mark pediments and metopes alike. On both the Sikyonian and the

Siphnian treasuries at Delphi writing was employed to make clear what the scene was, and there is little doubt that the narrative evoked mattered. These were not sculptures intended to appeal to a local audience easily kept informed by non-visual means; they were sculptures directly competing with other sculptures elsewhere and designed to make more than a parochial impression. Yet to do so they did not rely either on the Homeric poems or on Hesiod's *Theogony* – only with the Siphnian treasury frieze do battles at Troy enter the sculptor's repertoire: the common basis of Greek identity was a broad one, and the number of traditions which had been kept free from attachment to a particular city was large. That said, however, it is worth noting that at Athens the parochial does seem to have remained important; one might again compare the Athenian parts of the *Catalogue of Women*: neither the triple-bodied serpent-tailed figure from one Acropolis pediment nor the central frontal female figure shown inside a building on another, the so-called 'Olive Tree' pediment, can be paralleled or identified.

MONUMENTALISING THE CITY

The pattern of temple building

The buildings which bore these sculptures are part of a striking monumentalisation of the Greek city. Temple buildings already stood out among the structures of the eighth century BC; in the seventh century BC the advent of stone walls and elaborate tiled roofs further increased the prominence of religious buildings within the city (above, p. 199); in the sixth century BC such buildings spread, multiplied, and increased greatly in size and architectural sophistication, as stone sculpted metopes replaced painted terracotta ones, stone columns replaced wood, and cities lined up temples side by side in their sanctuaries. The increase in size and in number of structures may be illustrated in tabular form (Table 7).

The impact which sixth-century building might have on a city is particularly well illustrated at Selinous (Figures 70 and 71). Settlement at Selinous dates back to the middle of the seventh century, and habitations spread rapidly over a wide area. Shortly after 600 BC there are signs that here, as elsewhere at roughly this time (above, pp. 223 and 225), a new plan was imposed upon the settlement, involving both the establishment of a rectilinear grid of roads on the acropolis and on the Manuzza hill, and the building of two terraces to enlarge the sanctuary area. The so-called megaron building may date from this time. Around 560 BC there seems to have been some destructive event, followed by the building of a monumental terrace covering the eastern edge of the acropolis, and the building of the first really large temple, temple C, complete with sculpted metopes. This was followed almost immediately by temple D. Simultaneously two smaller structures, the temple of Demeter Malophoros and temple M, seem to have been under construction at the

Table 7 Major Greek temples down to 480 BC.

Approx. date	Name of temple	Order	No. of columns	Dimensions of stylobate (m)	Column height (m)
660	Corinth, Apollo				
650	Isthmia, Poseidon		7 × 18	14.4 × 39.3	
650	'Argive' Heraion, Hera		6 × 14	15.1 × 46.6	
650	Eretria, Apollo		5 × 16 (?)	11.7 × 40.5	
620	Thermon, Apollo	Doric	5 × 15	12.1 × 38.2	
610 (or 510?)	Corcyra, Kardaki (Mon Repos)	Doric	6 × 11	11.9 × 25.6	3.0
590	Olympia, Heraion	Doric	6 × 16	18.8 × 50.0	5.2
580	Corcyra, Artemis	Doric	8 × 17	c.23.5 × 49.2	
580	Kalydon, Apollo			10.4 × 15.6	
570	Metapontion, B (Hera)	Doric	9 × 17	19.9 × 41.6	
565	Syracuse, Apollo	Doric	6 × 17	21.6 × 55.3	8.0
560	Selinous, Demeter Malophoros	–	–	9.5 × 20.5	–
560	Samos, Heraion (Rhoikos)	Ionic	8 × 21	52.5 × 105.0	
560	Ephesos, Artemis	Ionic	8 × 21	55.1 × 115.1	12.1
555	Syracuse, Olympieion	Doric	6 × 17	22.4 × 62.1	8.0
550	Lokroi Epizephyrioi	Ionic	6 × 14	17.1 × 35.3	
550	Gela, Athenaion	Doric	6 × 12	17.3 × 35.2	
550	Selinous, Temple C	Doric	6 × 17	24.0 × 63.7	8.7
550	Selinous, Temple M	Doric		10.9 × 26.8	
550	Cyrene, Apollo	Doric	6 × 11	16.8 × 30.1	
540	Didyma, Apollo	Ionic	8/9 × 21	42.0 × 87.0+	15.45
540	Assos, Athene	Doric	6 × 13	14.0 × 30.3	4.8
540	Corinth, Apollo	Doric	6 × 15	21.5 × 53.8	7.2
535	Selinous, Temple D	Doric	6 × 13	23.6 × 55.7	8.3
530	Metapontion, AII	Doric	6 × 17	20.2 × 50.5	6.9
530	Poseidonia, 'Basilica'	Doric	9 × 18	24.5 × 54.3	6.4
530	Samos, Heraion (Polykrates)	Ionic	8 × 24	55.2 × 112.0	
530	Samos, South Building	Ionic	7 × 17	22.8 × 45.6	
530	Lesbos, Apollo Napaios	Aeolic	8 × 17	16.3 × 37.5	
530	Samos, North Building	Ionic	5 × 12	25.8 × 41.2	
525	Selinous, Temple FS	Doric	6 × 14	24.4 × 61.9	9.1
525	Athens, Athene Polias	Doric	6 × 12	21.3 × 43.2	7.4
520	Aigina, Apollo	Doric	6 × 11	16.4 × 31.4	
520	Delphi, Apollo	Doric	6 × 15	21.7 × 58.2	10.6
520	Orkhomenos, Kalpaki	Doric	6 × 12	14.5 × 27.0	
520	Selinous, Temple GT	Doric	8 × 17	50.1 × 110.1	14.7
520	Kalaureia, Poseidon	Doric	6 × 11	14.4 × 27.5	
520	Naxos, Apollo (unfinished)	Ionic	6 × 13	24.3 × 55.2	

continued ...

Table 7 continued

Approx. date	Name of temple	Order	No. of columns	Dimensions of stylobate (m)	Column height (m)
520	Paros	Ionic	Prostyle	large (only details survive)	
520	Delos	Ionic	Hexastyle large prostyle		
515	Athens, Olympieion (unfinished)	Doric	8 × 21	41.1 × 107.9	11.3
510	Karthaia, Athene	Doric	6 × 11	12.0 × 23.2	4.5
510	Akragas, Zeus Olympios	Doric	7 × 14	52.7 × 110.1	
510	Poseidonia, Athene	Doric	6 × 13	14.5 × 32.9	6.1
510	Poseidonia, Foce del Sele Heraion	Doric	8 × 17	18.7 × 39.0	
510	Eretria, Apollo	Doric	6 × 14	19.2 × 46.4	
500	Hermione, Poseidon	Doric	6 × 12	15.0 × 31.5	
500	Karthaia, Apollo	Doric	6 in antis	16.0 × 32.0	
500	Metapontion, Tavole Palatine	Doric	6 × 12	16.1 × 33.5	5.1
500	Akragas, 'Herakles'	Doric	6 × 15	25.3 × 67.0	10.07
500	Delphi, Athene Pronaia	Doric	6 × 12	13.3 × 27.5	4.6
500	Sounion, Poseidon	Doric	6 × 13	13.1 × 30.2	?
490	Aigina, Aphaia	Doric	6 × 12	13.8 × 28.8	5.3
485	Athens, Older Parthenon (unfinished)	Doric	6 × 16	23.5 × 66.9	?
490	Selinous, Temple A	Doric	6 × 13	16.0 × 40.0	
490	Selinous, Temple O	Doric	6 × 13	16.0 × 40.0	
490	Metapontion D	Ionic	8 × 20	14.8 × 38.4	
480	Himera, Victory	Doric	6 × 14	22.5 × 56.0	?
480	Syracuse, Athene	Doric	6 × 14	20.2 × 55.0	8.7
480	Selinous, Hera (ER)	Doric	6 × 15	25.3 × 67.7	10.2

western sanctuary site across the river Modione, and then within a very short time of the completion of temple D, building commenced in the eastern sanctuary site across the river Cotone, where temples FS and GT were constructed, the colossal GT dwarfing not only FS but also temples C and D. Nor did building work stop there: two further rather smaller temples on the acropolis, temples O and A, belong to the first quarter of the fifth century BC, as also does the large temple ER, once more with sculpted metopes, at the eastern sanctuary site.

Even if we include buildings other than temples, which are not represented in Table 7, no other city is known to have built as much as did the city of Selinous in the century from 580 BC onwards. But Akragas, 75 km south-east of Selinous and not founded until the early sixth century, Poseidonia (Paestum) in Campania, founded at about the same time as Selinous, and

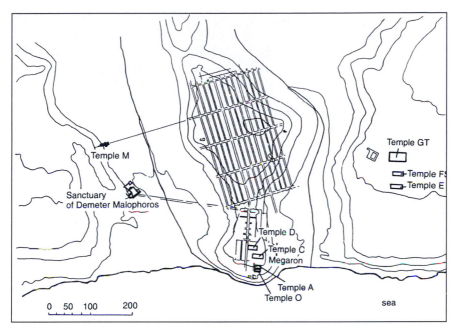

Figure 70 Plan of Selinous.

Figure 71 View across the acropolis at Selinous.

Figure 72 The quarries west of Selinous from which stone for the temples was dug.

Metapontion (which was also constructing the great stone ekklesiasterion) come close to rivalling Selinuntine activity, each building several very large temples. In a different way Samos, Ephesos, and Didyma also rival Selinous: only at Samos (below, p. 261) are there a number of separate large structures, several of them rather ill-known, but each of these three cities was building on a scale matching the very largest buildings in the west. On the Greek mainland only one city comes near to this display of energy in building: Athens. At Athens, as well as two phases of building of the temple of Athene Polias, surviving architectural sculptures – the so-called 'Bluebeard' pediment – show that a further, equally large, temple must have been built on the Acropolis in the period 570–550 BC. Then, around 515 BC, work was begun on the Olympieion, which was on the scale of the largest temples in the west and in Ionia. By comparison to the buildings on these sites even the building activity at places such as Delphi or by cities as wealthy as Aigina looks puny.

Explaining the pattern

How are we to understand the decision of some cities to build frequently and on a large scale, when other cities built rarely and modestly? There is clearly some correlation with the size and wealth of the city: Selinous and Athens, Akragas and Samos, all had very large hinterlands. Many of the cities have plentiful resources of adequate, if not excellent, building stone in their own territories too (Figure 72), although that is also true of many cities which do not build so extravagantly. But these are not only large and well-resourced

252

cities, they are well-connected cities. The extensive contacts of Samos, and the prominence of rich Athenian families outside their own city, will be considered at greater length below (and see above, p. 87); the extent to which Akragas was implicated in the wider Greek world is well revealed at the end of the archaic period when it is prominent among the sources of the athletic victors celebrated in Pindar's Victory Odes. But the marginal situation of all these cities except Athens is also important.

Juxtaposed to communities, Sicel, Italian, Phoenician, Lydian, from which they wished to distinguish themselves, and on the fringes of territory recognised as Greek, the citizens of these places may well have felt the need not only to impress their non-Greek neighbours but also to display to Greek visitors their Hellenic identity. Ethnic identity tends to become salient when a group comes under pressure, and these communities needed to display Greek identity as communities at home did not. The pressure manifested itself in Ionia in the form of direct political intervention, first from Lydia and then from Persia; in the west in the sixth century BC pressure was less direct. Such pressure there has long been suspected of being responsible for the burst of 'Greek' building at Segesta in the late fifth century BC; at Selinous that pressure is archaeologically manifest in the evident Phoenician influence displayed by the mosaic pavement showing the Phoenician goddess Tanit which was installed in front of temple A some time after the destruction of the city in 409 BC. The historical narrative reveals that Selinous had been feeling her way between the Greek and Phoenician worlds long before this. When Carthaginian and Greek clashed in Sicily in 480 BC, Selinous took no part on the Greek side (below, p. 327), and when the Carthaginians exiled Geskon, the son of their defeated general Hamilcar, Selinous took him in (Diodoros 13.43.5). The story that Selinous was going to send cavalry to help the Carthaginians against the Greeks, which came to circulate after the Carthaginian defeat (Diodoros 11.21–2), shows just how vital it was for Selinous to continue vigorously to assert its Hellenic identity (an assertion readily accepted by other Greek cities when they needed help – cf. Diodoros 11.68.1).

Regional styles of architecture

If the Greeks of Sicily and South Italy, on the one hand, and those of Ionia, on the other, used monumental temple architecture in part to identify themselves as belonging to a wider Greek community, and to distinguish themselves from the non-Greek communities with which they were in constant contact, this did not mean that they were simply following initiatives begun in the Greek mainland. The temples of Ionia, although they emulated each other closely, managed a basically similar arrangement (central chamber surrounded by a colonnade on a more or less imposing base) with very different articulation of proportions and details. The Ionic order (Figure 73, compare Figure 53) which they employed treated the foundations (not limited to three large steps as in Doric), the foot of the column (given a base as not in Doric), the flutes

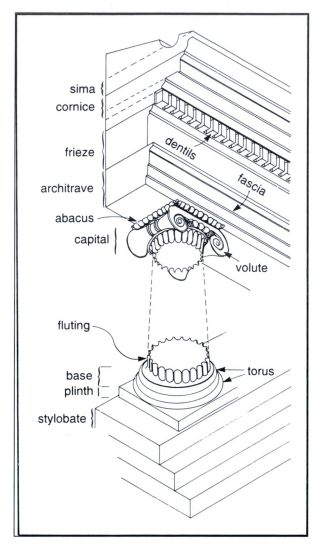

Figure 73 Diagram of the developed Ionic order.

of the columns (separated by fillets rather than simply an arris), the profile of the column (swelling only in Doric), the column capitals (with volutes rather than simply a quadrangular block on a 'cushion'), the architrave (divided into three faces in Ionic), and the frieze (of metopes and triglyphs only in Doric), all differently. The temples of Sicily and South Italy shared the Doric order with the peripteral temples of the Greek mainland, but they nevertheless developed variant features of plan and detail, building according to distinct rules, and working their architectural mouldings on a quite different scale. When Sicilian Gela built a treasury at Olympia in around 540 BC it used its own architects and imported the extremely striking terracotta facings (Figure 74) to the cornices; mainland Greek visitors to Olympia can have been in no doubt about the distinct architectural tradition of the west.

Architecture is, in fact, extremely revealing about the strength and limits of regionalism in Greek culture in the sixth century BC. While the basic scheme of temple architecture is recognisably the same from one end of the Greek world to the other, not only certain techniques (such as roofing), but also certain types of plan have a distinctly regional distribution. This is nicely seen in the archaic Doric temples of the Cyclades. These are almost all small and not peripteral – hence very few figure in Table 7, where the Cyclades are mainly represented by poorly preserved, but certainly large, Ionic temples. The Doric design preferred in the Cyclades has two, five, or six columns *in antis* (that is, between the decorated ends of the side walls) fronting a single or a centrally divided chamber. In some cases the building's width exceeds its length, as in the temple at Aliki at the southern tip of Thasos (see above, p. 223). The Doric temple at Aliki is in fact very close, in the proportions of its groundplan, to the Ionic temple at Sangri on Naxos (of *c.*520 BC), and the influence on Cycladic Doric of the more lofty proportions of Ionic buildings is seen particularly clearly in the Heraion at Delos of *c.*500 BC, whose columns are exceptionally tall and thin. This separatist tradition admits its first clear exception in the temple of Athene at Karthaia on Kea, a building close in both time and space to, but in marked contrast with, a temple of Apollo which, although unusually large, is essentially in the Cycladic tradition. The Athene temple at Karthaia, by contrast, marks the entry of the mainland tradition of Doric temple building into the Cyclades, and it is this mainland tradition which will come to dominate classical architecture in the area, as, typically, the fifth century BC witnesses the decline of regional cultural traditions.

Figure 74 Terracotta facings of the sixth-century Gela treasury at Olympia.

Cultural politics

The importance of the monumentalising of the city, and particularly of its sanctuaries, during the sixth century BC in publishing to neighbours, Greek and non-Greek, and to more distant cities with which relations are desired, claims to belong to a particular Greek or regional or local cultural world, can be seen graphically in the emulative actions of Kroisos king of Lydia. (Similar emulative actions claimed by Herodotos (1.14) for earlier Anatolian rulers, Midas and Gyges, are historically more suspect.) Kroisos became for the Greeks, as is very clear from the first book of Herodotos, the type of the man of immense wealth whose prosperity led him to fall, when he overestimated his military strength and attacked the Persians. Prior to that fall, however, Kroisos had made numerous dedications of great value at Greek sanctuaries, both in Ionia and in the Greek mainland. Herodotos lists such dedications in a treatment (1.50–2, 92 with Fornara 28) which also stresses that Kroisos does not really understand the Greek religious world, and particularly Greek oracles. Kroisos' 'testing' of Greek oracles (Herodotos 1.46–9) by sending messengers to ask what he, Kroisos, was doing at the time of the consultation, is something it would have been unthinkable for a Greek to do (see above, pp. 192–3). But, if Kroisos failed to understand the rationale of Greek oracles, he clearly understood very well the importance of Greek interstate sanctuaries as places at which to play cultural politics. Although the Persians' later very far from respectful treatment of Greek sanctuaries no doubt posthumously increased Kroisos' prestige, his success in marketing himself as a friend of the Greek world, who was finally able to understand, appreciate, and absorb Greek values, emerges not only from the sympathetic picture of Kroisos which Herodotos presents, but from the eagerness of Greek cities and individuals to cultivate his friendship: even the Spartans claimed to have tried to send him a great gift (Herodotos 3.47). And this of the man who completed the century-long Lydian encroachment on the Greeks of Asia Minor (*ANE* 567–72), and whose fall effectively put those Greeks into Persian hands!

If cities and ambitious foreign kings played politics through monumental building and dedication at sanctuaries, so could individual members of the élites of Greek cities. The glittering dedications of ivory, gold, and silver, sometimes in combination (Figure 75), which the sanctuary of Delphi received from eastern as well as mainland Greeks during the sixth century, unfortunately no longer carry the story of the circumstances of their dedication with them. But when the Athenian family of the Alkmaionidai, in exile from their homeland, financed the rebuilding of the temple of Apollo at Delphi in the second half of the sixth century BC, this was specifically cited in support of the claim that they had unduly influenced Delphi's oracular responses to the Spartans again the Peisistratid tyrants at Athens. That story presupposes that building temples earned local gratitude which might be expected to be repaid by political support, but there is little doubt that the building itself was constructed in order to keep the Alkmaionid name and

Figure 75 Silvergilt sacrificial ox from Delphi dating to the sixth century BC.

fame in wide circulation amongst such as frequented the great sanctuaries. When the oracular sanctuary of Apollo Ptoieus, in the territory of the small city of Akraiphnion in Boiotia, briefly acquired undue prominence as a result of the fire which destroyed the old Delphic temple, the Alkmaionids seem to have taken advantage of this and dedicated a monumental sculpture there to commemorate a chariot victory won at Athens (Text 40). Such victories could themselves be of such political moment that in the same period the Athenian Kimon thought it politic to have his chariot victory at the Olympic games announced as the victory of the Athenian tyrant Peisistratos (Herodotos 6.103, and see below, p. 269). Monumentalising such victories ensured that the glory won was neither just local nor just temporary. By 480, at latest, the Argives, at least, had created a public stud with which to achieve chariot-race victories at the Olympic games (*P. Oxy.* 222.31).

These last examples not only return us to the enhanced use of panhellenic games, with which this chapter began, but also confront us directly with political struggles within and between Greek cities. It is to these that I now turn.

FEUD AND FACTION BEYOND THE HISTORY OF THE CITY

In Chapter 6 I explored the feuding within the élite of individual cities, and the products of this feuding – laws and tyrants. The stories of early tyrants are much more interested in using them as examples of how individuals seize power than in exploring their actions, yet it is notable that their seizure of power is rarely held to have been significantly assisted from outside the city. In tradition, at least, seventh-century tyrants were largely self-generating, getting nothing except advice from other cities or other tyrants. Seventh-century cities regularly exploded, but the fall-out seems generally to have

I am a fine statue to delight Leto's son, Phoibos Apollo. Alkmaionides son of Alkmaion dedicated me after a victory with his swift horses, which Knopiadas drove at the festival of Pallas at Athens.

Text 40: IG i³ 1469. An Alkmaionid celebrates a chariot victory at Athens with a dedication at the sanctuary of Apollo Ptoieus near Akraiphnion in Boiotia.

determined its own future in some new area rather than to have affected the political life of neighbouring cities.

The traditions about faction, feud, and tyranny in the sixth century BC, by contrast, whether discussing the establishment, the continuation, or the dissolution of tyranny, are rich in claims that financial assistance was gained from outside, that foreign troops were used, that hostility to or from another city was an important factor, or that another city played a part in bringing tyranny to an end. The communities which in the seventh century BC had been feeling their way to the establishment of means of self-determination, and whose élites battled somewhat nervously among themselves to gain or restrict access to power, in the sixth century found their history to be ever more closely tied in to the history of the wider world of Greek cities. A short exploration of some better-attested examples will show the range of different ways in which sixth-century cities became implicated in one another's histories.

The case of Polykrates of Samos

Although we cannot reconstruct the political history of seventh-century Samos in any detail, the scraps of tradition which are preserved suggest that it too, like the cities examined in Chapter 6, saw dispute within the élite and individuals assuming extraordinary powers; one Phoibias is said, by a very late source (Theodoros Metokhites, *Miscellany* 668–9), to have been *aisumnetes* (elected dictator, compare Pittakos), and one Demoteles to have become *monarkhos* (sole ruler). Demoteles is said to have been assassinated, and a group called the 'Land Owners' (*Geomoroi*) took over. Plutarch (*Greek Questions* 57) tells that these were overthrown following a successful war against the Megarians, who had attacked Samian settlers at Perinthos: the Megarian prisoners were used by the victorious generals to murder the *Geomoroi*. Unconnected in the preserved traditions, but, if historical, possibly in the following years, were a war against Priene, which was reputed to have led to very large numbers of Samian deaths, and a war against 'the Aiolians' during which the general, one Syloson, is said to have insisted on the Samians celebrating an all-night festival at the Heraion as usual and then to have taken advantage of it to seize power (Polyainos, *Strategemata* 6.45).

What with the vague reference to 'the Aiolians', the existence of a later Syloson, and Polyainos (1.23) also claiming that Polykrates seized power during an important public sacrifice at the Heraion, we should beware of assuming any of this to be historical. But Samian settlement abroad in the late seventh century BC is well attested by the activity of Semonides (above, p. 214), and the 'scramble for the Hellespont', of which the action at Perinthos is part (Samians also settled nearby at Bisanthe, Prokonnesos, and Heraion Teikhos), seems to have been real enough. Involvement in warfare abroad is prominent in causing these political tensions: does this reflect what was the case *c*.600 BC in Samos, or does it simply reflect the manifest later connections between foreign policy and political turmoil at home (see below)? If the former is true, we might wonder, in particular, how far either settlement elsewhere or wars on behalf of those settlers or against cities across the water can be taken to be 'state' enterprises, and how far they represented the pursuit of sectional interests, which only marginally engaged the patriotism or loyalty of those who had to execute them. The abundant contacts with the Greek and the non-Greek world which the finds from the Samian Heraion display from the eighth century onwards (p. 87) may have been a source of enrichment for, and part of the lifestyle of, only a limited section of the population, and even the all-night festival at the Heraion may have been less than completely inclusive. If the Samian epic poet Asios is rightly ascribed to the sixth century BC, his description (Athenaios 525F, Text 41) of those at Hera's festival might effectively evoke the tone of such an occasion.

The richly detailed traditions in Herodotos (esp. 3.39–60, 120–42) about the tyranny of Polykrates at Samos in the second half of the sixth century contrast markedly with the earlier scraps, but they have given rise to just as much scholarly debate. That debate has invented a family tradition of tyranny before Polykrates (either an 'elder Polykrates' or a tyranny for Polykrates' father Aiakes, despite the fact that Herodotos says that Polykrates seized power by a rebellion) in order to cover a complete absence of any information about the political situation in Samos in the first half of the sixth century. I pass over such speculation here. My concern here is with the Samos which emerges directly from the stories told by Herodotos, who is exceptionally well-informed about this island on which, according to one ancient tradition, he spent part of his life (*Souda* s.v. Herodotos).

Polykrates left behind him a reputation for unusual prosperity, for willingness to intervene in both Greek and non-Greek affairs well outside Samos itself, and for ruthless calculation of his own advantage. Herodotos tells of a *coup* in which his two brothers share, followed by his killing one brother and exiling the other; of friendship with the Egyptian king Amasis (for whom see *ANE* 644–5), followed by the engineering of a request from Kambyses the Persian king for troops to join his campaign *against* Egypt (Polykrates sent forty ships manned with potential Samian rebels); of widespread Polykratean piracy in which cities as well as goods were taken and diplomatic gifts on their way between mainland Greek powers and non-Greek rulers were intercepted; and of Polykrates' death by crucifixion in Sardis as he goes to 'rescue' the Persian satrap there, Oroites, from Kambyses. That this is the general fifth-century view of Polykrates cannot be doubted: Thucydides (1.13; 3.104) remarks on

They combed their flowing locks and went, all dressed in fine garments, to the sanctuary of Hera. Their snow-white linen robes adorned with cicada-shaped golden brooches reach to the floor of the broad earth. Their hair, with golden grips, waves in the wind, and skilfully crafted bracelets encircle their arms.

Text 41: Asios frg. 13 quoted at Athenaios Deipnosophistai *525F. Asios describes the display of clothing and adornment at a festival at the Samian Heraion.*

Polykrates' capture of islands, specifying that he dedicated Rheneia to Apollo after capturing it.

What, historically, are we to make of these traditions? The traditions have two obvious effects: they stress the wealth and power of sixth-century Samos, and they stress that Samian 'misbehaviour' was Polykrates' responsibility. Of the former there can be no doubt. The temples of Hera, mentioned above, were only some of the magnificent monuments constructed in sixth-century Samos. Herodotos himself claims, and we should take his claim seriously, that he spends so long discussing Polykrates in 3. 39–60 because the Samians had been responsible for 'the three greatest monumental achievements of all the Greeks' – the temple, the kilometre-long tunnel masterminded by one Eupalinos bringing water to the city (see Figure 25), and the harbour mole. Such achievements both demanded explanation and invited the creation of explanatory stories – such as that the ditch round the fortification walls of Samos had been dug by Lesbians caught fighting on behalf of Miletos. Nor need we be seriously doubtful about Samian military, and particularly naval, power in the sixth century BC. But when attempts are made to impose a sequence on the actions ascribed to Polykrates, to see his attacks on 'the less wealthy towns of the Cyclades' as resulting from the fact that Persian acquisition of the Phoenician fleet in the 520s had prevented him raiding further east, then we need to take care.

Among the finds at the Heraion at Samos is a North Syrian bronze mould-made plaque from a horse harness, bearing an Aramaic inscription which reads: 'What Hadad [a god] has given to Lord Hazael from Umqi in the year when the Lord crossed the river' (Figure 76). The piece was made in the ninth century BC, but it was found in a late sixth-century context. What is more, a companion piece has been found in the sanctuary of Apollo at Eretria. The inscription seems to indicate that these pieces were originally booty captured by Hazael, and it has recently been suggested that they were then raided by the Greeks. While some might prefer to imagine an enterprising temple servant in an eastern sanctuary making a bit 'on the side' by disposing of some old dedications, these exotic pieces certainly seem to have been the result of some opportunist exchange. The story of Kolaios (above, p. 12) suggests that such opportunism was particularly attributed to Samians, and it is not hard to see how an illiberal view of such exchange – or the view propounded by the temple servant when he had to explain where the old treasures had gone – might regard it as amounting to piracy.

Figure 76 Hazael's horse-bronze from the Samian Heraion.

But did Polykrates put piracy on a new 'official' footing? The stories certainly claim that the Samians were able to get away with interventions which could be expected to bring reprisals, and there can be no doubt of the reality of the Samian military power which made such actions possible. But there is nothing in the stories which is not adequately explained by actions of an élite who know they have military power to protect them, being improved in the telling by those who were their victims. But such a view presupposes that the élite remained powerful, protected, but to some extent independent, under the tyrant. Is such a view justifiable?

That labour could be commanded in large quantities in Samos during the sixth century BC is clearly attested by the monuments. But the Rhoikos temple certainly antedates Polykrates, and there is some reason to believe that power and prosperity were not restricted to the person of the tyrant. The Samian Heraion stands out among Ionian sanctuaries for its monumental *kouros* statues, notably the *kouros* dedicated by Iskhes around 570 BC, which was originally some 4.75 m high: Samos seems to have gone on producing monumental *kouroi* when mainland *kouroi* had become standardly more or less life-sized. The group of four standing figures, one seated figure, and one reclining figure, known as the Geneleos group, of *c.*550 BC, has no parallel elsewhere, and nor has the dedication by a single man, Kheramyes, of two *kouroi* and one *kore c.*560 BC (Figure 77). It no doubt served well the purpose of those Samians who went to Sparta to ask for help in getting rid of Polykrates to claim that Polykrates had dispatched them to their death fighting against Amasis, but a high degree of collaboration between Polykrates and the élite,

Figure 77 Kheramyes' *kore* from the Samian Heraion.

rather than an élite constantly in terror for their lives, would seem best to fit the evidence. Polykrates was praised in the poetry of Ibykos and was already held by Herodotos to have entertained the poet Anakreon of Teos (who is said in one late source to have been his teacher); we should imagine that the performances of such poets were enjoyed by more than simply the ears of the tyrant alone. This is not to deny that there could be opposition as well as support from the élite. It would seem to have been disaffected members of the élite who in the 520s BC went off in the traditional manner to found a settlement at Puteoli in Italy which they called Dikaiarkheia (Eusebios (Jerome) under 524 BC), and the philosopher Pythagoras may have been an earlier refugee.

It is relations with Sparta that show most clearly the complexity of the situation. Sparta seems long to have had a somewhat special relationship with Samos. Certainly Samos received Spartan pottery and other goods extremely early (not long after 700 BC) and in much larger quantities than any other

262

Figure 78 Bronze lion dedicated by the Spartan Eumnastos.

place. It is also clear, from the famous discovery of a bronze lion, originally part of a large bronze vessel, manufactured in Sparta and inscribed round the mane, in Lakonian letters of *c.*550 BC, 'Eumnastos Spartiate to Hera' (Figure 78), that individual members of the élite moved from Sparta to Samos – and presumably in the other direction too, although there is less good evidence for that. When the Samian refugees came to Sparta (Herodotos 3.46–7, 1.70), with their story of Polykrates sending them to fight Egypt and of their unsuccessful attempt to fight their way back, the Spartans agreed to help. This decision is hardly made the less remarkable by the Spartan claim that they agreed in order to revenge the Samian interception of a bronze mixing-bowl which they were sending to Kroisos, and of a gift which Amasis was sending to them; that bronze mixing-bowl would have been sitting in the Heraion at Samos for some twenty years, during which time relations with Samos had evidently been continuing in a perfectly normal way, in both material and personal terms. The basis of the decision is perhaps more truly revealed by the story, the truth of which cannot be guaranteed, that one of the Spartans who excelled himself in the assault on Samos was given a public burial by the Samians (Herodotos 3.55); such a burial, especially given that the dead man's son was called 'Samios', may well imply that he was a guest-friend of the Samians. If so, this would bring out the complexity of guest-friendship, which involves potentially conflicting ties both to a city and to individuals: Sparta's ongoing relations with the Samian élite, rather than simply with Polykrates, are crucial to the special relationship between the two cities.

Support for this view of Polykrates' relations to the Samian élite comes from the traditions about what happened after his death. Herodotos (3.142, Text 42) tells that Maiandrios, whom Polykrates had left in charge when he went to Sardis, proposed to restore power to the citizens as a whole, only retaining for himself six talents of money and the priesthood of Zeus Eleutherios. But when one of the élite abused Maiandrios, he promptly changed his mind, arrested all the potential rivals, and made himself tyrant. This tradition, like the rest, has too much of the cautionary tale about it to be at all trustworthy – the story goes on to reveal Maiandrios to have had two brothers, one violent and the other mad … – but the existence of a proud élite, suspicious of one another and individually keen to rule, may reasonably be deduced.

The Samos of Polykrates might seem, on this basis, to be not so very different from the Mytilene of Pittakos, with a charismatic ruler keeping precarious control over a prospering but resentful élite. But there is no reason to doubt that Polykrates did die in Sardis, and Persian power politics cannot be neglected. Once more, the sequel to Polykrates' death needs to be examined. Five or six years after Polykrates' death a Persian expedition was sent to Samos with the intent of installing Polykrates' brother Syloson in power. Herodotos' account of this (3.139–49) makes personal motivation very central: he tells that the Persian king Darius agreed to undertake this because Syloson had once given him a splendid cloak; that the Samians could not agree to resist (another sign of rivalry among the élite) and initially agreed to come to terms; that Maiandrios' brother then persuaded them to turn to violence, as a result of which the Persian commander Otanes gave no quarter; that Maiandrios failed to bribe the Spartans to help him; and that Otanes later repopulated the island because of a dream and a disease of the genital organs. But Darius seems already to have begun looking west (Herodotos 3.133–8; see below, p. 302), and the policy which Persia will consistently pursue in Ionia in the late sixth century BC is one of giving power to individual members of cities who are prepared to support Persia, a pattern which the support for Syloson fits well. In the story of Darius' obligation to Syloson and the denial of Otanes' killing of large numbers of Samians, we see the claims of Persia to have acted honorably rather than arbitrarily, to be interested in fostering Greek cities rather than eradicating them. In the claims that Otanes drag-netted the island so as to hand it over to Syloson deserted, we see Samian insistence that Persia *was* violent. (In fact Samos was able, just four years later, to supply a fleet to assist Darius' Skythian expedition.) That both stories are current in the middle of the fifth century BC shows something of the extent to which Persia continued to be an important factor in Samian politics, even when Samos was part of the Athenian empire and Persian armed forces were officially excluded from the Aegean.

Maiandrios son of Maiandrios, to whom power had been delegated by Polykrates, had control on Samos. He wanted to be a man of exemplary justice, but did not manage it. For when he was told of the death of Polykrates what he did was the following: he first set up an altar of Zeus Liberator and set out the precinct around it which is still in the suburbs of the town. Next, when he had done that, he gathered an assembly of all the citizens together and gave this speech: 'As you are well aware, it was to me that Polykrates' insignia of office and all his power were handed over, and I could simply now rule over you. But I will not use force to do what I would be shocked by a neighbour doing. I did not approve of Polykrates lording it over men like himself or of anyone else doing the same. Polykrates has now met his destiny, and I am making magisterial office available and proclaiming to you equality before the law. But I think it right that the following privileges come to me: that six talents are reserved for me from Polykrates' property, and in addition, for myself and my descendants, the priesthood of Zeus Liberator to whom I established a sanctuary and since I extend liberty to you.' He made this announcement to the Samians, but one of them got up and said: 'You are not worthy to rule over us, you are base-born and worthless. You ought to be giving us an account of the money you have handled.' It was a distinguished man in the city, whose name was Telesarkhos, who said this. Maiandrios realised that if he shared office someone else would make himself tyrant in his stead, and so decided not to share it, but retired to the acropolis, sent for each man separately, as if he was going to give a financial account, arrested them and had them locked up.

Text 42: Herodotos 3.142–143.1. Herodotos' account of how dissent among the élite prevented the peaceful ending of tyranny on Samos.

The case of Kleisthenes of Sikyon

My second example is far less exotic, involving a community rooted in the Greek mainland rather than one on the fringes of the Greek world, a relatively small city, agriculturally prosperous but with no special resources. Aristotle (*Politics* 1315b11–21) held that the tyranny of Orthagoras and his sons at Sikyon was the longest lasting of all tyrannies. Aristotle put this down to the tyrants' moderate treatment of their subjects, keeping within the law, success in war, and general nurturing of the people. By contrast Nikolaos of Damascus (*FGH* 90 F 61, see in part Text 43), writing three centuries after Aristotle, has a story of Myron, who succeeded Orthagoras, being a rapist and adulterer who was killed by his brother Isodemos when he turned his attentions to his brother's wife, of Isodemos being outwitted and cheated of power by a further brother, Kleisthenes, and of Kleisthenes proving violent and cruel. The coexistence of such conflicting accounts is regular with tyrants (pp. 181–5 and see further below, p. 267 on Peisistratos), reflecting competing desires to counteract tyrannous ambitions in later leaders and to justify continuing to live under a tyrannous regime. Neither from them, nor from stories which claim Orthagoras became tyrant because of his success in war (*P. Oxy.* 11 1365/Fornara 10), which are surely part of the common

Myron, the ruler of Sikyon, who was descended from Orthagoras, was uncontrolled in other respects and particularly in his relations with women. He raped them not only secretly but openly. In the end he had an adulterous affair with the wife of his brother Isodemos. Isodemos became aware of this, and at first kept quiet, but, because he was troubled by it, he told his other brother when he returned from Libya. Isodemos was, they say, a simple and guileless fellow, but Kleisthenes was full of tricks. On this occasion, perceiving what needed doing, he said that he would not endure being treated like that even for a single day, but would punish the perpetrator with his own hand. By saying this he goaded Isodemos, plotting for tyranny in succession to Myron, once one brother was dead and the other could not sacrifice to the gods because he had his brother's blood on his hands. This became clear, for when Isodemos killed Myron after he had been tyrant for seven years, having found him in bed with his wife, and reported the fact to Kleisthenes with a great groan, Kleisthenes said that he felt troubled for both brothers, for the dead one because he had suffered death at his brother's hand, and for Isodemos because, since he had his brother's blood on his hands, he would not be able to sacrifice to the gods, and would have to get another to do this for him. And Isodemos was persuaded to speak the truth and, in order that he might not be forced from power because of this, after a year chose Kleisthenes as his partner in power. Kleisthenes managed what he plotted because of the simple-mindedness of Isodemos, and both ruled Sikyon. But the people took much more notice of Kleisthenes because he was frightening and active.

Text 43: FGH 90 F61. Part of Nikolaos of Damascus' account of how Kleisthenes got power at Sikyon.

stock of warnings about the dangers posed by military leaders with popular support, can we write a history of the Orthagorids.

Herodotos' stories about Kleisthenes of Sikyon, however, offer some important historical evidence. One story (6.126–31) concerns Kleisthenes, when he has just won the chariot race at the Olympic games, summoning suitors from other parts of Greece to compete for the hand of his daughter Agariste. As told by Herodotos the central episode in the wooing is an occasion when the Athenian Hippokleides gets drunk, and proceeds from respectable to far from respectable dancing; Kleisthenes tells him that he has danced away his marriage, and Hippokleides responds 'Hippokleides doesn't care.' Hippokleides may not have danced obscenely and the list of suitors may not be historically accurate (it seem to incorporate men who lived at rather different times), although marriage finally to the Athenian Megakles is historical enough. But the historical importance of this tale lies in its showing how tyrants moved easily in élite circles, and how members of the élite of one city were more than happy to cultivate relationships with a tyrant in another city. And from the point of view of the tyrant, the story nicely reveals the way in which a sixth-century tyrant might have his eye on cutting a figure in a world wider than the world of his own city (as at the Olympic games) and of taking immediate advantage of the personal status that brought.

The tyrant as but one member of the circle of rich and powerful Greeks needs, however, to be seen against the tyrant as one who promoted his own city in opposition to other cities. Herodotos' other story of Kleisthenes (5.67–8) involves him stopping *rhapsodes* singing the Homeric poems, changing central cult practices at Sikyon so as to displace the worship of the hero Adrastos and replace it partly with the worship of Adrastos' legendary enemy Melanippos and partly with worship of Dionysos, and altering the names of the Dorian tribes – he called his own tribe the Arkhelaoi (leaders of men) and the other tribes the Hyatai (Pigmen), Khoireatai (Swinemen), and Oneatai (Assmen). Herodotos sees these actions as anti-Argive: the Homeric poems celebrate the achievements of the Argives, Adrastos is an Argive, and the Dorian tribe names were shared with Argos (among other places). This interpretation is supported by the recent discovery that, at this very period, the Argives constructed in their agora a hero shrine to Adrastos and the other six with whom he had attacked Thebes, the famous 'Seven against Thebes'. That dispute over Adrastos' Sikyonian descent may also have left its traces in the tradition of his family line which has come down to us: Adrastos is said to have inherited Sikyon from his mother's father Polybos, who had no sons of his own, and that broken line of succession may well be a consequence of the sixth-century dispute. Kleisthenes may have been attempting to assert that Sikyon was older than such Dorian figures, and his tribe names, with their animal associations, may have been intended to parallel the old ethnic groups such as the Meropes, Dryopes, and Leleges whose names also could be interpreted in animal terms (bee-eaters, wood-peckers, storks). If so, then Kleisthenes' actions in this area too must point both outwards and inwards: inwards because myths of descent are central to ethnic identity; outwards because only by comparison to others' claims about descent do Sikyonian claims acquire significance. Herodotos says that the Sikyonians kept the tribal names for sixty years after his death, suggesting that the names were not seen as immediately insulting and that only a changed political agenda led them to be questioned.

The Peisistratids at Athens

Solon's legacy at Athens had been continued political competition among the élite, and further periodic breaking of the constitutional rules ([Aristotle,] *Constitution of the Athenians* 13; above, p. 213). Whatever Solon did to establish a free peasantry, it is clear that competition for political power among the wealthy had not abated, and that that competition should issue forth in the tyranny of Peisistratos hardly gives cause for surprise.

Ancient traditions about Peisistratos give a picture of the achievement of political power through deceit and of the exercise of political power in a popular way. Broadly speaking the former is Herodotos' story (1.59–64), the latter is what the Aristotelian *Constitution of the Athenians* (13–17) gives – despite relying on Herodotos for the early part of the account. Just as trickery and the abuse of women are combined in the traditions about the

Orthagorids at Sikyon, so they are combined in the Herodotean tradition of how Peisistratos achieved power. Herodotos tells how Peisistratos exploited religious sensibilities by having an imposing woman dressed in armour, like Athene in art, bring him back to the city (see above, p. 232), and how he exploited a political marriage alliance, made with the daughter of the same Megakles whom we have just met, by having intercourse with her 'not in the customary manner'. The relationship of these cautionary tales to history is somewhat uncertain, but they illustrate well an awareness on the part of those who related these tales that tyranny was but a variation on élite rule: Peisistratos is presented as tyrant even as he is described as working in alliance with a Megakles who had power enough to oblige him to leave the city.

The distinction between the Aristotelian and the Herodotean tradition emerges very clearly in the way they describe the political background to Peisistratos' attempts to seize power. Herodotos describes how Athenian politics before Peisistratos was dominated by conflict between two groups, the men of the coast and men of the plain. The champion of the former, he says, was Megakles son of Alkmeon, the champion of the latter Lykourgos son of Aristolaïdes. He then describes how Peisistratos 'awoke' a third group, collected supporters, and claimed to be the champion of the 'Hyperakrioi', the 'men over the hills'. The Aristotlian tradition takes this account and transforms it. In the *Constitution of the Athenians* there simply were three groups, and these groups were divided on political lines: Megakles' group wanted the 'moderate constitution', Lykourgos' group wanted oligarchy, and the third group, which he calls the 'Diakrioi', had a populist leader and attracted support from the discontented. This account is a rationalised reading of Herodotos' story, but in the rationalisation the whole nature of the conflict is transformed: personal followings, with the Hyperakrioi just a name given to his supporters by Peisistratos, become in [Aristotle] groups with real political programmes, and the name Hyperakrioi, which makes fun of the names of the other two groups, is transformed into Diakrioi, a name with reference to a real region of Attica. Consciously or not, [Aristotle] has played down rivalry among the élite, manifest perhaps in the diverse symbols on the earliest Athenian coins, and introduced conflict over the constitution and even a hint of class war.

But [Aristotle]'s further account, which is based on sources other than Herodotos, enlarges the stage on which Peisistratos plays still further. Not only does [Aristotle] have a series of stories about how good Peisistratos was to the ordinary man, relieving a poor farmer of taxes, extending loans to the poor, and helping them to prosper in peace, but he also stresses Peisistratos' involvement in wider Greek affairs. Herodotos tells how Peisistratos, after the failure of the alliance with Megakles, went to Eretria and got support from Thebes, Argos, and Naxos. [Aristotle] (and compare Herodotos 5.94.1) extends the scope to Macedonia, with particular reference to the Pangaion silver mines, and goes on to record that Peisistratos' third son was called Thettalos ('the Thessalian'), and that his third wife was daughter of Gorgillos of Argos and had previously been married to one Arkhinos of Ambrakia, a member of the Corinthian Kypselid family. Once more, these details cannot be proven, but that other Greeks were concerned about how Athens was ruled is shown beyond doubt by the Spartan invasion which finally expelled Peisistratos' son Hippias, after internal conflict had left Hippias' brother Hipparkhos dead, but had failed to shake Hippias' grip on power. [Aristotle] suggests that Peisistratid links with Argos were one reason for the Spartan attack, and certainly Hippias could command the support of Thessalian cavalry (see further below, pp. 276–7).

Received tradition in fifth- and fourth-century BC Athens chose to tell the story of the Peisistratids either to warn about the sorts of deceitful ways in which established politicians can arrogate power to themselves or to claim that the Peisistratids had not been so bad and the Athenians, individually and collectively, had not been as spineless as all that in failing to get rid of them. But stories told for other purposes, and other data preserved by chance, give a rather different picture. We have already met (p. 257) Kimon son of Stesagoras, who felt obliged to ascribe one Olympic victory to Peisistratos but was nevertheless secretly murdered by Peisistratos' sons as too much of a potential rival. That murder presumably dates to the 520s. A fragment of the Athenian archon list which happens to have been preserved (ML 6/Fornara 23) shows that in the same decade the eponymous archons, who were the most prominent of all magistrates at Athens and lent their names to the year for dating purposes, were successively Hippias (in 526/5), Kleisthenes son of Megakles, Miltiades son of that same Kimon, an unknown Kalliades, and then, probably, Hippias' son Peisistratos. This list nicely shows that the Alkmaionid claim, repeated by Herodotos (6.123), that they were in exile the whole time that Peisistratos and his sons were in power, was false; it also shows how the symbols of political power, and to some extent its reality, were shared around the élite in Athens during the tyranny.

Far from being absolute rulers, the Peisistratids are revealed as maintaining their supremacy by a delicate combination of threats and promises. Theirs was not a monopoly of power and patronage, and they were not the only people with charisma and the possibility of commanding loyal personal support. The rebuilding of the temple of Athena Polias in the 520s, the altars prominently dedicated to the Twelve Gods and to Apollo Pythios by the younger Peisistratos in celebration of his archonship (Thucydides 6.54.6, ML 11/Fornara 37), the construction of the massive temple to Olympian Zeus in the 510s and the replacement of coinage with family symbols with coinage bearing Athene's owl, should be seen as ways in which the Peisistratids ensured that theirs were the acts everyone was talking about in Athens. Herodotos' tradition relates that when, in c.515 BC, Miltiades' brother Stesagoras died in the Thracian Khersonesos, leaving a vacancy there in what was to all intents a family tyranny, the Peisistratids sent Miltiades out, as if he was their appointment to the post (compare Figure 84). Here again we should surely detect skilful jumping on the bandwagon by the Peisistratids. By this date

269

they had good reason to do so, for they were coming under serious threat from the activities of the Alkmaionidai, now certainly in exile, who in *c.*513 BC made an unsuccessful attempt to unseat Hippias by military means from the base of a fort at Leipsydrion in northern Attica. (For subsequent events see p. 276)

NETWORKING CITIES

The involvement in each other's histories which emerges from the traditions and the history of sixth-century tyrannies appears generally to have been opportunist, and often personal in basis. Individuals who arrogated power to themselves turned old personal guest-friendships with members of the élite of other cities into means of confirming their power. But the sixth century BC also saw the beginning of more formal associations, based on agreements between cities rather than between individuals, as cities formed groups to protect their interests against common enemies and wider threats. Such links were to prove crucial in the conflicts of the fifth century BC, and their pervasiveness then is one important factor in making the classical Greek world so different from the archaic Greek world. For this reason it is important here briefly to examine the beginnings of networking among cities.

The model of the *ethnos*

Networking was, in a sense, not a new phenomenon at all. In many areas of Greece – the northern Peloponnese and central and north-western Greece in particular, the sense of belonging to a people (*ethnos*) who inhabited a whole region was, throughout the archaic period (see above p. 129), as strong as the sense of belonging to a particular community determined to be distinguished from its neighbours. These political organisations, which embrace people dwelling in a number of separate and largely independent communities, should not be seen in negative terms, as if these are areas in which the city failed to develop, but as an alternative mode of social organisation, consciously chosen in areas where people saw not need for more than a rather limited range of functions to be performed collectively. One of those collective functions was religious cult. The eighth- and seventh-century BC multiplication of sanctuary sites and their monumentalisation are as striking in areas organised by *ethne* as in cities – compare the presence of Pherai in Thessaly among the sites at which a massive eighth-century increase of dedications can be noted (above, pp. 86–7), or the early temple building at Thermon in Aitolia (above, p. 200). By contrast, *ethne* were not primarily organised for warfare: with little sense of a common territory, and an expectation of settlement-mobility, common military action seems to have been a low priority, at least in the early archaic period.

Two developments can be seen in the sixth century BC. First, in the *ethnos* area of Boiotia separatist communities begin to emerge, without the loss of the sense of the importance of common identity. As a result, the Boiotians acquired a coinage at an early date, but the coinage was shared by a number of communities, who distinguished themselves by adding a letter (regularly the first letter of the name of the community) to the common type. They kept their common sanctuary, at Onkhestos, but acquired a strong sense of territory which they defended by fighting. Tensions between the independence of the individual community and the common identity of being Boiotian were to mark the history of Boiotia from the last quarter of the sixth century onwards, and are seen in conflict between Boiotian cities. The first signs of this came in *c.*519 BC when, according to Herodotos (6.108), the Plataians in south Boiotia, who apparently had never joined in the minting of Boiotian coins, under pressure from their Theban neighbours, approached Sparta for an alliance and were advised rather to ally with Athens, which they did.

The formation of alliances

The second sixth-century development is the networking of communities which were, and had long been, very conscious of their distinctiveness. In this networking common religious activity was a relatively low priority, and warfare was the most important common function. One of the manifestations of this is the existence of a number of inscriptions, notably from the sanctuary at Olympia, which record such agreements. So, from the mid-sixth century BC, we know of an agreement between Sybaris and her allies and a group who call themselves the Serdaioi of everlasting faithful friendship, between two other South Italian peoples, the Anaitoi and the Messapioi, for friendship for fifty years, and between Elis and her eastern neighbour in the Peloponnese, Heraia, to alliance for one hundred years. The Elis–Heraia agreement states that anyone who harms the writing should be fined a talent of silver just like anyone who breaks the treaty, and the fact of writing, along with the deposition in a distant sanctuary of agreements made by small communities in South Italy, is indicative of the seriousness with which these inter-state agreements were taken.

The case of the Peloponnesian League

The most striking networker is, however, Sparta. Unravelling the history of the league of cities committed to sharing offensive and defensive action with Sparta is extremely problematic. What is certain is that by the last decade of the sixth century most of the cities of the central and north-east Peloponnese, with the significant exception of Argos, were part of what scholars call the Peloponnesian League. Herodotos' story of the growth of Spartan influence in the Peloponnese (1.65–8) is of a Sparta which, after repeated unsuccessful attempts to subjugate her northern neighbour Tegea in the way she had

271

subjugated her western neighbour Messenia, turned to playing up claims on a common hero, Orestes, and after that regularly got the upper hand.

Herodotos' story is likely to have been influenced by events nearer to his own day than those which it describes. Sparta and Tegea came to blows in the decade following the Persian wars, and the Tegeans called in Sparta's traditional enemy Argos to help them (see below, p. 325). That episode must have been extremely worrying for Sparta, and telling themselves and others that Tegea had long had no hope of defeating them may have been particularly important for the Spartans' image. The continuing conflict makes it difficult to date the one piece of independent evidence which might corroborate Herodotos' story, Aristotle's record of an inscribed agreement between Sparta and Tegea, which is reported by Plutarch (*Greek Questions* 5). This agreement included a clause that the Tegeans 'were to expel the Messenians from the country and not to make [them? anyone?] worthy'. Plutarch reports that Aristotle interpreted the clause about not making worthy to mean 'not kill', apparently taking it to be an undertaking not to kill anyone (for example, Spartan sympathisers within Tegea). But the undoubted use of 'make unworthy' in other contexts to mean 'deprive of citizenship' makes it possible that Tegea is here undertaking to expel runaway helots and not enfranchise them. On Aristotle's interpretation, Tegea agrees to forgo *any* right to inflict capital punishment; the alternative view simply has Tegea accept that Sparta has a special interest in Messenians. Whichever is the case, it is clear that when this treaty was made the Tegeans traded some element of political freedom for some sort of support from Sparta. The treaty itself may date at any point from the late seventh to the early fifth century BC, but even if it is later rather than earlier in date, the trading for which it gives evidence was also involved in the agreement – to have the same friends and enemies and to follow where the Spartans led – that all cities made who leagued themselves with Sparta. Tegea was certainly a Spartan ally before the Persian wars, and the crucial position which it enjoys as Sparta's immediate neighbour to the north makes it likely that it was an early ally. So even if Herodotos' story which makes it crucial in the formation of Sparta's network of allies is motivated by fifth-century events, Tegea's decision to make an alliance may still usefully exemplify the choice which many Peloponnesian cities faced at some point in the sixth century.

Why did Tegea agree to such terms? While we might imagine that repeated military pressure from Sparta would engender a desire for peace at any reasonable price, it is possible that Tegea's actions should be understood in a rather wider context. Spartan subjection of Messenia and its population made it necessary for the Spartans to take an aggressive stance to other powers. But Sparta was not the only aggressive power in the Peloponnese. There is archaeological evidence that Sparta had, as early as the first quarter of the sixth century BC, given military assistance to the community at Halieis in the southern Argolid; a large number of ordinary Lakonian drinking cups of this date have been found on the acropolis at Halieis, and since such cups were not exported elsewhere it has been suggested that these point to a Spartan garrison. That the Halieis acropolis was then violently destroyed suggests that Spartan support had not been vainly invoked, even if it was incapable of providing the required protection. The aggressor at Halieis can hardly have been other than Argos. The pressure on Halieis is not likely to have been an isolated event, and it may be that the tradition about Argive expulsion of the people of Nauplion, and their resettlement by the Spartans at Methone in Messenia, latches on to violence of about this same time. Pausanias, in the second century AD, was able to collect a very large number of stories about myth-historical conflicts between the family of Temenos, based at Argos, and the peoples and rulers of other cities nearby – Epidauros, Troizen, Phleious, Sikyon, Hermione, and even Aigina (Pausanias 2.6, 13, 18–19, 26–9, 34, 38); these stories must surely reflect Argive ambitions and claims to rule over these cities in the archaic or classical period, and they may well be a product of sixth-century Argive activity. Faced with an aggressive Sparta and an aggressive Argos, Tegea had to make a choice.

Tegea's choice to ally with Sparta, and by implication to oppose Argos, had a profound effect on subsequent history. Tradition held that Argos had managed to defeat the Spartans at Hysiai (not so far from Tegea) in the seventh century BC, and that she held Sparta to a draw in the so-called Battle of the Champions in the sixth century BC (below, p. 275). Although such nearby communities as Mykenia and Tiryns (below, pp. 323–4) maintained a political independence of Argos into the fifth century BC, the power of Argos in the archaic period should not be underestimated. Tegea's decision to go with Sparta both itself strengthened Sparta's hand, and may have been crucial in persuading further communities in Arkadia, and further potential victims of Argos, to throw in their lot with the Spartans.

What role the development of a myth of common ancestry played in persuading Tegea we cannot now know. It is clear from Herodotos that the Spartans were later far from averse to pointing to such links, but although Herodotos' story implies that making use of the 'bones of Orestes' was a new ploy on the part of the Spartans, archaeological evidence casts some doubt on the novelty of the policy. The two most important cults of heroic figures at Sparta, from around 700 BC onwards, were cults of Menelaos and Helen (actually given divine, not merely heroic honours) at Therapne, just across the Eurotas from the main group of Spartan villages, and the cult of Agamemnon at Amyklai just to the south. Some scholars, indeed, believe that the placing of Agamemnon at Mykenai in the Homeric epics, and so in Greek tragedy and the later tradition, is in fact a late displacement of a figure originally at home in Lakonia. That the Spartan view of Agamemnon was not the same as the epic view seems indicated by cult being linked to the cult of an 'Alexandra' – an alternative name for the Trojan Kassandra of epic. But whatever the story told to explain Alexandra's presence, and whether she was conceived of as Trojan at all at Sparta, it seems that the Spartans had never completely cut themselves off mythologically from the panhellenic body of myth promoted by epic; the idea that Orestes had special Spartan connections can hardly have been new either to Spartans or to Tegeans in the sixth century BC, even if making something of the fact that Orestes was shared with Tegea was new.

Further support for the idea that the Spartans did make increasing use of traditions about their past in their relations with the rest of the Peloponnese comes from the story of Teisamenos, recorded in Pausanias. When discussing the myth-history of Akhaia, Pausanias (7.1.7–8) reports the tradition that the Dorians drove the Akhaians out of Sparta and Argos; that the Akhaians told the Ionians that they were happy to settle with them and not fight them; that the Ionians feared the *kudos* which the Akhaians' king, Teisamenos son of Orestes, possessed because of his ancestry and his personal qualities; and that, as a result, they fought the Akhaians, killing Teisamenos but losing the battle. Pausanias notes that Teisamenos' body was buried in Helike in Akhaia, but that later, on the command of the Delphic oracle, his bones were exhumed and taken to Sparta. Pausanias gives no date for the translation of Teisamenos' remains, but the similarity to the incident relating to Orestes makes association with the formation of Peloponnese-wide alliances in the later part of the sixth century attractive. Exhuming bones would provide to the states of the Peloponnese a clear symbol of Sparta's sense of herself as a power with a continuing history and of Sparta's determination not to play up ethnic separateness. We would see here precisely the converse of Kleisthenes of Sikyon's attention to those parts of the myth-history of his city which could be used to establish distinction from Argos.

But was it simply Sparta's showing herself to be user-friendly to the cities of the Peloponnese, at a time when there was widespread fear of Argos, which enabled Sparta to form so extensive a network of alliances in the second half of the sixth century BC? One ancient tradition holds that there was yet a further factor: that Sparta made a point of helping cities to get rid of their tyrants. That Sparta was prepared to go into action against Polykrates in Samos we have already seen (above, p. 263); that she would be involved in removing Hippias from Athens is not in doubt (see further below, p. 276). But was this part of a wider policy? The claim that it was is found in a papyrus fragment (*P. Ryland* 18, *FGH* 105 F1) and in Plutarch's essay *On the Malice of Herodotos* (ch. 21). We do not know the context from which the papyrus fragment comes, and for that reason its historical value cannot be assessed. Plutarch makes his claim in criticising Herodotos for stating that the attack on Polykrates was motivated by desire to punish past misdemeanours on the part of the Samians; Plutarch argues that, on the contrary, Spartan hostility to tyrants was a matter of principle. He then lists tyrants that Sparta helped to remove – the Kypselids from Corinth and Ambrakia, Lygdamis from Naxos, the Peisistratids from Athens, Aiskhines from Sikyon, Symmakhos from Thasos, Aulis from Phokis, Aristogenes from Miletos, and Aristomenes and Angelos in Thessaly. Several of these tyrannies are attested only in this passage, and where other sources do mention figures in Plutarch's list, variant traditions are betrayed which cast doubt on Plutarch's claims: so Aristotle (*Politics* 1304a31–2) has internal uprising throw out the tyrant of Ambrakia;

Nikolaos of Damascus (*FGH* 90 F60), who used the fourth-century historian Ephoros, has a similar explanation for the end of tyranny at Corinth. Such variants are not necessarily true, but, together with the surprising geographical range of Spartan intervention and the indisputable Spartan willingness to contemplate restoring tyranny to Athens (below, p. 278), they undermine trust in Plutarch's list. It is not to be denied that Sparta did, on occasion, play a part in ending tyranny, but the motivation for doing so is likely to have been case-specific, not blanket hatred of tyranny. Latykhidas' action in Thessaly is to be put in the context of his taking punitive action against those who had 'medised' in the Persian wars, and in other cases too it is what tyrants did and stood for, rather than their being tyrants, that we should see as motivating Spartan intervention. That Latykhidas' actions are included in Plutarch's list implies that that list was part of a tradition belonging, at the earliest, to the fifth century; Spartan eagerness to be seen to oppose, on principle, the 'tyrant city' of Athens is unlikely to be irrelevant to the telling of this tale.

Sparta's creation of a network of allies across the Peloponnese should be seen, therefore, as a product of opportunism rather than idealism. Sparta's unique oppression of the Messenians created a need to isolate Messenia, best served by ensuring that other cities easily accessible from Messenia had reasons to protect Spartan rather than helot interests. Argive aggression can be seen to have played into Sparta's hands, and the tradition (Herodotos 1.82) that there was a 'Battle of the Champions' between Argos and Sparta in the middle of the sixth century BC can be seen to symbolise the Spartans' upper hand. The story goes that 300 Argives fought 300 Spartiates, and that all but two Argives and one Spartiate were killed. The Spartiate is then held to have claimed the victory after the two Argives had run off to announce that *they* had won, and Argos to have disputed this claim. A general battle ensued in which the Spartans were victorious, and, at that point, the Argives swore to keep their hair shaved until they regained the territory while the Spartans gave up cutting their hair. Faced with the almost equal military power of Argos and Sparta the cities of the Peloponnese had to gamble as to which pole they should allow themselves to be drawn to. With the help of conciliatory myths, Sparta won in the clash of symbols. (For the further history of conflict between Argos and Sparta see p. 318.)

9

THE TRANSFORMATION
OF ARCHAIC GREECE
520–479 BC

Greece was part of the Mediterranean world, and even during the 'Dark Age' had never been completely out of touch with what was going on elsewhere in that world. During the period surveyed so far in this book, developments in Greece had been informed by contact with that wider world. But those contacts had generally been on terms which the Greeks had themselves been able to control – barring occasional acts of piracy. It was only in the sixth century BC, when the Persian king Kyros the Great conquered Lydia, that conditions began to change and that political power became a serious factor in Greek contacts. The effect of the interest taken in the Greek world by Persia was transformative – politically, militarily, and culturally. Without Persia the classical Greek world would not have been as we know it.

But classical Greece was not entirely a plant forced in a Persian-fired hothouse. The élite competition for political power that has been the focus of much discussion in earlier chapters itself led to institutional and constitutional innovations that came to transform the manner of government in a large number of Greek cities, and to be the focus for political debate and discussion not simply among the Greeks themselves but as a prominent part of the Greek legacy. Where hostile neighbours and élite factionalism organised around individuals had been the focus of political life in the seventh and sixth centuries BC, debate about the form of constitution and attitudes towards foreign powers came to be at its centre in the classical period, inaugurating a historical phase much more readily recognisable to modern western society.

DEMOCRACY

The end of tyranny at Athens

The end of tyranny at Athens was directly a product of Spartan action. Beginning in 511, Sparta launched, Herodotos tells us (5.63–76), not one but four campaigns against Athens in as many years. Hippias was able to defeat the first seaborne raid with the aid of Thessalian mercenary support (the story goes that the Thessalian cavalry maximised their effectiveness in

I'll carry my sword in a myrtle branch, like Harmodios and Aristogeiton when they together killed the tyrant and brought equality before the law to Athens.

Text 44: Athenaios Deipnosophistai *695ab. An Athenian drinking song celebrating the murderers of Hipparkhos for ending tyranny and bringing democracy.*

the plain behind Phaleron by cutting down trees). The second expedition was led by the Spartan king Kleomenes, who defeated the Thessalians, besieged 'the tyrants', and managed to capture the children of the Peisistratids. To free these hostages, the besieged agreed to leave the city and go off to Sigeion.

Why did Sparta do this? Athenians in the classical period told two stories about the end of tyranny. In one of them the focus fell not upon the Spartans, but upon two members of the Athenian élite, Harmodios and Aristogeiton, who, in 514 BC, had been responsible for the murder of Hipparkhos, but had not thereby shaken Hippias' power. Harmodios and Aristogeiton were celebrated in song (Text 44, Athenaios 695ab/Fornara 39A) and in sculpture as tyrant-slayers, and their descendants were given the privilege of meals at public expense in the public dining room known as the *Prytaneion* (*IG* i³ 131). So central did the act become to Athenian myth-history that the Athenians even erected a second set of sculptures to commemorate the act after the first set had been taken away by the Persians in 480 BC. Whatever the reasons for Harmodios' and Aristogeiton's actions (Thucydides 6.54–6 and later writers hold that a Peisistratid's unrequited love for Harmodios and a slight to Harmodios' sister were the immediate cause), and whether or not they aimed to kill Hippias, there is no doubt that they did not end the tyranny, still less alter Athens' constitution.

The second Athenian story admitted Spartan intervention, but held that they intervened because the Delphic oracle instructed them to free Athens, and that Delphi so instructed them because of Alkmaionid influence or bribery. The Spartans themselves became keen later, when some at least had doubts about the wisdom of having removed Hippias, to say that they had only done it to satisfy the oracle and that the oracle had been bribed. That claims for decisive Alkmaionid influence came to suit some people both at Athens and at Sparta does not, however, establish that the story was true, and we may legitimately doubt whether Spartan intervention can have been solely a product of Delphic urging.

We may prefer to set Spartan action into the wider context of Spartan networking (above, p. 271). Around 519 BC Sparta seems to have suggested that, for the small city of Plataia in south-west Boiotia, linking with Athens was a better bet than allying with Sparta, if she wanted to protect herself against Thebes. But if at that stage some in Sparta felt hesitation about extending their network of alliance outside the Peloponnese, it is not difficult to see how, ten years later, things may have looked a little different. The size and wealth of Athens, and the expectation of enthusiastic Athenian support for anything which would rid them of a tyrant, might well be thought encouragement enough to Sparta to attempt to include Athens within her network of allies. Past precedents for removing tyrants elsewhere to good effect may also have played a part (p. 275 above). That Spartan action at Athens utterly failed to bring Athens into the Spartan alliance is not good evidence that Sparta did not hope for such incorporation. It is, on the other hand, good evidence that the political situation at Athens was unusual.

The political revolution

The peculiarity of the political situation at Athens after the expulsion of Hippias lies in the role played by the people. It was entirely to be expected that the political vacuum should lead to quarrels among the élite, such as Herodotos reports between Isagoras son of Teisandros and Kleisthenes son of Megakles; we might compare what is said to have happened on Samos after the death of Polykrates. What neither parallels elsewhere nor earlier events in Athenian history could lead us to expect is the next move. Herodotos tells how, in response to a defeat by Isagoras, reasonably interpreted as Isagoras' election to the archonship, Kleisthenes redirected his energies to attracting popular support, canvassed a series of constitutional reforms, and created an enthusiastic following. His following was enthusiastic enough that, even after Kleisthenes, as an accursed Alkmaionid (above, p. 203), and 700 other families had been forced into exile, it faced and defeated a further invasion by Kleomenes designed to strengthen Isagoras' power.

Popular riot had clearly been something that might be envisaged from the time of the account of Thersites and the assembly of the Akhaians in *Iliad* 2, but it is not something which tradition reported for any earlier moment in Athenian history, or in the history of other Greek cities. But riot seems the only appropriate description of the situation in 508/507 BC. One way or another, a popular political movement had been created such as no Greek city had previously known, motivated by an issue and not by loyalty to a particular person. How had this situation been achieved?

There are three main candidates for the issue that galvanised the people: hostility to Sparta; rearmament; and the constitution. There is least to say about the first. That the riot manifested itself in opposition to Spartan interference is clear. Equally clear is Spartan dissatisfaction with what resulted: Kleomenes (Herodotos 5.74–5) led out the allies once more in an attempt to restore Isagoras to power, but this came to nothing because of the reluctance of the allies and of the other Spartan king, Damaratos, to take part. Later still (Herodotos 5.90–3) the Spartans again tried unsuccessfully to persuade the allies to campaign against Athens to restore Hippias to power. The extent to which Athens saw Sparta as a threat is underlined by the story that, at the same time as recalling Kleisthenes, the Athenians also sent an embassy to Sardis seeking Persian alliance (Herodotos 5.73). This embassy even considered submission to Persia not too high a price to pay for Persian support, although the Athenian people took a different view. The later polarisation of the Greek world between Athens and Sparta, and the temptation to Sparta and Athens to apply for Persian support in order to get the better of the other, will undoubtedly have encouraged the retrojection both of hostilities and of the Persian factor. But the facts of Spartan invasion and of Athenian resistance seem to warrant our accepting that both Athens and Sparta came to recognise, in the years immediately following Hippias' explusion, that inter-city relations in the Greek world had moved into a new phase.

The hostility to Sparta gives some plausibility to the suggestion that the Athenian people were galvanised by enthusiasm for a 'new model army'. But there are other factors also. Athenian tradition held that Peisistratos had battled his way to power at Pallene in 545 BC (above, p. 268) with the help of a mercenary army, and the role of Hippias' Thessalian cavalry support is made crucial to the failure and then success of the first two Spartan expeditions. One ancient tradition ([Aristotle,] *Constitution of the Athenians* 15.4, cf.18.4; Polyainos, *Strategemata* 1.21.2) held that Peisistratos had disarmed the Athenians in 545 BC, another that Hippias had disarmed them after 514 BC (Thucydides 6.56.2, 58). The variant traditions about disarming look suspicious, and there were good reasons for the Athenians to deny that they had been in a position to rise against the tyrants, but this does not necessarily mean that the stories are untrue. Certainly in 507/506 BC the Athenians did deploy an army against the Boiotians and the Khalkidians, who are said to have been going to support the abortive third invasion by Kleomenes, and deploy it to such effect that 700 Boiotians were captured and ransomed for more than twenty talents. Athens then established the enormous number of 4,000 settlers on the lands of the élite of Khalkis, an act showing both the extent of Athenian manpower and the importance which they attached to asserting their control in this area. The settling of further Athenians on Salamis (ML 14/Fornara 44B) may date to 507/506 BC too, another signal to Athens' neighbours and sign of Athenian 'nationalism' and military confidence.

The Athenians needed to recreate their armed forces, and they did so to good effect, but this does not itself mean that Kleisthenes was supported by the people because he offered a recipe for an effective new army. In his description of Kleisthenes' reforms Herodotos (5.66, 69, Text 45) lays stress on the creation of ten tribes in place of the four Ionian tribes. There is no doubt that these ten tribes were the basis of the classical Athenian army: Athenians fought in tribal units, so that if one part of the line was particularly hard hit the casualties might be largely from a single tribe (as would be the case at the battle of Plataia: Plutarch, *Aristeides* 19.4–5); all casualties in war were listed on public monuments which recorded individuals' names by tribe, without indication of parentage or deme. What is more, it is possible that the subdivision of the tribes into 'trittyes' or 'thirds' (on which further below) had a military aspect. Stones inscribed 'Up to this point the tribe *x* and the trittys *y*, from this point the tribe *z* and the trittys *f*' which have survived from the Athenian Agora, the Athenian Pnyx, where the assembly

That is what Kleisthenes of Sikyon did, and the Athenian Kleisthenes, grandson of the Sikyonian on his mother's side, and named after him, seems to me to have imitated the Kleisthenes with whom he shared his name, because he despised the Ionians and wanted to avoid having the same tribal divisions as the Ionians. He added the Athenian people, who had formally not been in the centre of things, to his own party, changed the names of the tribes and increased their number. He made ten tribal commanders instead of four and distributed demes into the tribes ten at a time. Once he had got the people on his side he had the upper hand over his rivals.

Text 45: Herodotos 5.69. Herodotos describes Kleisthenes' reforms at Athens as in the tradition of Kleisthenes of Sikyon's tribal changes.

met, and from the Peiraieus, show that in some circumstances in the fifth century BC the Athenians mustered by tribe and trittys (*IG* i³ 1117–31). That circumstance might be political, but since the stones occur in Athens' port at the Peiraieus as well as at the political centre, a military explanation might be more appropriate.

Much that Kleisthenes instituted cannot be explained either as a response to Spartan pressure or as designed to remodel the army. The tribes were the basis not only of the army, but also of a new Council of 500, to which each tribe contributed fifty members. These fifty members were not drawn randomly from the tribe, but were drawn from the villages of Attica which made up each tribe, according to a fixed quota which related to the village population (Figure 79). We do not know how the earlier Council of 400, a very shadowy institution perhaps created by Solon, operated, but there is no doubt that Kleisthenes invented the principle that every deme, that is every community of Attica, should be represented in the Council. This principle itself imposed some uniformity on communities in Attica, but Kleisthenes seems to have taken his interest in the nature of those communities yet further, requiring each of them to appoint a leader (demarch) annually, and giving them a role in determining their own members, and hence the membership of the citizen body, as well as their own cultic activities, finances, and even to some extent their judicial arrangements (*IG* i³ 2).

The creation of the deme was a political revolution. Kleisthenes did not create out of nothing the numerous communities in Attica which his measures recognised as 'demes'. Pre-existing villages, and perceptibly distinct communities within the town of Athens, were turned into 'demes', perhaps by the simple expedient of requiring every Athenian male over the age of 18 to register in what he regarded as his home community. Demes, on this view, were not parishes, not districts of Attica, to which one belonged because one resided within their boundaries. Demes will have had no physical boundaries as such, but were communities whose members were men who identified themselves as members of that community because that was where, no doubt normally for reasons of family history, they felt at home. Kleisthenes' creation of demes seems to have demanded

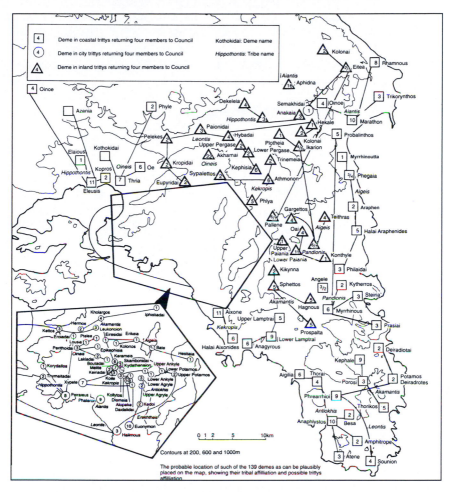

Figure 79 The Athenian demes of the classical period.

some grouping of small communities under a single name, and some assignment of names to communities previously referred to by reference to prominent families or local religious sanctuaries. That the family of the Boutadai came to call themselves the Eteoboutadai or 'true Boutadai' implies that they resented their family name being applied to all who lived in the community where they predominated, and scholars may be right to suspect that calling the community next to the important sanctuary at Brauron not 'Brauron' but 'Philaidai', even though many in the Philaid family registered themselves elsewhere, was a deliberate and political act on Kleisthenes' part. But the political significance of Kleisthenes' reforms lay only trivially in such acts; the important political act was to establish a structure for self-determination in each of the communities, and to give the community as a whole a sense of responsibility for all that went on

Figure 80 The late sixth-century theatre at Thorikos.

in the community (Figure 80). Community responsibility is seen nowhere more clearly than in the creation by demes of a calendar of cultic events, in which the date and nature of sacrifices performed within the community, or by the community at sanctuaries elsewhere, particularly in the town of Athens, was recorded and regulated. The best preserved of these calendars date to the late fifth and to the fourth century BC, but the calendar of the urban deme of Skambonidai is one of the earliest deme documents which we possess, and seems to date to shortly after the Persian wars (*IG* i³ 244, Text 46). Some sacrifices recorded on deme calendars will have been new creations, but we may also suspect that cultic acts which members of the community had previously engaged in as part of some other group came to be transferred to the deme.

The appeal of a promise that every community would henceforth be represented on the Council, and that every community would have a formal structure and recognised rights, becomes particularly clear when viewed against a background of factional strife and perhaps of manipulation of the boundaries of the citizen body. Although I have argued above (p. 268) that the 'men of the coast' and 'men of the plain' should be seen as personal factional followings for Megakles and Lykourgos, rather than as regional sectional interest groups, the use of such regional names will itself have encouraged fear and suspicion between men living in different areas of Attica. Such fear of Athenians in one part of Attica ganging up on Athenians in another part of Attica will have been further exacerbated if, as [Aristotle,] *Constitution of the*

...the demarch and the sacred officials are to sacrifice to Leos an unblemished victim, each member of the deme is to get a 3 (?) obol portion, and the resident foreigners are to obtain a share in the agora of the Skambonidai. . . . At the festival of the Synoikia, sacrifice on the Acropolis a perfect victim: meat to be sold raw. At the festival of the Epizephyra, sacrifice a perfect victim at the sanctuary of Apollo Pythios: meat to be sold raw.

Text 46: IG *i³* 244.C.2–10, 16–22. *Part of a calendar of sacrifices from the community of Skambonidai, part of the town of Athens.*

Athenians claims (13.5, cf. 21.2, 4), there was widespread expulsion of men from the citizen body following the overthrow of Hippias. The more arbitrary or prejudiced such expulsions seemed, both to victims and to those who had escaped expulsion, the greater will have been the appeal of promising to the deme a say on its own members and hence on who was and who was not a citizen. Kleisthenes' further promise, through the division of the tribes into three trittyes, that in each tribe demes from the city would constitute one third, demes from the inland region another third, and demes from the coastal region the final third, will have allayed any fears that the new system would allow regionalism in again by the back door by creating tribes wholly or predominantly from one region.

What were Kleisthenes' motives?

Seen from these points of view, popular support for Kleisthenes becomes easy to understand, but Kleisthenes' support for the people remains somewhat mysterious. Fear of Sparta, pressing need for a new army, and the promotion of the local community to a formal place in Athens' structures of government, may have appealed to the Athenian people at large, but what motivated Kleisthenes himself? Were there advantages for Kleisthenes personally, or was he an idealist and an altruist? Of our ancient sources, the Aristotelian *Constitution of the Athenians* (20–1) sees Kleisthenes as an idealist: the key to Kleisthenes' actions for [Aristotle] is the desire to mix up the people, obliterating old distinctions (and Aristotle in *Politics* 1319b19–27 implies a similar view). Herodotos, on the other hand, claims (5.69) that Kleisthenes replaced the four Ionian tribes with ten new tribes because he despised the Ionians, and did not want the Athenians to have the same tribes as the Ionians. Herodotos explicitly aligns Kleisthenes' action in this regard with that of his mother's father, Kleisthenes, the tyrant of Sikyon. I have suggested above (p. 267) that the changes to tribal names at Sikyon were part of the promotion of Sikyon in opposition to other cities. At Athens Kleisthenes' new tribal names, whether chosen by him directly or chosen by Delphi from a longer list which he submitted, as [Aristotle,] *Constitution of the Athenians* 21.6 suggests, can certainly be seen in the same light. The Ionian tribal names had no local reference, but the new tribal names were derived from eponymous tribal heroes who are important figures in Athenian myth-history: Erekhtheus, Aigeus, Pandion, Akamas, and Kekrops were among the legendary kings of Athens; Leos, son of Orpheus, sacrificed his daughters to save Athens at time of plague; Hippothoon was son of Poseidon; and Aias is the great hero of the *Iliad* from Salamis. To institute these new tribal names was to make all the various actions which Athenians performed in tribes, whether military, festival, or political, redolent of an Athenian past. The ground was laid for the promotion of Athenian autochthony, that is, of the Athenian claim always to have been in Attica from the beginning, which was so marked in the latter part of the fifth century BC. And Herodotos must be correct in thinking that such promotion of civic pride can only have weakened the sense of being part of the body of Ionian Greeks. When the pressure from Sparta might have caused division between Dorian and Ionian to become salient in Athens, Kleisthenes' tribal reform seems to have channelled Athenian opposition more narrowly.

Modern scholars have in general ignored Herodotos' specific explanation for Kleisthenes' action, but they have been keen to adopt his more general stance that Kleisthenes had personal motives and was not a democratic idealist. Observing the background of factional struggle, and the way in which Herodotos presents Kleisthenes' appeal to the people as a way of getting the better of Isagoras, they have scrutinised the details of the reforms for ways in which they might have damaged the interests of Kleisthenes' opponents and promoted the interests of his own family, the Alkmaionids. Attention has been directed in particular to the ways in which he combined demes into trittyes and into tribes. Neither Herodotos nor the Aristotelian *Constitution of the Athenians* tells us which deme was in which tribe. For the fourth century BC we know the tribal affiliation of each deme because the fifty members of a particular tribe who served on the Council of 500 for a year, and acted as its standing committee (*Prytaneis*) for one-tenth of the year, were regularly praised for their services, and had their names inscribed, by deme, on a commemorative monument. (It is from these lists that we know that each deme had a fixed number of members on the Council each year.) Combining these lists with what we know from a variety of sources, both literary and archaeological, about the location of individual demes, it is possible to observe how the location of one deme in a given tribe compares to the location of other demes in the same tribe (Figure 79). [Aristotle] in *Constitution of the Athenians* (21.4) says that each tribe was made up of one coastal, one inland, and one city trittys, and thus we might expect there to be three distinct blocks of demes in each tribe. In some tribes, Erekhtheis for instance, this does indeed seem to be the case. But in other tribes one or more deme appears to be isolated from the other demes in the tribe. Three striking examples are Probalinthos in Pandionis, Halimous in Leontis, and Pallene in Antiokhis. Do these isolated demes occur merely by chance, or are they evidence for Kleisthenic manipulation of his system?

Interpretation of these 'anomalous' arrangements is difficult. Although, as we will see (below, p. 306), the concept of a map was available at this time,

Kleisthenes will not himself have operated with an accurate map of Attica. His will have been a mental map based on his own knowledge of Attica, a map better at placing communities in a sequence along a route than at judging how two divergent routes related one to another. Yet the anomalies mentioned above seem greater than any geographical confusion in the mind of Kleisthenes could account for. What is more, all three of these demes which are isolated from other demes in the same tribe are demes which had important religious roles. Pallene was the centre of the 'League of Athene Pallenis' involving surrounding communities; Probalinthos with Marathon, Oinoe, and Trikorynthos formed the 'Tetrapolis', which had a joint religious calendar; Halimous was the most important cult centre of Demeter outside Eleusis and the town of Athens itself. 'Tetrapolis' became used as the name of the trittys of the tribe Aiantis which included Marathon, Trikorynthos, and Oinoe but not Probalinthos: was Kleisthenes deliberately bringing about a mismatch between political and religious units?

That Kleisthenes was determined to break the power of old religious units is not at all clear from what else we know about his reforms. Kleisthenes seems to have done nothing to end old religious associations and practices. When the Athenians inscribed their laws in the last decade of the fifth century BC, they included a religious calendar in which both the old Ionian tribes and the old trittyes of those tribes played a part: a surviving fragment mentions the tribe Geleontes and its trittys the Leukotainioi or 'White-ribboned men'. Similarly, although Kleisthenes made being recognised as a member of a deme the moment at which a man became a citizen, the older descent groups known as phratries continued not merely to exist but to function vigorously. A long inscription (*IG* ii^2 1237) from the beginning of the fourth century BC shows a phratry extremely concerned about its membership, and in fourth-century lawcourt speeches men regularly refer to their phratry membership in supporting their claims to be Athenian citizens. Again, although some of the eponymous heroes of the new tribes were figures for whom cult had to be created, others were figures that had an existing cult, and in those cases that existing cult acquired an additional role as a tribal cult, but the old cult personnel continued to have charge. Kleisthenes' general practice seems to have been additive not substitutive, and he was as liable to create new roles for old groups as to take their old roles away.

Another reason too for being cautious about deducing Kleisthenes' intentions from what we know of the tribal affiliations of demes in the fourth century BC is that there is a very serious possibility that the fourth-century situation was not purely the result of Kleisthenic actions, but that the framework which Kleisthenes had created had been modified at some subsequent date. There are two reasons for thinking that this might be the case, one demographic and the other archaeological. Of the 139 demes of which we know in the fourth century BC, no fewer than a quarter returned not more than one member a year to the Council. Since, after the initial registration at the time of Kleisthenes, deme membership was hereditary in the male line, and not determined by residence, the size of a deme in the fourth century will have depended upon the demographic history of the community registered as demesmen at the end of the sixth century. A deme which could only justify one member on the Council of 500 is likely to have had an adult male population of around 50 to 100 (0.2–0.4 per cent of a total citizen population of 25,000) in 507 BC. The chance that thirty-five communities of that size at that time all had a similar demographic history through the fifth century is extremely small, especially given the possible local effects of the plague and the way in which particular tribes suffered particularly heavily in particular battles. Demography seems to require either a revision of bouleutic quotas or the transfer of men from one deme to another, perhaps on grounds of residence, at some point in the fifth century.

Archaeological evidence suggests even more radical change during the fifth century BC. Intensive archaeological survey work in one area of southern Attica has recovered a greater density of archaeological remains per hectare in that area than has been revealed by similar work in any other area of Greece. Individual buildings, grave terraces, and extensive agricultural terracing of a rather unpromising landscape, have been traced. Ceramic evidence is not plentiful, but neither it nor the building remains give any indication that this area was occupied prior to the fifth century BC. Yet there is no doubt that in the fifth and fourth centuries this was the location of the deme Atene, a deme which returned three members to the Council annually. It seems inconceivable that a community of some 500 or more people can have lived in this area in the late sixth century BC and left no archaeological trace. But the alternative is to believe that some reform during the fifth century, and before 432/431 BC when the first member of the deme is attested in a dated inscription, not only changed the numbers of councillors which a deme was expected to produce annually, but even introduced new demes whose members must have been descendants of men registered in other demes. Whether those changes were great enough to render credible Herodotos' apparent belief that there were just 100 demes in 507 BC we cannot currently tell.

There is no reason to be surprised at the possibility that there was a fifth-century reform of the Kleisthenic system which is not recorded in literary sources. Epigraphic evidence has shown that there were various procedural changes in the institutions of Athenian democracy during the fifth and fourth centuries BC which are not recorded even in the Aristotelian *Constitution of the Athenians*, and the sort of changes envisaged here would not involve any important question of principle. But even if the changes had very limited consequences for contemporaries, they have profound consequences for our understanding of Kleisthenes. For the combined numerical and geographical constraints which were built into the Kleisthenic system meant that new demes and new quotas had significant knock-on effects. Since each tribe had to return 50 members to the Council, introducing a new deme, or increasing a deme's quota, meant either making equivalent reductions to the quotas of other demes in the same tribe, or moving a deme from that tribe to another in which quota reductions could be made. Thus, even at the level of tribal affiliation, the existence of anomalies in the fourth century might well be a product of fifth-century adjustments rather than Kleisthenic decisions. When we consider trittyes, the fact that in the fourth century BC the inland group of demes in a particular tribe does not return the same number of members to the Council as the coastal or city group of demes would seem to be an inevitable result of any creation or enlargement of individual demes.

The arguments that have been used to suggest that Kleisthenes tried to benefit his own family of the Alkmaionidai do not depend in the same way on details which are likely to have been affected by post-Kleisthenic changes. The claim is that Kleisthenes put together, into the same tribe, coastal and city communities which were the traditional strongholds of the Alkmaionidai. This claim rests heavily upon interpreting the 'Coastal' group, identified as Megakles' supporters in the narratives of Peisistratos' rise to power, to imply strong Alkmaionid support in the area for which 'Coast' was used as a technical term, the south-west coast of Attica around the deme of Anaphlystos (modern Anavyssos). In as far as the family can be traced in the fifth century BC, and the Alkmaionids play remarkably little part in political life after the 480s, its members belonged to three city demes, Alopeke, Agryle, and Xypete, which were in three separate tribes. This does not mean that they did not continue to own land in the Anavyssos area, where most local communities belonged to Antiokhis, the same tribe as Alopeke, and landownership is likely to have involved local patronage through seasonal employment, leasing to tenants, and so on. But was having a good deal of influence within a single tribe likely to be advantageous to a politically ambitious family? We know very little of the role that the tribes were initially given, but it seems likely that they effectively decided certain military offices from a very early date and that they also had a considerable say in who financed the festivals in which tribal events took place (see further below, p. 291). There would certainly have been chances to enhance one's social standing through dominant influence in a tribe. But that is a rather different matter from dominance of the political stage. The subsequent record of the family certainly does not suggest that the Alkmaionids enjoyed a uniquely favoured position there.

None of the arguments for a Kleisthenes who, under the guise of giving power to the people, really tried to destroy the power of opposing members of the Athenian élite while institutionally entrenching the influence of his own family, seems to stand up to close scrutiny. Does this mean that Kleisthenes was an altruistic idealist after all? Hardly so. Just as a number of different concerns may have led the people to back Kleisthenes, so his reforms may have been designed to deal with a number of immediately pressing problems. We should expect Kleisthenes, as a politician with twenty years of varied experience behind him, to have a fairly shrewd idea of the immediate consequences of proposing these reforms. The popular backing which he received, and the military success over the Boiotians and Khalkidians, argue that he predicted those immediate consequences accurately. But he need have had no positive long-term view in mind. Whether he had or not, the long-term consequences were profound.

Political life in Kleisthenic Athens

What sort of a state did Kleisthenes create? For Herodotos (5.78, Text 47) what transformed Athens from a weak state ruled by tyrants to a state which could dominate all neighbours was *isegoria* – equality of speech. The songs which celebrated Harmodios and Aristogeiton as tyrannicides hailed them as bringers of *isonomia* – equality in law – to Athens. How soon Athenians came to describe their constitutional order as *demokratia* – power to the people – is disputed: although the first attested use of the word comes only after the Persian wars it may have been employed earlier. But what was it about Kleisthenes' reforms which made it possible to describe Athens in terms of equality of speech and law and of the people's power? We are hampered in understanding the effect of the institutional innovations – the new tribes, the Council of 500, the demes – by our ignorance about how the old Council of 400 had been chosen and about its powers. Certainly the quotas for the new Council, and the insistence, if it was imposed at the beginning, that no Athenian could serve on it for more than two, separated, years did ensure that a large number of Athenians had close contact with the running of the state. The powers of the Council were closely defined: the Council Oath introduced in 501 BC made it very clear that the Council was a deliberative, not an executive body, with strictly limited judicial competence; and a further statute of limitations, known only in fragmentary form from its reinscription for the Athenian law code in the last decade of the fifth century, may indicate subsequent reinforcement of the Council's judicial incapacity. The restrictions on the Council's power make clear that already by 501 BC the Assembly was in charge, determined to assert that the people were sovereign, and that even so representative a body as the Council was but the adviser of the people.

What gave the Assembly its pre-eminence in Athens? There was certainly an assembly in Athens prior to 507 BC, and assemblies had been a feature of Greek life back at least to the time of the Homeric epics. The Great Rhetra at Sparta shows a concern there with the regular meeting of an assembly and with its powers in the years around 700 BC (above, p. 167). The stories which were later told about the rise of tyrants also imply the possibility of the popular voice determining political events. A law from Khios, dated to the first half of the sixth century BC, shows that the people there were powerful enough to have created a 'popular council' which was elected and met monthly (ML 8/ Fornara 19), and at Olympia in the sixth century we even find reference to a Council of 500 and a full assembly working together (Buck 64), but there, as at Sparta, there is a limit imposed upon their interference. Two important factors that ensured that at Athens the Assembly was the most important political body were the powerlessness of magistrates and the rapid formation of an ethos of participation.

They dedicated a tithe of the ransom-money from the prisoners in the form of a bronze four-horse chariot. This stood on the left as one first entered the Propylaia on the Acropolis. The inscription on it read: 'The Athenians in deeds of war tamed the people of Boiotia and Khalkis, and ended their violence with gloomy chains of iron; then they dedicated these horses as a tithe to Pallas.' So the Athenians now grew more powerful. But it is not in one act but everywhere that the importance of equal rights to political involvement (isegoria) is clear: the Athenians, when ruled by tyrants, were no better in war than their neighbours, but freed from tyrants they were far superior. This shows that when they were constrained they let themselves be defeated, since they were working for an overlord, but when they were freed each one was keen to do the deed for himself.

Text 47: Herodotos 5.77.4–78. Herodotos uses the Athenian defeat of Boiotians and Khalkidians as a sign that democracy unlocked new Athenian military power.

The powerlessness of Athenian magistrates emerges particularly clearly from comparison with Sparta. It is not just that Athens had no equivalent of the two kings, who achieved office by virtue of birth (the heir to the throne did not go through the *agoge* lest pre-eminent birth conflict with apparent failure in deed) and continued in office till death. Athens also had no equivalent of Sparta's annual magistrates, the ephors, whose power was such that Herodotos (5.39–40) could tell the story of them ordering the king to divorce his wife and marry another in order to ensure male heirs (see below, p. 317), that an ephor was crucial in persuading Spartans to fight Athens in 432 BC (Thucydides 1.85–7), and that Aristotle could blame the decline of Sparta in the fourth century BC partly on the poor quality of the ephors (*Politics* 1270b6–35). Spartan kings, who were expected to lead all military expeditions abroad, and ephors had powers which no individual magistrate at Athens possessed; jobs such as receiving embassies, which were done in Sparta by ephors, were in Athens in the hands of the Council of 500. But kings and ephors also had an influence which transcended their statutory powers. In the case of kings, this was achieved through their special treatment – double portions at meals, particularly elaborate funerals, and the like – and through the accumulation of experience which lifelong office-holding gave. In the case of ephors it was at least in part a product of their election tending to reflect the opinion prevailing at the time. This becomes clear at moments when the popular mood swung sharply after the ephorate elections but the ephors persisted in carrying through a policy about which there was now popular doubt (the clearest case comes with the trial of King Pausanias in 403; Pausanias 3.5.1–2). The tendency to ascribe special importance to individuals by virtue of their office extended also to members of the Gerousia, the council of twenty-eight elected over-60-year-olds. Diodoros (11.50) has a tale, not necessarily true, about one of the Gerousia, Hetoimaridas, playing a crucial role in preventing Sparta attacking Athens in the 470s; and Xenophon (*Hellenika* 3.3.8) tells how, in the crisis over one Kinadon getting all non-Spartiates at Sparta to band together against the Spartiates, the ephors carefully consulted members of the Gerousia individually.

Only one magistracy at Athens allowed either long-term occupation of the same office or any sense of being elected on a platform. This was the generalship, only instituted in 501 BC and only acquiring its predominant military role after 490 BC. Unlike other magistrates, generals were not chosen by lot: in military matters individual incompetence could not be made up for by having a large board to do the office. And unlike other magistracies the generalship could be held repeatedly, with no limit. Yet off the battlefield the general seems to have had no powers and no special privileges; it was an innovation proposed by critics of democracy to put the general *ex officio* on the Council of 500 ([Aristotle,] *Constitution of the Athenians* 30.2). Although on occasion the generals together seem to have sponsored some decree (e.g. *IG* i³ 92, honouring a Thessalian in 416/415), no electoral hustings seem to have developed. Some individuals certainly did hold the generalship for long years in succession (Perikles and Nikias are clear fifth-century cases), but where we have a full or nearly full listing of generals for more than one year in succession a high degree of turnover is clear. How remarkably separate politics and generalship were at Athens is shown up by the contrast with late fifth-century Syracuse, where the contamination between the two areas is prominent in the careers of Hermokrates and of Dionysios I.

It is the ethos of participation at Athens that must be invoked to explain how even generals remained politically subordinate. Athenians took up the possibilities of self-government enthusiastically. We find the structures of central government mimicked in the structures of deme, phratry, religious and other groups. And not just the structures. The very rhetoric employed in meetings in the local community echoed, and was echoed by, that of the Assembly. Surviving evidence does not allow this process to be easily dated, but the inscription on stone of community decisions in demes comes as early as the inscription of assembly decisions: the Assembly's laws about cult practices at Eleusis from the 460s are matched by the deme of Skambonidai's laws from the same decade (*IG* i³ 6, 244); the Parthenon accounts from the 440s come in the wake of the accounts of the temple of Nemesis at Rhamnous from the same decade (*ML* 53, 54/Fornara 90B, 114). The customary practices which were quickly developed for central government became simply *the* way of operating assumed by Athenian citizens in any context whatsoever.

Athens' ethos of participation depended both on displacing the traditional élite and on fostering a high degree of self-confidence in the ability of every citizen, if not individually, then certainly when part of a group. The new-style Athenian army, and its immediate successes, must have played an important part in this confidence, a part reinforced by the ongoing struggle with and over Aigina (see below, p. 307). Kleisthenes' new local institutions, in which no Athenian family had any claim to special status on the basis of past traditions, weakened the role of the élite. Whether the institution of ostracism, in which once a year the Athenians might be asked to write on a sherd of pottery the name of the citizen they wanted expelled from the city for ten years, played a part in this too depends upon whether or not it is to be dated with the 507 BC reforms. Ancient tradition ([Aristotle,] *Constitution of the Athenians* 22.3–4) held that ostracism was not used until 488/487 BC, and there has been some doubt as to whether such a weapon would have been left untried for so long. Alternatively its very institution may be seen as a product of citizen confidence, boosted by their victory over the Persians at Marathon (below, p. 314), that they could do without individuals whom they could not trust to work through the newly established channels. This latter view gains some support from the fact that, in the year following the first use of ostracism (487/486), the Athenians went over to selecting archons by lot from a shortlist, rather than by direct election.

In laying stress, quite properly, on the unprecedented involvement which the Kleisthenic constitution gave to the ordinary man, it is important not to overlook that his constitution was equally unprecedented in the degree to which political power was institutionalized. We have seen that as early as the seventh century communities were keen to flag up the strict limits to the competences which they afforded to magistrates (above pp. 174–6). But in every archaic city there was room for personal qualities and connections to impact upon political decisions. Family connections continued to be an important source of power in every Greek city – hence the power of the story of the competition for the hand of Agariste, daughter of Kleisthenes of Sikyon (p. 266). Now in Kleisthenic Athens the possible scope for the personal becoming the political was severely cut back. And not the least consequence of this was the disappearance of women from political consideration. For although women had had formal powers in no archaic Greek community that we know of, their informal political importance had been very significant. Athens became the place in the Greek world least generous with the rights it afforded to women, allowing them only the most restricted property rights and insisting that in lawcourts they should be represented by a man. More than ever before, at Athens women's roles came to be restricted to the religious sphere, but even in religion the new democracy increased the opportunities for involvement by men without altering the roles of women.

Religious festivals and the origin of the Great Dionysia

It is important not to overlook the political importance of the religious festivals, on the number of which Athenians came to pride themselves (Thucydides 2.38.1; [Xenophon,] *Constitution of the Athenians* 3.8). Some of those festivals had their origins in the seventh century BC, others came into their classical form during the sixth century BC (see above, p. 232). But the years immediately following Kleisthenes' reforms certainly saw the institution of a number of festivals, and in particular a number of festivals with competitive elements, such as the Herakleia, the Prometheia, the Hephaisteia, and the festival of Pan (this last definitely created in the wake

Figure 81 Amphora dated to *c.*530 BC showing what appears to be a dramatic chorus performing on stilts.

of the victory at Marathon: Herodotos 6.105). Old festivals, including the Oskhophoria, Thargelia, and Panathenaia, were reorganised, at least to the extent of making the new tribes, singly or in pairs, the competitive unit for at least some events. Tribal competition was both a way of fostering solidarity in those new and artificial units and a way of ensuring that victory gave glory without giving power. The importance of this aspect is well revealed by the stories about athletes whose unusual and often frightening powers required that they be given hero-cult. The earliest such figure, Philippos of Kroton (Herodotos 5.47) in *c.*520, seems only marginally distinguished from the familiar glorious victor (above, p. 93), but other tales, such as that told about Kleomedes of Astypalaia (Pausanias 6.9.6–8, Text 48) focus on the damage done by such a hero if his powers are not rightly acknowledged, and we may suspect that they, like stories of how tyrants got power, functioned as cautionary tales, forewarning and forearming Greek cities against athletic *kudos*. All the enhanced competitions at Athens, and the *kudos* resulting from victories achieved in them, were open only to men.

One addition to the festival calendar, which was to have momentous consequences in a world wider than simply classical Athens, the dramatic festival at the Dionysia, may also have been introduced with the new democracy. Here too the enhanced possibility of gaining glory by competitive festal success was limited to men: women could not act on stage (men took

At the Olympiad before this [492 BC], they say that Kleomedes of Astypalaia, when boxing with Ikkos of Epidauros, killed Ikkos in the fight. He was condemned by the Hellanodikai for breaking the rules, and deprived of his victory. The distress of this drove him out of his mind, and he returned to Astypalaia, attacked a school in which there were some sixty children, and removed the pillar which held up the roof. The roof fell in on the children and Kleomedes was stoned by the citizens and fled to the temple of Athene. He got into a box which was lying in the temple, and pulled the lid shut. The people of Astypalaia tried to open the box but laboured in vain. In the end they broke the wood of the box, but did not find Kleomedes either alive or dead. They sent men to Delphi to ask what had happened to Kleomedes and the Pythia announced to them 'Kleomedes is the last hero of Astypalaia. Honour him with sacrifices, he is no longer mortal.' So from that time the Astypalaians give cultic honours to Kleomedes as to a hero.

Text 48: Pausanias 6.9.6–8. Pausanias tells the story of how his overpowering strength turned Kleomedes of Astypalaia first into an unmanageable murderer and then into a hero.

the female roles) and there is some doubt as to whether they could even watch the acting. Drama of some sort had been a feature of some festivals in earlier times: we might remember the masks at the sanctuary of Orthia in Sparta (above, p. 170 and Figure 45), and the initiation of girls to womanhood at Brauron in Attica also involved some sort of dressing up. Choruses of costumed men performing to the music of the pipes appear on Athenian vases from soon after 550 BC (Figure 81), but scripted plays performed by one or more actors with a responding chorus seem to have been developed in Athens in the later part of the sixth century BC. The choruses on vases correspond more closely to later comedy than to tragedy, but we know comic competition to have been institutionalised at Athens only in the fifth century BC, and performance of tragedies is similarly likely to have preceded by some appreciable time the institution of a competition between dramatists, each of whom produced three tragedies.

Athens' own later record on stone of victories probably went back only to 502/501 BC, and the list of victorious tragedians is unlikely to have gone back any further. The entries in the Byzantine encyclopedia the *Souda* which record a production by Thespis in 535/533 BC, by Khoirilos in 523/520 BC, and by Phrynikhos in 511/508 BC place these landmarks at such regular intervals as to invite suspicion, and this suspicion is reinforced by the claim in the entry for Thespis that he had fifteen predecessors. Changes to the festival continued to be made in the fifth century, and it seems quite probable that the competition between tragic poets first became the central feature of the City Dionysia only in the last two or three years of the sixth century.

This landmark in the history of European literature was surely also a landmark in the way Athenians regarded themselves. Although the earliest surviving tragedy dates from after the Persian wars, from the very earliest years of the competition the concerns dramatised at the Dionysia were concerns current in the city – something that the Homeric poems performed at the

Panathenaia by rhapsodes could never achieve. Tragedy both presupposed and fostered a popular concern with political issues in the broadest sense, encouraging critical scrutiny of both individual and community actions. Just how directly the Athenians' own decisions were scrutinised on the stage emerges from the Athenians' fining the playwright Phrynikhos for 'reminding them of their own troubles' in his play the *Capture of Miletos* about the recent taking of that city by the Persians in 494 (Herodotos 6.21).

Warfare, festival competitions, and local responsibilities – if only the choice of a community leader (demarch) annually – ensured that Kleisthenes' new institutions existed not just on paper but as part of people's lives. The new constitution impinged upon all group activities. By doing so it succeeded in replacing the factional struggles among members of the élite with widespread involvement in determining the future of the city. The factionalism which those who framed the American Constitution believed could only be overcome through representative government in which the representatives were men of virtue, the Kleisthenic constitution overcame by combining more or less arbitrarily chosen local representatives in the Council with an eagerness to become involved in political decision-making that was sufficiently widespread to ensure that the Assembly was not dominated by any particular group. By exploiting the distrust to which multiple Spartan interventions gave rise, by encouraging something close to nationalism, both through the military campaigns against their northern neighbours and by the institution of tribal names with local resonances, and by creating an institutional framework which could be employed at every level of society, Kleisthenes managed to instil in the Athenians that 'special way of thinking' which Rousseau insisted was essential to successful government, a way of thinking which put common interests above separate and particular interests.

Democracy and material culture

Archaeology provides some evidence for the effect that Athens' democracy had on the way in which people thought and acted. At the level of the city it is clear that the democratic polis, although not taking over the projects of the tyrants (the temple to Olympian Zeus, above, p. 269, was never completed), oversaw the construction of impressive religious monuments as a necessary part of the construction of a proper image of Athenian power. It is possible that the rebuilding of the temple of Athene Polias, complete with marble sculptures, may date to the last decade of the sixth century rather than to the 520s (the only arguments available are stylistic). It is certain that, at some time shortly before or shortly after the battle of Marathon, the Athenians not only began building an even larger temple on the Acropolis, the predecessor of the Parthenon on the same site, but also constructed a treasury building at Delphi complete with a full set of marble sculptures – thirty metopes, both pediments, and half-a-dozen figures set on the corners of the roof and the gable top as acroteria (Figure 82). Then, after the battle of Marathon, they

Figure 82 Metope of Theseus and Antiope from the Athenian treasury at Delphi.

added a stoa at Delphi in which spoils were displayed. Athens' treasury at Delphi both directly competed with the earlier Siphnian treasury, with its striking sculpted Ionic frieze, and also competed, as a work of the Athenian *polis*, with the temple of Apollo on the terrace above, which had been restored by the Alkmaionidai.

More striking still are developments in the private sphere. Most immediate is the dramatic change in burial practices. The number of adult burials recovered by archaeologists for most of the seventh and sixth centuries BC averages about one a year. At the end of the sixth century the number of known burials rockets to something like nine a year, with almost as many child burials known as adult burials. Although there is some talk in the Aristotelian *Constitution of the Athenians* (21.4) about 'new citizens', this change is very unlikely to reflect population change and must rather reflect the provision of an archaeologically visible burial to a greater proportion of the people. The implication of this is that the events of the last decade led to a significant proportion of Athenians feeling that their personal status had been enhanced.

Less immediate, and less easy to quantify, are changes in the provision of funerary monuments. During the sixth century BC rich graves had been marked in three ways: by carved pillars or stelai, usually showing a young man or soldier in profile; by *kouroi* (cf. above, p. 197); and by painted plaques. The tradition of plaques seems to die out by 500; *kouroi* seem to have gone on being used occasionally down to around 480; stelai with athletic or military figures seem to

295

die out around 500. Although the cessation of commemoration is not sharply defined in the archaeological record, it is possible that it should be associated with legal regulation. Cicero states that 'sometime after Solon' a law was passed restricting tombs to what ten men could build in three days, and perhaps banning all sculpted markers (*De Legibus* 2.64–5). It is certainly tempting to connect the end of funerary monuments with the changing position of the élite at Athens, and with the new ways in which they had to negotiate their position.

Harder still to assess are the factors behind changing imagery. Sculpted dedications on the Acropolis seem to go on in very much unchanged form: indeed the sequence of late sixth- and early fifth-century *korai* from the Acropolis is unparalleled. But in pottery, along with a technical change from black-figure to red-figure vases which happens gradually over the last two decades of the sixth century and the first decade of the fifth, there is a change in iconographical preferences. The dominance of mythological scenes is shaken, and the mythological scenes painted by red-figure artists tend to be different from those that were the favourites with the black-figure artists of the middle of the sixth century. The change in drawing technique is certainly itself one factor in changing the iconography: red-figure offered a chance to treat figures differently, and in doing so undermined old iconographic schemes; if new schemes were needed they might as easily be new schemes for new subjects as new schemes for old ones. But the technical change does not seem sufficient to explain the increasing interest in non-mythological scenes, scenes of the symposion, of the palaistra, of revelling (Figure 83). These are scenes of the élite at play, scenes which it is not difficult to imagine picture life around the court of Hipparkhos and Hippias. But the scenes continue uninterrupted into early democracy. They are a useful reminder that, while

Figure 83 A symposium scene on a large late sixth-century Athenian cup. The is one of a number of puzzling vessels where male participants are dressed in characteristically female clothing. The threatening of the serving boy with the slipper, and the shaping of the foot of this cup in the form of male genitals suggest that the scene is sexually charged.

Kleisthenes' reforms may have immediately encouraged those of lower status to aspire to commemorate their own standing, and while legislation may have curbed the public display by the rich, the private lifestyle of the élite may have been but little affected, or indeed simply more widely emulated. Both in dedicatory sculpture and in the iconography of vase painting, the most marked revolution comes after 480 BC rather than after 507 BC, and that story must be told elsewhere.

The successful creation of popular government in Athens had a massive impact not just on Athens but on Greek history. The diffusion of democratic institutions was only one relatively minor part of that impact; far more important was the way in which constitution subsequently became an issue in relations between cities. I have argued above that tyranny was less a peculiar form of government than a particular development of élite-dominated constitutions, have pointed to the easy relations which tyrants enjoyed with members of the élite in other cities, and have expressed doubt about whether Sparta in the sixth century BC had any principled opposition to tyranny as such. By contrast, in the fifth century BC, though more after the Persian wars than before, oligarchy and democracy became poles on which cities hung their flags (see Thucydides 1.19, 3.82).

PHILOSOPHY

By the late fifth century, when Herodotos was writing his *Histories*, theoretical debate about the merits and disadvantages of different forms of government was well developed. That debate is directly reflected in the discussion about whether Persia would be better off with monarchy, oligarchy, or democracy, which Herodotos (3.80–2) insists took place prior to Darius' accession to the Persian throne in 522 BC; it is also implied by the way in which Herodotos presents archaic tyrants as having precisely the habits for which they are condemned in that discussion. Herodotos may well have taken over the terms of the constitutional debate from contemporary political philosophy: the influence of the professional philosopher Protagoras, whose views are well known from Plato's fourth-century dialogues, has often been suspected. But Herodotos' stories about archaic tyranny surely reflect popular perceptions, and there is no doubt that theoretical debate about the political order went back well before Kleisthenes' reforms.

Those reforms themselves need to be seen in the context of philosophical debate. That he chose to have ten tribes, rather than twelve, is unlikely to have been an arbitrary decision. Tens and fifties were by no means unparalleled elsewhere, but they certainly became the hallmarks of a secular and democratic organisation (as at Elis and Sybaris in the fifth century), and they distinguished Kleisthenic Athens both from the organisation of Ionia, with its twelve cities (Herodotos 1.145–6), and from the Peisistratids with their promotion of the altar of the twelve gods. Fascination with numbers and regularities is to be found in several Greek thinkers: as early as Hesiod some dates of the month are regarded as good and others bad; the symbolic associations of particular numbers seem to underlie the complex numerological relationships found in Greek medicine; the followers of the philosopher Pythagoras are held to have associated justice with the number four, marriage with the number five (the sum of the male number, three, and the female number, two); and Aristotle (*Metaphysics* 1093a13ff.) has occasion to be critical of those who find significance in the number seven because there were seven vowels in the Greek alphabet, seven notes to the scale, seven Pleiades, and at age 7 children lose their teeth. We do not need to posit any direct connection between Kleisthenes and Pythagorean philosophy to suppose that the potential power of number symbolism was not lost on him.

The congruence of political debate and constitutional change with philosophical thought extends much more broadly than this matter of numbers. As early Greek thinkers came to try to understand how the world came to be in its present form without recourse to such arbitrary divine interventions as Hesiod's *Theogony* presupposes, analogies from the political world, as well as analogies from the natural world, played an important part in their thought. So Anaximander of Miletos in the middle of the sixth century, when explaining that all things came from 'the boundless' and reverted to 'the boundless', is said in Simplicius' commentary on Aristotle's *Physics*, written in the sixth century AD, to have maintained that 'the source of coming-to-be for existing things is that into which destruction too happens, "according to necessity; for they pay penalty and retribution to each other for their injustice according to the assessment of Time"'. Anaximander was himself responding to the suggestion of Thales of Miletos that water was what all things came from. Aristotle suggests that Anaximander offered his alternative of 'the boundless' because of the difficulty of explaining how the opposite of water, fire, could possibly come to be out of water. Similarly the counter-suggestion by Anaximenes that all things not only came from but were air seems to have been motivated by the need to explain how it is that the original substance turns into other things; for Anaximenes the advantage of considering air as the original substance lay in his belief that fire was just rarefied air, earth and stones very much thickened air. But whatever Anaximander's and Anaximenes' motives, the important thing to note is the process of argument. Settling disputes by argument in a lawcourt or a public meeting is a concept familiar already in the *Iliad*, and the rhetorical sophistication of Homeric epic must not be underestimated (see above, p. 147); but the application of such arguments to the natural world represented an important breakthrough, which is traditionally seen as marking the beginning of Greek philosophy.

It is hard to believe that argument as such was anything new in archaic Greece. But what the arguments among members of the élite led to was the attempt to establish rules which would have both general application and an overall consistency and coherence. Although there was widespread recognition, reflected in stories about tyrants seizing power, that even the

Xenophanes says that the sun is made up of tiny bits of fire that are gathered together each day, that the earth has no bounds and is not surrounded by Ocean or by air, and that there are endless suns and moons and they are all made of earth.

Text 49: Hippolytos, Refutation of All Heresies *1.14.5. Hippolytos gives an account of Xenophanes' physical theories.*

best laws were useless unless there was an adequate agency to enforce them, it is clear that the quality of general rules mattered, as was not the case where monarchy or despotism was firmly established. It is a measure of the wide-ranging importance of this commitment to, and interest in, general rules that, despite the advanced mathematical skills of both Babylonians and Egyptians, it was the Greeks who first developed the concept of a mathematical *proof.*

Was the exchange between political and philosophical debate all one way? The surviving reports of the thought of two late sixth-century Ionian figures, Xenophanes of Kolophon and Herakleitos of Ephesos, suggest that it was not. Xenophanes took up the attempt by the Milesian philosophers, Thales, Anaximander, and Anaximenes, to reduce the variety of the natural world to order; in Xenophanes' version all things come from earth and water (Text 49). But his importance lies in the way he applies the same kinds of argument to the supernatural world. Xenophanes became notorious for his criticism of the immorality of the gods in Homeric epic and in Hesiod's poems (frg. 11), and for his suggestion that men make gods in their own image, and that if cattle had gods they would picture them as cattle (frg. 15). Far from being an atheist, Xenophanes maintained that there was a god, and that that god was single, not at all like men, and moved things by thought (frgs 23–6). The mode of thought which, applied to the physical world, emphasised the relatedness of disparate matter, when applied to the metaphysical world emphasised the relativity brought about by the observer's viewpoint: 'If god had not created yellow honey, they would say that figs were much sweeter' (frg. 38).

Questioning the absolute, and emphasising the importance of context, is still more prominent in the views and words attributed to Herakleitos. He drew attention to the fact that sea water is pure and healthy for fish, polluted and deleterious for men (frg. 61), and that it is only the existence of disease that makes health pleasant (frg. 111), and by doing so brought out the relativity of human observation in a pointed and paradoxical way. As Xenophanes indicates the arbitrariness of men's images of the gods, Herakleitos indicates the arbitrariness of cult practices – where blood can be deemed to pollute in one circumstance but purify in another (cf. frg. 5). Not surprisingly, Herakleitos was sceptical of the possibility of gaining secure knowledge through the senses, noting that 'nature loves to keep itself hidden' (frg. 123), and he employed the language of the lawcourts in claiming that eyes and ears are evil witnesses unless their language can be understood (frg. 107). But, despite making some claims to superior wisdom, Herakleitos seems to have regarded the coexistence of opposites as an essential part of the world order, rather than simply a by-product of human weakness: 'all things happen by strife and necessity' (frg. 80), and there would be no musical scale without the existence of the opposites high and low (Aristotle, *Eudemian Ethics* 1235a25ff.).

According to Diogenes Laertios (9.5), Herakleitos' book *On Nature* was divided into three discourses, on the universe, on politics, and on theology. Although that division is unlikely to be original, it emphasises that subsequent Greeks saw Herakleitos' thought as having direct political relevance. By emphasising that the values which individuals and groups adopted were not absolute but relative, dependent upon a particular context, Herakleitos posed a challenge to contemporaries and to subsequent generations to root their behaviour in values which could be defended by argument: 'those who speak with sense must rely on what is common to all, just as a city on law and much more strongly' (frg. 114). Herakleitos' challenge to see conventions as the product of a particular viewpoint was subversive of blind obedience to rulers or to existing rules, but it gave a reasoned basis for promoting public debate in which everything could be questioned. In the hands of Xenophanes and Herakleitos philosophical speculation did not merely build upon experience of dispute settlement and the public consideration of ethical problems, but offered a rational justification for preferring public debate and for challenging accepted views.

PERSIA

Just as I have argued above that living in the face of a rather different civilisation encouraged the extravagant display of Greek identity in the massive temples of Sicily and Ionia, so it seems unlikely that the presence of the alien worlds of Lydia and Persia had no role in stimulating early Greek philosophy. The beginnings of philosophy occurred in Miletos, a city very heavily involved not just with its Lydian neighbours and with the near east but also with the Black Sea, where it claimed large numbers of Greek settlements as its colonies. The international contacts of Herakleitos' home city of Ephesos ran well back into the eighth century, as finds from the temple of Artemis have revealed (above, p. 84). But just as these developments stimulated in Ionia had their most dramatic and lasting effects in the Greek mainland, so also in the political sphere it was the mainland Greeks, who resisted Persian conquest, who were the more changed by their contact with Persia than the Ionians, who enjoyed direct Persian rule.

The defeat of Kroisos of Lydia by Kyros (II) the Great in the 540s (above, p. 243) was part of an extraordinary twenty-five years of conquest by that ruler and his successor, during which they subjugated all four of the major near-eastern kingdoms – the Medes, the Lydians, the Babylonians (freeing the captive Jews in the process, hence the image of Cyrus (Kyros) in Isaiah 44–6), and the Egyptians (*ANE* 656–64). So Kroisos' defeat not only brought the Greeks for the first time into direct contact with the Achaemenid Persians, it brought them into contact with a power which quickly came to extend all the way to Afghanistan.

The death of Kyros' successor, Kambyses, led to a constitutional crisis in 522 BC from which Darius emerged as Persian king (*ANE* 649, 664–7, 676–80, 686–8). Darius' own description of his establishment of his power is preserved in the so-called Behistun inscription, in which he tells of his triumph over all manner of 'pretenders' to the throne. The succession crisis and its aftermath reflect not only the insecure grip on the recently conquered, but also resentment at the cost of conquest and some religious conflict. Darius' firm action in dealing both with revolt and with provincial governors (satraps, *ANE* 689–92) who quarrelled with their neighbours – the Lydian satrap was replaced – quickly put him firmly in control and enabled him to turn his attention to further conquest. The Ionian cities, whose status in the years since Kroisos' defeat is not entirely clear, are to be found assisting Darius in his attack on Skythia (see below, p. 303), traditionally dated to 513 BC, and some of these had certainly been persuaded into allegiance to Persia by a display of power by one of Darius' officers, Otanes, in around 517 BC.

The Persian conquest of Lydia opened up a new world of opportunity for the Greeks. From the beginning the Persians ruled their empire through satraps, and despite the construction of a very impressive network of communications (see Herodotos 5.52–3), the very size of the empire inevitably meant that these satraps, and the financial officials who both assisted and to some extent checked them, had enormous independence. For the Greeks this combination of local rulers, powerful but always wary of their reputations, and a Persian king with great power and also constant fear of disloyalty among the satraps, offered great opportunities. We have already (p. 259) seen Polykrates playing off the advantages of displaying loyalty to Persia with the possibilities offered by supporting a rebel, and Herodotos' account of events in Ionia from the Persian defeat of Kroisos onwards is full of stories of intrigue.

All the stories which Herodotos tells about Ionian dealings with Persia are tinged with hindsight. The success of the Greeks of the mainland in defeating the Persian invasions of 490 and 480, and the shaping of the Persians into the quintessential 'other' (*ANE* 447–9), the negation of all that was Greek and in particular the opponent of liberty, cast a shadow over the variously compromised and collaborative dealings which Ionian cities had had with Persia. The stories of how Ionian cities and their rulers faced up to Persia in the half-century before the Persian wars were recast in a political atmosphere where only total and united resistance to the 'barbarian' was acceptable. But if few incidents can be held beyond the powers of later invention, and none exempt from later distortion, nevertheless the stories can nicely illustrate the sorts of choices which Persian presence and Persian pressure offered to the Greeks of Asia Minor.

The stories illustrate the choices and opportunities both for communities and for individuals. Communities had the choice of showing themselves friendly to Persian rule or making the most of their independence. Herodotos (1.154–61) tells how the Lydian Paktyas, whom Kyros had left in charge of the finances at Sardis, took advantage of his position to hire mercenaries and lead a rebellion. Greek cities first had to decide whether to back Paktyas, and then, when he was defeated by a force under the Mede Mazares and sought refuge among the Greek cities, those cities had to debate the morality and the politics of giving him over to his enemies. Herodotos' story dramatises the incident in terms of consultations of the oracle at Didyma by the people of Kyme, but, whatever the truth of that, the dilemma for the Greek cities is clear. Even for those disinclined to display subservience to Persian demands, Paktyas was too hot a property to handle, and having been passed on from one place to another he was eventually given over to Mazares by the Khians – who extorted some land on the mainland opposite as their reward.

The issue of what attitude to take to the Persians could split communities. Herodotos (1.163–7) tells how Phokaia first exploited its links with the western Mediterranean, and in particular with metal-rich Tartessos in Spain, to build a strong fortification wall, and then, faced with a Persian siege, part of the population decided on permanent migration. This group settled in the west – first in Corsica, and then, after five years or so, in Italy, finally ending up at Velia. But the other group, perhaps after a brief withdrawal, remained at Phokaia, and it was one of their citizens who, rather disastrously, became commander of the Ionian fleet in the Ionian Revolt against Persia. An exactly similar series of events is recorded for Teos: again, pressure of Persian attack is said to have caused a group to go off and found Abdera in Thrace, but Teos continued to exist, refounded or reinforced from Abdera, and supplied a substantial naval force of seventeen ships in the Ionian Revolt (Herodotos 1.168, 6.8).

The choices and opportunities offered to individuals were there for both great and small. The records which have survived on clay tablets from Persepolis reveal Ionian Greeks occupying positions of responsibility and also Greeks in more humble positions (Fornara 45–6). There are female Greek irrigation workers, Greeks transporting building materials, Greek craftsmen. How any of them got to Persepolis we cannot tell, but we may suspect a mixture of ambition and compulsion. Certainly that seems to be the case with the most famous of all Greek workers at the Persian court in this period, the doctor Demokedes of Kroton, whose story Herodotos tells at length (3.125, 129–37). Demokedes' services are supposed to have been bid for by Aigina, Athens, and Polykrates of Samos; he then is said to have accompanied Polykrates on the mission on which Polykrates was killed, and from there to have been taken to Darius and forced to serve him, rising to be a man of wealth and influence, and eventually using that influence to turn Darius' thoughts towards the invasion of Greece in order to have himself given a mission which would allow him to return home. We may suspect that much of this story is what Demokedes wanted people to think, but its value in showing the potential for personal advancement which Persia offered to Greeks is not lessened thereby. And the more such stories circulated, the more others would be encouraged to follow where Demokedes claimed to have gone before.

But the opportunities for individuals were not all dependent on uprooting and making an impression with a satrap or at the Persian court. Persian backing was also a card which members of the élite could play who wished to establish themselves as tyrants. We have already seen this happening at Samos with Syloson (above, p. 264). By the time of Darius' Skythian expedition it is clear that individual members of the élite in many Greek cities had followed the same route, establishing themselves as tyrants with a more or less close link to the Persian powers. Darius seems to have seen the value of having Greek cities under rulers dependent upon him for their positions, and to have been prepared to humour them (compare the apparent rebuke of the Ionian satrap Gadatas for giving minor offence to Greeks, ML 12/Fornara 35, *ANE* 699).

The consequences for Greek liberty of the pursuit of personal advantage by individual Ionians are well brought out by the story, very probably entirely apocryphal, of the debate among Greek rulers as to whether or not to sabotage Darius' Skythian campaign. Herodotos (4.87–142) tells how, sometime in the 510s, Darius turned his attention to Skythia, gathered an Ionian navy, had a Samian engineer named Mandrokles construct a bridge of ships across the Bosporos, marched a vast army into Thrace, and headed north to the Danube, subduing the Getai on the way. Darius then crossed the Danube and, persuaded by an Ionian adviser, left the Ionians to guard the bridge constructed over the Danube until his return. While Darius was being frustrated by the freedom-loving Skythians, who decided that the best way to defeat him was to avoid conflict, keep on the move, and from time to time use cavalry to raid Persian positions and supplies, the Ionians had a conference. At this conference Miltiades, the Athenian ruler in the Thracian Khersonesos, recommended that they should do for Darius by breaking down the bridge, deserting, and leaving the Persians for the Skythians to deal with. But Histiaios of Miletos maintained that, since all the Ionian commanders at the Danube owed their position to the Persians, and since without Persian pressure the people over whom they ruled would prefer democracy and would overthrow them, it was in their own best interests to continue loyal to Darius. This conference dramatises very real issues: Ionian rulers owed their positions to their situation on the edge of the Persian empire. Their personal advantage arose from precisely the situation which meant effective subjection for those they ruled. That personal advantage had the appearance of both prosperity and freedom, particularly when personal loyalty led to grants of additional territory; but that freedom was in fact as constrained as was the freedom of those they governed.

It was not only ambitious Ionians who sought to advantage themselves with the Persian king. Once the Persians were to hand in Asia Minor it became possible for politically active Greeks on the mainland to contemplate doing a deal with them. Not only does Herodotos (3.133–7) have the story of Demokedes of Kroton turning Darius' attention to mainland Greece in order to achieve his own liberty, but he relates how a number of Greeks expelled from their own cities turned east, including most notably Hippias from Athens and Damaratos king of Sparta. Others, secure in internal political terms but threatened externally, took the same course, such as the Aleuadai, who had hereditary control in Thessaly.

As soon as individual politicians from mainland Greek cities could contemplate enlisting Persian support to their own advantage, attitudes to Persia became a subject on those cities' political agenda. The nicest example of this concerns Athenian behaviour in the face of Kleomenes' invasions. Herodotos (5.73) tells how, at the same time as they prepared themselves to resist Kleomenes' second invasion, the Athenians sent an embassy to Sardis to the satrap Artaphernes for assistance. Artaphernes offered support in return for 'earth and water' (that is, tokens of submission). The ambassadors, of their own accord, agreed, but, as Herodotos puts it, got themselves into big trouble at home by doing so. What is so nice about this story is the way it shows up the possibilities of innocence: the ambassadors see themselves as securing what Athens most needs – support against Sparta; the Athenians, who in the mean time have got rid of Kleomenes, see them as giving away Athens' most valued possession – autonomy. At the beginning of the last decade of the sixth century BC mainland Greece still retained an innocence with regard to Persia which the Ionian Greeks had lost more than a quarter of a century before. It would not maintain it into the new century.

The Ionian Revolt

However far their own interests clouded their judgement, political observers in Ionia must have realised that if Darius was interested in Skythia he could hardly fail to be interested in Thrace, Macedonia, and the rest of mainland Greece – especially given the mineral resources which the coins of Thraco-Macedonian cities and tribes were beginning to put so magnificently on display (above, p. 244). When Darius withdrew from Skythia, he left his general Megabyzos in Europe. Megabyzos took Perinthos, moved west, making the whole of Thrace friendly to Persia, and received tokens of submission from Amyntas of Macedon, who also married his daughter to a Persian (Herodotos 5.1, 18). Herodotos' account of Darius' campaign in Skythia makes it a forerunner of the Persian invasion of Greece, in which the Persians are defeated by a liberty-loving people and by their own excessive numbers. But the success of first Megabyzos and then Otanes (Herodotos 5.25–6), and the Persian ability even to transplant the whole community of the Paionians from Thrace to Phrygia, shows that for those living in Thrace and Macedonia the Persians represented a formidable threat.

Darius made no further military offensives in the west during the last decade of the sixth century BC, but that did not significantly relieve the pressure on the Greek cities. However, it did remove the distraction of military demands, and so allow resentment against the perceived agents of Persian control, the tyrants in the individual cities, to grow. And in 499 BC a partially coordinated revolt broke out among the Greek cities of Ionia. For the causes and the course of this revolt Herodotos is our only source. But his account derives from oral traditions which were not only formed after the Persians had taken control of Ionia, but which had adapted themselves to explain why Ionian resistance to Persia failed while mainland Greek resistance was successful. What is more, Herodotos himself uses the Ionian Revolt, sandwiched as it is between the Skythian campaign and the Persian invasions of mainland Greece, to bring out by contrast the distinctive features of mainland Greek success. On the role of individuals and of particular cities, and on motives, Herodotos may faithfully report what was said in the middle or later part of the fifth century BC, but we need to be very wary of assuming that what was said faithfully recorded what actually happened.

The origins of the Ionian Revolt were political. The tyrants in Ionian cities needed to be seen to have Persian support in order to maintain their positions, and they needed to bring themselves to the notice of Darius if they were to be able to lay claim to greater rewards. This meant that there were times when such men had to gamble, knowing that if their attempt to show themselves indispensable to Persia went wrong they would have to quit. Such seems to be the case with Aristagoras the ruler of Miletos. Aristagoras' predecessor as tyrant, Histiaios, had got himself summoned to the Persian court in return for past services – we cannot tell whether this was genuinely a reward or whether he had acquired so great a power and influence that he had become a threat. Herodotos has Histiaios play a starring role in the causes of the revolt, telling how he sent a slave with a message to revolt tattooed on his scalp, and there is no doubt that he did return to Ionia during its course. But the revolt is comprehensible simply in terms of a gamble by Aristagoras, without invoking external provocation.

Aristagoras gambled that he could enhance his position by enabling the Persians to extend their influence westwards into the Aegean through the capture of the island of Naxos. The opportunity to do this was provided by Naxian exiles who approached Aristagoras for assistance, and Aristagoras no doubt calculated that the political instability in Naxos, from which the tyrant Lygdamis had been expelled less than twenty years before, would make military intervention easy. But the campaign went wrong – Herodotos tells of the barbaric discipline applied to Greeks by the Persian commander leading to a quarrel between that commander and Aristagoras (Herodotos 5.33). Far from enabling the Persians to make a significant addition to their empire, Aristagoras found himself having led them to useless expense. Having failed to double his standing, Aristagoras had little choice but to quit.

In quitting, Aristagoras exploited the fragility of his own position. Since he could not strengthen his position via Persian support, he jumped on to the bandwagon of popular rule – the same bandwagon that had driven members of the élite into exile from Naxos. He resigned his position at Miletos in favour of some form of popular government, and encouraged other Ionian cities to expel their tyrants (Herodotos 5.37–8). This initiative had marked success, but the Persians could be expected to react to such expulsion of their friends, and so matters could not be left there.

The great problem for the Ionians was knowing what they had to do to prevent the Persians using military might to reinstall their friends or install something worse. Should they launch an all-out offensive? If so, how and against whom? Herodotos' stories of Hekataios of Miletos advising that a revolt could work only if the Ionians established naval supremacy, of Aristagoras going to Sparta to seek support for a campaign against Sousa, and of the Ionians burning the temple at Sardis, reflect the various approaches that were possible. All the signs are that no coherent policy was formulated or could command universal backing; some were content with the expulsion of the tyrants, others wanted to attack the local manifestation of Persian power in the satrap's headquarters at Sardis, and others again had still grander ideas. Equally, the slowness with which the Persians responded suggests some indecision on their part over the seriousness of the events in Ionia.

The precise course and chronology of the five years of the Ionian Revolt are impossible to recreate from Herodotos' account. But certain features are clear. Concern about Persia had sufficiently penetrated to the Greek mainland to ensure a small amount of naval support from Athens and Eretria, even if nothing from Sparta, where Aristagoras was said to have produced a map of the world on bronze which served only to heighten Spartan fear when he revealed its scale (Herodotos 5.49–50). Dissatisfaction with the Persian presence extended beyond the Greek cities of Ionia: Carians and Cypriots both joined in the revolt. Popular government seems less likely to have been high on the agenda in those places, and we should not ignore the importance of the financial demands which Persia imposed. The Ionians did achieve some striking military successes, particularly at sea, and the Persians were compelled to muster large armies and fight on more than one front at the same time. For the decisive battle, at Lade off Miletos, Herodotos (6.8) records that 353 ships were contributed by nine Ionian cities; but they faced some 600 Persian vessels. The Ionians were defeated, and the recriminations which followed meant that even Herodotos felt unable to establish who fought well and who ill, but the defeat should not be allowed to overshadow the achievement: this was by far the largest naval engagement in which the Greek world had ever been involved.

The revolt had some horrific consequences, but the transformation that it brought even to Ionia was not entirely negative. At Miletos those men not killed in the siege were deported to Mesopotamia and established near the mouth of the Tigris; the women and children were sold into slavery;

the temple at Didyma was burnt (Herodotos 6.19–21). Archaeologically the traces of destruction are clear; it was complete enough to make space for a new planned city at Miletos a decade or so later, and some areas of the city were never reoccupied. Other acts of wanton violence by the victorious Persians led to stories of boys being castrated and girls sent off to Darius' court (Herodotos 6.32). But the Persians also introduced positive changes: Artaphernes created a new taxation system based on a measured survey of land, and Mardonios, Darius' son-in-law, sent west to campaign again in Thrace and Macedonia, introduced a form of government which Herodotos is happy to describe as democracy (Herodotos 6.42–3). We do not know exactly how Artaphernes' taxation system worked, but it seems possible that economically, as well as politically, the real losers in the revolt were the élite, who could now no longer achieve personal power through cultivating the Persians, and who may have had to pay more fairly the price which their resources warranted.

The Ionian Revolt had not brought escape from the Persian Empire, but it is not clear that there were many who believed that to be the aim. It had brought an end to Persian-backed tyrants (though they reappear in due course). Ionia was not to enjoy independence, but in the individual cities the immediate liberty of those who survived to tell the tale was arguably enhanced. The Greeks themselves came to write as if it was only the revolt that had drawn Persian attention to mainland Greece and as if the Persian invasions were solely the consequence of Eretrian and Athenian involvement in the burning of Sardis. But if the revolt affected the timing of the Persian attempts to invade Greece, we have already seen enough evidence to suggest that Persian eyes had been set on westward expansion some time before.

Persian impact on mainland Greek politics

The Persian empire had an impact on mainland Greek cities well before any Persian invasion. The proximity of Persian power changed the rules under which the cities of Old Greece operated. This emerges particularly clearly if we look at relations between Athens and Aigina. Little can be gathered about the past relations between these two cities from Herodotos' story of an old enmity (5.82–8), a story which may well simply reproduce the political alignments c.500 BC which it is supposed to explain. There does appear to have been a period in the seventh century BC when there were close material cultural links between the two places – middle proto-attic pottery is found in both places and it is not clear in which it was made. But during the sixth century BC their worlds had been very different: Aigina had strong Egyptian and strong Cycladic interests (above, p. 244) and was turned to the sea to a greater extent than was Athens. It is a measure of Aigina's central importance as a middleman in trade that Xerxes, at Abydos on the Hellespont in 480 BC, is said to have seen grain-carrying ships heading for Aigina and the Peloponnese (Herodotos 7.147).

Athens and Aigina were rivals in prosperity, but contrasted markedly in size and, after 508/507, also in political disposition. The prosperity of Aigina is nicely symbolised at just this time by the building of the temple of Athene Aphaia. The temple itself was by no means enormous, but it was richly adorned with pedimental sculptures. The excavated remains make it clear that the original sculptural scheme was drastically revised after the east pediment had been completed and crowned with akroteria. The original scheme seems to have shown a local myth – the nymph Aigina raped by Zeus – and a battle between Greeks and Amazons. The replacement showed the sack of Troy by Herakles and Telamon to the east, and the part played by Aias, son of Telamon, in the later Greek sack of Troy to the west. The east pediment was completed last, perhaps shortly before 480 BC, and in composition and treatment of bodies in movement and of drapery it seems consciously to outdo the other pediment. The radical and costly change in plan does not seem to have been required for architectural or structural reasons, and we must suspect political motivation. That motivation may have been of two kinds. We know little of Aiginetan politics, but Pindar wrote some eleven odes for ten different Aiginetan victors, and this suggests an élite keen to surpass each other in conspicuous expenditure, both on competing in the games in the first place and on celebrating their victories. The continued Aiginetan commitment to the values which competing in the games represented, and which Pindar set forth, forms something of a contrast with what Athenians were choosing in the same period, and suggests a rather different structure to Aiginetan politics. For although Pindar celebrates two Athenian victors, one an equestrian victor, and although we know of other victories in the games not celebrated in extant poetry, the exposure achieved by the Aiginetans is of a quite different order. But political rivalry with Athens may have been as important as rivalry between different members of the Aiginetan élite in determining the changes of plan in the Aphaia sculptures. The changed subject matter replaced a myth in which Aigina was symbolised as a woman desirable to the gods with episodes which put Aigina at the centre of legendary warfare in which the Greeks were united, and drew attention to the Aiakidai, the children of Aigina, in whose line was Aias, much celebrated in Pindar's odes for Aiginetan victors (*Nemean Odes* 4, 7, and 5). This is in the face of the Athenian claim to Aias made when Kleisthenes named one of his new tribes after him. The investment in the temple of Aphaia and the iconography chosen both help to make clear why Athens might have a wary eye on her neighbour.

Herodotos (5.79–81, 89–90) tells how in *c.*507 BC the Thebans, in response to defeat by the Athenians, consulted an oracle and were advised to seek help 'from those nearest'. Eventually they decided that the Aiginetans were nearest because mythology held that Thebes and Aigina were both daughters of Asopos; but when Aigina responded by offering the support of its heroes, the Aiakidai, Thebes insisted it needed more material aid. The Aiginetans then began raiding the coasts of Attica. The Athenians also got oracular advice: they should wait thirty years, build a sanctuary to Aiakos, and then they would beat the Aiginetans. The Athenians decided to build the sanctuary and attack straightaway, but were prevented by Kleomenes' final abortive invasion attempt. So far this story is of a conflict whose course can be understood entirely in terms of local rivalry between cities, in which myths of common descent and rival claims to heroes play a part. The involvement of the oracle is typical of conflicts with neighbours, where community consensus is important but liable to be undermined by personal ties, and where the timing of hostile action is underdetermined by events. Anything in this story from the last decade of the sixth century BC could have related to events half a century earlier.

Athens' next clash with Aigina happens in a new world. When the Aiginetans, along with other islanders, showed a willingness to offer tokens of submission to the Persians in the wake of their suppression of the Ionian Revolt, Athens reacted strongly, contacted Sparta, and procured an expedition against Aigina by Kleomenes (Herodotos 6.49). The events that follow, if Herodotos' story is at all reliable, suggest that internal political issues at Sparta were influential in Kleomenes' action: Kleomenes' fellow-king Damaratos was party to a move by the Aiginetans to claim that Kleomenes' expedition to Aigina was unconstitutional; Kleomenes responded by having Damaratos replaced as king on the grounds that he was a bastard and not the son of King Ariston. But issues of external politics were involved too. On the one hand, Kleomenes' action should be seen as a disciplining of a member of the Peloponnesian League and enforcing the requirement that League members 'have the same friends and enemies'. On the other hand, the action took a definite stance *vis-à-vis* Persia. Athens had shown her colours by supporting the revolting Ionians; Sparta had not. If Sparta was to take a stand against Persia she needed a dramatic action. The Athenian request over Aigina should be seen as deliberately precipitating a basic policy decision in Sparta, and the deposition of Damaratos arguably had more to do with foreign policy than with the stories about the circumstances of his birth or about Kleomenes' bribing of oracles which Herodotos retails – stories surely produced by the political debate rather than its causes.

The details and the chronology of what followed are much debated. Herodotos has Kleomenes and Damaratos' successor, Latykhidas, take rich Aiginetans as hostages and deposit them at Athens, and has the Aiginetans after Kleomenes' death persuade the Spartans to make Latykhidas attempt, unsuccessfully, to get them back (Herodotos 6.73, 85–6). That the Spartans had indeed attempted to deal with Aigina by taking hostages is rendered credible by the following account of plans for a popular coup on Aigina aborted by Athenian failure to provide military help in time. The events in Ionia, and the stand taken by Athens, suggest an identification between popular government and a policy of opposing Persia. Less certain are the claims that Sparta regretted her actions: indications to the contrary seem provided by the supply by Corinth of twenty ships to strengthen the Athenian attack on Aigina, and the presence fighting for Aigina of 1,000 volunteers from Argos, the one significant Peloponnesian city outside Sparta's League, and recently a victim of Spartan aggression. In the land and sea encounters that followed both sides enjoyed some success, but the Athenians seem to have had to turn their attention to the Persian expedition before they even had time to commemorate their war dead (cf. Pausanias 1.29.7).

In traditional circumstances an equally matched war between Athens and Aigina might have been looked on with some delight by neighbours and rivals. Provided that neither side utterly crushed the other, little was to be lost, and much gained, by third parties from such conflicts. The Persian factor changed all that. The threat that Aigina's naval power, which even with Corinthian help Athens could only just match, might assist in establishing Persian overlordship on the Greek mainland hastened Greek states into action. The alignment against Aigina anticipated the alignment against Persia – with one exception: the Aiginetans themselves. For the fighting of the 490s had two important consequences: it became clear to the Aiginetans how strong the Greek opposition was and to the Athenians how strong Aigina was. For the Greek action seems to have been sufficiently decisive to change Aigina's attitude to Persia. The Aiginetans were to play a key role in the defeat of the Persian navy. But it was sufficiently indecisive to bring two far-reaching changes to Athenian policy.

In 493/492 BC as archon Themistokles persuaded the Athenians that they should fortify the Peiraieus (Thucydides 1.93.3). This marked the move from using the beach at Phaleron as the prime place to land ships to the provision of full harbour facilities and naval shipsheds in the Peiraieus, a place wonderfully endowed by nature with several fine harbours, one of them enormous. Such facilities were part of what made classical Athens the major entrepôt of the central Mediterranean. Ten years later in 483/482, still appealing to Athenian fears of Aiginetan seapower, Themistokles took a second initiative: he persuaded the Athenians to divert profits from the Athenian silver mines to strengthening the Athenian navy by building 100 or more new triremes (Herodotos 7.144; [Aristotle,] *Constitution of the Athenians* 22.7). This created a navy on a quite new scale, and it signalled a decisive change not just in foreign policy but in the economic investment in warfare.

Warfare in the archaic period had been cheap. Putting members of the community into the field armed with their own armour and weapons was not an expensive business, especially when campaigns were short and rarely involved going much outside one's own territory. Cavalry, potentially very much more expensive, were little used. Naval warfare was rare and small scale. Nor were the stakes particular high in economic terms. An army profited from what it could run off with, but the best chance was to drive off large herds – otherwise gains were limited to what could be carried. But to put 100 triremes into action demanded organising almost 20,000 men to crew them, training them to row together – no simple matter – and then keeping them supplied during what might be a lengthy period away from home. It was not simply a capital commitment to building hulls that the Athenians undertook in 483/482, it was a marked change in public financial investment in warfare.

How and why did Athens transform its stake in warfare? It is easy to make light of the Athenian decision to build 100 or more triremes. All that was involved, it might seem, was pooling the windfall from striking rich new seams of silver in the Laurion mines. Instead of taking home a few drachmas each, the Athenians got themselves a communal resource. But the sum of money involved, reportedly 100 talents, would have given the equivalent of a month's wages to every Athenian citizen, so this was a significant vote against individual interests. More particularly it must have gone with a decision, implicitly at least, to maintain and man these vessels, a decision which will have required of some Athenians a commitment to row and from other a commitment to finance the ships. In the fourth century the Athenian navy is maintained by requiring the rich to pay for the upkeep as a form of taxation. Although we do not know exactly what mechanism was employed during the Persian wars, it seems unlikely that rich Athenians did not find a new call on their resources. Athenians were effectively committing themselves to putting their bodies and their wealth behind the city's foreign policy in a way never previously required. In doing so they made, for the first time, the military machine a significant economic engine. Together the development of the Peiraieus and the massive expansion of the Athenian navy not only transformed Athens into the major Greek power, they created a new economic order.

Conflict with Persia: the first round

Mardonios' expedition to Thrace and Macedonia in 492 BC (p. 307) had ended with the fleet being wrecked off Athos; it is said, writes Herodotos (6.44), that about 300 ships were destroyed and more than 20,000 men killed. Although it is clear throughout that numbers larger than could be adequately supplied or controlled were involved on the Persian side, no reliable figures for Persian troops or Persian casualties can be recovered from Greek sources for any of the succeeding conflicts. It may not have been in the power of any Greek, and was certainly not in their interest, to give an accurate picture of the Persian army and its doings. The story of the Persian wars was repeated for the lessons it offered, lessons about the power of unity, the ability of a few to face up to and defeat the many, the toughness engendered by poverty, the superiority of Greek cunning. It also offered material for allegations of treachery, on the part of individual political enemies within a city and on the part of cities. The conflict with Persia was myth as soon as it was history. The Persians appeared on the Athenian stage within a decade in Aiskhylos' *Persians*, the earliest extant Greek tragedy, produced in 472 BC, and the war was, even before that and perhaps in 479–8, made the subject of an extended elegy by Simonides (*P. Oxy.* 3965) which explicitly aligned it with the Trojan wars. The Persian war became the organising feature around which the Greek past was shaped, encouraging a new polarisation in Greek views of themselves and of others.

'What did this city do in the Persian wars?' was the first historical question whose answer mattered that could be asked of all Greek communities.

What can a historian today say about the Persian wars? We can have little confidence that we can satisfactorily answer any of the questions which the Greeks themselves answered. Too much was invested in antiquity in answering the question of how the Greeks beat the Persians for us to be able to disembed truth from partial tradition. What we can do is to exploit the tensions between competing traditions, and by doing so throw light on the nature of city-state politics in these years, and hence on the classical legacy left by the war. This is true both of the 490 and of the 480/479 invasion, but the smaller number of participants in 490 makes it particularly clear in that case (Figure 86).

In 490 BC a Persian naval expedition under Datis and Artaphernes gathered in Cilicia and then made its way via Samos and Ikaria to Naxos. The Naxians are said to have offered no resistance, and the Persians burnt and looted before proceeding eastwards and besieging Karystos on southern Euboia. A siege of Eretria followed, and resistance there collapsed after six days. A few days later the Persians set sail for Attica; guided, it is said, by the ex-tyrant Hippias, they landed, as Peisistratos had done in 545 BC, in the plain of Marathon. In a long battle the Persians were defeated by the Athenians, who had the support of a small force from Plataia. A Persian attempt to use their fleet to attack the town of Athens itself before the Athenian army arrived back was defeated by Athenian anticipation.

Such a narrative already incorporates a number of tendentious claims; the details which enliven Herodotos' account reveal even more about subsequent politics. The positive interpretation of the Persians encamping on Rheneia, rather than looting Delos, suggests that some were keen to justify their own failure to assist in resisting the attack by claiming that its aims were limited to Eretria and Athens, the two mainland cities involved in the Ionian Revolt. The naming of the traitor who betrayed Eretria to the surrounding Persians, and the story that the Alkmaionidai gave a treacherous shield signal to the Persians at Marathon show how the magnitude of the danger did not prevent events being manipulated to local political advantage. The stress in the story of Athenian military decision-making on the role of the ten tribal generals, the *strategoi*, and particularly on one of them, Miltiades, although control of the army was formally with the polemarch Kallimakhos, who was uniquely celebrated in a dedication on the Athenian Acropolis (ML 18/Fornara 49), surely reveals something of the arguments used to get military power fully transferred from polemarch to *strategoi* (never after this do we hear of a polemarch playing any part in a battle). The respectful telling of how the Spartans wanted to help, but could not leave Sparta in time because they had to wait for a full moon, is coupled with the story that the Athenian messenger to Sparta, the runner Philippides or Pheidippides, met on the way in Arkadia the god Pan, who promised support in return for cult (Herodotos 6.105–6); and this coupling, which makes the sending of the messenger to Sparta bear fruit in the long term, turns Sparta's immediate failure to assist into the prelude to greater assistance. The role that came to be attributed to the local hero, Ekhetlaos, said to have intervened in the battle wielding a ploughshare (Pausanias 1.32.4 and cf. Herodotos 6.117.3), may have been a reaction to the introduction of the cult and festival of the Arkadian god Pan.

Politics after Marathon

Athens and Sparta

Marathon was crucial militarily for the whole of Greece, but this should not overshadow its massive political importance at Athens and at Sparta. Political life in Athens had been lively in the 490s and was to be livelier still in the 480s. Although after 506 BC the Athenians seem always to have decided on markedly anti-Persian policies, this did not mean that there was no political debate. The question of who in a democracy could or should be entrusted with what powers was one to which Kleisthenes' reforms had offered no easy answer. In 496/495 BC the man elected to the eponymous archonship was one Hipparkhos son of Kharmos, almost certainly Hippias' grandson. Although the powers of the archon may already have been relatively unimportant, Hipparkhos' election strongly suggests that the proper attitude to take to the Peisistratids and their rule was open for negotiation. If, as many have suspected, this is the Hipparkhos celebrated as 'beautiful' (*kalos*) in a number of inscriptions on early red-figure vases, it may be that he owed his election to support from the élite circles in which he moved. In 494/493 BC Miltiades returned to Athens. He had had a somewhat colourful career ruling in the Thracian Khersonesos (above pp. 269 and 303), which had included capturing Lemnos for the Athenians, and had ended up with his being a man much sought after by the Persians. Put on trial in Athens for tyranny, he was acquitted, elected general, and became one of the heroes of the accounts of the battle of Marathon. Although it is hard to be sure what the issues were, these events suggest strongly opposed, but almost equally matched, views about the suitability of a man with Miltiades' record as a democratic citizen (Figure 84).

That a return to factional politics threatened Athens is surely confirmed by the events of the 480s. Following Marathon, Miltiades, with a fleet of seventy ships and an army, sailed to Paros, set siege to the city, and demanded 100 talents to lift the siege. Miltiades himself suffered a leg injury, and the siege was lifted after twenty-six days with nothing achieved. On his return to Athens the dying general was prosecuted by Xanthippos, condemned, and fined 50 talents, which his son Kimon paid (Herodotos 6.132–6). This is another episode so politically charged that the stories told later cannot be trusted. We may, for example, suspect that the claim that Miltiades had not told the Athenians the purpose for which he wanted the force, and the conflicting claim that he said he wanted to punish Paros for supporting the

Figure 84 Late sixth-century plate attributed to the painter Paseas and showing a mounted archer in northern dress. In the background is written the slogan 'Miltiades is beautiful'.

Persians at Marathon, but in fact wanted to punish a personal enemy who had slandered him to a Persian official, were both told as part of a denial of Athenian responsibility. But the episode well reveals the extreme actions which a political leader could persuade the, perhaps rather cocksure, Athenians to adopt, and the readiness of other political leaders to take advantage of military set-backs to score political points.

In this atmosphere, the first use of ostracism, and perhaps its invention (above, p. 290), in 488/487 BC can be understood in one of two contrasting ways: either as giving an additional weapon which one faction could use against another, or as a means of preventing factional politics leading to riot and revolution. In favour of the latter is the way in which the change to selecting archons by lot from a large number of elected candidates occurred in the following year, 487/486 BC, a move which can only have defused factional politics. In any case Hipparkhos son of Kharmos was the first victim, and ostracisms seem then to have been held annually down to 483/482 BC In the year after Hipparkhos' ostracism the victim was the Alkmaionid Megakles, with whose banishment the claims about Alkmaionid treacherous behaviour at Marathon (Herodotos 6.121–4) should probably be associated. It is a measure of how little some members of the élite thought that politics at Athens had changed from the days of Peisistratos' tyranny that Megakles went off and immediately won a chariot victory at the Pythian games in 486 BC. He got Pindar to write a short ode celebrating this and expressing regret at Athenian ingratitude for Alkmaionid services.

We get further shadowy indications of what the political issues were from the identity of subsequent victims: Xanthippos, the prosecutor of Miltiades, a man who had married an Alkmaionid and may, to judge from an elegiac couplet on one surviving ostrakon, have been associated with them; and Aristeides 'the Just', whom ostraka claim both to be a 'friend of Datis the Mede' and 'the man who refused the suppliants'. In addition, ostraka cast against others, not known certainly to have been ostracised, also identify them as Alkmaionids, refer to them as 'one of the traitors' or, in one case, draw a picture of a Persian on the back of the sherd (Figure 85). Attitudes to Persia were clearly at issue, but they had become entwined with family-based

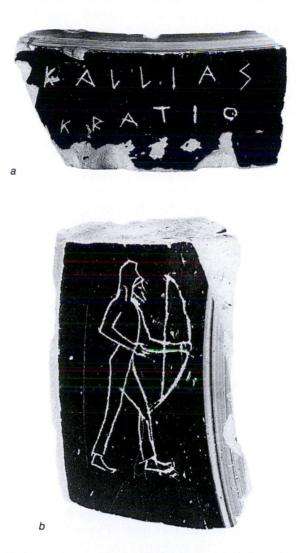

a

b

Figure 85a and b An ostrakon cast against Kallias Kratiou who is figured on one side as a Persian archer.

315

élite struggles. Ostracism tells us who the losers were, but the greater threat to democracy may well have been posed by the winners.

The allegations of treachery and Persian sympathy consistently made against those ostracised in the 480s suggest that, after the upset of Miltiades' conviction, it was those arguing for a foreign policy focused on actively eradicating Persians from the Greek world who could deliver the votes that mattered. Ancient accounts offer only one candidate as the chief promoter of this policy: Themistokles. Themistokles' prominence seems to be confirmed by the way in which more ostraka survive which name Themistokles than anyone else, and by the dump of prepared ostraka (191 written by fourteen hands) found in a well in the Agora, which seem to have been prepared for an ostracism in the 480s. Themistokles used his influence to initiate an expansion of the Athenian fleet (above, p. 310), and when the Persians had once more to be faced in the field he was in a position to determine Athenian action and exercise a power not dissimilar to that which Miltiades had commanded after Marathon. How he would have used that influence had war not intervened we cannot know, but we should not be oversanguine about the strength of democracy at Athens. It should be noted, not least to make it clear how far the Athenians themselves realised claims of Persian sympathy to be merely political abuse, that when Persian invasion threatened the ostracised were all recalled ([Aristotle,] *Constitution of the Athenians* 22.8).

Kings, ephors, and politics at Sparta

If political tension increased at Athens under the threat of Persian invasion, the same may have been even more true at Sparta, where it is time to draw together the threads which have occasionally been glimpsed running through the account above. The Great Rhetra (above, p. 167) gives a glimpse of three political forces in Sparta: the two kings, the Council of Elders (Gerousia), and the people. Whatever their date of origin, by the time we see Spartan politics in action in any detail, in the second half of the sixth century BC, there was also a further force to be reckoned with, the five ephors, who were elected annually. One sixth-century ephor, named Khilon, was credited by ancient sources with considerable individual influence over Spartan foreign policy, and the formal powers of ephors, receiving embassies, calling out the army, and so on, feature frequently in Herodotos' account of Kleomenes' reign.

There is no doubt, however, that the crucial figures in Sparta were the kings. Herodotos recognises this by devoting considerable space to a description of the powers and privileges of Spartan kings (Herodotos 6.56–60). Kings were set apart at Sparta: heirs to the throne did not go through the competitive training other boys received in the *agoge* (Plutarch, *Agesilaos* 1.2), kings received double portions in the common messes (*sussitia*), they had a special guard when they marched at the head of the army, because of their priestly role they received the perquisites from sacrifices, they enjoyed positions of honour at games, appointed the officials who consulted the Delphic oracle, oversaw heiresses and adoptions, and were given extravagant funerals at which all Spartan households had to be represented. This treatment of the kings as special both reflected and preserved the kings' political position. In a society where Spartiates might be more or less wealthy, but had to achieve a reputation through their performance in the *agoge* and valour in war, the kings enjoyed a status that was not achieved but endowed. But although the kings were dignified by special rights and elaborate pomp, and were assimilated to religious officials whose efficiency could not be called into question, Spartan politics show a continuous challenge to the kings to justify their position by effective action.

One of the most striking features of Herodotos' account of Sparta in these years is the prominence of marital irregularities. He tells us that Kleomenes was the product of a bigamous union which the ephors of one year, worried about Anaxandridas not producing an heir, had insisted upon. Anaxandridas' first wife then produced three sons, Doricus, Leonidas, and Kleombrotos, and the conflict over Kleomenes' acceding to the throne resulted in Dorieus leading an unsuccessful colonising expedition. The other king, in the Eurypontid line, at the time of Kleomenes' accession was Ariston. Herodotos' story, which is suspiciously parallel to stories told about the Persian court, tells (5.61–3, 66–70) how Ariston married twice without producing any children and then got a third wife by having his friend, named Agetos, promise to give him anything he asked for, and then asking for Agetos' wife. This wife bore Damaratos at a sufficiently short interval after the marriage to enable rumours to be circulated denying that Damaratos was Ariston's son, and to effect his expulsion from the throne (above, p. 309). But this was only after Damaratos had himself stolen the daughter of Sparta's most famous sixth-century ephor, Khilon, who was betrothed to another descendant of Eurypontid kings, Latykhidas, to be his own wife (Herodotos 5.65). When Damaratos was deposed, it was Latykhidas who became king in his stead. Latykhidas himself had a son, Zeuxidamos, who predeceased him, having engendered a son Arkhidamos who was married to Latykhidas' daughter by a second marriage. Rather similarly Kleomenes himself, who had no sons, married his daughter to his half-brother, Leonidas, who succeeded him.

One might think that, for two generations or so of two families, the number of infelicitous relationships is extraordinarily high. But what these infelicities indicate is surely less that those who play for high stakes politically also play for high stakes in their sexual relations, than that, in a system where the most influential political role is inherited, and where that political role still demands that a high level of practical skill be displayed (notably in commanding armies), the degree of residual community concern about the genetic background and the efficient action of any king will be such that irregular relationships will be encouraged, while any possible irregularity will also be exploited if there is ever any doubt about competence of action. The more active Sparta was in the wider world in which the leadership of the kings was traditionally required, the more the pedigree and behaviour of kings would come under scrutiny. The stories of scandal which surround these generations of Spartan kings are a direct product of a situation which was politically fraught.

One big issue in Sparta was the nature and extent of the Peloponnesian League (above, p. 271). That issue was neither settled by the new procedures which the abortive invasion of Attica caused to be adopted, nor overshadowed by the question of attitudes to Persia which arose over the behaviour of Aigina. In the 490s the big issue at Sparta seems to have been whether an all-out effort should be made to overcome Argos, the last remaining important Peloponnesian state which stood outside the League. I say 'seems' for two reasons: first, although Spartan action against Argos at some time during Kleomenes' thirty-year reign is certain, Pausanias (3.4.1) says that it took place early in the reign, while Herodotos (5.76–83; 7.148.2) implies a date of around 494 BC; second, what happened on the Argos campaign became so central to a campaign to get rid of Kleomenes that none of the stories about it can be trusted. One fact is clear: Sparta did not succeed in conquering Argos. It suited Spartans hostile to Kleomenes to attribute successes to trickery, and to allege not only that he finally failed in his mission because of bribery, but that he acted in sacrilegious fashion, burning a sacred grove when Argive soldiers were within, using force to sacrifice at the Argive Heraion, etc. It suited Argives, keen to justify not joining the Greek war effort against Persia, to claim that the Spartans had inflicted serious losses (Herodotos 7.148; cf. Pausanias' story (2.20.7–8) of the Spartans being repulsed solely through the actions of the Argive women led by the poetess Telesilla), and later, keen to justify a political revolution, to claim that the losses had led to powers being handed over to 'slaves' who needed to be expelled when the sons of those killed came of age (Herodotos 5.83).

Sparta's concern about Argos was not merely a concern for tidiness, or a desire to be rid of a rival power around which opposition to Sparta might crystallise (as to some extent it did in the later fifth and early fourth centuries BC). There are signs that Sparta was actively worried about her grip on her allies and on her helot population. After the Argos campaign, hostility to Kleomenes in Sparta became such that, whether or not he was formally exiled, the story goes that he absented himself from Sparta, went to Arkadia, and tried to get the Arkadians to combine behind his personal leadership. Both the absence from Sparta and the Arkadian conspiracy may be a fiction created by Kleomenes' enemies to justify putting him under guard and perhaps executing him – the story says he went mad and committed suicide by self-mutilation (Herodotos 5.74–6). Even if this is a fiction it was a fiction designed to be credible. After the Persian wars Pausanias, who was regent for Leonidas' son, and whose behaviour had been under scrutiny for other reasons also, was held to have been conspiring with helots and promising them freedom and citizenship – another indication of Spartan sensitivity about home affairs (Thucydides 1.132.4, where Thucydides expresses confidence that the story was true). Whether there was substantive evidence to back up these suspicions is less certain. Plato in *Laws* (698e) has a character say that it was a 'Messenian war, or some other distraction' that kept the Spartans from giving aid at Marathon, and some modern scholars have thought he says this on good authority.

Do any of these Spartan stories of intrigue relate to Persia? Although only the Aigina affair is explicitly linked in to attitudes to Persia by Herodotos, the case for seeing Persian pressure as pervasive is strong. In 481 BC the Greeks debated whether defence against a Persian invasion should take place at the Isthmus of Corinth or further north. This was an issue that political observers must have seen coming, and the power of Athens made it almost inevitable that the answer would have to be further north. The Spartans had to get into a position where they could send a substantial army out of the Peloponnese without the threat of unrest at home or among their allies. The Persian threat made strong government at Sparta an issue, a strong grip on the Peloponnese an immediate necessity rather than a longer-term hope, and helot unrest a sinister spectre. As at Athens, so at Sparta, Persia gave a focus around which, directly or indirectly, factionalism could focus.

Conflict with Persia: the second round

No one can have expected that Marathon would be the end of a story, but the next episode was delayed by a decade as a result of the death of Darius and a revolt in Egypt. Herodotos chooses to devote his attention to Persian preparations for invasion, and after Marathon pays no attention to events in Greece itself until the end of the 480s. This is extremely effective as a literary device, since it has Greek preparations take place in the shadow of the mighty army which has just been described, but it misleadingly compresses the timetable of Greek reactions. The previous section on Athens, where there is non-Herodotean information available, and on Sparta, where the story of events before 490 BC can, in a sense, stand proxy for events after, has made some attempt to fill the void.

The military events

The military story of the 480/479 BC invasion can no more be told in detail than can the story of the battle of Marathon. The Persian numbers reported in ancient sources vary, but none commands belief. Ignorance of troop numbers itself makes battle reconstruction futile, but in any case stories about what happened in the battles became so politically charged that no confidence can be placed in any claims about what went on. A graphic example of this concerns the sea battle at Salamis. Herodotos reports (8.94) the Athenians' claim that the Corinthian contingent at Salamis fled when battle commenced, and only rejoined the fleet when battle was over. He says that the Corinthians denied this and other Greeks supported them. Plutarch (*On the Malice of Herodotos* 39) reports that the Corinthians put up a memorial to their valour in this battle on Salamis, that is, on Athenian territory. A monument bearing the first two lines of the inscription reported by Plutarch has been discovered (ML 24/Fornara 21), and whether that monument was indeed put up in 480 BC, or whether an existing monument was 'reinterpreted' as part of the Corinthian story, it is clear that even the behaviour of a significant contingent in the Greek fleet was subject to dispute within a short time of the events.

The military story that can be told is therefore thin (Figure 86). The Persians won a battle in the narrows at Thermopylai, just south of modern Lamia,

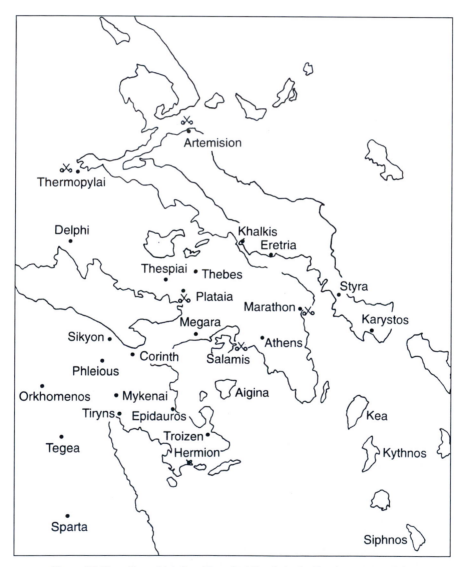

Figure 86 The cities which fought against Persia in the Persian wars and the battle sites of that war.

the Athenians evacuated their territory, and the Persians sacked the Athenian Acropolis as they occupied the whole of Greece as far as the Isthmus of Corinth. The Persian fleet first faced the Greeks off Cape Artemision between northern Euboia and the Gulf of Pagasai, suffered some losses in an initial engagement, much more severe losses in a following storm, and in a final engagement inflicted significant losses as well as suffering them (Herodotos 8.6–16). The Greek fleet withdrew because of the defeat at Thermopylai, and gathered in the waters between Attica and Salamis. Enticed in here, the Persians were comprehensively defeated. Winter ended that campaigning season and Xerxes' own presence in Greece, and the following season saw Greek victory completed with a battle at Plataia in south-west Boiotia, where the Greek army showed itself superior when fighting in a wide-open landscape.

The politics of Greek disunity

The political story is very much richer. One basic issue divides the Greeks in the myth of the Persian wars which Herodotos hands down to us: whether they consider that the Persian threat overrides issues to do with their relationship with other Greek states, or whether relationships with other Greek states take top priority. Herodotos (7.132) gives a list of those who offered tokens of submission to the Persians, and records the oath of the other Greeks to dedicate a tithe of the collaborators' property to Delphi if they beat the Persians. This is a fascinating testimony because the sanctuary at Delphi was controlled by an Amphiktyony, a group of surrounding communities, and Herodotos' account suggests that already at the time of the oath these communities were split between resisters and 'medising' collaborators. Perhaps it was precisely this fact, that the power of victory would be displayed in the midst of the collaborators, which encouraged the choice of Delphi – although victory was also commemorated at the other great panhellenic sanctuary at Olympia. But it is equally likely that juxtaposing at this point the oath and the list of cities which 'medised' is itself a contentious product of post-war politics.

In Herodotos' history, the initial meeting of resisting Greeks in 481 BC decided as a matter of urgency to put an end to inter-state conflicts, and also to ask both Argos and Gelon of Syracuse for help. Herodotos' long accounts (7.148–67) of why neither Argos nor Gelon agreed to help shows how observers preferred their own explanations for actions to any official explanation put forward. Argos and Gelon are both alleged to have insisted that they would only fight if they could be (at least joint) leaders, and this and the other stories told illustrate the way in which for these cities relations with other Greek cities were more important than resisting Persia. We should note that in order to get the (true) story that Gelon was facing a massive Carthaginian threat (see below, p. 327), Herodotos had to go to Sicily (7.165.1).

The leadership issue was not employed only to cast aspersions on Argos and Gelon, but was also made a source of positive virtue by those who agreed to Spartan command. The issue is played out in Herodotos particularly with regard to Athens: the Athenian envoy is given the speech refusing Gelon leadership (7.161); Herodotos himself says that Athens gave up her claim to leadership in the interests of promoting unity (8.3); and a debate is staged at Plataia as to whether Athens or Tegea should get the second most important position, the left wing (9.26–8). The emphasis here is part of a larger theme running through Herodotos' account: the theme of Athenian selflessness. The Athenians challenge the Delphic oracle (see below, p. 333) in their determination to resist (7.140–4); they evacuate their own territory after Thermopylai (8.40–1) – by the fourth century BC they could display the decree which ordered this evacuation (Demosthenes 19.303; cf. ML 23/ Fornara 55); they refuse Persian overtures after Salamis (Herodotos 8.136, 140–4).

But there is another aspect to the portrayal of Athenian involvement also, for their role is anything but passive. That aspect is encapsulated in the actions of one man, Themistokles. Themistokles masterminds Athenian resistance, effectively controls all that happens with the fleet (largely by trickery), and is declared by Herodotos (8.123–4) the winner of a vote by commanders after Salamis on who had displayed most valour – even though no prize was awarded! The mixture of cleverness and dishonesty, good judgement and greed, which Themistokles displays in the story reflects the way in which Athenian political claims required that Athens' part was crucial, but also that granting a crucial role to a single individual could not be tolerated in the subsequent political debate, which eventually led to Themistokles' ostracism (see *GW* 12, 21–2). There are some signs in Herodotos that other stories gave the Athenian Aristeides a role of some importance: he is made the man who reveals to the Greeks that they have no choice but to fight at Salamis (8.79–82), his part in eradicating the Persians who had landed on the little island of Psyttaleia is specially mentioned (8.95), and he is the Athenian general at Plataia. Other writers made yet more of Aristeides: there is a second encounter between him and Themistokles, the Psyttaleia episode is made an important part of the battle of Salamis (Aiskhylos, *Persai* 447–71), he is the man responsible for rejecting Persian overtures after Salamis (Plutarch, *Aristeides* 10), he is part of the subsequent embassy to Sparta, he speaks against conceding the wing position at Plataia to the Tegeans, and he is the man summoned by name by Alexander of Macedon when he deserts the Persian side to give intelligence to the Greeks. These parts attributed to Themistokles and Aristeides belong to the script of Athenian political history in the 470s.

The political use of resistance and of the charge of collaboration shapes the whole of Herodotos' account. The rather sketchy account of the sending of a large army to the Tempe valley in Thessaly, an army withdrawn before the Persians arrive, may well be entirely fictional and part of the emphasis on Thessalian medism (Thessaly and Thebes were the two powers at whom

These fought the war: Lakedaimonians, Athenians, Corinthians, Tegeans, Sikyonians, Aiginetans, Megarians, Epidaurians, Orkhomenians, Phleiasians, Troizenians, Hermionians, Tirynthians, Plataians, Thespians, Mykenians, Keans, Melians, Tenians, Naxians, Eretrians, Khalkidians, Styrians, Eleans, Poteidaians, Leukadians, Anaktorians, Kythnians, Siphnians, Ambraciots, Lepreans.

Text 50: ML 27. The record of those who fought against the Persians in 480–79 BC inscribed on the 'Serpent Column' at Delphi. The column was taken to the hippodrome of his new city by Constantine, and is still be be seen in Istanbul.

post-war retribution was most directly aimed). Herodotos (7.6, 172) himself actually endeavours to undermine that emphasis by stressing that the Thessalians had little choice, and that it was the ruling family of the Aleuadai who were chiefly responsible (see also *GW* 95–7). Herodotos provides not only a list of those who were with the Spartans at Thermopylai (7.202), but also a list of those who remained to the death – Thespians, Spartans, and Thebans. To be included on the list of those present was not enough for some cities: Pausanias (10.20.2) records that the people of Mykenai insisted that their contingent of eighty men was there to the last too. In Herodotos the Theban presence is made evidence against rather than for them: only there because Leonidas would not let them go, they break away and surrender (7.233). Later they are specified as giving wise tactical advice to the Persian general Mardonios at Plataia (9.31), and fighting with great enthusiasm in that battle (9.40, 67).

The dedication mentioned by Herodotos (9.81) which the victorious Greeks made at Delphi, and on which they recorded the names of all the cities who had contributed to the victory, survives (Text 50, ML 27/Fornara 59). Its list only goes to reinforce the politics of the war. Various cities which Herodotos records to have participated in the war do not get on to the column – Kroton in southern Italy, Pale on Kephallenia in the Ionian sea, the Opountian Lokrians. Of the two cities which Herodotos says arrived too late for the battle of Plataia, Mantineia and Elis, Elis is on but Mantineia not (even though Herodotos says that there were Mantineian troops at Thermopylai). Both communities blamed, and claimed to have disciplined, the generals for the lateness. Herodotos has Seriphos, Siphnos, and Melos all providing galleys fighting with the Greeks at Salamis: Melos got on to the column from the beginning, Siphnos was added, but Seriphos does not appear. The late addition of Tenos, because a Tenian trireme deserted to the Greek side at Salamis, is mentioned by Herodotos (8.82).

Herodotos names, at Thermopylai and at other points in the war, the individuals outstanding for bravery, and also for treachery. Individual deeds could chalk up credit, or blame, for a city, and could also be cashed in for influence at home. So, for example, we are told that the only Greek to desert from the Persians at Artemision was Antidoros the Lemnian (Herodotos 8.11). In the case of the Greek who revealed the alternative route which enabled the

Persians to turn the pass at Thermopylai, Herodotos not only gives the name of the man he regards as having been responsible, he names others who were also blamed. Herodotos (7.213–15) says the culprit was Ephialtes of Malis, and that he fled to Antikyra where he was murdered by Athenades of Trakhis but for another reason (that is, no patriotic credit to Trakhis for the deed!), but that others blame Onetes of Karystos and Korydallos of Antikyra. Is it by chance that Antikyra features in both stories, or that Karystos heads the list of the islanders who helped the Persians (8.66), and was the object of a Greek campaign after Salamis (Herodotos 8.112, 121)?

The uses of the war in post-war politics did not stop at claims to have fought alongside the Greeks. Greek cities also invited each other to despise communities for their non-military actions. Herodotos records, for instance (9.78), the barbaric suggestion made by Lampon of Aigina after the battle of Plataia that, since Xerxes had had Leonidas decapitated and his head displayed on a pole after Thermopylai, the Greek general Pausanias should do likewise with the Persian war casualties. And he goes straight on to allege (9.80) that it was the Aiginetans who profited from the dishonesty of those Spartan helots who had been set the task of gathering the great booty which fell into Greek hands after Plataia, preposterously claiming that it was from this that the great wealth of Aigina stemmed.

Enough Greek cities collaborated in the war effort against Persia to secure success, but, as Herodotos makes clear, Greek unity is largely a myth. In addition to Athens and the Peloponnesian League the number of mainland Greek cities who joined the struggle on the Greek side was small, their combined forces practically insignificant. What Herodotos' account of the war reveals is how slight and how temporary a concession was made in the infighting of Greek cities. Even those cities which fought together rapidly turned to claiming of one another that they had tried to desert, or to casting aspersions on the motives which led others to fight: Herodotos' view (8.30) that it was only hatred of Thessaly that made Phokis not 'medise', and that had Thessaly resisted Phokis would have 'medised', surely reflects a widely used structure of argument. Far from the war leading to greater Greek unity, it only gave additional arguments which could be deployed to enable points to be scored off neighbouring cities.

The consequences of Greek victory

Neither fighting together nor siding with the Persians had a long-term effect on inter-city relations. The actions taken against cities that 'medised' were limited, and so too were the benefits for the loyal. For all Mykenai's loyalty to the cause, little seems to have been done by those who had fought beside her to prevent Argos taking her over in the 470s (Diodoros 11.65). A city's record in the war was only as powerful an influence on its future as was the argument which that record provided. Fifty years later, during the Peloponnesian war, Sparta would humour medising Thebes, which claimed it was only a few Thebans who had dictated the decision to support Persia, by destroying Plataia, claiming that the Plataians had never done anything to help the Spartans in that war ... (Thucydides 3.52–68).

What then had the Greeks saved themselves from by defeating the Persian invasion? They had saved themselves from an imposed end to inter-city conflict. The liberty which they had gained was the liberty to continue to interfere with each other's liberty. The Greek cities of Ionia had maintained a degree of autonomy with regard to domestic issues, and even with regard to their armies and navies, but strict limits could be expected upon the degree to which one city could take aggressive action against another. They had also saved themselves from prolonged domination by a particular political group. Even after the settlement of the Ionian Revolt, which seems to have favoured popular government, Greeks undoubtedly believed that Persia would give power to those who ingratiated themselves with them. The Thebans who joined the Greek cause at Thermopylai were led by a man who was Sparta's guest-friend in Thebes, and the later Theban claim that just one group had determined the 'medising' policy is likely to have had some truth in it. Compared with these potential political impositions, the economic burdens which threatened were trivial. Persia would undoubtedly have imposed a tax, although the level of that tax in Ionia might have been light enough for some cities to pay both the tax to Persia and tribute to Athens in the later part of the fifth century BC (cf. Thucydides 8.5).

The defeat of the Persian invasion did not lead to a return to the status quo. Even though, both strategically and tactically, the Greek military successes were to an uncomfortable degree a result of luck, rather than judgement, the resistance to the Persian invasion did have a long-term military effect. It boosted military confidence among both land and sea forces. Is it by chance that the Tegeans are found fighting with the Argives and against the Spartans within a few years of the war (Herodotos 9.35)? They were held to have precipitated the Greeks' entry into battle at Plataia (Herodotos 9.61), to have suffered the third largest number of casualties (all of sixteen men! 9.70.5), and to have played an important part in following up the routed Persians (9.70.3). It is certainly not by chance that the Athenians enjoyed a naval supremacy after the war which they had not been able to claim before it.

The resistance to Persia was by no means as glorious as Greeks subsequently made it out to be, but it was a learning experience. The extreme malleability of a single event, which conflicting accounts of the war so pungently illustrated, was indeed one of the things that launched Herodotos' researches 'so that what men have done should not be rubbed out by the passage of time', in the words of his preface. But one city drew a more sinister lesson from the same observation that history, and so also the argument from history, was in the hands of the successful. Athenian action in continuing the war strongly suggests that the Athenians had quickly learnt one important lesson from the Persian war: that a cause which exerted moral pressure on cities could be used to render those cities subject, in the name of liberty.

Greeks and Phoenicians in the west

If the Persian wars fundamentally changed the political history of mainland Greece (and see further p. 331), the contemporary war against the Carthaginians in Sicily stands right at the beginning of political history there. A tradition, which goes back to the fifth century BC, held that there was a battle between Greeks, Elymians, and Carthaginians around 580 BC over Greek attempts to settle at Lilybaion in western Sicily (Diodoros 5.9, *FGH* 555 F 1), but our knowledge of political events in Sicily prior to about 500 BC is patchy in the extreme, and improves only when Herodotos tells us what he thinks we need to know in order to understand the Greek appeal to Gelon and his refusal to help the Greek war effort (7.153–67 and see *GW* 44–8). Herodotos explains how Gelon came to exercise power: he was massively successful as a general in the campaigns by which his brother Hippokrates, tyrant of Gela, gained control of most of eastern Sicily; on Hippokrates' death he used a popular uprising against Hippokrates' sons to gain power at Gela himself; and subsequently he took sides with the Syracusan nobility against the people, and so established control of Syracuse also.

Sicilian tyrants get portrayed in the tradition in rather stereotyped ways (see *GW* 41–54), but this story about Gelon does reveal two special features of Sicilian history. One is the prevalence of bitter conflict between rich and poor, often manifesting itself in armed struggle. The other is the capacity of the armies of powerful cities to sweep through whole swathes of Sicilian territory, subduing all before them. Populations are uprooted, cities wander homeless, individual rulers come to command vast resources. Even in the decade between Gelon seizing power (traditionally 491 BC at Gela, 485 BC at Syracuse) and the battle of Himera, supposedly on the same day as the battle of Salamis, the cities of Kamarina, Sicilian Euboia, and Megara Hyblaia (above, p. 227) were rubbed off the map; the people of Kamarina were entirely moved to Syracuse, and in the other two cities the nobility were moved to Syracuse and the people sold into slavery (Herodotos 7.156). These big bold gestures relate to events in Old Greece rather as the large architectural mouldings and brash colours of Sicilian temples relate to the delicate details of the mainland temples (above, p. 253 and compare Figure 74). They stand as a reminder that the city-state was by no means a single phenomenon, and that different conditions – generally large, fertile, and adequately watered territories, the presence of a non-Greek native population, access to the world of the Punic west – created very different conditions of political as well as of economic and social life.

Gelon's seizure of power at Gela had been followed within a couple of years by Theron's seizure of power at Akragas. Swiftly the two linked themselves by marriage ties: Gelon married Theron's daughter Damareta and Theron married Gelon's niece. Theron had designs on western Sicily just as Gelon had on eastern, and although the fulfilment of his desires would make Theron a dangerous rival, they would necessarily involve conflict with the

Carthaginians, and Gelon had perhaps already clashed with the Carthaginians in the first years of his rule. Whether or not the need for a united front against Carthage played a part in prompting Gelon's and Theron's alliance, it was certainly in the face of a Carthaginian offensive that the alliance made its most lasting mark.

War against the Carthaginians was triggered by Theron's attack on Himera. The ruler of Himera called in his own son-in-law Anaxilas of Rhegion, who had already battled with the tyrants of Gela over Zankle, and together they summoned the Carthaginians. Under Hamilcar the Carthaginians invaded in force – though Herodotos' figure of 300,000 North African troops (7.165) is as wild as his figure for the number of Persians. Hamilcar summoned Selinous, which fear of Akragas had driven into alliance with him, and Theron summoned Gelon. Gelon caught the Carthaginians unprepared and scored a massive victory – he is said to have burned nine-tenths of the Carthaginian fleet as it lay beached (Diodoros 11.21–2) – and the Carthaginians immediately sued for peace.

Ancient sources disagreed as to whether it was pure coincidence that war against the Phoenicians in the west should occur at precisely the same time as war against the Persians in mainland Greece. Aristotle regarded it as the paradigm coincidence (*Poetics* 1459a25), but the fourth-century BC historian Ephoros claimed that there was a Persian–Carthaginian understanding (cf. Diodoros 11.1.4). Herodotos, who himself indicates no causal link, does give evidence that the Persians had some interest in the western Mediterranean (3.136), and at the very least it seems improbable that the Carthaginians were not aware of events further east in the Mediterranean when they decided to help Himera. Corinth and Corcyra are said to have intervened a little earlier to settle a war between Hippokrates and Syracuse (Herodotos 7.154), and attempts by the western Greeks to draw in the Greeks of the mainland were as much to be expected as appeals from the mainland to Sicily.

The achievement of victory at Himera at the very moment that the Persians were being driven from the Greek mainland enabled Gelon and the Sicilians to parade their achievement in terms of the defence of liberty as they displayed the spoils at Delphi (Simonides frg. 106, ML 28/Fornara 54). When Pindar wrote an ode to celebrate Gelon's younger brother Hieron's victory in the chariot race at the Pythian games in 470 BC he juxtaposed the Sicilian victories at Himera, and at sea against the Etruscans in 475 BC, to those at Salamis and Plataia (Text 51, *Pythian Odes* 1.75–80). Herodotos' treatment, on the other hand, very much downplays that parallelism, and he is surely right. The circumstances in Sicily and in mainland Greece were entirely different: on the Greek mainland it is doubtful, despite the stories told about Argos (Herodotos 7.152), that any Greek city felt sufficiently pressured by another to want Persia as overlord to relieve that pressure; but in Sicily the city of Himera had a stark choice between incorporation into Theron's 'empire', or even total destruction by him, and getting non-Greek aid. Whereas in mainland Greece Persians and other barbarians were relatively

Son of Kronos, I beg you give a gentle sign that the Phoenician and the Etruscan war cry may stay at home, now they have seen the lamentable loss of ships off Cumae and what they suffered as they were subdued by the leaders of the Syracusans, who cast men in the prime of life from the swift ships into the sea and rescued Greece from heavy slavery. From Salamis I will try to win a reward from grateful Athenians, and in Sparta from the battle in front of mount Kithairon in which the Persian archers were made to labour. But from the lush banks of the river Himera will I win a reward from the sons of Deinomenes when I have finished my hymn, for it is there that they showed their mettle and the men of the enemy came to grief.

Text 51: Pindar Pythian Odes *1.71–80. Pindar puts the Deinomenid victory at Himera on a level with Athenian achievements at Salamis and Spartan achievements at Plataia.*

rare visitors, the Greeks of Sicily lived cheek by jowl with both native Sicilians and the Phoenicians whose cities were dotted around the west of the island. The Carthaginian empire was quite different from the Persian empire, and might reasonably be seen as offering opportunities for economic prosperity as part of a vigorous network rather than as a matter of political oppression. The real parallel for the activities of Gelon and Theron against the Carthaginians was still to come – in the activities of the Athenians against the Persians.

It was in the interests of Gelon and other Sicilian tyrants, as it would be in the interests of the Athenians, to present their victory as a matter of liberation. In a similar way, it was in their interests to pursue success in the Olympic and Pythian games and so present themselves as simply parallel to the élite of Greece itself. This strategy left both poetic and sculptural monuments. On the poetic level, the Sicilian tyrants and their culture have left a massive mark on Pindar's odes written for victories in panhellenic games. It is not just that Hieron, Gelon's successor, is the recipient of two of Pindar's *Pythian Odes* (1 and 2), only one of them in fact celebrating a Pythian victory, but that whereas the odes from the 490s and 480s celebrate only two victors from Sicily, as against six from the Greek mainland, the odes probably from the 470s celebrate twelve Sicilian or South Italian victors and only seven from the mainland. The world of the competitive aristocracy, which even Athenians had continued to inhabit in the 480s, when Pindar wrote to celebrate victories by Megakles and by Timodemos of Akharnai, was, after the Persian wars, a world lacking in Athenians and dominated by the new Greek world; in the 470s and 460s Pindar three times wrote for the élite of Cyrene (including the odes discussed in Chapter 1: p. 8).

The highly conspicuous way in which the Sicilian élite presented themselves to the mainland Greek world is equally magnificently represented by the bronze statue celebrating the victory of Gelon's other brother, Polyzalos, tyrant of Gela, at Delphi in 478 or 474 BC, a statue known as the Delphic Charioteer (Figure 87). Although there has been debate as to whether the sculptor responsible for this piece was from the Greek mainland or from Sicily, the sculpture is entirely at home in the history of Greek art. The choice of

Figure 87 The Delphic charioteer: part of a bronze chariot group erected to celebrate a victory by Polyzatos of Gela in the Pythian games at Delphi shortly after the Persian wars.

Figure 88 Enigmatic statue, perhaps of a charioteer or a cult official, from Motya in Sicily.

moment – after rather than during the race – the serious countenance of the figure, and the simple firm treatment of the folds of the charioteer's garment, all place this with the sculptures produced in the quarter century after the Persian war, sculptures like those on the east pediment of the temple of Zeus at Olympia, rather than with late archaic *kouroi* or even the sculptures of the temple of Athene Aphaia on Aigina from the 490s or 480s.

But the contrasting picture of Greek Sicily, the picture of a world apart where city-state politics operated according to different rules and where contact with non-Greek traditions was frequent and intimate, can also be represented by an image, one that is in many respects parallel but represents a tradition which could never converge. From Motya, an island in a lagoon off the west coast of Sicily on which the Phoenicians had settled and which

Theron took in the aftermath of the battle of Himera (Pausanias 5.25.5), comes a marble statue of a young man of around the date of the Charioteer (Figure 88). This statue has excited no small art-historical controversy. Some interpret the draped standing figure as another charioteer, but a very different one. The most striking difference is in the drapery; rather than a single layer of heavy drapery hanging symmetrically and cleanly in deep folds away from the body, several layers of light-weight drapery display folds that that stretch over the contours and cling, rather than fall, producing a figure that is strongly tactile, and indeed sensual. How is this drapery, married as it is to a head which might almost have come off the west pediment of the temple of Zeus at Olympia, to be explained? Some seek an explanation in the subject matter, supposing this to be not a charioteer but some Carthaginian priest or king; others look to its origin and see the whole statue as a product of an environment in which Phoenician and Greek influences mingled freely and productively. Since marble statuary is very rare from fifth-century Sicily, and since the find context offers little help, the statue is bound to remain something of a mystery. The clothing of a Greek body with an alien form neatly sums up Greek Sicily.

Between them, the Delphic Charioteer and the Motya youth indicate the two faces of the western Greeks. One face maintained that they were part of the world of mainland Greek cities, sharing their values. The other face belonged in a world where Greeks were only one group among many, competing and cooperating by turns with rather scant regard for ethnic origins. The continuing history of the cities of Sicily repeatedly displays the tension between these two sides, as Greeks from the mainland, both in what they do and in what they write about Sicily, assume that it is the Delphic Charioteer with which they have to come face to face, only to discover that somehow in Sicily the familiar always becomes unfamiliar, and the rules are different. The importance of the events of 480 BC in this ongoing story lies in the fact that only by understanding the difference between what went on in the Greek mainland and what went on in Sicily can we understand the divergent histories of the two areas. Along with the Persians, the mainland Greeks repelled the cultures of the east: classical Greece was culturally isolated in a way that archaic Greece had not been. But the defeat of the Carthaginians at Himera meant no such divorce for the western Greek world: the Carthaginians maintained a presence in Sicily and, unlike the Persians, they would before long be back there active as a military force. In the mean time contact with that world had commercial advantages. Defeating the Carthaginians was only one in a number of military encounters with non-Greeks: in 475 BC Hieron would defeat the Etruscans at sea off Cumae (ML 29/Fornara 64, Diodoros 11.51 and Text 51), and in the 450s and 440s Sicilian Greeks had to cope with a native Sicel uprising. The world of classical Greek Sicily was in many ways but the archaic world writ large. The same could not be said of the world of mainland Greece.

EPILOGUE

The war against Persia did not end in 479 BC. Greeks continued to campaign to liberate Greek cities, in Thrace and Ionia, from Persian control for another decade and a half. Even after the successful naval battle at Eurymedon, in the Gulf of Antalya, in which the Persian navy was decisively beaten, fighting against Persia continued with an expedition to Egypt and intervention in Cyprus. But the continuing war was an exercise which could no longer even pretend to stem from a united Greek front. It was an Athenian enterprise supported by Greek cities of the Aegean and its seaboard, at first willingly and for their own advantage and later because they had no option.

Modern accounts of the Persian wars all end in 479 BC because that is where Herodotos ended. Arguably, Herodotos' reasons for ending at that point have nothing to do with Persia or with war, and everything to do with politics. The Athenians hijacked the cause of Greek liberty, and any account of events after 479 BC involved taking a stand on a story which was still actively political at the time Herodotos was writing (7.139; compare Thucydides 3.10.3; 6.76.3). In telling the story of events in Greece until 479 BC Herodotos might reasonably, if vainly, hope that past events could be rescued from politics; for events after 479 BC he could be under no such illusion. Only an observer brought up in Athens itself, as Thucydides was, could become so used to the Athenian version as to overlook its tendentious political construction.

Yet history did change in 479 BC. It changed not just in the sense that there would be no other Herodotos, and that what it was to write history came to be dominated by the example of Thucydides' writing about contemporary history. It changed because after 479 BC tradition both lost its innocence and became subject to external tests. For both these developments the Athenian empire and her democracy were primarily responsible: it was with the empire that massive public documentation in permanent form, records inscribed on stone, was first undertaken by a Greek city, and it was with democracy that political and lawcourt debates so developed as to lead to written speeches. Thucydides' personal observations, along with the existence of records made at the time of what people said and decided and of the arguments they used, make the writing of history after 479 BC a quite different matter.

There are many ways in which this change in Greek history might be explored, but the changing role of the Delphic oracle in history is perhaps what is most revealing. Archaic Greek history, whether as written by Herodotos or as recorded by later writers, overflows with oracle stories, as if no public enterprise was complete without them. Accounts of classical Greece, by contrast, feature oracle stories only infrequently. This is not just a matter of Thucydidean 'rationalism', for oracles are no more plentiful in the works of Xenophon or the speeches of Demosthenes. In the second century AD Plutarch shaped two of his dialogues around the issues of 'Why oracles are no longer given in verse' and 'The abandonment of oracles'. To understand why indeed oracle stories fade out of classical Greek history is to understand something very important about archaic Greek history.

The politics of the archaic Greek world, with its élite factions and its tyrants on the one hand, and its non-participating but militarily essential and potentially riotous masses on the other, created the conditions in which an oracle was a highly desirable thing. Desirable to be able to get the backing of divine authority; even more desirable to be able to tell the story of how one's past actions had been predicted, promoted, even invented, by the god. Those individuals and groups who told stories to justify their political position, and those individuals and groups who told stories to justify assailing the political position of others, had equal use for what the oracle might have said in the past.

The politics of the classical world, or at least the politics of the classical world about which we are best informed, were different. The record of classical Greece is dominated by classical Athens, and Athenian democracy had very little space for oracular consultation on matters other than the religious. This was less a matter of taste than of political necessity: democracy depended upon confidence that the best way to get the right answer was to discuss it in a mass meeting and follow the decision made by the majority present. Whereas an individual ruler or a small group could decide to consult an oracle before taking a decision, the very decision not simply to decide by debate and discussion was problematic for democracy. And for a democratic assembly to decide what to do first and then consult an oracle would both imply that there was something provisional about what had been decided and lay open the possibility that the oracle might overturn the democratic decision. But if the people's decisions could be declared wrong by superior authority how could confidence in democratic decision-making be maintained? Individual Athenians certainly did seek oracular guidance, and oracular support for their views, both on private matters and on affairs of state – often from oracular sources easier and cheaper to consult than Delphic Apollo – and the Athenian state frequently consulted on matters that only gods could ever know about, but its consultations were limited to matters of cult narrowly defined, and it did so before coming to a public decision on the matter, not after (compare e.g. ML 73/Fornara 140).

The Delphic oracle became marginal to Greek history after 479 BC, however, not just because of Athenian democracy but because events began to become history before they became tradition. Thucydides certainly depended upon what others told him, and his history is certainly vulnerable to the personal distortions of his informants, but the events of the Peloponnesian war made it into Thucydides' notes before cities had time to take them up and shape them to their subsequent interests. By contrast, the Delphic oracle, precisely because it stood outside the direct powers of any city, was an ideal instrument with which oral tradition could think about the past of a city. Citing a Delphic oracle lent an inevitability to the events described, and lifted them above mere quibbling about the possible roles of particular individuals in past events. Spartans were brought up in a regime of obedience, but any revolutionary thoughts there might be were more effectively stifled by claiming that the laws under which classical Sparta operated were laws which had a Delphic *imprimatur* than simply by claiming they were the bright ideas of one Lykourgos.

The uses of the oracle can best be revealed by one of the most remarkable of all the traditions about Delphic consultation, the tradition about Athenian consultation on the eve of the Persian wars (Herodotos 7.139–145.1). The story goes that, when those whom the Athenians sent to consult the Delphic oracle entered the temple, the Pythia immediately delivered a long oracle, twelve lines of hexameter verse, telling them that they were doomed and should flee from the Persians. The Athenian ambassadors were thrown into a panic by this, but on the advice of a man from Delphi they took up suppliant boughs and asked for a better oracle. The oracle then produced another dozen lines of hexameter verse telling them not to await the Persians but to trust in the 'wooden wall', and calling Salamis 'divine'. When this oracle was announced at Athens a debate ensued about what was meant by the 'wooden wall'; some insisted that it must be the old wooden fortifications of the Acropolis, but Themistokles convinced the majority that it was the ships. A minority stuck to the other interpretation, were not even persuaded by the claim that Athene's sacred snake had deserted the Acropolis, and were found in the temple of Athene Polias by the invading Persians (Herodotos 8.41, 51). Oracles were persuasive devices, but they could not persuade all the people all the time.

Herodotos introduces the story of Athens' consultation of the oracle when he has just allowed himself a rare authorial verdict that had it not been for the Athenians the Greeks would not have defeated the Persian invasion. He makes the transition by noting that not even fearful oracles from Delphi caused the Athenians to panic and desert Greece. That introduction makes very clear the value of this story to the Athenians: it highlighted the tenacity with which they resisted Persia, and at the same time removed the possibility of other Greeks exonerating their own behaviour with reference to Delphi. What is more, by making the Delphic oracle speak before it is spoken to (compare the Cyrene story, p. 13), it not only makes for a more dramatic narrative which emphasises the unusual importance of the events but also avoids making clear what it is that the Athenians asked.

Not the least remarkable thing about this consultation is how so developed a tradition could arise with regard to an incident which occurred within the living memory of those to whom Herodotos spoke. There are two important points to make here. One is that the only Athenians who knew what actually happened at Delphi were the ambassadors: all that any city ever heard was the report of those it had sent to Delphi. The second point is that what made an impact at Athens was the public debate about what to do, a debate which ended with the majority convinced that evacuation and trusting to naval strength was the best option. If an oracle about wooden walls and/or Salamis played a part in that public debate, it is not difficult to see how the story could get elaborated to make the oracle the central feature, and to add an earlier, even less favourable response from Apollo. After the events it was in no one's interests to question the Athenian decision, and in no one's power to deny Themistokles a major part in the taking of that decision. The forces which led to the Decree of Themistokles (above pp. 322–3) and the forces which led to these twenty-four lines of Delphic hexameters were not essentially different. Least of all was it in the interests of Delphi, now or on any other occasion, to deny responsibility for advice which was held to be good – particularly since other Delphic responses had encouraged defeatism in the face of the Persians.

Falsifying the historical record, replacing historical fact by fiction, tends to be seen in the twentieth century as one particularly frightening aspect of totalitarian regimes. Winston Smith, in George Orwell's novel *Nineteen Eighty-Four*, is employed altering reports in old issues of *The Times* to obliterate discrepancies between past and present; his job is to make predicted production figures match actual output, to remove all record of acceptable actions by persons now disgraced, and so on: 'A number of *The Times* which might, because of changes in political alignment, or mistaken prophecies uttered by Big Brother, have been rewritten a dozen times still stood on the files bearing its original date, and no other copy existed to contradict it' (p. 36). Those in whose interest it is to remember a different version of the past disappear, are 'vaporized', and those left who are old enough to remember differently have no interest in anything but personal anecdotes, as Smith discovers when he engages an aged 'prole' in conversation in a public house. Smith reflects that 'It might very well be that literally every word in the history books, even the things that one accepted without question, was pure fantasy. . . . Everything faded into mist. The past was erased, the erasure was forgotten, the lie became truth' (p. 63).

Much of our 'knowledge' of the past, even today, does not rest upon a base in documentary evidence. It is not simply that, even without physical manipulation of the sort Winston Smith is engaged in, past records allow any amount of reinterpretation – as debates about the Holocaust show. Most of what we believe about the past remains oral tradition: we grow up used to hearing certain sorts of things said about certain sorts of events, and with a roll-call of heroes and villains such as *1066 and All That* mocks. No falsification of records was involved in the invention of the myth of French resistance during the Second World War, and the unmasking of the extent of collaboration has not seriously shaken the hold of that myth on the people of western Europe, outside as well as inside France.

The world of archaic Greece was a world entirely constructed from tradition. The only documentation contemporary with the events of the seventh and sixth centuries BC which was available to later Greeks was poetic, and even when this emanated from characters who were themselves of considerable historical moment it was historically extremely inexplicit (see above pp. 204 and 207 on Solon). Just as the regime of Orwell's Oceania believes it to be important for its own ongoing credibility that accurate predictions were made in the past, so archaic Greek traditions incorporated Delphic oracles which revealed accurately, if inexplicitly, events to come, and thereby justified the status quo.

Orwell invents a history textbook which depicts the capitalist past in terms which mix accurate information (capitalists in great big beautiful houses with as many as thirty servants to look after them), exaggeration (if anyone disobeyed a capitalist he could have him thrown into prison), and fantasy (every capitalist having the right to sleep with any woman working in one of his factories). The traditions which face the historian of archaic Greece are a similar mixture, and our ability to distinguish fact from fantasy is slight. After 479 BC we are in a different position, able to make quite confident judgements about what actually happened in a significantly higher proportion of instances. The comparative absence of the Delphic oracle from the stories of classical Greece is one indicator of that difference.

Classical Greece had two pasts, the actual past and the past it shaped for itself out of the pasts which successive generations had already shaped for themselves. In this book I have attempted to tell both these stories, to indicate what I believe there is good reason to think actually happened in the centuries down to the Persian wars, and to indicate what the Greeks themselves thought they knew about that past. Our understanding of the achievements of classical Greece is seriously attenuated if we neglect either story, for Greeks of the fifth and fourth centuries BC, like ourselves, were moulded both by what had happened and by what they believed had happened. Our understanding of the tragic events which have followed the break-up of Yugoslavia is seriously attenuated if we fail to take adequate account of the role played by both the changeable and the unchangeable past. At one point (pp. 67–8) Winston Smith is afflicted with doubts about whether perhaps his belief that the past is unchangeable might be false, but he stiffens his resolve on realising that he is not the only person to hold that view. The temptation for the historian is always to ignore that the past is changeable. This book has been written in the conviction that remaining ever conscious that the past is both changeable and unchangeable is both an academic duty and a political necessity.

BIBLIOGRAPHICAL NOTES

There are a number of rich and stimulating treatments of the Greece from *c*.800 BC to the Persian wars. The most accessible is O. Murray, *Early Greece* (2nd edition, London, 1993). A. M. Snodgrass, *Archaic Greece: An Age of Experiment* (London, 1980) is particularly important on the eighth century. L. H. Jeffery, *Archaic Greece: The City States c.700–500* BC (London, 1976) is a remarkable condensation of a mass of literary traditions. J. Hall, *A History of the Archaic Greek World ca. 1200–479* (Oxford, 2007) offers a picture complementary to that offered here, sharing my starting date. Stimulating reflections on the interpretation of the archaeology of the period are to be found in I. Morris, *Archaeology as Cultural* History (Oxford, 2000). My *Greek History* (London, 2004), in the Routledge Classical Foundations series, situates archaic Greek history into its broader historical context. A particularly enjoyable way in to the material evidence is provided by J. Boardman, 'The Greek world' in *Cambridge Ancient History: Plates to Volume Three* (Cambridge, 1984) and by *Cambridge Ancient History: Plates to Volume Four* (Cambridge, 1988). I have made reference to these works in the chapter bibliographies only when they are a vital point of reference for a particular topic, but the reader's enjoyment of this book will, I hope, be enhanced by frequent comparison with these other works.

CHAPTER 1

On cultural imperialism see especially E. Said, *Orientalism* (2nd edition, London, 1995) and M. Herzfeld, *Anthropology through the Looking-Glass: Critical Ethnography in the Margins of Europe* (Cambridge, 1987).

For a general introduction to the sources for ancient history see M. H. Crawford (ed.), *Sources for Ancient History* (Cambridge, 1983). The story of Greek historiography is well told by Simon Hornblower in the Introduction to S. Hornblower (ed.), *Greek Historiography* (Oxford, 1994) 7–54. On the social construction of oral history see E. Tonkin, *Narrating our Pasts* (Cambridge, 1992). The way in which individuals and societies forget their pasts and the importance of this are well brought out by J. Carsten, 'The politics of forgetting: migration, kinship and memory on the periphery of the southeast Asian state', *Journal of the Royal Anthropological Institute* NS 1 (1995), 317–35. The best introduction to oral tradition in the Greek world is J. K. Davies,

'The reliability of oral tradition', in J. K. Davies and L. Foxhall (eds), *The Trojan War: Its Historicity and Context* (Bristol, 1984) 87–110. For a detailed exploration of the Athenian case see R. Thomas, *Oral Tradition and Written Record in Classical Athens* (Cambridge, 1989).

Throughout this book I take Herodotos to have reported what he was told, although I believe him to have done so selectively, and according to his own purposes. Critics who prefer to believe that other fifth-century Greeks could not have told stories which were false, while Herodotos systematically invented his informants and their stories, seem to me to ignore entirely the reasons why people tell and retell stories, and I will not further discuss their views. On Herodotos the best short guide is J. Gould, *Herodotus* (London, 1989); there is much of value also in D. Lateiner, *The Historical Method of Herodotus* (Toronto, 1992) and R. Thomas, *Herodotus in Context: Ethnography, Science and the Art of Persuasion* (Cambridge, 2000). I discuss Herodotos as a source for archaic Greek history further in 'Archaic Greek History' in I. de Jong and H. van Wees (eds), *Brill's Companion to Herodotus* (Leiden, 2002), 497–520.

On the shaping of traditions about 'colonisation' see C. Dougherty, *The Poetics of Colonization: From City to Text in Archaic Greece* (Oxford, 1993), esp. ch. 6 for Cyrene; I. Malkin, *Myth and Territory in the Spartan Mediterranean* (Cambridge, 1994), chs 5–6 for Cyrene; and M. Giangiulio, 'Constructing the past: colonial traditions and the writing of history. The case of Cyrene', in N. Luraghi (ed.), *The Historian's Craft in the Age of Herodotus* (Oxford, 2001) 116–37. On Tartessos see J. G. Chamorro, 'Survey of archaeological research on Tartessos', *AJA* 91 (1987), 197–232. On the setting of Cyrenaica see P. Horden and N. Purcell, *The Corrupting Sea: A Study of Mediterranean History* (Oxford, 2000), 65–74. On the settlement of Cyrene see J. Boardman, *The Greeks Overseas* (London, 1980), 153–9; J. Boardman, 'Evidence for the dating of Greek settlements in Cyrenaica', *ABSA* 61 (1966), 149–56; S. Stucchi, 'I vasi greci arcaici e la Cirenaica: importazioni ed influenze', *Rendiconti della Accademia nazionale dei Lincei* 39 (1984), 161–71; D. White *et al.*, *The Extramural Sanctuary of Demeter and Persephone at Cyrene, Libya*, vol. 2 (1985) esp. 9–107. It follows from what I say in the text that I think many archaeological accounts very much too beholden to the literary texts. For a critical examination of my own account here see I. Malkin '"Tradition" in Herodotus: the foundation of Cyrene', in P. Derow and R. Parker (eds), *Herodotus and his World* (Oxford, 2003), 153–70, in response to which I have endeavoured further to clarify my case in the text here.

For perceptive general remarks on the relationship between archaeology and the history told by literary texts see A. M. Snodgrass, *An Archaeology of Greece* (Berkeley, CA, 1987), 36–66.

CHAPTER 2

On Waterhouse's painting see R. Jenkyns, *The Victorians and Ancient Greece* (Oxford, 1980), 190, and A. M. Snodgrass, *An Archaeology of Greece: The Present State and Future Scope of a Discipline* (Berkeley, CA, 1987), 70–1.

The historical geography of the Mediterranean has been set on a new footing by P. Horden and N. Purcell, *The Corrupting Sea: A Study of Mediterranean History* (Oxford, 2000). The fullest descriptive geography of Greece remains A. Philippson, *Die griechischen Landschaften*, 4 vols (Frankfurt, 1952–6).

For an introduction to the geology of Greece see D. Ager, *The Geology of Europe* (London, 1980), 500–14, and for an introduction to the climate see D. Furlan, 'The climate of southeast Europe', in C. Wallén (ed.), *Climates of Central and Southern Europe: World Survey of Climatology*, vol. 6 (London, 1977). Greek plant and animal life is usefully set into a wider context in J. Blondel and J. Aronson, *Biology and Wildlife of the Mediterranean Region* (Oxford, 1999).

The information on Methana is drawn from M. C. Forbes, 'Farming and foraging in prehistoric Greece', in M. Dimen and E. Friedl (eds), *Regional Variation in Modern Greece and Cyprus: Towards a Perspective on the Ethnography of Greece*, Annals of the New York Academy of Sciences 268 (New York, 1976). Note also H. Forbes, '"We have a little of everything": the ecological basis of some agricultural practices in Methana, Trizinia', ibid., pp. 236–50; P. James *et al.*, 'The physical environment of Methana', and H. Forbes, 'Turkish and modern Methana', in C. Mee and H. Forbes (eds), *A Rough and Rocky Place: The Landscape and Settlement History of the Methana Peninsula, Greece* (Liverpool, 1996), 5–32, 101–17.

For climate and food supply see P. Garnsey, *Famine and Food Supply in the Graeco-Roman World: Responses to Risk and Crisis* (Cambridge, 1988), especially 8–14, and R. Osborne, *Classical Landscape with Figures: The Ancient Greek City and its Countryside* (London, 1987), 27–52, where fuller figures for rainfall at Athens and Eleusis will be found.

The most thorough study of the historical plant communities of any area in Greece is O. Rackham, 'Observations on the historical ecology of Boeotia', *ABSA 78* (1983), 291–351. Note also O. Rackham, 'Land use and the native vegetations of Greece', in M. Bell and S. Limbrey (eds), *Archaeological Aspects of Woodland Ecology*, British Archaeological Reports, International Series 146 (Oxford, 1981), 177–98; O. Rackham, 'Ancient landscapes', in O. Murray and S. R. F. Price (eds), *The Greek City from Homer to Alexander* (Oxford, 1989); and L. Foxhall, M. Jones, and H. Forbes, 'Human ecology and the classical landscape', in S. Alcock and R. Osborne (eds), *Classical Archaeology* (Oxford, 2007), 91–117. The standard work on trees and timber is R. Meiggs, *Trees and Timber in the Ancient Mediterranean World* (Oxford, 1982).

The rather static view of the development of the landscape offered here is essentially that championed by Rackham. For a rather more dynamic view, with more extensive discussion of prehistory, see Tj. H. van Andel and C. N. Runnels, *Beyond the Acropolis: A Rural Greek Past* (Stanford, CA, 1987), 13–98; and M. H. Jameson, C. N. Runnels, and Tj. H. Van Andel, *A Greek Countryside: The Southern Argolid from Prehistory to the Present Day* (Stanford, CA, and Cambridge, 1994), ch. 3.

For an extremely vivid eyewitness account of the damage which violent storms can do, even to a well-maintained landscape, see D. G. Hogarth, *Accidents of an Antiquary's Life* (London, 1910), 79–85, which tells of an extraordinary storm in May 1901 at Zakro in east Crete.

Climatic data on Sicily come from F. Pollastri, *Sicilia: Notizie e commenti ecologici di agricoltura siciliana* (Palermo, 1948–9), vol. 2, tav. 7. Climatic data for Libya are taken from Amilcare Fantali, *Le pioggie della Libia* (Rome, 1952). On the human consequences of the environment of Cyrenaica see D. L. Johnson, *Jabal al-Akhdar, Cyrenaica: An Historical Geography of Settlement and Livelihood* (Chicago, IL, 1973).

The best map of Mediterranean agricultural practice in this period is Horden and Purcell, *Corrupting Sea,* chs 6–7. I have discussed the agricultural constraints in general terms in R. Osborne, *Classical Landscape with Figures: The Ancient Greek City and its Countryside* (London, 1987). On change in crops and on the constraints upon human performance in antiquity see R. Sallares, *The Ecology of the Ancient Greek World* (London, 1991), with review by P. Halstead in *Nature* 350 (11 April 1991), 538. Greek agricultural practices and their social consequences have been discussed at length by V. D. Hanson, *The Other Greeks: The Family Farm and the Agrarian Roots of Western Civilization* (New York, 1995), whose stress on the importance of tree crops, and on the mentality which intensive family farming develops, is salutary. Compare also P. Halstead and J. O'Shea, *Bad Year Economics* (Cambridge, 1989); P. Halstead, 'Traditional and ancient rural economy in Mediterranean Europe: plus ça change?', *JHS* 107 (1987), 77–87; and, on the pressure points of the farmer's year, P. Halstead and G. Jones, 'Agrarian ecology in the Greek islands: time stress, scale and risk', *JHS* 109 (1989), 41–55. The best introduction to general issues of demography is W. Scheidel, 'Demography', in W. Scheidel, I. Morris and R. Saller (eds), *The Cambridge Economic History of the Greco-Roman World* (Cambridge, 2007), 38–86. The importance of changing demand and changing labour supply over a family's life-cycle is well discussed by T. W. Gallant, *Risk and Survival in Ancient Greece* (Stanford, CA, and Cambridge, 1991). I discuss labour demands and use of slaves further in 'The economics and politics of slavery at Athens', in A. Powell (ed.), *The Greek World* (London, 1996), 27–43. On the place of pastoralism see S. Hodkinson, 'Animal husbandry and the Greek polis', in C. R. Whittaker (ed.), *Pastoral Economies in Classical Antiquity* (Cambridge, 1988), 35–74. On olives see L. Foxhall, *Olive Cultivation in Ancient Greece: Seeking the Ancient Economy* (Oxford, 2007). On the importance of semi-luxuries see L. Foxhall, 'Cargoes of the heart's desire: the character of trade in the archaic Mediterranean world', in N. Fisher and H. van Wees (eds), *Archaic Greece: New Approaches and New Evidence* (London, 1998), 295–310, and L. Foxhall, 'Village to city: staples and luxuries. Exchange networks and urbanization', in R. Osborne and B. Cunliffe (eds), *Mediterranean Urbanization 800–600 B.C.* (Oxford, 2005), 233–48. Not all scholars accept that farming in archaic and classical Greece was intensive; see S. Isager and J. E. Skydsgaard, *Ancient Greek Agriculture: An Introduction* (London, 1992), who signal their differences at 108–14, and A. Moreno, *Feeding the Democracy: The Athenian Grain Supply in the Fifth and Fourth Centuries BC* (Oxford, 2007). Much ancient evidence is usefully collected and discussed in A. Burford, *Land and Labor in Ancient Greece* (Baltimore, 1993).

CHAPTER 3

There are two classic syntheses of the archaeology of the Dark Age: A. M. Snodgrass, *The Dark Age of Greece* (Edinburgh, 1971; reissue with new foreword, 2000), and V. R. d'A. Desborough, *The Greek Dark Ages* (London, 1972). An up-to-date synthesis is provided by O. Dickinson, *The Aegean from Bronze Age to Iron Age* (London, 2006), and a detailed survey of the Aegean by I. Lemos, *The Protogeometric Aegean: The Archaeology of the late Eleventh and Tenth Centuries BC* (Oxford, 2002). Fundamental on the nature of community organization, but difficult, is C. Morgan, *Early Greek States Beyond the Polis* (London, 2003).

On Late Helladic IIIC see also J. Hooker, *Mycenaean Greece* (London, 1977), ch. 7, 'The end of the Mycenaean Age 1200–1051 BC', 140–82 and J. Maran, 'Coming to terms with the past: ideology and power in Late Helladic IIIC', in S. Deger-Jalkotzy and I. Lemos (eds), *Ancient Greece: From Mycenaean Palaces to the Age of Homer* (Edinburgh, 2006), 123–50. The Perati cemetery finds are published by S. Iakovidis, *Perati: To Nekrotapheion* (Athens, 1969) (in Greek). On Elateia and Phokis see C. Morgan, 'What is *ethnos* religion', in L. Mitchell and P. J. Rhodes (eds), *The Development of the Polis in Archaic Greece* (London, 1997). On the cemetery at Ialysos see C. Mee, *Rhodes in the Bronze Age* (Warminster, 1982), 96. On Cyprus see Desborough, *Dark Ages,* 49; Dickinson, *Aegean* 62–3; A. B. Knapp, *Prehistoric and Protohistoric Cyprus: Identity, Insularity and Connectivity* (Oxford, 2008), 281–97; on Philistine pottery see Snodgrass, *Dark Age*, 107–9. On Emborio see M. F. S. Hood, 'Mycenaeans in Chios', in J. Boardman and C. E. Vaphopoulou-Richardson (eds), *Chios: A Conference at the Homereion in Chios 1984* (Oxford, 1986), 169–80. On Lefkandi see below. On Mende see *Archaeological Reports* 39 (1982–3), 54; on Torone see J. K. Papadopoulos, *The Early Iron Age Cemetery at Torone*, 2 vols (Los Angeles, CA, 2005). On Cyprus and iron metallurgy see A. M. Snodgrass, 'Iron and early metallurgy in the Mediterranean', in T. A. Wertime and J. D. Muhly, *The Coming of the Age of Iron* (New Haven, CT, and London, 1980), 335–74, esp. 340–55, and S. Sherratt, 'Commerce, iron and ideology: metallurgical innovation in 12th–11th century Cyprus', in *Proceedings of the International Symposium 'Cyprus in the 11th Century BC'* (Nicosia, 1994), 59–107. On the Skales cemetery at Palaipaphos see V. Karageorghis, *Palaepaphos–Skales: An Iron Age Cemetery in Cyprus* (Konstanz, 1983). The case for Cypriot influence on the origin of Attic protogeometric is made by Desborough, *Dark Ages*, 54–5. The basic study of protogeometric pottery is V. R. d'A. Desborough, *Protogeometric Pottery* (Oxford, 1952). On Crete in this period see Desborough, *Dark Ages*, 112–29, and J. N. Coldstream, 'Knossos: an urban nucleus in the Dark Age?', in D. Musti *et al.* (eds), *La transizione dal Miceneo all'alto arcaismo: Dal palazzo alla città* (Rome, 1991), 287–99, with A. Peatfield, 'After the "Big Bang": What? or Minoan Symbols and Shrines beyond Palatial Collapse', in S. Alcock and R. Osborne (eds), *Placing the Gods: Sanctuaries and Sacred Space in Ancient Greece* (Oxford, 1994), 19–36.

For the idea of 'systems collapse' see A. C. Renfrew, 'Systems collapse as social transformation', in A. C. Renfrew and K. L. Cooke (eds), *Transformations: Mathematical Approaches to Culture Change* (New York, 1979), 275–94.

On questions of cult continuity the picture has changed substantially; compare Snodgrass, *Dark Age*, 394–401, with F. de Polignac, *Cults, Territory, and the Origins of the Greek City-State* (Chicago, IL, 1995) 27–31; A. D'Agata 'Cult activity on Crete in the Early Dark Age: changes, continuities and the development of a "Greek" cult system', in Deger-Jalkotzy and Lemos, *Ancient Greece*, 397–414, and M. Prent, *Cretan Sanctuaries and Cults: Continuity and Change from the Late Minoan IIIC to the Archaic Period* (Leiden, 2005). On Kalapodi in central Greece see R. Felsch *et al.*, 'Apollon und Artemis oder Artemis und Apollon? Bericht von den Grabungen im neu entdeckten Heiligtum bei Kalapodi 1973–77', *Archäologischer Anzeiger* (1980), 38–123; R. Felsch *et al.*, 'Kalapodi: Bericht über die Grabungen im Heiligtum der Artemis Elaphebolos und des Apollon von Hyampolis 1978–82', *Archäologischer Anzeiger* (1987), 1–99. On Kato Symi on Crete see A. Lebessi and P. Muhly, 'The sanctuary of Hermes and Aphrodite at Syme in Crete', *National Geographic Research* 3 (1987), 102–12. For the material from the Polis cave on Ithaka see W. D. E. Coulson 'The protogeometric from Polis reconsidered', *ABSA* 86 (1991), 43–64. On Delphi see *BCH* 117 (1993), 626–31. Although A. Mazarakis-Ainian, *From Rulers' Dwellings to Temples: Architecture, Religion and Society in Early Iron Age Greece (1100–700 B.C.)* (Göteborg, 1997) collects much useful material, I am not persuaded by its main thesis.

On changes in tombs see Snodgrass, *Dark Age*, 140–212, and, for Attica in particular, A. J. M. Whitley, *Style and Society in Dark Age Greece* (Cambridge, 1991) and I. Morris, *Burial and Ancient Society: The Rise of the Greek City State* (Cambridge, 1987).

For a general survey of Homer and Hesiod on the Dark Age see Snodgrass, *Dark Age*, 2–5. On the interpretation of Hesiod's myth of the five races see J.-P. Vernant, 'The Hesiodic myth of the races: an essay in structural analysis', in J.-P. Vernant, *Myth and Thought among the Greeks* (1965, Eng. trans. London, 1983), 3–32. I discuss Homer and Hesiod further in Chapter 5.

The issue of the nature of 'ethnic' divisions in archaic Greece has been much discussed recently, in particular in the work of Jonathan Hall. See J. Hall, *Ethnic Identity in Greek Antiquity* (Cambridge, 1997), and J. Hall, *Hellenicity: Between Ethnicity and Culture* (Chicago, 2002), especially ch. 3 for Ionian and Dorian migrations. On the Ionian migration, see also Snodgrass, *Dark Age*, 373–8. The ancient source material is accumulated and synthesised in G. L. Huxley, *The Early Ionians* (London, 1966), 23–35. The most important ancient accounts are to be found in Strabo, *Geography* 14.1.3–6 (written in the first century BC, but quoting earlier authors), and in Herodotos, especially 1.146–7. On the Dorian invasion see Snodgrass, *Dark Age*, 296–323; Dickinson, *Aegean* 50–5; and Hooker, *Mycenaean Greece*, 163–80 and appendix 1 (213–22) which collects the literary sources for the invasion. On Sparta in particular see I. Malkin, *Myth and Territory in the Spartan Mediterranean* (Cambridge, 1994), ch. 1. Note also P. A. Cartledge, *Sparta and Lakonia* (London, 1979), ch. 7, 'The first Dorians *c.*1050–775', pp. 75–101, but Cartledge may overestimate the discontinuity in the pottery (see W. D. E. Coulson, 'The Dark Age pottery of Sparta', *ABSA* 80 (1985), 29–83; 'The Dark Age pottery of Sparta II. Vrondama', *ABSA* 83 (1988), 21–4; and W. D. E. Coulson, *The Dark Age*

Pottery of Messenia (Göteborg, 1986), 71–8). With the approach taken here compare G. Grote, *History of Greece* (3rd edition, London, 1851), vol. 2, pp. 7–8.

On the history of the near east in the Dark Age see *Cambridge Ancient History* (2nd edition), vol. 3/1 (Cambridge, 1982), chs 6–9. On the Phoenicians the most accessible and up-to-date discussion in English is Maria Eugenia Aubet's *The Phoenicians and the West: Politics, Colonies and Trade* (Cambridge, 1993; 2nd edition, 2001); note also S. Frankenstein, 'The Phoenicians in the far west: a function of neo-Assyrian imperialism', in M. T. Larsen (ed.), *Power and Propaganda* (Copenhagen, 1979), 263–94.

On Lefkandi see M. R. Popham, L. H. Sackett, and P. G. Themelis (eds), *Lefkandi I: The Iron Age. The Settlement and the Cemeteries* (London, 1979 (plates), 1980 (text)); R. W. V. Catling and I. S. Lemos (eds), *Lefkandi II, Part I: The Pottery* (London, 1990); M. R. Popham, P. G. Calligas, and L. H. Sackett (eds), *Lefkandi II, Part 2: The Excavation, Architecture and Finds* (London, 1993); M. R. Popham with I. Lemos, *Lefkandi III: The Early Iron Age Cemetery at Toumba* (London, 1996); and *Archaeological Reports* (1981–2), 15–18; (1982–3), 12–15; (1983–4), 17; and (1984–5), 15–16. See also Desborough, *Dark Ages*, 187–99, J. N. Coldstream, *Geometric Greece* (London, 1977; revised edition, 2003), 40–3, 63–6, 90, and Lemos, *Protogeometric*, 140–6, 161–8. J. Crielaard, '*Basileis* at sea: elites and external contacts in the Euboean Gulf region from the end of the Bronze Age to the beginning of the Iron Age', in Deger-Jalkotzy and Lemos, *Ancient Greece* 271–97, makes the case for exceptional continuity of settlement and contacts in this region. On contact with the east see M. R. Popham, 'Precolonization: early Greek contact with the East', in G. R. Tsetskhladze and F. De Angelis (eds), *The Archaeology of Greek Colonisation* (Oxford, 1994), 11–34. For the earliest finds of Greek pottery in the east see Coldstream, *Geometric Greece*, 66–8, 92–5.

For Athens in this period see Desborough, *Dark Ages*, 133–60, and Coldstream, *Geometric Greece*, 26–35, 55–63, 73–81. I. Lemos, 'Athens and Lefkandi: a tale of two sites', in Deger-Jalkotzy and Lemos, *Ancient Greece,* 505–30, usefully compares Athens and Lefkandi.

For early protogeometric pottery at Tyre see P. Bikai, *The Pottery of Tyre* (Oxford, 1979), plates xxii and xxx. On the arrangement of cemeteries see I. Morris, *Burial and Ancient Society*, 57–96, and D. C. Kurtz and J. Boardman, *Greek Burial Customs* (London, 1971) 34–67. For the wall at Old Smyrna see R. V. Nicholls, 'Old Smyrna: the Iron Age fortifications and associated remains on the city perimeter', *ABSA* 53–4 (1958–9), 35–137. For the cemetery at Tsikalario on Naxos see Coldstream, *Geometric Greece*, 92.

For Crete in this period see Desborough, *Dark Ages*, 225–39; Coldstream, *Geometric Greece*, 48–50, 68–70, 99–102, and the papers by Coldstream, Whitley, and Wallace in Deger-Jalkotzy and Lemos, *Ancient Greece,* 581–664. For full publication of the cemeteries of the period see J. K. Brock, *Fortetsa: Early Greek Tombs near Knossos* (Cambridge, 1957); J. Boardman, 'Protogeometric graves near Agios Ioannis near Knossos', *ABSA* 55 (1960), 128–48; R. W. Hutchinson and J. Boardman, 'The Khaniale Tekke tombs', *ABSA* 49 (1954), 215–30; J. Boardman, 'The Khaniale Tekke tombs II', *ABSA* 62 (1967), 57–75; L. Vagnetti, 'A Sardinian askos from Crete', *ABSA* 84 (1989), 355–60; M. S. F. Hood and J. Boardman, 'Early Iron Age tombs at Knossos', *ABSA* 56 (1961), 68–80; J. N. Coldstream, 'Five tombs at Knossos', *ABSA* 58 (1963), 30–43; J. N. Coldstream, 'Some new tomb vases from early hellenic Knossos', *Stele N. Kontoleontos* (Athens, 1979), 408ff.; J. N. Coldstream, P. Callaghan, and J. H. Musgrave, 'Knossos: an early Greek tomb on lower Gypsadhes hill', *ABSA* 76 (1981), 141–66; *Archaeological Reports,* 23 (1976–7), 11–18; 25 (1978–9), 43–55; 29 (1982–3), 51–3; and compare 34 (1987–8), 67; J. N. Coldstream and H. W. Catling, *Knossos North Cemetery: Early Greek Tombs* (London, 1996); J. N. Coldstream, 'Knossos: an urban nucleus in the Dark Age?', in D. Musti, *et al.* (eds), *La transizione dal Miceneo all' alto arcaismo: Dal palazzo alla città* (Rome, 1991), 287–99. On Cretan relations with the east see G. Hoffman, *Imports and Immigrants: Near Eastern Contacts with Iron Age Crete* (Ann Arbor, MI, 1997), N. Stampolidis and A. Kotsonas, 'Phoenicians in Crete', in Deger-Jalkotzy and Lemos, *Ancient Greece,* 337–60. On the site at Karphi see S. Wallace, 'Last chance to see? Karfi (Crete) in the twenty-first century: presentation of new architectural data and their analysis in the current context of research', *ABSA* 100 (2005), 215–74.

CHAPTER 4

For a general survey of the archaeology of archaic Greece see I. Morris, 'Archaeology and archaic Greek history', in N. Fishser and H. van Wees (ed.), *Archaic Greece: New Approaches and New Evidence* (London, 1998), 1–91. On north-western Crete see M. Andreadhaki Vlasaki, 'The Khania area *c.*1200–700 BC', in D. Musti *et al.* (eds), *La transizione dal Miceneo all' alto arcaismo: Dal palazzo alla città* (Rome, 1991), 403–23; on Knossos see J. Coldstream, 'Knossos in early Greek times', in Deger-Jalkotzy and Lemos, *Ancient Greece,* 581–96; the archaeological evidence from the Argolid is usefully collected in A. Foley, *The Argolid 800–600 BC: An Archaeological Survey* (Göteborg, 1988), but for the southern Argolid her work is superseded by M. H. Jameson, C. N. Runnels, and Tj. van Andel, *A Greek Countryside: The Southern Argolid from Prehistory to the Present Day* (Stanford, CA, and Cambridge, 1994); I derive the figures for graves and sanctuaries from J. M. Hall, 'Ethnic Identity in the Argolid 900–600 BC' (Cambridge Ph.D. thesis, 1993).

On demographic trends see, in favour of growth, A. M. Snodgrass, *Archaeology and the Rise of the Greek State* (Cambridge, 1977) and *Archaic Greece: The Age of Experiment* (London, 1980), 21–4; R. Sallares, *The Ecology of the Ancient Greek World* (London, 1991), 42–293, esp. 84–8, 122–9, 160–92; against, I. Morris, *Burial and Ancient Society: The Rise of the Greek City-State* (Cambridge, 1987); the question is reviewed in a wider perspective by W. Scheidel, 'The Greek Demographic Expansion: Models and Comparisons', *JHS* 123 (2003), 120–40. On age-class systems generally see B. Bernardi, *Age Class Systems: Social Institutions and Polities Based on Age* (Cambridge, 1985): my quotation is taken from p. 170. The case for the importance of age-classes through into classical Greek history has been powerfully stated by James Davidson: see J. Davidson, 'Revolutions in human time: age-class in Athens and the Greekness of Greek revolutions', in S. Goldhill and R. Osborne (eds), *Rethinking*

Revolutions through Ancient Greece (Cambridge, 2006), 29–67: my quotation about the 'helicocritical gaze' comes from p. 58.

On the interpretation of burials see generally R. Huntington and P. Metcalf, *Celebrations of Death: The Anthropology of Mortuary Ritual* (Cambridge, 1979); E.-J. Pader, *Symbolism, Social Relations and the Interpretation of Mortuary Remains* (Oxford, 1982); J. O'Shea, *Mortuary Variability: An Archaeological Investigation* (New York, 1984). On Greece and Rome see I. Morris, *Death Ritual and Social Structure in Classical Antiquity* (Cambridge, 1992). A systematic survey of Greek practices is provided by A. M. Snodgrass, *The Dark Age of Greece* (Edinburgh, 1971), ch. 4, for the eleventh to the eighth century, and by D. C. Kurtz and J. Boardman, *Greek Burial Customs* (London, 1972) for all periods. The case of eighth-century Athens is discussed in detail by I. Morris, *Burial and Ancient Society: The Rise of the Greek City-State* (Cambridge, 1987) and A. J. M. Whitley, *Style and Society in Dark Age Greece: The Changing Face of a Pre-Literate Society 1100–700* (Cambridge, 1991). I discuss the Dipylon cemetery and its monumental grave markers further in 'Monumentality and ritual in archaic Greece', in D. Yatromanolakis and P. Roilos (eds), *Greek Ritual Poetics* (Cambridge, MA, 2004), 37–55, esp. 44–8. The disappearance of arms and armour from Athenian graves is put into a longer history of carrying arms by H. van Wees, 'Greeks bearing arms: the state, the leisure class, and the display of weapons in archaic Greece', in N. Fisher and H. van Wees (eds), *Archaic Greece: New Approaches and New Evidence* (London, 1998), 333–78. For Argos see P. Courbin, *Tombes géométriques d'Argos I* (Paris, 1974); Morris, *Burial and Ancient Society* 183–8; Whitley, *Style and Society*, 189–91. On grave plots see S. C. Humphreys, *The Family, Women and Death* (London, 1983; revised edition, Ann Arbor, MI, 1993), ch. 5.

On geometric art see below.

The development of our understanding of the importance of cult activity can be well appreciated by comparison of J. N. Coldstream, *Geometric Greece* (London, 1977), ch. 13 with A. M. Snodgrass, *Archaic Greece: The Age of Experiment* (London, 1980), and F. de Polignac, *Cults, Territory, and the Origins of the Greek City-State* (Paris, 1984; Eng. revised edition, Chicago, IL, 1995). For assessments of the impact of de Polignac: N. Marinatos and R. Hägg (eds), *Greek Sanctuaries: New Approaches* (London, 1993) and S. Alcock and R. Osborne (eds), *Placing the Gods. Sanctuaries and Sacred Space in Ancient Greece* (Oxford, 1994); for the eighth century (and before) see in particular the contributions of C. Sourvinou-Inwood and C. Morgan to the former, and of F. de Polignac and C. Morgan to the latter. My discussion of Perachora and Isthmia is heavily indebted to Morgan's papers. On Isthmia see now C. Morgan, *Isthmia VIII: The Late Bronze Age Settlement and Early Iron Age Sanctuary* (Princeton, NJ, 1999). On the Artemision at Ephesos see A. Bammer, 'A *Peripteros* of the geometric period in the Artemision of Ephesus', *Anatolian Studies* 40 (1990), 137–60. For Phokian and Arkadian sanctuaries see C. A. Morgan, *Early Greek States Beyond the Polis* (London, 2003), 113–34, 155–62, and M. E. Voyatzis, *The Early Sanctuary of Athena Alea at Tegea and Other Archaic Sanctuaries in Arkadia* (Göteborg, 1990). For Peloponnesian pins see I. Kilian-Dirlmeier, *Nadeln der frühhelladischen bis archaischen Zeit von der Peloponnes* (Munich, 1984). For pins and fibulae from Lindos see C. Blinkenberg, *Lindos: Fouilles de l'Acropole 1902–1914*, vol. 1. *Les*

Petits Objets (Berlin, 1931). For pins and fibulae from Pherai see K. Kilian, *Fibeln in Thessalien* (Munich, 1975) (at Snodgrass, *Archaic Greece*, p. 53, and Morris, *Burial and Ancient Society*, p. 191, Philia is a mistake for Pherai). For vases from Hymettos see M. K. Langdon, *A Sanctuary of Zeus on Mt. Hymettos* (Princeton, NJ, 1976). For terracottas from Kombothekra see U. Sinn, 'Das Heiligtum der Artemis Limnatis bei Kombothekra', *AM* 96 (1981), 25–71. For Olympia and Delphi see C. A. Morgan, *Athletes and Oracles: The Transformation of Olympia and Delphi in the Eighth Century* BC (Cambridge, 1990). On imported dedications at Greek sanctuaries see I. Kilian-Dirlmeier, 'Fremde Weihungen in griechischen Heiligtümern vom 8. bis zum Beginn des 7. Jahrhunderts v. Chr.', *Jahrbuch des Römisch-Germanischen Zentralmuseums Mainz* 32 (1985), 215–54.

On athletic victors see L. Kurke, 'The economy of *kudos*', in C. Dougherty and L. Kurke (eds), *Cultural Poetics in Archaic Greece* (Cambridge, 1993), 131–63.

On hero cults, J. Coldstream, 'Hero cults in the age of Homer', *JHS* 96 (1976), 8–17, argues for the influence of epic; A. M. Snodgrass, *Archaic Greece* (London, 1980), ch. 1, especially 37–40 and 74–5, argues that cults mark peasant claims to land; A. J. M. Whitley, 'Early states and hero cults: a reappraisal', *JHS* 108 (1988), 173–82, makes the case for the political importance of hero cult, especially at Argos; I. M. Morris, 'Tomb cult and the Greek renaissance: the past in the present in the eighth century BC', *Antiquity,* 62 (1988), 750–61, stresses the use of the past in struggles between an aristocratic élite and the emergent *polis*; and C. Antonaccio, 'The archaeology of ancestors', in C. Dougherty and L. Kurke (eds), *Cultural Poetics in Archaic Greece* (Cambridge, 1993), 46–70, and C. Antonaccio, *An Archaeology of Ancestors: Tomb Cult and Hero Cult in Early Greece* (Lanham, MD, 1995), distinguishes sharply between tomb and hero cult. The field is valuably reviewed by F. de Polignac, *Cults, Territory, and the Origins of the Greek City-State* (Chicago, IL, 1995), 128–49. My discussion has been influenced by D. Boehringer, *Heroenkulte in Griechenland von der geometrischen bis zur klassischen Zeit: Attika, Argolis, Messenien* (Berlin, 2001).

The world outside: for an overview of this whole topic see J. Boardman, *The Greeks Overseas* (3rd edition, London, 1980). For the Phoenicians in the west Mediterranean, see M. E. Aubet, *The Phoenicians and the West: Politics, Colonies and Trade* (Cambridge, 1993; 2nd edition, 2001). For relations between Greeks and Phoenicians generally see S. P. Morris, *Daidalos and the Origins of Greek Art* (Princeton, NJ, 1992), ch. 5. On Lyre Player Seals see J. Boardman, 'The Lyre Player group of seals: an encore', *AA* (1990), 1–17. On Al Mina see J. Boardman, 'Al Mina and history', *OJA* 9 (1990), 169–90, J. Boardman, 'The excavated history of Al Mina' in G. Tsetskhladze (ed.), *Ancient Greeks West and East* (Leiden, 1999), 135–61. Note also J. Y. Perreault, 'Les *emporia* grecs du Levant: mythe ou réalité?' in A. Bresson and P. Rouillard (eds), *L'Emporion* (Paris, 1993), 59–83, and J. Luke, 'The Nature of Greek Contacts with the Levant in the Geometric Period' (Cambridge Ph.D. diss., 1994).

On the invention of the alphabet and early Greek alphabets see L. H. Jeffery, *The Local Scripts of Archaic Greece*, revised with supplement by A. W. Johnston (Oxford, 1990). The earliest inscriptions are usefully collected in B. B. Powell, *Homer and the Origin of the Greek Alphabet* (Cambridge, 1991). On writing on pots see R. Osborne and A. Pappas, 'Writing on archaic Greek pottery', in Z. Newby and R. Leader-Newby (eds), *Art and Inscriptions in the Ancient World* (Cambridge, 2007), 131–55. On the Cretan 'poinikastas' see L. H. Jeffery and A. Morpurgo Davies, ΠΟΙΝΙΚΑΣΤΑΣ and ΠΟΙΝΙΚΑΖΕΙΝ: a new archaic inscription from Crete', *Kadmos* 9 (1970), 118–54. On literacy and its consequences see R. Thomas, *Literacy and Orality in Ancient Greece* (Cambridge, 1992), and M. Detienne (ed.), *Les savoirs de l'écriture: En Grèce ancienne* (Lille, 1988). These works argue strongly against the classic claim that literacy did make a difference, made by J. Goody and I. Watt in 'The consequences of literacy', in J. Goody (ed.), *Literacy in Traditional Societies* (Cambridge, 1968), 27–68. For discussion of the impact of adopting the alphabet from Greece in Etruria and Latium see *BR*, 103–5.

On trade in metals and oxhide ingots see N. H. Gale, 'Copper oxhide ingots: their origin and their place in Bronze Age metals trade in the Mediterranean', in N. H. Gale (ed.), *Bronze Age Trade in the Mediterranean* (Jonsered, 1991), 197–239, against, on the matter of the origin of the oxhide ingots on Sardinia, the important views of D. Ridgway, *The First Western Greeks* (Cambridge, 1992), 26–9, but see also 148. For a broad view of the development of exchange in the Mediterranean in this period see A. Sherratt and S. Sherratt, 'The growth of the Mediterranean economy in the early first millennium BC', *World Archaeology* 24 (1992–3), 361–78. I attempt a review of the archaic Greek economy in 700 BC in my 'Archaic Greece', in I. Morris, R. Saller, and W. Scheidel (eds), *Cambridge Economic History of Greece and Rome* (Cambridge, 2007), 279–86.

On Pithekoussai see D. Ridgway, *The First Western Greeks* (Cambridge, 1992), who discusses population at 101–3, Levantine presence at 111–18. For full publication see G. Buchner, *Pithekoussai* (Rome, 1993). Evidence for interactions between Pithekoussai and the Phoenician and Carthaginian worlds is reviewed by R. F. Docter and H. G. Niemeyer, 'Pithekoussai: the Carthaginian connection. On the archaeological evidence of Euboeo–Phoenician partnership in the 8th and 7th centuries BC', *Apoikia: Scritti in onore de Giorgio Buchner, AION* NS 1 (1994), 101–15. On 'Nestor's cup' see now O. Murray, 'Nestor's cup and the origins of the symposion', *Apoikia: Scritti in onore de Giorgio Buchner, AION* NS 1 (1994), 47–54. I argue for Pithekoussai's importance for the volume of eighth-century shipping in 'Pots, trade and the archaic Greek economy', *Antiquity* 70 (1996), 31–44. On ships see L. Casson, *Ships and Seamanship in the Ancient World* (Princeton, NJ, 1971); and on ships in epic see G. S. Kirk, *The Iliad: A Commentary*, vol. 1 (Cambridge, 1985), on *Iliad* 1.434 and 486–8. On mobility see N. Purcell, 'Mobility and the *polis*', in O. Murray and S. R. F. Price (eds), *The Greek City from Homer to Alexander* (Oxford, 1990), 29–58 and P. Horden and N. Purcell, *The Corrupting Sea: A Study of Mediterranean History* (Oxford, 2000), ch. 9. On Demaratos see *BR*, 124–5. On developments in Etruria and Latium see *BR*, ch. 4; S. Stoddart, 'Divergent trajectories in central Italy 1200–500 BC', in T. Champion (ed.), *Centre and Periphery: Comparative Studies in Archaeology* (London, 1989), 88–101; A. Bietti Sestieri, *The Iron Age Community of Osteria dell' Osa: A Study of Socio-Political Development in Central Tyrrhenian Italy* (Cambridge, 1992), and C.J. Smith, *Early Rome and Latium: Economy and Soceity c.1000–500 B.C.* (Oxford, 1995), chs 2–3. For the parallels between princely burials in Italy and the Eretrian West Gate burials see B. D'Agostino, 'Grecs et "indigènes" sur la côte Tyrrhénienne au VIIe siècle: la transmission des idéologies entres élites sociales', *Annales, Economies, Sociétés, Civilisations* 32 (1977), 3–20. On the interpretation of the Eretria burial see F. de Polignac, *Cults, Territory and the Origins of the Greek City-State* (Chicago, IL, 1995), 130–7.

On early settlement abroad more generally see A. J. Graham, 'Pre-colonial contacts: questions and problems', in J.-P. Descoeudres (ed.), *Greek Colonists and Native Populations* (Oxford, 1990), 45–60. The classic accounts of 'colonisation' are A. J. Graham, 'The colonial expansion of Greece', *Cambridge Ancient History* (2nd edition), vol. 3, part 3 (Cambridge, 1982), 83–162, and A. J. Graham, *Colony and Mother City in Ancient Greece* (2nd edition, Chicago, 1983). I make the case against 'colonisation' at greater length in 'Early Greek colonisation? The nature of Greek settlement in the West', in N. Fisher and H. van Wees (eds), *Archaic Greece: New Approaches and New Evidence* (London, 1998), 251–70. Compare also M. I. Finley, 'Colonies – an attempt at a typology', *Transactions of the Royal Historical Society* 26 (1976), 167–88. Since the focus of my criticism of 'colonisation' centres on the role of the supposed 'mother city' in deciding to found a settlement and determining its subsequent development, the criticisms of I. Malkin, 'Exploring the validity of the concept of "foundation": a visit to Megara Hyblaia', in V. Gorman and E. Robinson (eds), Oikistes: *Studies in Constitutions, Colonies, and Military Power in the Ancient World Offered in Honor of A. J. Graham* (Leiden, 2002), 195–225, are largely beside the point. For discussion of motives for 'colonisation' see A. Gwynn, 'The character of Greek colonisation', *JHS* 38 (1918), 88–123, and G. L. Cawkwell, 'Early colonisation', *Classical Quarterly* 42 (1992), 289–303. On the literary tradition about settlements abroad see C. Dougherty, 'It's murder to found a colony', in C. Dougherty and L. Kurke (eds), *Cultural Poetics in Archaic Greece* (Cambridge, 1993), 178–98. On the role of Delphi in the foundation of colonies see C. A. Morgan, *Athletes and Oracles: The Transformation of Olympia and Delphi in the Eighth Century* BC (Cambridge, 1990), ch. 5, and I. Malkin, *Religion and Colonisation in Ancient Greece* (Leiden, 1987), together with my discussions in Chapter 1 and the Epilogue. On burial practices in Sicily and their relationship to those of 'mother cities' see G. B. Shepherd, 'The pride of most colonials: burial and religion in the Sicilian colonies', in T. Fischer-Hansen, *Ancient Sicily*, Acta Hyperborea 6 (Copenhagen, 1995), 51–82, and *Death and Religion in Archaic Sicily* (Cambridge, 2010).

For geometric art in general a useful introduction is provided by S. Langdon (ed.), *From Pasture to Polis: Art in the Age of Homer* (Columbia, MO, 1993). I offer a more extensive account than here in *Archaic and Classical Greek Art* (Oxford, 1998), ch. 2. The fullest guide to geometric pottery is J. N. Coldstream, *Greek Geometric Pottery* (London, 1968), in which much relevant material is easily accessible. On the question of what the figure scenes represent see J. N. Coldstream, 'The geometric style: birth of the picture', in T. Rasmussen and N. Spivey (eds), *Looking at Greek Vases* (Cambridge, 1991), 37–56; A. M. Snodgrass, 'Towards an interpretation of the geometric figure scenes', *AM* 95 (1980), 51–8; J. Boardman, 'Symbol and story in geometric art', in W. G. Moon (ed.), *Ancient Greek Art and Iconography* (Madison, WI, 1983), 15–36; and A. M. Snodgrass, *An Archaeology of Greece* (Berkeley, CA, 1987), ch. 5, 'The first figure scenes in Greek art', 132–69. Scenes of the laying out of the corpse are collected by G. Ahlberg, *Prothesis and Ekphora in Greek Geometric Art* (Göteborg, 1971). On Attic gold bands see D. Ohly, *Griechische Goldbleche des 8 Jahrhunderts v. Chr* (Berlin, 1953).

The issue of the 'rise of the *polis*' was put on the agenda by V. Ehrenberg 'When did the polis rise?', *JHS* 57 (1937), 147–59. It has become bound up with the distinct, if related, question of the origin of the state; see I. Morris, 'The early polis as city and state', in J. Rich and A. Wallace-Hadrill (eds), *City and Country in the Ancient World* (London, 1991), 24–57. On *ethne* see C. Morgan, *Early Greek States beyond the Polis* (London, 2003). For the question of urbanization see my 'Urban sprawl: what is urbanization and why does it matter?', in R. Osborne and B. Cunliffe (eds), *Mediterranean Urbanization 800–600 BC* (Oxford, 2005), 1–16. On the city-state as a phenomenon see M. H. Hansen (ed.), *A Comparative Study of Thirty City-State Cultures* (Copenhagen, 2000). The work of the Copenhagen Polis Center is vitiated by its fixation with the term *polis*.

CHAPTER 5

On the development of Greek epic poetry see M. L. West, 'The rise of the Greek epic', *JHS* 108 (1988), 151–72, with his reply to critics in *JHS* 112 (1992), 173–5, and R. Janko, *The Iliad: A Commentary*, vol. 4. *Books 13–16* (Cambridge, 1992), 8–19. Hesiod's language is explored by G. P. Edwards, *The Language of Hesiod in its Traditional Context* (Oxford, 1971). The oral background to Homeric poetry was first probed in detail by Milman Parry, *The Making of Homeric Verse* (Oxford, 1971). The limits to what is involved in formulaic composition are well explored in the introduction to that volume by Adam Parry. A succinct account of the problems can be found in R. B. Rutherford's introduction to his commentary on *Homer Odyssey Books XIX and XX* (Cambridge, 1992), 47–57. See also J. Griffin, *Homer Iliad IX* (Oxford, 1995), introduction. On the differing language of different characters see J. Griffin, 'Words and speakers in Homer', *JHS* 106 (1986), 36–57, and R. Martin, *The Language of Heroes* (New York, 1989), with which one might usefully compare J. Burrows, *Computation into Criticism: A Study of Jane Austen's Novels and an Experiment in Method* (Oxford, 1987).

On the historical interest of the Homeric and Hesiodic poems in general see K. Raaflaub's useful synthetic article, 'Homer to Solon: the rise of the polis', in M. H. Hansen (ed.), *The Ancient Greek City-State* (Copenhagen, 1993), 41–105.

On the *Theogony*, M. L. West, *Hesiod Theogony Edited with Prolegomena and Commentary* (Oxford, 1966), is fundamental. Parallel near-eastern texts can be found in S. Dalley, *Myths from Mesopotamia* (Oxford, 1989), and in J. B. Pritchard (ed.), *Ancient Near Eastern Texts Relating to the Old Testament* (Princeton, NJ, 1969). Maximal claims about the indebtedness of Hesiod to the east are made in M. L. West, *The East Face of Helicon: West Asiatic Elements in Greek Poetry and Myth* (Oxford, 1997), ch. 6.

On the *Works and Days*, M. L. West, *Hesiod Works and Days Edited with Prolegomena and Commentary* (Oxford, 1978), is basic. The traditional side of Hesiod's poetry is stressed by G. Nagy, 'Hesiod', in T. J. Luce (ed.), *Ancient Writers* (New York, 1982), 43–72, against such biographical speculations as R. M. Cook, 'Hesiod's father', *JHS* 109 (1989), 170–1. The case for Hesiod's being a peasant world is most strongly argued by P. C. Millett, 'Hesiod and his world', *PCPS* 210 (1984), 84–115 (contrast V. D. Hanson, *The Other Greeks* (New York, 1995), 95–108). The most thorough study of Hesiod's society is A. Edwards, *Hesiod's Ascra* (Berkeley, CA, 2004). The 'myth of the generations' has been very much discussed: see particularly J.-P. Vernant, *Myth and Thought among the Greeks* (London, 1983), chs 1–2.

On the worlds of *Iliad* and *Odyssey*, a sea-change in modern scholarship was set in train by M. I. Finley, *The World of Odysseus* (London, 1954). For a traditional, object-centred approach, by no means completely outdated, see H. L. Lorimer, *Homer and the Monuments* (London, 1950). Reactions to Finley have taken two main forms: questioning his identification of the world portrayed in the poems as a Dark Age world, either by denying that it is a world of any single date or by claiming that it is a world of a different date; and questioning his claims that a simple and uncontested 'heroic' value system is embodied in the poems. For the former attack see A. M. Snodgrass, 'An historical Homeric society?', *JHS* 94 (1974), 114–25; A. G. Geddes, 'Who's who in Homeric society?', *Classical Quarterly* 34 (1984), 17–36; I. M. Morris, 'The use and abuse of Homer', *Classical Antiquity* 5 (1986), 81–138; and E. S. Sherratt, '"Reading the texts": archaeology and the Homeric question', *Antiquity* 64 (1990), 807–24. For the latter, O. Taplin, *Homeric Soundings* (Oxford, 1992), which also has an important discussion of the context of original performance. For a useful general review see J.-P. Crielaard, 'Homer, history and archaeology: some remarks on the date of the Homeric world', in J.-P. Crielaard (ed.), *Homeric Questions* (Amsterdam, 1995), 201–89. The best discussion of Homeric warfare is H. van Wees, 'The Homeric way of war', *Greece and Rome* 41 (1994), 1–18, 131–55, although he has not convinced me that the Homeric way of warfare is militarily plausible. See also H. van Wees, 'Leaders of men', *Classical Quarterly* 36 (1986), 285–303, and 'Kings in combat', *Classical Quarterly* 38 (1988), 1–24.

The nature of Homeric values has been subject to a separate debate, centred on whether competitive virtues are the only virtues recognised in the poems: see A. W. Adkins, *Merit and Responsibility* (Oxford, 1960), and A. A. Long, 'Morals and values in Homer', *JHS* 90 (1970), 121–39 (with reply by Adkins, *JHS* 91 (1971), 1–15). My discussion of speech and counsel follows M. Schofield, '*Euboulia* in the *Iliad*', *Classical Quarterly* 36 (1986), 6–31. Much discussion of Homeric politics has attempted to discover Homer's class sympathies. For a different and more productive approach see J. Haubold, *Homer's People: Epic Poetry and Social Formation* (Cambridge, 2000). The classic discussion of the importance of lack of agriculture and sacrifice among non-human communities in the *Odyssey* is P. Vidal-Naquet, 'Land and sacrifice in the *Odyssey*: a study of religious and mythical meanings', in R. L. Gordon (ed.), *Myth, Religion and Society* (Cambridge, 1981), and in P. Vidal-Naquet, *The Black Hunter* (Baltimore, MD, 1986).

On the context in which the *Iliad* and *Odyssey* came to be composed see Taplin, *Homeric Soundings*, ch. 1, and J. Griffin, *Homer Iliad 9* (Oxford, 1995), 4–8. On the handing down of the Homeric poems see R. Sealey, *Women and Law in Classical*

Greece (Chapel Hill, NC, 1990), 127–35; G. Nagy, *Pindar's Homer* (Baltimore, MD, 1990), 21–4; W. Burkert, 'The making of Homer in the sixth century BC: rhapsodes versus Stesichorus', in *Papers on the Amasis Painter and his World* (Malibu, CA, 1987), 43–62; and R. Janko, *The Iliad: A Commentary*, vol. 4. *Books 13–16* (Cambridge, 1992), 20–38. On the destruction of Thebes as a key event for dating the *Iliad*, see W. Burkert, 'Das hunderttorige Theben und die Datierung der *Ilias*', *Wiener Studien* 10 (1976), 5–21, and M. L. West, 'The Date of the Iliad', *Museum Helveticum* 52 (1995), 203–19. On the date of the Lelantine war see V. Parker, *Untersuchungen zum Lelantischen Krieg und verwandten Problemen der frühgriechischen Geschichte*, Historia Einzelschriften 109 (Stuttgart, 1997).

CHAPTER 6

I discuss the art of this period more generally in *Archaic and Classical Greek Art* (Oxford, 1998), chs 3–4. For the Chigi vase see P. Arias, B. Shefton, and M. Hirmer, *A History of Vase Painting* (London, 1962), plates IV, 16 and 17, and pp. 275–6. On the relief *pithoi* see M. E. Caskey, 'Notes on relief pithoi of the Tenian-Boiotian Group', *AJA* 80 (1976), 19–41, and N. Kontoleon, 'Die frühgriechische Reliefkunst', *Archaiologiki Ephemeris* (1969), 215–36. The phenomenon of orientalizing and the theoretical problems of the concept are explored over a wide range of material in C. Riva and N. Vella (eds), *Debating Orientalization: Multidisciplinary Approaches to Change in the Ancient Mediterranean* (London, 2006). For the material discussed here see S. P. Morris, *Daidalos and the Origins of Greek Art* (Princeton, 1992), and W. Burkert, *The Orientalising Revolution: Near Eastern Influence on Greek Culture in the Early Archaic Age* (Heidelberg, 1984; Eng. trans. Cambridge, MA, 1992), with R. Osborne, 'A la grecque', *Journal of Mediterranean Archaeology* 6/2 (1993), 231–7. I owe my knowledge of parallels between *Odyssey* and *Mahabharata* to conversation with Dr N. Allen. On orientalising in Corinthian pottery see T. Rasmussen, 'Corinth and the orientalising phenomenon', in T. Rasmussen and N. Spivey (eds), *Looking at Greek Vases* (Cambridge, 1991). On changing patterns of trade see A. and S. Sherratt, 'The growth of the Mediterranean economy in the early first millennium BC', *World Archaeology* 24 (1992–3), 361–78, and H. Matthäus, 'Bronzene Kandelaber mit Blattüberfall: Zeugnisse phönikischer Expansion im Mittelmeergebiet', in P. Aström (ed.), *Acta Cypria*, part 2 (Jonsered, 1992), 214–54.

On warfare all discussions must now engage with H. van Wees, *Greek Warfare: Myths and Realities* (London, 2004). A. M. Snodgrass, *Early Greek Armour and Weapons* (Edinburgh, 1964), remains fundamental, although his early date for the hoplite shield is not secure. On early cavalry see P. Greenhalgh, *Early Greek Warfare: Horsemen and Chariots in the Homeric and Archaic Ages* (Cambridge, 1973). On the visual evidence for hoplites see J. Salmon, 'Political hoplites?', *JHS* 97 (1987), 84–101; H. van Wees, 'The development of the hoplite phalanx', in H. van Wees (ed.), *War and Violence in Ancient Greece* (London, 2000), 125–66. My arguments here are closely parallel to those of V. D. Hanson, *The Other Greeks* (New York, 1995), 221–44.

Sparta: on the context in which Tyrtaios was performed see E. Bowie, '*Miles ludens:* the problem of martial exhortation in early Greek poetry', in O. Murray (ed.), *Sympotica* (Oxford, 1990). On the Messenians as a late construct see N. Luraghi, *The Ancient Messenians: Constructions of Ethnicity and Memory* (Cambridge, 2008), and J. Siapkas, *Heterological Ethnicity: Conceptualizing Identities in Ancient Greece* (Uppsala, 2003). On the problems of writing about early Sparta see C. G. Starr, 'On the credibility of early Spartan history', *Historia* 14 (1965), 257–72, and for the way in which later tradition distorts even our understanding of the structure of Spartan society S. Hodkinson, *Property and Wealth in Classical Sparta* (London, 2000). On all the material from the sanctuary of Orthia see R. M. Dawkins (ed.), *Artemis Orthia* (London, 1929); on the masks see J. B. Carter, 'Masks and poetry in early Sparta', in R. Hägg, N. Marinatos, and G. Nordquist (eds), *Early Greek Cult Practice* (Stockholm, 1988), 89–98, and M. H. Jameson, 'Perseus, the hero of Mycenae', in R. Hägg and G. Nordquist (eds), *Celebrations of Death and Divinity in the Bronze Age Argolid* (Stockholm, 1990), 213–23, who discusses and illustrates the rather different head-masks from Tiryns. On the institutions of archaic Sparta, see S. Hodkinson, 'The development of Spartan society in the Archaic period', in L. Mitchell and P. J. Rhodes (eds), *The Development of the Polis in Archaic Greece* (London, 1997). On Alkman and the choral activities of young women see C. Calame, *Choruses of Young Women in Ancient Greece* (London, 1997). On Sparta and hoplites see P. A. Cartledge, 'Hoplites and heroes: Sparta's contribution to the technique of ancient warfare', *JHS* 97 (1977), 11–27. On ivory at Sparta see J. B. Carter, *Greek Ivory Carving in the Orientalizing and Archaic Periods* (New York, 1985). For more general introductions to Sparta see W. G. Forrest, *A History of Sparta 950–192 BC* (London, 1968); M. I. Finley, 'Sparta' in M. I. Finley, *The Use and Abuse of History* (1975), reprinted in M. I. Finley, *Economy and Society of Ancient Greece*, ed. R. P. Saller and B. D. Shaw (London 1981); P. A. Cartledge, *Sparta and Lakonia: A Regional History* (London, 1979); and particularly for illustrations of the archaeological material, L. Fitzhardinge, *The Spartans* (London, 1981).

Law: the best introduction is M. Gagarin, *Writing Greek Law* (Cambridge, 2008). See also K.-J. Hölkeskamp, 'Written law in archaic Greece', *PCPS* 38 (1992), 87–117; M. Gagarin, *Early Greek Law* (New Haven, CT, 1986); and R. Sealey, *The Justice of the Greeks* (Ann Arbor, MI, 1994). Comparison with the Twelve Tables at Rome is revealing: see *BR*, ch. 11. For Cretan laws in particular see also J. Whitley, 'Literacy and law-making: the case of archaic Crete', in N. Fisher and H. van Wees (eds), *Archaic Greece: New Approaches and New Evidence* (London, 1998), 311–31.

On Theognis see T. Figueira and G. Nagy, *Theognis of Megara* (Baltimore, MD, 1985), and R. Lane Fox, 'Theognis: an alternative to democracy' and H. van Wees, 'Megara's Mafiosi: timocracy and violence in Theognis', in R. Brock and S. Hodkinson (eds), *Alternatives to Athens: Varieties of Political Organization and Community in Ancient Greece* (Oxford, 2000), 35–51 and 52–67; on Alkaios the standard work is D. L. Page, *Sappho and Alcaeus* (Oxford, 1955); illuminating on the politics of Alkaios' language is L. Kurke, 'Crisis and decorum in sixth-century Lesbos: reading Alkaios otherwise', *Quaderni Urbinati di Cultura Classica* 47 (1994), 67–92.

On tyranny, A. Andrewes, *The Greek Tyrants* (London, 1956), has long dominated the field. A bold argument against the use of the term 'tyrant' at all is offered by G. Anderson, 'Before *tyrannoi* were tyrants: rethinking a chapter of early Greek history', *Classical Antiquity* 24 (2005), 173–222. On traditions about tyranny see J.-P. Vernant, 'From Oidipous to Periander: lameness, tyranny, incest in legend and history', *Arethusa* 15 (1982), 19–38; J. F. McGlew, *Tyranny and Political Culture in Ancient Greece* (New York, 1993), ch. 2; and, on the Periander story, C. Sourvinou-Inwood, '"Myth" and history: on Herodotos 3.48 and 50–53', *Opuscula Atheniensia* 17 (1988), reprinted in her *'Reading' Greek Culture* (Oxford, 1991), 244–84. On traditions about tyrants as sages see R. P. Martin, 'The seven sages as performers of wisdom', in C. Dougherty and L. Kurke (eds), *Cultural Poetics in Archaic Greece* (Cambridge, 1993), 108–28. On the classical use of the metaphor of the 'tyrant city' see C. J. Tuplin, 'Imperial tyranny: some reflections on a classical Greek political metaphor', in P. A. Cartledge and F. D. Harvey (eds), *Crux: Essays Presented to G. E. M. de Ste Croix on his 75th Birthday* (Exeter and London, 1985), 348–75. For parallels between Greek tyrants and the rulers of Rome in the sixth century see *BR*, 145–6.

On Greeks and the Black Sea see G. Tsetskhladze, 'Greek penetration of the Black Sea', in G. Tsetskhladze and F. De Angelis (eds), *The Archaeology of Greek Colonisation* (Oxford, 1994), 111–35, who argues that the earliest Greek settlements there belong to the seventh century BC; and D. Braund, *Georgia in Antiquity: A History of Colchis and Transcaucasian Iberia 550 BC–AD 562* (Oxford, 1994), ch. 3.

On Thasos see A. J. Graham 'The foundation of Thasos', *ABSA* 73 (1978), 61–98, S. Owen, 'The "Thracian" landscape of archaic Thasos', in S. Owen and L. Preston (eds.), *Inside the City in the Greek World: Studies of Urbanism from the Bronze Age to the Hellenistic Period* (Oxford, 2009), and the further comments in Chapter 7 below; on Abdera, A. J. Graham, 'Abdera and Teos', *JHS* 112 (1992), 44–73. For settlement in South Italy see D. Yntema, 'Mental landscapes of colonization: the ancient written sources and the archaeology of early colonial Greek southeastern Italy', *Bulletin Antieke Beschaving* 75 (2000), 1–50, and see further in Chapter 7 below.

Settlement in Greece: on Kea see J. F. Cherry, J. L. Davis, and E. Mantzourani (eds), *Landscape Archaeology as Long-Term History* (Los Angeles, CA, 1991), chs 11 and 22, with T. Whitelaw, 'Colonisation and competition in the *Polis* of Koressos: the development of settlement in north-west Keos from the archaic to the late Roman periods', in L. Mendoni (ed.), *Papers from the Kea-Kythnos Conference* (forthcoming); on Melos, C. Renfrew and M. Wagstaff (eds), *An Island Polity: The Archaeology of Exploitation in Melos* (Cambridge, 1982), with R. W. V. Catling, *Classical Review* 34 (1984), 98–103; on the southern Argolid see M. H. Jameson, C. N. Runnels, and Tj. van Andel, *A Greek Countryside* (Stanford, CA, 1994), fig. 4.21 and pp. 372–81; on Attica, R. Osborne, 'A crisis in archaeological history? The seventh century in Attica', *ABSA* 84 (1989), 297–322, and R. Osborne, 'Archaeology, the Salaminioi, and the politics of sacred space in archaic Attica', in S. Alcock and R. Osborne (eds), *Placing the Gods: Sanctuaries and Sacred Space in Ancient Greece* (Oxford, 1994), 143–60.

On Delphi, C. A. Morgan, *Athletes and Oracles* (Cambridge, 1990), chs 4 and 5, is fundamental. On the remains at Delphi see M. Maass, *Das antike Delphi* (1993), but for early occupation see also *BCH* 117 (1993), 626–31. On the oracles see also R. Parker, 'Greek states and Greek oracles', in P. A. Cartledge and F. D. Harvey (eds), *Crux: Essays Presented to G. E. M. de Ste Croix on his 75th Birthday* (Exeter and London, 1985), 298–326, and S. Price, 'Delphi and divination', in P. E. Easterling and J. V. Muir (eds), *Greek Religion and Society* (Cambridge, 1985), 128–54. The line taken here owes much to J. Fontenrose, *The Delphic Oracle* (Berkeley and Los Angeles, CA, 1978), a much-misrepresented work with an extremely useful collection of material. For a more credulous line see, for example, I. Malkin, *Religion and Colonisation in Ancient Greece* (Leiden, 1987), ch. 1.

On Daedalic sculpture the classic treatment was R. Jenkins, *Dedalica* (London, 1936). See also S. P. Morris, *Daidalos and the Origins of Greek Art* (Princeton, NJ, 1992), ch. 9, and J. Hurwit, *The Art and Culture of Early Greece* (Ithaca, NY, 1985), 179–202.

On *kouroi* and *korai* the basic collections of evidence are G. M. A. Richter, *Kouroi* (3rd edition, London, 1970), and G. M. A. Richter, *Korai* (London, 1968), but see also K. Karakasi, *Archaic Korai* (Los Angeles, CA, 2003). On Egyptian influence E. Guralnick's claims in 'Proportions of kouroi', *AJA* 82 (1978), 461–72, do not stand up to statistical scrutiny. On the Ptoion sanctuary see J. Ducat, *Les kouroi du Ptoion: Le sanctuaire d'Apollon Ptoieus à l'époque archaïque* (Paris, 1971). For calculation of the numbers of *kouroi* and a discussion of the implications for the scale of shipping, see A. M. Snodgrass, 'Heavy freight in archaic Greece', in P. Garnsey, K. Hopkins, and C. R. Whittaker (eds), *Trade in the Ancient Economy* (London, 1983), 16–26.

On the development of Greek temples see J. J. Coulton, *Greek Architects at Work* (London, 1977), ch. 2, and B.Barletta, *The Origins of the Greek Architectural Orders* (Cambridge, 2001). Note also the rather different approach of M. Wilson Jones 'Tripods, triglyphs and the origin of the Doric frieze', *American Journal of Archaeology* 106 (2002), 353–90. On the development of temple roofs see N. Winter, *Greek Architectural Terracottas from the Prehistoric through to the Archaic Period* (Oxford, 1993).

CHAPTER 7

On the early chapters of the *Constitution of the Athenians* see P. J. Rhodes, *A Commentary on the Aristotelian 'Athenaion Politeia'* (Oxford, 1981), 65–79. On Kylon, ibid. 79–84, and S. Hornblower, *A Commentary on Thucydides*, vol. 1 (Oxford, 1991), 202–10. An excellent general picture of Athens at this time is provided by R. Seaford, *Reciprocity and Ritual* (Oxford, 1994), 92–102, 106–9. For a collection of studies of Solon see J. Blok and A. Lardinois (eds), *Solon of Athens: New Historical and Philological Approaches* (Leiden, 2006); on Solon's self-presentation in his poetry see E. Irwin, *Solon and Early Greek Poetry: The Politics of Exhortation* (Cambridge, 2005). On Solon in the fourth century BC see R. Thomas, 'Law and lawgiver in the Athenian democracy', in R. Osborne and S. Hornblower (eds), *Ritual, Finance, Politics: Athenian Democratic Accounts Presented to David Lewis* (Oxford, 1994), 119–34, and E. Ruschenbusch, '*Patrios Politeia:* Theseus, Drakon, Solon und Kleisthenes in Publizistik und Geschichtsschreibung des 5. und 4. Jahrhunderts v. Chr.', *Historia* 7 (1958), 398–424. On the monuments on which Solon's laws were inscribed see P. J. Rhodes, *A Commentary on the Aristotelian 'Athenaion Politeia'* (Oxford, 1981), 131–5. Rhodes also provides the best introduction to Solon's legislation and to the 'crisis' which he faced. The testimonia to and quotations from Solon's laws are collected by E. Ruschenbusch, *ΣΟΛΩΝΟΣ ΝΟΜΟΙ: Die fragmente des Solonischen Gesetzeswerkes mit einer Text- und Uberlieferungsgeschichte*, Historia Einzelschriften 9 (Wiesbaden, 1966). On issues arising from the nature of Solon's law see R. Osborne, 'Law in action in classical Athens', *JHS* 105 (1985), 40–58.

The best treatment of the inappropriateness of 'aristocracy' as a term is A. Duplouy, *Le prestige des elites: Rechereches sur les modes de reconnaissance sociale in Grèce entre les Xe et Ve siècles avant J.-C.* (Paris, 2006). Against the fantasies of 'middling' and 'aristocratic' ideology see E. Kistler, 'Kampf der Mentalitäten: Ian Morris' "Elitist" versus "Middling-Ideology"?', in R. Rollinger and C. Ulf (eds), *Griechische Archaik: Interne Entwicklungen, Externe Impulse* (Berlin, 2004), 145–75; D. Hammer, 'Ideology, the symposium, and archaic politics', *American Journal of Philology* 125 (2004), 479–512. On Solon's 'classes' see L Foxhall, 'A view from the top: evaluating the Solonian property classes', in L. Mitchell and P. J. Rhodes (eds), *The Development of the* Polis *in Archaic Greece* (London, 1997), 113–36; and H. van Wees, 'Mass and elite in Solon's Athens: the property classes revisited', in Blok and Lardinois, *Solon,* 351–89. On the possibly Solonian date for the Genesia see F. Jacoby, Γενεσια: a forgotten festival of the dead', *Classical Quarterly* 38 (1944), 65–75. On SOS amphorae see A. W. Johnston and R. E. Jones, 'The SOS Amphora', *ABSA* 73 (1978), 103–42. On pottery as evidence for patterns of trade see R. Osborne, 'Pots and trade in archaic Greece', *Antiquity* 70 (1996), 31–44.

On women in archaic Greece see E. Fantham *et al.*, *Women in the Classical World* (Oxford, 1994), ch. 1. On Semonides (and Hesiod), see N. Loraux, 'On the race of women and some of its tribes', in her *Children of Athena* (1984; American. trans. Princeton, NJ, 1993), R. Osborne, 'The use of abuse', *Proceedings of the Cambridge Philological Society* 47 (2001), 47–64, T. Morgan, 'The wisdom of Semonides frg. 7', *Proceedings of the Cambridge Philological Society* 51 (2005), 72–85. On the *Homeric Hymn to Demeter* see H. P. Foley, *The Homeric Hymn to Demeter* (Princeton, NJ, 1994); N. J. Richardson, *The Homeric Hymn to Demeter* (Oxford, 1974); and R. C. T. Parker, 'The *Hymn to Demeter* and the Homeric Hymns', *Greece and Rome* 38 (1991), 1–17. On Sappho see M. Williamson, *Sappho's Immortal Daughters* (Cambridge, MA, 1996), and E. Greene, *Reading Sappho: Contemporary Approaches* (Berkeley, CA, 1996). On early Attic black-figure pottery see my *Archaic and Classical Greek Art* (Oxford, 1998), 87–95.

On the nature of archaic Greek cities see F. de Polignac, 'Forms and processes: some thoughts on the meaning of urbanization in early archaic Greece', in R. Osborne and B. Cunliffe (eds), *Mediterranean Urbanization 800–600 B.C.* (Oxford, 2005), 45–70. On Thasos see above on Chapter 6 and Y. Grandjean, *Recherches sur l'habitat Thasien à l'époque grecque*, Etudes Thasiennes 12 (Paris, 1988), esp. 463–89. On Metapontion see J. C. Carter, *Discovering the Greek Countryside at Metaponto* (Ann Arbor, MI, 2006).

On Megara Hyblaea see G. Vallet, F. Villard, and P. Auberson, *Mégara Hyblaea*, vol. 1. *Le quartier de l'agora archaïque* (Rome, 1976); G. Vallet and F. Villard, *Mégara Hyblaea*, vol. 2. *La céramique archaïque* (Rome, 1964); G. Vallet, F. Villard, and P. Auberson, *Mégara Hyblaea*, vol. 3. *Guide des fouilles* (Rome, 1983); F. De Angelis, *Megara Hyblaia and Selinous: The Development of Two Greek City-States in Archaic Sicily* (Oxford, 2003); and the papers by Villard, Tréziny, and de Polignac in *La Colonisation grecque en Méditerranée occidentale* (Paris, 1999). The ceramic art of Megara Hyblaia is well situated in relationship to what was being done elsewhere in Greece by P. Devambez and F. Villard, 'Un vase orientalisant polychrome au Musée du Louvre', *Fondation Piot: Monuments et Mémoires* 62 (1979), 13–41.

CHAPTER 8

On the festival circuit see C. A. Morgan, *Athletes and Oracles* (Cambridge, 1990); on the Panathenaia see J. Neils (ed.), *Goddess and Polis* (Hanover, NH, 1992); on political unrest in Panathenaic years see T. J. Figueira, 'The ten *Archontes* of 579/8 at Athens', *Hesperia* 53 (1984), 447–73 at 466–9; on Peisistratos, and on the more general issue, see W. R. Connor, 'Tribes, festivals and processions; civic ceremonial and political manipulation in archaic Greece', *JHS* 107 (1987), 40–50. For the notion of symbolic capital see P. Bourdieu, *Outline of a Theory of Practice* (Cambridge, 1977), ch. 4 and especially 171–83. For further use of that idea in a similar context see R. Osborne, 'Looking on – Greek style: does the sculpted woman girl speak to women too?' in I. Morris (ed.), *Classical Greece: Ancient Histories and Modern Ideologies* (Cambridge, 1994), 81–96 especially 88–95.

On the Homeric hymns see J. S. Clay, *The Politics of Olympus: Form and meaning in the Major Homeric Hymns* (Princeton, NJ, 1989); on the Hesiodic *Catalogue of Women* see M. L. West, *The Hesiodic Catalogue of Women* (Oxford, 1985); R. L. Fowler, 'Genealogical thinking, Hesiod's *Catalogue*, and the creation of the Hellenes', *Proceedings of the Cambridge Philological Society* 44 (1998), 1–19; and R. Hunter (ed.), *The Hesiodic Catalogue of Women: Constructions and Reconstructions* (Cambridge, 2003).

On Athenian pottery and the Etruscan market see my 'Why did Athenian pots appeal to the Etruscans?', *World Archaeology* 33/2 (2001), 277–95, and C. Reusser, *Vasen für Etrurien: Verbreitung und Funktionen attischer Keramik im Etrurien des 6. und 5. Jahrhunderts vor Christus* (Zurich, 2002). On regional pottery styles see F. Blondé and J. Y. Perreault (ed.), *Les ateliers de potiers dans le monde grec aux époques géométrique, archaïque et classique, BCH* Supplément 23 (1992).

On coinage the best introduction is C. J. Howgego, *Ancient History from Coins* (London, 1995); the coins themselves are best accessed through C. M. Kraay, *Archaic and Classical Greek Coins* (London, 1976); for Lydian coinage see G. le Rider, *La naissance de la monnaie: Pratiques monétaires de l'Orient ancien* (Paris, 2001). For the origins and effects of coinage see D. Schaps, *The Invention of Coinage and the Monetization of Ancient Greece* (Ann Arbor, MI, 2004), and the bold speculations of R. Seaford, *Money and the Early Greek Mind: Homer, Philosophy, Tragedy* (Cambridge,

2003). For other forms of money than merely coinage see S. von Reden, 'Coinage, law and ritual: money and the Greek Polis', *JHS* 117 (1997), 154–76. For the 'mercenary hypothesis' see R. M. Cook, 'Speculations on the origin of coinage', *Historia 7* (1958), 257–62. On the availability of small change see H. Kim, 'Archaic coinage as evidence for the use of money', in A. Meadows and K. Shipton (ed.), *Money and its Uses in the Ancient Greek World* (Oxford, 2001), 7–22. I attempt to describe the economy of archaic Greece *c.*500 BC in my 'Archaic Greece', in I. Morris, R. Saller, and W. Scheidel (eds), *Cambridge Economic History of Greece and Rome* (Cambridge, 2007), 286–95.

On architectural sculpture see J. Boardman, *Greek Sculpture: The Archaic Period* (London, 1978), ch. 7; A. Stewart, *Greek Sculpture: An Exploration* (New Haven, CT, 1990), 113–16, 128–30, and my 'Archaic and classical Greek temple sculpture and the viewer', in B. A. Sparkes and K. Rutter (eds), *Word and Image in Ancient Greece* (Edinburgh, 2000), 228–46. On the Siphnian treasury and its frieze see R. Neer, 'Framing the gift: the politics of the Siphnian Treasury at Delphi', *Classical Antiquity* 20 (2001), 273–336.

The standard handbook on Greek architecture remains W. B. Dinsmoor, *The Architecture of Ancient Greece* (3rd edition, London, 1950). The best introduction is J. J. Coulton, *Greek Architects at Work* (London, 1977). Data are conveniently gathered in R. Schmitt, *Handbuch zu den Tempeln der Griechen* (Frankfurt, 1992). On the development of Doric architecture in the archaic period see F. E. Winter, 'Tradition and innovation in Doric design' I and II', *AJA* 80 (1976), 139–45; 82 (1978), 151–61. On the temples at Selinous see F. de Polignac, *Cults, Territory, and the Origins of the Greek City-State* (Chicago, IL, 1995), 111–13; on Selinous generally see F. de Angelis, *Megara Hyblaia and Selinous: The Development of Two Greek City-States in Archaic Sicily* (Oxford, 2003). On the distinct use of Doric architecture in the Cyclades see M. Schuller, 'Die dorische Architektur der Kykladen in spätarchaischer Zeit', *JDAI* 100 (1985), 319–98.

On the Alkmaionid monument at the Ptoion sanctuary see A. Schachter, 'The politics of dedication: two Athenian dedications at the Sanctuary of Apollo Ptoieus in Boeotia', in R. Osborne and S. Hornblower (eds), *Ritual, Finance, Politics* (Oxford, 1994), 291–306.

The history of Samos is readily accessible in G. Shipley, *A History of Samos 800–188 BC* (Oxford, 1987). On Eupalinos' tunnel see T. E. Rihll and J. V. Tucker, 'Greek engineering: the case of Eupalinos' tunnel', in A. Powell (ed.), *The Greek World* (London, 1995), 403–31, and H. J. Kienast, *Der Wasserleitung des Eupalinos auf Samos* (Bonn, 1995). For Iskhes' *kouros* see H. Kyrieleis, *Der Grosse Kuros von Samos* (Bonn, 1996). For Hazael's bronze see W. Burkert, *The Orientalizing Revolution* (Cambridge, MA, 1992), 12 n. 15, 16 with n. 14, and fig. 2; and S. P. Morris, *Daidalos* (Princeton, NJ, 1992), 133–4, 147, and fig. 25. On Samos and Sparta see P. A. Cartledge, 'Sparta and Samos: a special relationship?', *Classical Quarterly* 32 (1982), 243–65.

On guest-friendship see G. Herman, *Ritualised Friendship and the Greek City* (Cambridge, 1987).

On Peisistratos see B. Lavelle, *Fame, Money and Power: The Rise of Peisistratos and 'Democratic' Tyranny at Athens* (Ann Arbor, MI, 2005). On the Peisistratids see D.

M. Lewis, 'The tyranny of the Peisistratidae', *Cambridge Ancient History*, vol. 4 (2nd edition, Cambridge, 1988), 287–302.

On ethnic identity and the manipulation of stories of descent see J. M. Hall, *Ethnic Identity in Greek Antiquity* (Cambridge, 1997). The Argive monument to the Seven against Thebes was published by A. Pariente, 'Le monument argien des "Sept contre Thèbes"', in M. Piérart (ed.), *Polydipsion Argos* (Paris, 1992), 195–229. On the *ethnos* see above on Chapter 4, C. A. Morgan, 'Ethnicity and Early Greek States: Historical and Material Perspectives', *PCPS* 37 (1991), 131–63, and J. McInerney, *The Folds of Parnassos: Land and Ethnicity in Ancient Phokis* (Austin, TX, 1999).

On Spartan foreign policy in the sixth century see for differing views W. G. Forrest, *A History of Sparta* (London, 1968), 85–95, and G. L. Cawkwell, 'Sparta and her allies in the sixth century BC', *Classical Quarterly* 43 (1993), 364–76. There is much of relevance to the Peloponnesian League in G. E. M. de Ste Croix's *The Origins of the Peloponnesian War* (London, 1972). Aristotle's reading of the terms of the treaty with Tegea has been defended by T. F. R. G. Braun, 'Khrestous poiein', *Classical Quarterly* NS 44 (1994), 40–5, against the reinterpretation of F. Jacoby 'Khrestous poiein', *Classical Quarterly* 38 (1944), 15–16. On Spartans at Halieis see M. H. Jameson, C. N. Runnels, and Tj. van Andel, *A Greek Countryside: The Southern Argolid from Prehistory to the Present* (Stanford, CA, 1994), 70–1.

On the politics of heroes' bones see D. Boedeker, 'Hero cult and politics in Herodotus: the bones of Orestes', in C. Dougherty and L. Kurke (eds), *Cultural Poetics in Archaic Greece* (Cambridge, 1993), 164–77; and R. Buxton, *Imaginary Greece* (Cambridge, 1994), ch. 10, which valuably puts the incident into a wider context. On the cult of Agamemnon and Menelaos at Sparta see Pausanias 3.19. For the archaeological finds at the Menelaion see H. W. Catling, 'Excavations at the Menelaion Sparta 1973–6', *Archaeological Reports* 23 (1976–7), 24–42. For the archaeological finds at the shrine of Agamemnon and Kassandra at Amyklai see *Praktika tis Archaiologikis Etaireias* (1956), 211–12; (1960), 228–31; (1961), 177–8.

CHAPTER 9

On the circumstances of the Kleisthenic reforms see J. Ober, 'The Athenian revolution of 508/7: violence, authority and the origins of democracy', in C. Dougherty and L. Kurke (eds), *Cultural Poetics in Archaic Greece* (Cambridge, 1993), 215–32, and P. B. Manville, *The Origins of Citizenship in Ancient Athens* (Princeton, NJ, 1990), 172–209. On how Kleisthenes managed his reforms in institutional terms see A. Andrewes, 'Kleisthenes' reform bill', *Classical Quarterly* 27 (1977), 241–8. On the question of whether the reforms created democracy see my 'When was the Athenian democratic revolution', in S. Goldhill and R. Osborne (eds), *Rethinking Revolutions through Ancient Greece* (Cambridge, 2006), 10–28. On the question of the possible military background to the reforms see H. van Effenterre, 'Clisthène et les mesures de mobilisation', *Revue des Études Grecques* 89 (1976), 1–17, and P. Siewert, *Die Trittyen Attikas und die Heeresreform des Kleisthenes* (Munich, 1982), with D. M. Lewis, *Gnomon* 55 (1983), 431–6. The contemporary reforms of Servius Tullius at Rome provide a fascinating parallel: *BR*, ch. 7, esp. 194–5. For the victory over the Boiotians and Khalkidians and the monument erected on the Acropolis see Herodotos 5.77, Pausanias 1.28.2, and ML 15/Fornara 42. On the Council of 500 see P. J. Rhodes, *The Athenian Boule* (Oxford, 1972; revised edition, 1985). On the deme system as a whole see J. S. Traill, *The Political Organisation of Attica* (Princeton, NJ, 1975) and, with care, J. S. Traill, *Demos and Trittys* (Toronto, 1986). On demes see R. Osborne, *Demos: The Discovery of Classical Attika* (Cambridge, 1985), and D. Whitehead, *The Demes of Attica* (Princeton, NJ, 1986). On the religious life of the deme see R. Parker, 'Festivals of the Attic demes', *Boreas* 15 (1987), 137–47. On the tribal heroes and their religious implications see E. Kearns, 'Change and continuity in religious structures after Cleisthenes', in P. A. Cartledge and F. D. Harvey (eds), *Crux: Essays Presented to G. E. M. de Ste Croix on his 75th Birthday* (Exeter and London, 1985), 189–207, and E. Kearns, *The Heroes of Attica* (London, 1989). The case for Kleisthenic manipulation of tribes, trittyes, and demes was first made in detail by D. M. Lewis, 'Cleisthenes and Attica', *Historia* 12 (1963), 22–40; see also G. R. Stanton, 'The tribal reform of Kleisthenes the Alkmeonid', *Chiron* 14 (1984), 1–41. On the phratry see S. D. Lambert, *The Phratries of Attica* (Ann Arbor, MI, 1993). On possible archaeological evidence for post-Kleisthenic deme creation see H. Lohmann, *Atene: Forschungen zu Siedlungs- und Wirtschaftsstruktur des klassischen Attika* (Cologne, 1993), with R. Osborne, *Gnomon* 69 (1997), 243–7.

For the bouleutic oath see P. J. Rhodes, *The Athenian Boule* (Oxford, 1972; revised edition 1985), 194–9, and P. J. Rhodes, *A Commentary on the Aristotelian 'Athenaion Politeia'* (Oxford, 1981), 263–4. The most recent treatment of the statute of limitations is F. X. Ryan, 'The original date of the δῆμος πληθύων provisions of *IG* i³ 105', *JHS* 114 (1994), 120–34, who suggests that it is Solonian.

On the powers of kings and magistrates at Sparta see D. M. Lewis, *Sparta and Persia* (Leiden, 1977), ch. 2, and P. Carlier, 'La vie politique à Sparte sous le règne de Cléomène 1er: essai d'interprétation', *Ktema* 2 (1977), 65–84.

Participation is one of the keystones of Athenian democratic ideology presented in funeral orations: see Thucydides 2.35–46 at 37 (the speech in the mouth of Perikles in 431), and N. Loraux, *The Invention of Athens* (Paris, 1981; Eng. trans. Cambridge, MA, 1986). On the symmetry between central and local government see R. Osborne, 'The Demos and its divisions', in O. Murray and S. R. F. Price, *The Greek City from Homer to Alexander* (Oxford, 1989), 265–93. For the resolution of the competing claims of mass and élite in classical Athens see J. Ober, *Mass and Élite in Classical Athens: Rhetoric, Ideology and the Power of the People* (Princeton, NJ, 1989). On competitive festivals at Athens see R. Osborne, 'Competitive festivals and the polis: a context for dramatic festivals at Athens', in A. H. Sommerstein, S. Halliwell, J. Henderson, and B. Zimmermann (eds), *Tragedy, Comedy and the Polis* (Bari, 1993), 21–38. On the cult of Pan see Ph. Borgeaud, *The Cult of Pan in Ancient Greece* (Rome, 1979; Eng. trans. Chicago, IL, 1988), ch. 7. On hero athletes see L. Kurke, 'The economy of *kudos*', in C. Dougherty and L. Kurke (eds), *Cultural Poetics in Archaic Greece: Cult, Performance, Politics* (Cambridge, 1993), 131–63. On the possibility that tragic competition at the Dionysia was a democratic innovation see W. R. Connor, 'City Dionysia and Athenian democracy', in J. R. Fears (ed.),

Aspects of Athenian Democracy (Copenhagen, 1990), 7–32, and M. L. West, 'The early chronology of Attic tragedy', *Classical Quarterly* 39 (1989), 251–4.

On the art and archaeology of Athens 520–480 see M. Robertson, *The Art of Vase-Painting in Classical Athens* (Cambridge, 1992); A. Stewart, *Greek Sculpture: An Exploration* (New Haven, CT, 1990), chs 10–11; G. M. A. Richter, *The Archaic Gravestones of Attica* (London, 1961), and my *Archaic and Classical Greek Art* (Oxford, 1998), ch. 8. I have explored some of the implications of the end of the use of *korai* as dedications in R. Osborne, 'Looking on – Greek style', in I. Morris (ed.), *Classical Greece: Ancient Histories and Modern Ideologies* (Cambridge, 1994), 81–96.

On philosophical aspects of Kleisthenes see P. Lévêque and P. Vidal-Naquet, *Clisthène l'Athénien: Essai sur la représentation de l'espace et du temps dans la pensée politique grecque, de la fin du VIè siècle à la mort de Platon* (Paris, 1964; Eng. trans., 1996). On number in Greek thought see G. E. R. Lloyd, *The Revolutions of Wisdom: Studies in the Claims and Practice of Ancient Greek Science* (Berkeley, CA, 1987), ch. 5 (and pp. 74–5 on mathematical proof). The classic case for the political background being crucial to the emergence of Greek philosophy is made by G. E. R. Lloyd, *Magic, Reason and Experience* (Cambridge, 1979), ch. 4. See also G. E. R. Lloyd, *Demystifying Mentalities* (Cambridge, 1990). Ancient texts on early Greek philosophy are most conveniently available in J. Barnes (ed.), *Early Greek Philosophy* (Harmondsworth, 1989).

On Persia and the Greeks' relations with the Persians see *The Cambridge Ancient History* (2nd edition), vol. 4 (Cambridge, 1988), chs 1–3 and 8–11; and A. R. Burn, *Persia and the Greeks* (1962; revised edition, London, 1988). On the nature of Persian rule see D. M. Lewis, *Sparta and Persia* (Leiden, 1977), ch. 1; P. Briant, *From Cyrus to Alexander: A History of the Persian Empire* (1996; American trans. Winona Lake 2002). On ongoing relations between Greeks and Persians see M. Miller, *Athens and Persia in the Fifth Century B.C.* (Cambridge, 1997). On fifth-century barbarisation of Persia see E. Hall, *Inventing the Barbarian* (Oxford, 1989). On Teos and Abdera see A. J. Graham, '"Adopted Teans"' *JHS* 111 (1991), 176–8, and 'Abdera and Teos', *JHS* 112 (1992), 44–73. On Simonides' Plataia elegy see D. Boedeker and D. Sider (eds), *The New Simonides: Contexts of Praise and Desire* (Oxford, 2001).

On Athens and Aigina see A. Podlecki, 'Athens and Aigina', *Historia* 25 (1976), 396–413. On the politics of the Aiginetan victory odes see S. Hornblower, *Thucydides and Pindar: Historical Narrative and the World of Epinikian Poetry* (Oxford, 2004), 207–354. On the Peiraieus see R. Garland, *The Piraeus from the Fifth to the First Century B.C.* (2nd edition, Bristol, 2001). On the economic aspects of ancient warfare see V. D. Hanson, *Warfare and Agriculture in Classical Greece* (2nd edition, Berkeley, CA, 1998). On all aspects of the trireme see J. Morrison, J. Coates, and B. Rankov, *The Athenian Trireme: The History and Reconstruction of an Ancient Greek Warship* (Cambridge, 2000). On financial aspects see V. Gabrielsen, *Financing the Athenian Fleet: Taxation and Social Relations* (Baltimore, MD, 1994).

For military accounts of the Persian wars see, in addition to the items cited above, J. F. Lazenby, *The Defence of Greece 490–479 BC* (Warminster, 1993), G. L. Cawkwell, *The Greek Wars: The Failure of Persia* (Oxford, 2005), and C. Hignett, *Xerxes' Invasion of Greece* (Oxford, 1963). N. Whatley's classic piece on battle-reconstruction, written in 1920, deserves still be read rather than simply cited: 'On the possibility of reconstructing Marathon and other ancient battles', *JHS* 84 (1964), 119–39. On the politics of Greek resistance see P. A. Brunt, 'The Hellenic League against Persia', *Historia* 2 (1953–4), 135–63, reprinted in P. A. Brunt, *Studies in Greek History and Thought* (Oxford, 1993). On the construction of tradition about the Persian wars see R. Thomas, *Oral Tradition and Written Record in Classical Athens* (Cambridge, 1989), 221–7; N. Loraux, *The Invention of Athens* (Cambridge, MA, 1986); and E. Bridges, E. Hall, and P. J. Rhodes (eds), *Cultural Responses to the Persian Wars* (Oxford, 2007).

On Athenian politics of the 490s and 480s there is much that is stimulating, though much that has no basis in ancient evidence, in B. M. Lavelle, *The Sorrow and the Pity: A Prolegomenon to a History of Athens under the Peisistratids, c.560–510 BC*, Historia Einzelschriften 80 (Stuttgart, 1993). See also A. J. Holladay, 'Medism at Athens 508–480 BC', *Greece and Rome* 25 (1978), 174–91. On ostracism see ML 21, Fornara 41, P. J. Rhodes, *A Commentary on the Aristotelian 'Athenaion Politeia'* (Oxford, 1981), 267–83; S. Forsdyke, *Exile, Ostracism and Democracy: The Politics of Expulsion in Ancient Greece* (Princeton, NJ, 2005); P. Siewert with S. Brenne, *Ostrakismos-Testimonien I: Die Zeugnisse antiker Autoren, der Inschriften und Ostraka über das athenische Scherbengericht aus vorhellenistischer Zeit (487–322 v.Chr.)*, Historia Einzelschriften 155 (Stuttgart, 2002); and S. Brenne, '"Porträts" auf Ostraka', *AM* 107 (1992), 161–85.

On events in Sicily see T. J. Dunbabin, *The Western Greeks: The History of Sicily and South Italy from the Foundation of the Greek Colonies to 480 BC* (Oxford, 1948), chs 13 and 14; D. Asheri, 'Carthaginians and Greeks', *Cambridge Ancient History* (2nd edition), vol. 4 (Cambridge, 1988), 739–80. On the Delphic Charioteer see J. J. Pollitt, *Art and Experience in Classical Greece* (Cambridge, 1972), 45–48; on the Motya statue see R. R. R. Smith, 'Pindar, athletes, and the early Greek statue habit', in S. Hornblower and C. Morgan (eds), *Pindar's Poetry, Patrons and Festivals* (Oxford, 2007), 83–139.

EPILOGUE

On the changing nature of Greek history see M. Detienne, *The Creation of Mythology* (Paris, 1981; Eng. trans. Chicago, IL, 1986), ch. 3. I make further observations on this theme in 'The polis and its culture', in C. C. W. Taylor (ed.), *Routledge History of Philosophy*, vol. 1 (London, 1997), ch. 1. On Thucydides and religion see S. Hornblower, 'The religious dimension to the Peloponnesian War, or what Thucydides does not tell us', *Harvard Studies in Classical Philology* 94 (1992), 169–97. Specifically on oracles see N. Marinatos, 'Thucydides and Oracles', *JHS* 101 (1981), 138–40.

On the Delphic oracle see above pp. 190–5 and, taking issue with my argument here, H. Bowden, *Classical Athens and the Delphic Oracle: Divination and Democracy* (Cambridge, 2005), esp. 154–7, with a convenient list of Athenian consultations at 168–9.

George Orwell's *Nineteen Eighty-Four* was first published in 1949. I cite it from the edition published by Penguin Books (1954 and reprints).

INDEX

361

Tenos 156, 188, 323

terraces 22–3

textiles, role in trade 106

Thales of Miletos 298

Thapsos cups 191

Thasos 120, 186, 220–4, 229, 274

Theagenes of Megara 203

theatre, 129; at Athens 293–4; in Attica 282

Thebes 20, 308; and Peisistratos 268; and Persia 322–5; and Plataia 271, 277; and Sikyon 267; and Sparta 324–5. *See also* Boiotia

Thebes, Egyptian 152, 199

Themistokles 310, 316; decree of 334; ostracism of 322; and Persian wars 322; and 'wooden walls' oracle 333

Theodoros Metokhites, on Samos 258

Theognis of Megara 178–81, 185; and Solon 204

Theogony 3, 47, 131, 133–7, 148, 248, 298; on birth of Athene 157; and *Catalogue of Women* 233–4; on Herakles 232; and near-eastern epic 135–6; on women 214; *see also* Hesiod

theology, of *Theogony, Iliad* and *Odyssey* 134–6, 157; *see also* gods

Theophrastos 21; on law 177

Theopompos 168

Thera, assembly on 13; 'colony' of Sparta 9; and Cyrene 8–16; homosexual inscriptions from 104; and Samos 12–13

Thermon, temple at 199–200, 270

Thermopylai, battle of 320, 322, 323–5, 325

Theron of Akragas 326–8

Thersites 133, 278

Theseus 49, 128, 295

Thesmophoria 218

Thespiai 323

Thespis 293

Thessaly 20, 43, 47, 59, 274; absence of tomb cult in 97; and Athens 276–7, 279; continuation of tholos tombs in 35; dedications in seventh century 195; epic poetry in 131; and Peisistratids 268–9; and Persians 304, 322–4; pottery from at Knossos 63; servile population in 32

tholos tombs 35, cult at 97–8

Thorikos 98, 282

Thrace 186, 303; and Persia 304, 307, 311, 331

Thracians, on Thasos 220, 222

Thucydides, archaeology of 47–8; on Athens 182, 291; and contemporary history 4, 331–3; and Delian League 331;

Delphic oracle in, 332–3; on divide between democracy and oligarchy 297; on Harmodios and Aristogeiton 277; on Hippias 279; on Kylon 202–3; and Lelantine war 139; and Pausanias the regent 318; on Peiraieus 310; on Peisistratids 269; on Polykrates 259; on Spartan ephor 289; on Spartan treatment of Plataia 325

timber, from north Aegean 120

tin 106, 120; problem of access to 46

Tiryns 174–5, 189, 273; in Dark Age 41; masks from 351

Titans, 134–5

Tocra, foundation of, 15; Greek pottery at 15–16

tomb cult 97–8

Torone 39, 59

town-planning, 130; at Megara Hyblaia 227–8, 229; at Metapontion 225–7; at Miletos 307; at Thasos 222–4

trade 10, 12–13, 54, 57, 64, 66, 105–8, 110, 119, 120, 122, 158, 185, 213; in agricultural products 27–9, 229–30; coinage and 243, 245; and dedicatory practices 86–7; in grain 307; in metals 106–8, 229; in pottery 60, 63, 98–101, 106–8, 153, 159, 191, 213, 224, 234–5, 296–7; Solon and 211; in *Works and Days* 138

tragedy 2, 311; beginnings of 293–4; *see also* drama

transport, and agriculture 25–6, 28–9

Trapezous 185

treasuries, at Delphi 247–8, 294–5; at Samian Heraion, 84; at Olympia 200

tribes, Athenian 279–80, 283–7, 292; Dorian 47, 50, 267; Ionian 50, 283

Triphylia 173

tripod 157; as dedications 88–91, 191; *see also* Apollo

Triptolemos 216

triremes, funding of 245; wood for 20

trittys, at Athens 279–80, 283, 284–5, 287

Troizen, and Argos 273

Trojan horse 10, 228

Trojan War 9, 47, 85–6, 133, 140–8, 248, 311; and settlement at Cyrene 9–10

Troy 140–1, 142–3, 146, 308; appearance in epic tradition 133

tyrannicides, at Athens 277, 288

tyranny 180–5, 232, 297; at Athens 276–7, 297; of one city over another 182, 275; and élite 261–2,263–5, 267–70;